William Nassau Molesworth

The History of England

from the Year 1830 - 1874

William Nassau Molesworth

The History of England
from the Year 1830 - 1874

ISBN/EAN: 9783741184789

Manufactured in Europe, USA, Canada, Australia, Japa

Cover: Foto ©ninafisch / pixelio.de

Manufactured and distributed by brebook publishing software (www.brebook.com)

William Nassau Molesworth

The History of England

THE
HISTORY OF ENGLAND

FROM THE YEAR 1830—1874.

BY

WILLIAM NASSAU MOLESWORTH, M.A.

AUTHOR OF "THE HISTORY OF THE REFORM BILL OF MDCCCXXXII," ETC.

SEVENTH THOUSAND.

VOL. I.

LONDON:
CHAPMAN AND HALL, 193, PICCADILLY.
1877.

[All rights reserved.]

PREFACE TO THE FIRST EDITION.

For reasons that are assigned at the beginning of my History I have commenced it with an account of the great reform struggle of 1831 and 1832; and I have embodied in the present volume my History of that contest; but greatly abridged, in some parts altogether re-written, in all carefully revised and corrected, and with a few additions. There is, however, one passage of that work which I have left entirely untouched—that, namely, which narrates the interview of Lords Grey and Brougham with William IV. on the morning of the 22d of April 1831, and which gave rise to a protracted controversy. I have made a slight correction in the observations with which the anecdote was prefaced; but the story of the interview itself is told word for word as it was given in the first edition of my History of the Reform Bill of 1832. I felt that after the generous and honourable alacrity with which Lord Brougham came forward to rescue me from the embarrassing position in which the present Lord Grey's flat denial of my narrative had placed me, and to make himself distinctly responsible for the correctness of my narrative, I should be laying myself open to a charge of being wanting in the grateful respect I owe to the memory of that great man, if I were now to withdraw the passage from any desire to shorten this part of my work. I am now enabled to give that anecdote stamped with what Lord Grey justly termed 'the high authority of Lord Brougham;' an evidence in its favour which I say advisedly, and after having, I believe, read all that has been written on the subject, is not only unshaken, but rather corroborated by the efforts that have been made to confute it.

In that large portion of my work which is altogether new I propose to follow with regard to the debates on questions of great national importance the plan adopted in my History of the Reform Bill of 1832. I have given the report of the speeches which throw most light on the question, and on the manner in which it was received and regarded by different parties, in a very shortened form. Exordia, perorations, flights of rhetoric, even flights of eloquence, have been remorselessly pruned away, and the residue has been greatly condensed; but the style, and, as far as possible, the very words, of each orator have been carefully preserved.

I am aware that there are other histories which cover a portion more or less considerable of the ground over which this work is intended to extend; but their point of departure is different, and so also are the presiding ideas under which they are written.

W. N. M.

Spotland Vicarage, Rochdale,
May 30, 1871.

CONTENTS OF VOLUME I.

CHAPTER I.

INTRODUCTORY.

	PAGE		PAGE
The Subject of the Work	1	Indignation of the Protestant Party	29
Growth of Abuses	2	Sir C. Wetherell	29
Reform by the Long Parliament and Cromwell	3	Distress	31
Re-appearance of the Question in 1745	4	Opening of Parliament at commencement of 1830	32
The elder Pitt on Reform	4	The Marquis of Blandford's Reform Bill	33
Mr. W. Pitt's Motion for a Select Committee on Parliamentary Reform	5	Other attempts	34
		Death of George IV.	34
Mr. Pitt renews his attempt in 1783	7	William IV.	34
		Position of the Government on the eve of the General Election	36
Mr. Pitt's last effort	8		
Mr. Grey	9	Revolution in France	37
Petition of 'the Friends of the People'	9	Opening of the New Parliament	38
The Corn-laws	10		
'The Blanketeers'	11	Declaration of the Duke of Wellington against Reform	39
Agitation and consequent alarms	12		
Proceedings of the Government	13	The Guildhall Dinner	40
Great Manchester Reform Meeting	14	Unpopularity of the Government	41
Lord J. Russell's Motion	17	Defeat of the Government	43
The Wellington Administration	19	Resignation of the Wellington Administration	43
Mr. Huskisson's removal from the Ministry	19	Influence of Freedom of Speech and of the Press on the Measures of Parliament	45
Catholic Emancipation	20		
Daniel O'Connell	21		
Embarrassment of the Government	22	Earl Grey accepts Office	46
		Mr. Brougham	47
The Clare Election	23	Earl Grey's Explanations	49
Effects of Mr. O'Connell's Election	24	Committee to frame a Reform Bill	49
Necessity of concession	26	Distress and Discontent	51
Perplexity of the Government	26	Machine-breaking and Rick-burning	52
Concession resolved	28		
The Catholic Emancipation Bill introduced	28	State of the Country	53

CHAPTER II.

FIRST INTRODUCTION OF THE REFORM BILL.

	PAGE
Re-assemblage of Parliament, and announcement of the Reform Bill	57
Lord J. Russell	57
Retrenchment	59
Appearance of the House of Commons	61
Introduction of the Reform Bill	62
Lord J. Russell's Speech	63
Sir R. H. Inglis's Speech	76
Mr. Hume's Speech	79
Mr. Hunt's Speech	80
Sir C. Wetherell's Speech	84
The Attorney-General's Speech	86
Lord Palmerston's Speech	86
Sir R. Peel's Speech	88
Mr. Stanley's Speech	94
Mr. Croker's Speech	97
Mr. O'Connell's Speech	98
Lord J. Russell's Reply	101

	PAGE
Reception of the Bill by the Country	102
Political Unions	106
The Press	107
Meetings and Petitions	108
Public Feeling	109
Second Reading	109
Lord J. Russell's Explanations	111
General Gascoyne's Motion	112
Lord Althorp's Speech	113
Mr. Stanley's Speech	114
Mr. O'Connell's Speech	116
Obstacles to a Dissolution	119
Question of a Dissolution	120
Interview of Lords Grey and Brougham with the King	122
Scene in the House of Lords	124
The King's Speech	126
Scene in the House of Commons	127

CHAPTER III.

SECOND INTRODUCTION OF THE REFORM BILL.

	PAGE
General Election	130
Reëlection of the Speaker	132
The King's Speech	133
Re-Introduction of the Reform Bill	135
Second Reading	137
Prosecution of Cobbett	139
Anomalies of the old system exhibited	142
The Night of Divisions	143
The Bill in Committee	144
Alderman Thompson's 'Inadvertence'	145
Sir A. Agnew's Motion	146
Mr. Mackinnon's Motion	147
The Committee	149
The Coronation	156
Report of the Committee	157

	PAGE
Third Reading	157
The Bill passes the House of Commons	158
What will the Lords do?	159
The Bill carried up to the House of Lords	159
Asserted Reaction	160
Earl Grey's Speech	161
Lord Wharncliffe's Speech	165
Lord Melbourne's Speech	165
Duke of Wellington's Speech	166
Lord Lyndhurst's Speech	166
Speeches of the Chief Justice and the Archbishop of Canterbury	168
Earl Grey's Reply	168
The Division	170

CHAPTER IV.

THE REFORM BILL CARRIED.

	PAGE		PAGE
Effects of the rejection of the Bill	171	The Bill passed in the House of Commons	206
Popular Irritation	172	The Waverers	207
Scene in the House of Lords	173	The Second Reading	208
Procession	178	The Committee	209
Riotous Proceedings	179	Lord Lyndhurst's Motion	211
Lord Brougham condemns the Outrages	181	Lord Ellenborough's Programme	212
Lord Ebrington's Resolution	182	Resignation of the Ministry	215
The Birmingham Meeting	182	Altercation between Lords Carnarvon and Grey	215
Impatience of the Nation	184	Lord Ebrington's Resolution	216
Lord Brougham's Explanations	185	State of the Nation	216
Prorogation of Parliament	186	Meetings	217
Asserted Reaction	186	Efforts to embarrass the coming Administration	218
The Political Unions	187	Attempts to form a Ministry	219
The Bristol Riots	189	Failure of the attempts to form a Ministry	220
Disturbed State of the Country	197	Earl Grey re-called	221
Parliament re-assembles	199	Explanations	223
The Reform Bill introduced by Lord J. Russell	200	The Bill in Committee	225
Sir R. Peel's Observations	202	The Amendments of the Lords accepted by the Commons	225
Second Reading	203	Results of the Bill	227
What will be done with the Lords?	203	The Royal Assent	227
Close of the year 1831	205	Periodical Literature	228
The New Year	205	Death of Sir Walter Scott	229
Re-assemblage of Parliament	206		

CHAPTER V.

THE FIRST REFORMED PARLIAMENT.

	PAGE		PAGE
The Revision	230	East India Company's Charter	252
The Elections	231	Abolition of Slavery	254
Opening of the Parliament	233	Factory Bill	240
The King's Speech	234	Bribery and Corruption	202
Debate on the Address	234	The Ballot	262
State of Ireland	236	Triennial Parliaments	263
The Coercion Bill	239	End of the Session	265
The Irish Church	242	Death of William Wilberforce	266
Irish Tithe Bill	245	The British Association	269
Financial Measures of the Government	246	Church Reform	272
Proposed Reduction of the Malt-tax	248	The Oxford Tracts	273
House and Window-duties	249	The Opening of the Session of 1834	283
The Bank Charter	251	Scene in the House of Commons	284
		Charges against Baron Smith	287

CONTENTS OF VOLUME I.

	PAGE
Mr. Ward's Motion	287
Changes in the Cabinet	289
Irish Church Commission	291
Irish Tithe Bill	293
The Coercion Bill	294
Mr. Littleton and Mr. O'Connell	297
Resignation of Earl Grey	301
Lord Melbourne Premier	302
The Irish Tithe Bill again	303
Church Questions	304
Admission of Dissenters to University Degrees	304
Church Rates	305
The New Poor-law	309
Mr. Chadwick's Recommendations	310
The Bastardy Clauses	314
Introduction of the New Act	314
Results	319
Agricultural Distress	319
Financial Statements	320
Ineffectual attempts at Legislation	321
Position of the Ministry	323
Dissatisfaction of the King	324
The King's Reply to the Irish Bishops	325
Dismissal of the Melbourne Administration	326
Destruction of the two Houses of Parliament	327
Death of S. T. Coleridge	330

CHAPTER VI.
CORPORATION REFORM.

	PAGE
The Appeal to the Country	333
Election of a Speaker	334
Rumours of another Dissolution	335
The Marquis of Londonderry	337
Report of the Ecclesiastical Commissioners	339
Defeats of the Government	340
Lord J. Russell's Resolution	341
Sir J. Graham's Speech	345
Mr. W. E. Gladstone's Speech	349
Mr. O'Connell's Speech	352
Sir R. Peel's Speech	353
Defeat and Resignation of the Ministry	356
Lord Melbourne again in Office	359
Corporate Abuses	361
The Corporation Reform Bill	361
Lord J. Russell's Speech	362
Committee	369
Sir W. Follett's Motion	360
The Bill in the House of Lords	372
Irish Tithes	373
Loss of the Irish Tithe Bill	375
Orange Lodges	376
Improvements made in the Reform Bill	380
Agricultural-distress Debates	380
Death of Cobbett	381
The Budget of 1836	382
Irish Corporation Reform Bill	384
Tithe Bills	385
Registration of Births, Deaths, and Marriages	386
Ecclesiastical Reforms	388
Amendment of Corporation Reform Act	391
Counsel for Prisoners	392
The New Houses of Parliament	395
Agricultural Distress	396
The Budget	397
Reduction of the Newspaper Stamp Duty	398
Opening of the Session of 1837	403
Irish Corporation Reform	403
The Westminster Election	405
Church Rates	407
The New Poor-law	409
The Privileges of the House of Commons	413
Canadian Affairs	414
Monetary Derangements	416
British Intervention in the Affairs of Spain	417
State of Public Business	417
Death of the King	419
Character of William IV.	419

A HISTORY OF ENGLAND,

ETC.

CHAPTER I.

INTRODUCTORY.

I INTEND to write the history of England during the forty years over which my memory ranges. I do not attempt to write a history of the British Empire or of the British Isles, but simply of England; and therefore I shall not refer to Scotch, Irish, colonial, or foreign affairs, unless they seem to me to have appreciably accelerated, retarded, or modified the course of English events. I commence with the Reform Bill of 1832. I choose it as my point of departure for many reasons. It is the earliest important occurrence in the history of this country which my memory clearly embraces. It effected a great and enduring change in the Constitution without violence or illegality. It inaugurated a long series of improvements, which are distinctly traceable to it as their source. It has conferred a continuously increasing power on public opinion as distinguished from popular clamour. Lastly, it was the commencement of an era which has been a period of unexampled peace and prosperity, as well as of rapid and manifest political, material, intellectual, moral, and religious development.

During the years 1831 and 1832 the attention of the nation was monopolised by the Reform struggle, and the struggle at the hustings which succeeded it. To this subject, therefore, our attention will be almost exclusively directed in the earlier part of this volume. But before entering on it, we will briefly sketch the origin and course of the agitation which led to the introduction of the Reform Bill of 1831.

The abuses of which the reformers complained were not of modern growth. Many of them were as old as our representative system, which, dating from ages in which anarchy and oppression were struggling with each other as in one vast weltering chaos, was sure to present numerous anomalies and incongruities. Some of these were from time to time corrected; but others grew up in their place. In the earlier periods of our parliamentary history there was no fixed rule for the selection of the towns represented in the Lower House. The King appears to have issued his writ to such as he chose to select, being usually, though not invariably, guided in his choice by their importance and populousness; and as in those times the House of Commons was not an object of jealousy to the Crown, but, on the contrary, often proved a useful ally to the sovereign in the contests which arose between him and his barons, there was no motive for the improper exercise of this power, and little danger that it would be seriously abused. But when the House of Commons began to be recognised as a great estate of the realm, it was felt that bounds must be set to this arbitrary discretion; and the sovereign readily relinquished a prerogative from which he did not derive much advantage. Thus, by the tacit consent of all parties, this discretionary power of the Crown gradually fell into disuse. It is perhaps to be regretted that it was not formally transferred to the legislature or to the House of Commons, instead of being left, as it was, in such a position that any step taken by the Parliament would be regarded by the Crown as a usurpation of its prerogative, and any attempt on the part of the Crown to exercise its dormant rights would arouse in the Commons a jealousy which would have been neither unreasonable nor unfounded. A discretionary power which needed regulation was practically annulled; and the consequence was, that towns which had grown into importance were wholly unrepresented, while others which had decayed still sent members to the House of Commons. Thus a distribution of the representation originally made with tolerable fairness had, even in the time of Charles I., become so evidently anomalous as to attract the attention of the Long Parliament, which increased the number of members returned by the counties and the metropolis; gave representatives to Manchester, Leeds, and Halifax, towns even then rising into importance; disfranchised a considerable number of decayed boroughs; and conferred the elective franchise on every owner of land, whatever the nature of his tenure of it might be. It also gave representatives to Scotland and Ireland, which was thought a fair and desirable arrangement, and one against which no serious objection could be urged. The civil war prevented these changes from being carried into effect at the time when they were mooted; but the plan was subsequently adopted by Cromwell in summoning the Parliament of 1654; and Clarendon, in his history of the time, admits that 'it was not thought an ill temperament, and was then generally looked upon as an alteration fit to be more warrantably made and at a better time.'

It is curious to remark how little opposition or objection was offered to this great change in the constitution of the country, especially when we look at the storm that was raised by the introduction of the Reform Bill; a measure which, considering the period at which it was introduced, and the great increase of anomalies in the representation which had taken place during the interval, we shall see to be a much less violent change than that which Cromwell so boldly adopted. The Parliament elected under it was certainly not distinguished by excessive deference for the Protector. It began its career by calling his authority in question; its whole existence was one prolonged struggle against him; it took every opportunity of criticising his acts; and was dissolved at the earliest possible moment, because it was found to be utterly unmanageable. And yet not a single member seems ever to have thought of objecting to the great change which the Protector had made in the constitution of the House. On the contrary, as far as we are able to judge at this distance of time, not only did they cordially adopt this change, but proceeded to make farther gradual alterations.*

From this time the reform question underwent a long eclipse. The reaction against Cromwell and the Long Parliament prejudiced men's minds against all changes

* I find the following entry in Whitelock's diary: 'Wednesday, Dec. 6. Debates about disfranchisement of certain boroughs, and transfer of their franchise to other places.'

which they had made; and the question did not again emerge into distinct daylight until the year 1745, when Parliament was called together in October, on account of the rebellion in Scotland.

The alarm and distress produced by that event seem to have engendered a feeling favourable to Parliamentary reform, which found an utterance in the following amendment to the address: 'That for the firmer establishment of his Majesty's throne on the solid basis of his people's affections, it should be our speedy care to frame such bills as may effectually secure to his Majesty's subjects the perpetual enjoyment of their undoubted right to be freely and fairly represented in parliament frequently chosen, and exempted from undue influence of every kind.' This amendment, proposed by Sir Francis Dashwood, afterwards Lord De Spencer, and seconded by Sir J. Phillips, was negatived without a division.

Foremost among its opponents was the elder Pitt. 'The amendment,' he said, 'being offered at a time so exceedingly improper as the present, is fraught with a dangerous tendency. There is only one motive to which this motion can be ascribed, and that is, to make ministers odious in the eyes of the people, if they put a negative on it. But I will venture to say that the contrary will be the fact; for although motions of this kind are always popular, yet in this hour of distress and difficulty, when rebellion rages in the kingdom, and an invasion from France is expected, when the people are seriously intent on measures of the highest consequence, they cannot think favourably of those who attempt to draw off their attention from subjects of danger to points of speculation. Shall we employ ourselves in framing bills to guard our liberties from corruption, when we are in danger of losing them and everything else that is dear to us by the force of arms? Would not this be like a man's amusing himself with making regulations to prevent his servants from cheating him at the very time that thieves were breaking into his house? But why are we to introduce this subject into the address? No county, nor city, nor corporation, have requested their representatives to bring in any such bills; the people are everywhere engaged in making subscriptions and forming associations for defending their sovereign and themselves against those who have traitorously conspired to rob him of his crown and them of their liberties. Do gentlemen wish to give a turn to the spirit of the people, to create a contention about the constitution, that the kingdom may fall an easy prey to the enemy? If, sir, I did not know the honourable gentlemen who made and seconded this motion, I should really suspect their having some such design; and however much I may, from my own personal knowledge, be convinced that they have no such design, they may be assured that, if they do not withdraw their motion, the suspicion will be strong against them amongst those persons who have not the honour of their acquaintance.'

This language seems uncalled for. The adoption of such a motion might, and probably would, have had the effect of uniting the people more cordially and enthusiastically in defence of the throne. Be this as it may, the motion was in perfect accordance with the popular principles which Pitt always professed; and one is rather surprised to find him condemning it as ill-timed, without, at the same time, stating that in the abstract he cordially approved it. On other occasions he gave utterance to sentiments entirely in harmony with the amendment which he now so strongly reprobated. For instance, in the year 1766, we find him, in a speech against the American Stamp Act, making use of the following memorable expressions:

'There is an idea in some that the colonies are virtually represented in this House. I would fain know by whom an American is represented here. Is he represented by any knight of the shire in any county in this kingdom? *Would to God that respectable representation was augmented to a greater number!* Or will you tell him that he is represented by any representative of a borough; a borough which perhaps its own representatives never saw? *This is what is called the rotten part of the constitution. It cannot continue a century. If it does not drop, it must be amputated.*'

On the 22nd January, 1770, this great man, now become Earl of Chatham, in supporting a motion proposed by the Marquis of Rockingham, that the House of Lords should take into consideration the state of the nation, made the following remarks on the subject of parliamentary reform: 'Whoever understands the theory of the British constitution, and will compare it with the fact, must see at once how widely they differ. We must reconcile them to each other, if we wish to save the liberties of the country; and we must reduce our political practice as near as possible to our principles. The constitution intended that there should be a permanent relation between the constituent and the representative body of the people. Will any man affirm that, as the House of Commons is now formed, that relation is in any degree preserved? My lords, it is not preserved; it is destroyed. Let us be cautious, however, how we have recourse to violent expedients.

'The boroughs of the country have, properly enough, been called the rotten parts of the constitution. I have lived in Cornwall, and, without entering into an invidious particularity, have seen enough to justify the appellation. But in my judgment, my lords, the boroughs, corrupt as they are, must be considered as the natural infirmity of the constitution. Like the infirmities of the body, we must bear them with patience, and submit to carry them about with us. The limb is mortified; but its amputation might be death.

'Let us try, my lords, whether some gentler remedy may not be discovered. Since we cannot cure the disorder, let us try to infuse such a portion of new health into the constitution as may enable it to support the most inveterate diseases. The representation of the counties is, I think, still preserved pure and uncorrupted. That of the greatest cities is on a footing equally respectable, and there are many of the large trading towns which still preserve their independence. The infusion of health which I now allude to would be to permit every county to elect one member more in addition to their present representatives. The knights of the shire approach nearest to the constitutional representatives of the country, because they represent the soil. It is not in the little dependent boroughs, it is in the great cities and counties that the strength and vigour of the constitution resides; and by them alone, if an unhappy question should ever arise, will the constitution be honestly and firmly defended. I would increase that strength, because that is the only remedy we have against the profligacy of the times, the corruption of the people, and the ambition of the Crown.' After meeting some objections to his proposal, drawn from the terms in which the act of union between

England and Scotland was drawn, he concluded his observations on the subject of parliamentary reform, by suggesting that one additional member should be given to every county in England and Scotland. The year following he declared himself a convert to triennial parliaments. It is highly probable that if that illustrious man had lived and retained his health, a measure such as he indicated would have been carried during the period of discontent and suffering which attended and followed the close of the American war.

The project thus announced by the great earl towards the close of his glorious career was taken up by his son, William Pitt, who, on the 7th of May, 1782, moved for a select committee on parliamentary reform. His speech on the occasion is said to have been warm and animated; but the only passage which has been preserved is one in which he thus inveighed against the corrupt influence of the Crown, &c. 'It is an influence, sir, which has been pointed at in every period as the fertile source of all our miseries— an influence which has been substituted in the room of wisdom, of activity, of exertion, and of success—an influence which has grown with our growth, and strengthened with our strength; but which, unhappily, has not diminished with our diminution, or decayed with our decay.' This motion was seconded by Alderman Sawbridge, a veteran reformer: and in a house of upwards of 300 members was lost by only 20 votes. The motion was opposed by Mr. Burke with characteristic vehemence. In his great speech on American taxation he had stigmatised the defects of our parliamentary representation as 'the shameful parts of our constitution;' but now he seemed to think that no change whatever was needed.

Mr. Pitt renewed his attempt in the following year. This time, however, he brought forward a specific plan, contained in three resolutions, the first of which was intended to pledge the House to measures for the prevention of bribery; the second proposed that whenever the majority of the voters in any borough should be convicted of gross corruption, the borough should lose its right of returning a member, and the uncorrupted minority should become county voters; the third proposed to give additional members to the counties and to the metropolis. This proposition was rejected by a majority of 144.

In the year 1785, Mr. Pitt, being then prime minister, made a last attempt to amend the representation. His plan was, to purchase from thirty-six boroughs of small population their right of sending members, to transfer the seats thus acquired to counties or populous places; and to establish a permanent provision for extinguishing from time to time, by similar means, the franchises of boroughs which might have become decayed and depopulated. The scheme, though introduced by a minister who carried almost all his measures by triumphant majorities, was negatived by 248 to 174. This result has thrown great suspicion on the sincerity of his zeal for reform; the numbers certainly seemed to show that he had not used any great exertions to secure votes for his motion. It is not improbable that abuses which he viewed with abhorrence, while they helped to sustain administrations to which he was hostile, were regarded by him with more indulgence when they strengthened his own power. Be this as it may, he made no farther efforts in favour of changes of which he had once been the zealous advocate, and from the time of the French Revolution he became their uncompromising opponent; instituting prosecutions against men whose only crime was that they still held the opinions which he had formerly professed, and used language in advocating them scarcely, if at all, more violent than that which he himself had once employed. His desertion, though it greatly weakened the reform party, did not discourage them. The French Revolution, while it terrified many of the aristocratic friends of reform, encouraged its supporters among the people, and animated them to fresh exertions in a cause akin to that which seemed to be triumphing on the other side of the Channel. The consequence was, that in the year 1793, the question excited more popular enthusiasm, and met with a more earnest opposition, than on any previous occasion. Mr. Grey, who had taken up the standard which Mr. Pitt had flung away, was sustained by unprecedented demonstrations of popular sympathy. On the 2nd of May petitions were presented to the House of Commons praying for a reform in the representation of the people, from Sheffield, signed by 8,000 persons, but rejected on account of the disrespectful manner in which it was worded, from

Birmingham, signed by 2,720 persons. On the 6th of the same month a very large number of petitions were presented, many of them very numerously signed, and, among them, one from the city of Edinburgh, the signatures to which were so numerous that it extended over the whole length of the floor of the House. But of all the petitions of this time, that which obtained and deserved the greatest attention was one from "the friends of the people," which was presented by Mr. Grey. It gives, in great detail, a most clear and temperate statement of the abuses and grievances of which the petitioners complained. Any person wishing to become thoroughly acquainted with the real views and designs of the reformers of this period, should carefully peruse this most able document.*

Mr. Grey advocated the prayer of the petition. Referring to one portion of it in which the petitioners offered to prove that upwards of 97 members were actually nominated, and 70 more indirectly appointed by Peers and the Treasury, and that 91 Commoners procured the election of 139, so that 306 members, that is, an absolute majority of the House of Commons, were returned by 160 persons. Mr. Grey said, "I assert that this is the condition of England: if you say it is *not*, do justice to yourselves by calling on us for the proof, and expose your calumniators to reproach; but if it be the condition of England, shall it not be redressed?" A long debate followed, in the course of which the prayer of the petition was supported by Mr. Erskine, Mr. Francis, Mr. Fox, and Mr. Sheridan, and was opposed by Mr. Windham and Mr. Pitt. In fact, the question never received a fuller consideration in Parliament, or stirred the heart of the country more strongly, until the great final struggle. But the overwhelming majority of the House of Commons, led by Mr. Pitt, gave the most decisive testimony to the truth of Mr. Grey's assertions, by refusing to accept the challenge he had thrown out. The excesses of the French Revolution produced in this country a strong reaction against parliamentary reform, and a feeling of bitter hostility towards reformers, who were supposed to regard that event with favour. The war with France, which followed, threw the question back for

* See Appendix to my *History of the Reform Bill of 1832.*

many years. It was indeed brought forward again by Mr. Grey in 1795 and 1797, but each time with diminished support in the country, and larger hostile majorities in Parliament. Persecuted by the government, and odious to the mob, the reformers of this generation were put to silence, and the question did not again emerge until the conclusion of the peace which followed the battle of Waterloo.

This peace brought with it but little alleviation of the distress which the war had produced. Indeed, it had been preceded by a measure calculated to prevent the people from obtaining their proper share of the benefits which ought to have attended it. The landed interest had profited greatly by the war; they had enjoyed an almost complete monopoly, which caused a great rise of the profits of the farmer and the rent of the landlord. But the peace which followed the first overthrow of Buonaparte put an end to this monopoly, and the consequence was an immediate fall of rents and profits, attended by great agricultural distress. The monopoly had caused a great extension of agricultural operations; the cessation of the monopoly necessarily produced a collapse. Instead, however, of accepting this necessity, and endeavouring to accommodate themselves to it, the dominant landed interest made the prevalent distress a pretext for protecting, as it was termed, British agriculture, by duties on the importation of foreign corn. And thus, in the interval which preceded the last paroxysm of our struggle with France, was begun that policy of 'protection' once so strenuously upheld, and now so universally condemned.

This law relieved the agricultural interest at the expense of almost every other interest in the nation; and those who suffered from it were not slow in discovering the cause of their distresses. In the north of England, where the manufacturing interest was already strong, the discontent was great and general; but it was felt to be useless to attack the obnoxious measure as long as the government of the country was entirely in the hands of those at whose instigation and for whose supposed advantage it was adopted, and therefore the old cry of parliamentary reform began to be uttered more and more loudly; and the expedients which were adopted by the suffering classes to make their wishes and wants known soon excited considerable attention and no little alarm.

Early in the year 1817 the starving colliers of Bilston had conceived the idea of making their way to Carlton House, the residence of the Prince Regent, with two carts of coals, fondly hoping that they would be admitted to tell their tale of woe to his royal highness, and that the spectacle of their misery would induce him to do something for their relief. The Manchester workmen, improving on this idea, determined that they would walk up to London to make known their distresses to the authorities there, to ask them to provide some legislative remedy, and especially to give them the great panacea of parliamentary reform. It was proposed that each petitioner should take a blanket with him, that they might sleep on the way in any sheltered place they might find, and the food which would be required. They were long remembered by the name of the Blanketeers. The project of these poor simple-minded men, instead of exciting compassion, filled the minds of the government and the upper classes with alarm. It was regarded as an attempt to overthrow the institutions of the country. The Habeas Corpus Act being at that time suspended, the leaders of the proposed expedition were seized and imprisoned. The greater part of those who had intended to join it yielded at once; a few, however, persisted in their intentions; but troops had been placed along the proposed line of march, and they were intercepted, searched, and either sent back or imprisoned. Nothing was found on them to justify these proceedings, except 'two unusually long knives.'

In 1819, Sir F. Burdett brought the question of reform once more under the notice of Parliament. He based his motion on the old maxim of the common law, which declares that 'the people of England have a property in their own goods, which are not to be taken from them without their own consent.' From this ancient dictum Sir Francis inferred that every person paying taxes ought to have a voice in the election of a representative in the House of Commons. He did not, however, bring forward a specific plan, but contented himself with moving 'That the House should take the subject of the representation into its consideration early in the next session.' This motion was rejected by a very considerable majority. Outside the House, and especially in the manufacturing districts, the question found more favour. Early in this year an application had been made to the boroughreeve and constables of Manchester to call a public meeting of the inhabitants, to petition Parliament to repeal the Corn Bill, but which was really intended to afford an opportunity of expressing the public opinion in favour of parliamentary reform. Notwithstanding their refusal, it was resolved that the meeting should be held, and Mr. Hunt, the great radical agitator and orator, accepted an invitation to preside over it. He was accompanied into the town by a great multitude who had gone out to meet him, and who carried banners on which were inscribed, among other mottoes, 'Hunt and liberty,' 'The rights of man,' 'Universal suffrage,' 'No corn laws.' The meeting, at his suggestion, instead of applying to the Parliament, adopted a remonstrance addressed to the Prince Regent. The example thus given in Manchester was followed by nearly all the great towns of the empire; and though the language employed at these meetings was often very violent, the persons who attended them conducted themselves in an orderly and unexceptionable manner. In many places the women, as well as the men, took an active part in the agitation. At Blackburn a *female* Reform Society was established, and issued circulars to the wives and daughters of the workmen, inviting them to form 'sister societies,' for the purpose of co-operating with the men, and instilling into the minds of the rising generation a 'deep-rooted hatred of our tyrannical rulers.' Attempts were also made to establish a regular communication between the various societies in different parts of the kingdom, and thus to enable them to act in concert for the promotion of their common designs.

Unfortunately the government of that day never thought of inquiring whether there was not some discoverable and removable cause for the wide-spread and deep-rooted discontent which these proceedings evinced. They made no attempt to alleviate the distresses of the people, or convert, by wise legislation, their disaffection into loyalty. Their only remedies were strong measures of repression, which exasperated the discontents and increased the sufferings of the people. Greatly alarmed by the accounts, often much exaggerated and highly coloured, which they received of the proceedings and organisation of the reformers, they resolved to put down the agitation with a strong hand. On the 7th of July a circular letter was issued by the Secretary of the Home Department to the Lord Lieutenants of the 'disturbed' counties, as they were now called, recommending them to take prompt and effectual measures for the preservation of the public tranquillity, to excite the magistrates to a vigilant and active discharge of their duties, and to give directions to the yeomanry to hold themselves in readiness, if their services should be required.

The persons to whom this circular was sent fully shared the alarms of the government, and were only too ready to adopt the measures which it indicated. On the other hand, the persons against whom it was levelled were rather exasperated than alarmed. At Birmingham a meeting was held on the 12th of July, at which it was estimated that at least 15,000 persons were present. It was there resolved that the meeting would proceed to elect 'two legislatorial attorneys and representatives of Birmingham.' Their choice fell on Major Cartwright, a veteran reformer, and Sir Charles Wolseley. Neither of them was present, but the latter accepted the office, and promised that he would claim a seat in the House of Commons. A similar meeting was held shortly after at Leeds; but as no one could be found who was willing and qualified, in the opinion of the leaders of the movement, to represent the town in the House of Commons, the election was postponed until a suitable delegate could be obtained.

The government lost no time in picking up the gauntlet of defiance which the reformers had thus boldly thrown down. Sir C. Wolseley was arrested at his own house, and carried to Knutsford to answer for some words he had used in speaking at a public meeting held at Stockport. Several other arrests of a similar character were made about the same time. A proclamation was issued in which it was stated that seditious and treasonable speeches had been delivered to persons assembled at meetings held to petition for reform, and that attempts had been made to bring into hatred and contempt the government and constitution established in this realm, and particularly the Commons'

House of Parliament. The proclamation farther declared that 'many wicked and seditious writings had been printed, published, and laboriously circulated;' and it concluded by charging all persons in authority to use their best endeavours to repress the disorders of which it complained, and to bring their perpetrators to justice.

Undeterred by these proceedings, the leaders of the Manchester reformers summoned a meeting in that town to choose a representative, after the example of Birmingham; but Hunt and others dissuaded them from this design, which the authorities declared to be clearly illegal. It was, however, resolved that a meeting should still be held for the unquestionably legal purpose of petitioning for reform of the House of Commons, and Hunt consented to attend and speak on the occasion.

This meeting was regarded by both the friends and foes of reform as a great crisis in the impending struggle. On the one hand, the minds of the magistrates were filled with exaggerated apprehensions, which they communicated to the government; and, on the other hand, the reformers made great exertions to render the demonstration as imposing as possible, and multitudes were drawn to the spot by the expectation of some attempt on the part of the authorities to prevent the meeting from being held.

Such were the dispositions on both sides on the morning of the 16th of August, the day appointed for the holding of the great meeting. From all the surrounding towns and villages clubs came in, many of them marching in military order to the place of meeting,—a large field near St. Peter's Church, then on the outside of the town, but now in its very heart. On that spot stands the Free-Trade Hall, appropriately commemorating the peaceful triumph of a struggle of which its sight witnessed the bloody and turbulent commencement. For though the reform of Parliament was the means, cheap bread, through the repeal of the Corn-laws, was one of the principal ends which the persons attending this meeting proposed to themselves. Most of the clubs carried flags, and some of them were preceded by bands of music. Every little circumstance that could serve to inflame the fears of those who dreaded reform and reformers was carefully noted. It was observed that one of these bodies marched in military style, timing their steps to the sound of a bugle. Another was preceded by a standard bearing the motto of William Wallace, 'God armeth the patriot.' Other devices inscribed on their banners were —'Annual Parliaments,' 'Universal Suffrage,' 'Vote by Ballot.' Among the clubs were two composed of female reformers, one of which numbered 150 members. Many other females accompanied their friends to the ground. Altogether it was computed that at least 80,000 were present; and when we consider the great population which even then inhabited the districts around Manchester, the feeling in favour of reform that pervaded the bulk of that population, and the importance attached by both sides to this meeting, we can hardly think this estimate excessive. Had this multitude really entertained the designs imputed to them by the anti-reformers, they might unquestionably have annihilated the handful of soldiers, most of them very ill-disciplined, and of special constables, who were at the disposal of the magistracy, and might have wreaked on Manchester, or on the portion of its inhabitants that were obnoxious to their displeasure, any mischief they might have contemplated. But they harboured no such intentions. They had come to display their force, not to exert it; and there can now be no doubt that, had they been permitted to carry out their proceedings without molestation, they would have returned to their respective homes without molesting any one. But the insolence and fears of the authorities prevented this happy result. Before the commencement of the meeting, a body of special constables took up their position on the field, and the multitude opened to afford them a passage. Mr. Hunt, who did not reach the ground until some time after the hour fixed for the commencement of the meeting, was received with enthusiastic shouts, and called to the chair by acclamation. He had not proceeded far with his opening address when the yeomanry made their appearance and advanced at a brisk trot, creating great consternation in that part of the crowd which was nearest to them. They halted for a moment to re-form their ranks, which had been thrown into disorder by the rapid movement. No sooner had they recovered themselves than they drew their swords, which they flourished in a threatening manner The multitude replied to this demonstration with three cheers. Meanwhile the Riot Act had been read, but in such a manner that it does not appear that the meeting heard it, nor were they then or afterwards commanded to disperse. As soon as tranquillity was in some degree restored, Mr. Hunt resumed his speech, which the arrival of yeomanry had interrupted. While he was telling his hearers that the appearance on the ground of the yeomanry was only a trick to disturb the meeting, they, without regarding the danger to which they exposed the crowd, rode forward to the waggon which served as a platform, and their commanding officer called on Hunt to surrender. Hunt coolly replied, that he was ready to give himself up to any civil officer who would produce a warrant for his apprehension, and exhorted the people to behave peaceably, and not to attempt any resistance; advice which, notwithstanding the irritating and ill-advised conduct of the authorities, was followed. Hunt then gave himself up. Flushed with this success, the yeomanry then raised the cry of 'Have at the flags!' and at once rode on the mob, cutting at them with their swords. The persons thus assailed attempted to escape; but the human mass behind them rendered retreat impossible, and formed a living wall at which the yeomanry rode, cutting their helpless and unresisting victims with their swords, or trampling them under the feet of their horses. At length the crowd broke, and fled in all directions. A few of those who remained, in their natural indignation at this cruel and cowardly attack, flung stones and bricks at their assailants, without, however, inflicting any serious injury. Altogether between three and four hundred persons were cut or otherwise wounded. Hunt was conveyed to prison, amidst the threats and insults of the yeomanry and special constables, and his life was in imminent danger from his excited captors. This *massacre*, as it was termed at the time, greatly embittered the minds of the working classes, and produced a feeling of hostility towards those above them in wealth and station, which worked much mischief for many years after. The affair was never properly investigated, and it is impossible to say whether the magistrates or the yeomanry were most guilty; but there can be no doubt that both were highly blameworthy. It was an act of reckless inhumanity to choose such a moment for the arrest of Hunt and his associates. It was still more improper to employ in such a service a body of ill-disciplined yeomanry when regular troops were at hand. The latter acted with mingled coolness and firmness, and inflicted no injury whatever on the crowd. Had they been employed to make the arrest, the meeting might have been dispersed, not perhaps without complaint, but without bloodshed, and without engendering that feeling of burning indignation which the conduct of the yeomanry provoked.

The effect of these events was to increase the alarm and exasperation which prevailed on both sides. The government brought into Parliament an array of bills, empowering them to seize arms, suppress drilling, punish seditious libels, and employ other coercive measures. These bills were carried by large majorities, while every motion for inquiring into the distress of the people was voted down by the supporters of the ministry.

These untoward circumstances did not deter Lord J. Russell from bringing the question of reform before the House of Commons. His motion was made on the 4th of December; but the resolutions moved were withdrawn in consequence of an intimation from Lord Castlereagh that the government were disposed to take up the question. Lord John therefore contented himself with moving the disfranchisement of the borough of Grampound, where corruption had already been proved. But even this miserable instalment of reform was denied, the Whigs, either from indifference or despair, gave a very feeble support to Lord J. Russell, and when the post of prime minister was filled by Mr. Canning, who, though liberal in his views on some questions, entertained a strong and decided antipathy to a parliamentary reform, they allowed the matter to be shelved, without any serious remonstrance. Nor was the disposition manifested by the people at this moment such as to encourage the advocates of reform in the House of Commons. The repressive measures of the government were producing their intended effects, and the peace now at length begun to be followed, not indeed by plenty, but by a very marked alleviation of the sufferings of the people, the consequence of which was that their discontent diminished, and the cry for reform waxed fainter and fainter. Under such circumstances it was useless to continue a hopeless struggle, in the face of a hostile and overwhelming majority. The question was therefore allowed to fall into abeyance, and was only raised by proposals so very moderate as to seem like the mockery of reform; but nevertheless too violent for those to whom the very name of reform was odious. Still, the agitation was not dead. The political atmosphere was charged with electricity, which though not seen made itself to be felt. Everywhere there was an uneasy sensation of dread and distrust, like the feeling that precedes a storm. Ministry after ministry had fallen, apparently without any adequate cause; and the King, when he summoned to the chief place in his councils George Canning—a man whom he greatly disliked—yielded to a necessity which many felt, but none could explain. Canning, during his brief administration, found himself surrounded by embarrassments and difficulties which undermined his health, and would probably have resigned if his premature death had not anticipated his fall from power. His followers still retained office, under the nominal leadership of Lord Goderich; but in less than six months the inherent weakness of the government, and the dissensions of some of its members, caused it to fall to pieces.

This ministry was succeeded by another, which seemed to be endowed with stronger vitality. At the head of it was the Duke of Wellington, whose practical good sense, distinguished services, and great military renown gave strength and prestige to his administration. But he brought to the cabinet the habits of command he had learned in the camp, and exacted from his ministerial colleagues the same unreasoning obedience he had been accustomed to receive from his military subalterns. A short time before, he had declared that he should be mad to aspire to the office of prime minister; yet he now accepted that office, or rather was persuaded to take it, as being the best possible defender of a state of things which his sovereign and he were both anxious to sustain, but which the tide of events was rapidly carrying to its inevitable downfall. The duke was much guided and influenced by Mr. Peel; an excellent administrator, a skilful debater, and perhaps the only man in the House of Commons capable of leading that assembly in conjunction with the duke. He was the real head of the government, because his chief felt that he could not safely take a step without his aid and guidance. In some few matters belonging more immediately to his own position as premier, the duke acted without his advice; and it was when thus acting that he took a step which led to the breaking up of that strong party which had hitherto successfully resisted every proposal for the reform of Parliament, and might perhaps have continued to defy the popular demands, at the imminent though unseen risk of a violent overthrow of our institutions.

The duke had admitted into his cabinet several followers of Mr. Canning, at the head of whom stood Mr. Huskisson; a man who, though destitute of the brilliancy and eloquence of his chief, was a good debater, and enjoyed a considerable reputation in the House and in the country as a financier and political economist. His views on Catholic emancipation, reform, and other questions, were much more advanced than those of the prime minister; and an event soon occurred which brought them into direct collision. The borough of East Retford had been convicted of corruption, and the question of the manner in which its franchises should be disposed of was brought before the House of Commons. On the one hand, it was proposed that they should be given to the town of Birmingham; on the other that they should be transferred to the hundred in which East Retford is situated. The duke and the majority of the cabinet supported the latter alternative; Mr. Huskisson voted for the former. Immediately after doing so, he wrote a note to the duke, in which he briefly explained the grounds of his vote, and offered to withdraw from the ministry if his explanation should be deemed unsatisfactory. The duke, impatient, as we have already remarked, of all insubordination on the part of his colleagues, especially on the question of reform, and probably dissatisfied with Mr. Huskisson's views on other questions, treated his letter as a resignation, and at once obtained the King's acceptance of it. Mr. Huskisson disavowed the interpretation that had been put on his words, and offered farther explanations. The duke, however, refused to listen to anything but the unconditional withdrawal of the letter, thus placing Mr. Huskisson in the position of either quitting the administration, or degrading himself in the eyes of Parliament and the country. He chose, though not without hesitation, the former alternative; and the other members of the Canning party followed his example. His removal from the ministry gave great dissatisfaction both in the House of Commons and out of doors; and this feeling was increased when it was known that Sir G. Murray, a military man, was chosen to succeed him.

The question which at the moment when these events were occurring occupied and almost engrossed the attention of the government was the state of Ireland. The overwhelming majority of the inhabitants of that country were Roman Catholics; but the law placed the whole political power in the hands of the Protestant minority, not only excluding the Catholics from almost every office of trust and power, but preventing them from sending representatives of their own faith to the imperial Parliament. A strong and growing feeling of the flagrant iniquity of this state of things filled the minds of the oppressed majority; and many Protestants in Ireland as well as in England, convinced of the injustice and impolicy of these odious and invidious disabilities, desired their abolition. Mr. Pitt and most of his successors in office had been anxious to effect their removal; but could not overcome the prejudices and scruples of George III. and George IV., both of whom considered that they were bound by the coronation oath to resist any change in this respect, and the latter of whom had exacted a promise from some of those whom he had summoned to form a government that the subject should not be mentioned to him during their administration. On this point the Duke of Wellington shared the opinions of his sovereign. He had on several occasions declared his hostility to Catholic emancipation: and it was probably owing to his well-known opinions on this point that no such pledge as we have just referred to was exacted from him. Had it been required, he would probably have given it, and having given it, would certainly have adhered to it. Mr. Peel was even more strongly pledged to resist the Catholic claims. He had opposed Mr. Canning on the express ground of that gentleman's avowed desire to remove the disabilities under which the Catholics laboured, although it was known that he was precluded from bringing forward a measure for their removal. Indeed, Mr. Peel was regarded as the leader and champion of the Protestant party in the House of Commons and in the country; and to that opinion he owed the honour—and at that period, even more than at present, it was regarded as a very high honour—of representing the University of Oxford. Still, there was a certain pervading spirit of liberality which tinctured his opinions, inspiring hope into the Catholics, and producing an uneasy feeling of distrust among his own followers. Most of the other members of the cabinet shared the views of their chief; but their opinions were of comparatively small importance.

The Catholics were not idle. A 'Catholic Association' had been formed, and placed itself at the head of one of the most formidable agitations that had ever been carried on in any country. A sort of military organization was given to the discontented party, uniforms were made for them, and they increased daily in numbers, in boldness, and in violence. The police, which was necessarily composed chiefly of Catholics, shared the prevalent passions and discontent. The Irish soldiers, who formed no inconsiderable portion of the army, were Catholics almost to a man, had been tampered with by the malcontents, and could not be relied on in case of an insurrection.

The leader of this formidable agitation was a man well calculated to bring it to a successful termination. Daniel O'Connell possessed a varied and persuasive eloquence, of a kind admirably adapted to stir the passions of that generous and excitable race who had chosen him for their champion. At one moment he addressed them in terms of the most winning *bonhomie*, at another he denounced the tyranny of their Saxon oppressors, and proclaimed the wrongs of his country in accents of the most withering indignation. He possessed a rare mixture of caution and audacity; and his legal education—for he was a barrister—enabled him to approach the very verge of treason without bringing himself within the grasp of the law. He possessed in an eminent degree all the wit, humour, and readiness for which his countrymen have always been remarkable. His versatile genius enabled him with equal ease and success to negotiate with the lord-lieutenant and his government, and to guide the turbulent and impulsive spirits at whose head he was placed, and whose deliverance he had undertaken to achieve. Most men, if placed in a similar position, would have been unable to ride the storm they had conjured up, and would have become its victims; but so great was the ascendancy that O'Connell had acquired over the lower orders of his fellow-countrymen, and so unbounded the confidence they reposed in him, that he was able to goad them almost to madness, and then, if it suited the purpose of the moment, to restrain them in the wildest transports of their fury. In a word, he wielded the wild and excitable millions of the Catholic population with an ease that seemed almost magical. Having it in his power to throw them into instant rebellion, he took care that they should exhibit just violence enough to terrify their opponents without breaking out into open insurrection or coming into collision with the force of the British empire. The embarrassment which this state of things had caused to the British government was thus correctly described by Mr. Peel, when he subsequently introduced a measure for its removal:

'For thirty-five years the state of government in this country on the Catholic question has been disunion. Lord Fitzwilliam went to Ireland in 1794, and his government came to a termination on account of a difference about the Catholic question. In 1801, Mr. Pitt's government came to an end, and on the same ground—a difference about the Catholic question. He resumed the government in 1804, composing his cabinet in a manner which showed that it was not formed on the principle of unqualified resistance. After his death succeeded a new ministry, which endured about eighteen months, and then came to a termination— still on the same ground, a difference about the Catholic question. It is true that during the five years that followed, under the ministry of Mr. Perceval, government resisted the consideration of this question; but the resistance did not proceed on permanent grounds, for during the greater part of that interval Lord Castlereagh and Mr. Canning were members of the government, and consented to act only in deference to the conscientous scruples of his late Majesty. So soon as the restrictions on the Regency had expired, the same Parliament which had been elected in 1807 determined, by a very large majority, to take the question into consideration. Since then, up to the commencement of the present session, the Catholic question has been made what is called a neutral question; any member of every government was allowed to take his own course with respect to it, the consequence of which has been most unfortunate, though perhaps unavoidable. During the whole of that period the government was divided—sometimes equally; sometimes the proportion was seven to six against concession; sometimes it was six to seven in favour of concession. Usually, however, the cabinet was equally divided. This divided government had been but an apt representative of the divided opinion of the legislature which I am addressing. Four out of the five last Parliaments have, at some time or other, come to a decision in favour of the Catholic question. One House of Commons did resist the consideration of the question; but that single house, out of five, resisted its consideration by a majority of only 243 to 241. From a list of the divisions during the last ten years, I find that in 1819 there was a majority of 2 against the question; in 1820 there was a majority of 6 in its favour; in 1821 a bill was passed by a majority of 9; in 1822 the bill for the admission of Roman Catholic Peers into the House of Lords was passed by a majority of 5; in 1824 the question was not brought forward; in 1825 a bill was passed by a majority of 21; in 1826 there was a general election; and in 1827 the present House of Commons decided against the question by a majority of 4; but in the last session they had decided in its favour by a majority of 6.'

Such was the state of affairs and parties at the time when Mr. Huskisson and his friends were expelled from the ministry. Among those who had been introduced into it, to supply their places, was the Honourable Vesey Fitzgerald, member for the county of Clare. His acceptance of office rendered it necessary that he should go back to his constituents. He was personally popular with all parties, and, though a Protestant, was favourable to Catholic emancipation. He was therefore supported by almost every man of wealth and property in the county of Clare. As for the forty-shilling freeholders, they had always hitherto voted according to the bidding of the great landed proprietors, who by long custom considered themselves as having a right to command their votes. His return, therefore, seemed a matter of certainty, and no opposition was anticipated. Nevertheless, the Catholic Association determined to contest the seat, and put forward as their chosen candidate Mr. O'Connell himself, who, though disqualified from sitting in the House of Commons, might be elected as a representative, and in that capacity protest with greater effect against the injustice with which he and his co-religionists were treated. Every exertion was made to secure his election; and to encourage his supporters, he solemnly declared to them, on his reputation as a lawyer, that there was nothing in the state of the law to prevent him taking his seat, if elected. He backed this assertion by the opinion of Mr. Butler, a Roman Catholic barrister of some reputation and considerable learning. His candidature roused the enthusiasm of his countrymen to the highest pitch. From almost every altar in the county the people were solemnly urged to vote for O'Connell, and they who hesitated were denounced as renegades to their religion, and traitors to the liberties of their country. The county was traversed in every direction by agitators who inculcated the same doctrines in language still more inflammatory. The result was, that the hitherto irresistible influence of the territorial aristocracy was annihilated. The great landowners, almost to a man, supported Fitzgerald, the poor but more numerous freeholders voted with equal unanimity for O'Connell. Mr. Fitzgerald saw from the first that his cause was hopeless, and after a five days' poll, on which his opponent had a very decided majority, he withdrew from the contest.

This event produced an immense effect throughout the whole empire, but especially in Ireland. The poor miserable half-starved and less than half-civilised Irish peasant saw in it the dawn for him of a social and political millennium. A first great victory had been gained over his oppressors, and he hailed it as an omen of many future successes. Henceforth his enthusiasm became wilder, his confidence in his great leader more unbounded. If the signal for rebellion had been then given, it would have been promptly and generally obeyed, and a civil war would have ensued, which, though it might ultimately have been crushed by the superior power of England would certainly have assumed very formidable proportions.

On the other hand, nothing could exceed the consternation with which the Protestants regarded this great defeat of their party. It revealed to them the full extent of the Catholic combination, and the intense passion and enthusiasm by which it was animated. They saw with dismay the hitherto submissive serfs now rising in a body against their landlords; and they could not help fearing that the movement, though now carried on within the limits of strict legality, might end in an outburst of violence, of which they would probably be the victims. Some of them were so alarmed that they either became avowed advocates of emancipation or shrank from all show of opposition to it. Others were goaded by terror and party spirit into still more violent resistance to concession. Their exasperation was at its height, and their imprudent insolence was not unlikely to lead to conflicts which neither O'Connell nor the Catholic Association, could prevent or restrain. In England, too, the effect produced was immense, and, on the whole, highly favourable to Catholic emancipation.

O'Connell was not the man to allow his victory to remain unimproved. He lost no time in following it up by more vigorous efforts and a hotter agitation. Ireland was traversed from one end to the other by the agents and emissaries of the Catholic Association, making inflammatory speeches, organising threatening demonstrations, and employing every means that could be devised to embarrass the government and increase the prevailing disaffection. O'Connell himself came over to England to fulfil his pledge of taking his seat in the House of Commons; but as the session was drawing to a close, and as nothing was to be gained at the time by pressing his claim, he prudently deferred the attempt until the commencement of the following session.

It was clear that the government could not allow this state of things to continue without making an effort to put an end to it. Blow after blow, humiliation after humiliation, was inflicted on them, and they were unable to do anything. While the Catholic party daily gained strength, they became weaker and weaker in their means of resisting it. They were humiliated in the eyes of friends and foes alike. It was therefore becoming more and more necessary that the agitation should be met either by repression or by concession. The former course was the one which the antecedents of the chief members of the government seemed to require; but it was one that involved fearful peril and responsibility. It was likely to lead to a civil war, which would produce as its first effect the massacre of those Protestants for whose supposed benefit it was undertaken. The foreign relations of the country were far from satisfactory, and there was reason to fear that the outbreak of an Irish insurrection would be followed by demands which the government could not grant without humiliation, and could not resist without extreme danger. And if a war should arise, what would be the position, and prospects of the government, with England discontented, Ireland holding out her hands to our enemies, and an army composed in a very great proportion of disaffected Irish troops? The policy of repression was not to be thought of, the policy of doing nothing could not be persevered in much longer—there remained, then, nothing but the policy of concession. For the sake of the whole empire, for the sake of Ireland, for the sake, above all, of the Irish Protestants and the Irish Protestant Church, it was necessary that something should be done to satisfy the just demands of the Irish Roman Catholics.

Still, this policy was attended with no small difficulties. We have already pointed out how strongly the Duke of Wellington and Mr. Peel were committed against Catholic emancipation, and the decided objection which the King entertained to it. It seemed therefore that the only course which the duke could honourably and properly take, under the circumstances, was to admit that he had hitherto been in error, to make way for his parliamentary opponents, and to support them in those measures which they felt to be required; and, perhaps, if he had adopted it he would have best consulted his own reputation and the interests of his party. But even to this course, very plausible objections might be urged. The cabinet had only been in existence for about half a year, and it would have been a very serious calamity, after the many administrative changes that had taken place, to break up the only strong government which had existed for some time. It would also have the effect of throwing the King into the hands of the Whig party, to which in his younger days he had been attached, but with which he had broken in a manner that did not redound to his own credit, and which he now regarded with a feeling of aversion that would render it very humiliating to him to be compelled to call them in to advise him. The duke, whose loyalty knew no bounds, was ready to make almost any sacrifice in order to save his sovereign from what he regarded as a degradation. He feared too that the Whigs, if called to power, would stipulate for permission to introduce a bill for the reform of Parliament; a measure which the duke and the King regarded with even greater aversion than Catholic emancipation. Besides, the duke and Mr. Peel were sincerely anxious to maintain the Protestant ascendancy in Ireland, and they thought that this might be effected by certain securities, with which it was intended that the emancipation should be accompanied, but which their parliamentary opponents would probably object to introduce. Thus the duke felt himself bound, by his sense of what was due to his sovereign and his country, to retain the office on which he had so recently entered.

Such were the circumstances under which Mr. Peel began to feel that his own consistency and the duty he owed to his party must be sacrificed to the higher duty which he owed to his sovereign and his country. The events which were taking place in Ireland convinced him of the necessity of yielding to the demands of the Irish Catholics; and he hoped that the concession might be accompanied by other measures, which would tend to remove the danger with which he and his friends believed that the Church of England and Ireland, but especially the latter, was menaced by Catholic emancipation. He lost no time in imparting this conviction to the Duke of Wellington, and urging him to take the steps which, in his opinion, were imperatively required. At the same time, knowing that his change of opinion would be attributed to a sordid love of pay and power, and justly feeling that he ought not to propose a concession of which he had hitherto been the chief opponent, he begged to be allowed to withdraw from the administration, promising that, as an independent member of Parliament, he would give his warm support not only to the particular measures which he thought were required by the circumstances of the times, but also to the general policy of the government. For the reasons we have already assigned, the Duke of Wellington was fully prepared to enter into the views of his colleague, but he too felt the embarrassment of his position. However, the duke, Mr. Peel, and Lord Lyndhurst, then Lord Chancellor, carefully examined the question in all its bearings, and the course which it would be advisable to adopt had been chalked out by them, but no definite resolution had been adopted; and as late as the 11th of December the Duke of Wellington wrote a letter to the Roman Catholic Primate of Ireland, in which he expressed a hope that the day might come when Catholic emancipation might be safely granted, but at the same time intimated that the day was still at a considerable distance; little thinking probably, at the time when he wrote, that in less than a month the measure to which he referred would have been adopted by himself, and the government over which he presided. The approach of the session necessitated a decision, but the subject had not yet been mentioned to the King. Mr. Peel, however, drew up, for his Majesty's information, a paper in which he stated his reasons for thinking that Catholic emancipation should be conceded without delay, and the securities by which, in his opinion, it ought to be accompanied, to prevent the dangers which were apprehended from it. Armed with this document, the Duke of Wellington succeeded in wringing from his sovereign a reluctant consent to the introduction of a measure based on Mr. Peel's arguments, and accompanied by the securities which he recommended. Hereupon Mr. Peel once more begged to be allowed to resign, and renewed his promise of independent support to the government. The duke, however, felt that he could not hope to carry the measure unless Mr. Peel, who was its author, would take charge of it as a minister of the Crown. Amidst all these negotiations, the final decision was only arrived at within a few days of the opening of the session; and though some vague rumours of what was in agitation were circulated through the country, the intentions of the government were not known until they were revealed by the royal speech at the opening of Parliament, which was delivered by commission.

Accordingly, in the month of March, a measure of Catholic emancipation was introduced into the House of Commons, accompanied by two other bills, one of which disfranchised the forty-shilling freeholders, by whose means chiefly Mr. O'Connell had won his election; the other enacted the suppression of the Catholic Association. Thus the ministry hoped to restore contentment and tranquillity to Ireland, to secure the Church of Ireland, and to put the Irish Catholics in all important respects on a footing of equality with their Protestant fellow-countrymen. The last two measures encountered no serious opposition. The Protestant party, for whose protection they were framed, had no reason to object to them; and the Catholics and their friends knew that by opposing them they might imperil the success of that great measure of justice for which they had been struggling so long, and which was now unexpectedly offered to them by their chief opponents. But the Emancipation Bill encountered a most formidable opposition both in the House and out of doors. The great Orange-Tory party, taken unawares, and complaining, with some show of reason, that they had been betrayed by their leaders, whose irresolution certainly wore the appearance of calculated treachery, protested bitterly against the haste with which the measure was pressed forward, and clamoured for a dissolution, which would have enabled them to appeal to the Protestant prejudices of their countrymen, and might very probably have given them a majority against the bill. They were absolutely furious, and ready to ally themselves with any party who would assist them in defeating the measure and wreaking vengeance on its framers. The clergy opposed it almost to a man, and used their influence with their flocks against it. The majority of the Dissenters adopted the same course.

Nor were these feelings confined to those who had lately been the supporters of the ministry. They found vehement expression in their own ranks. The Attorney-General, Sir C. Wetherell, to whom offers of high office had been made if he would support the measure, not only refused to follow his colleagues in their unexpected change of opinion, but even to draw the bill. It might have been expected that the Duke of Wellington, who had so summarily ejected Mr. Huskisson and his friends for a much lighter act of insubordination, would not have tolerated this refusal; but the events that had followed Mr. Huskisson's dismissal had taught him caution. He knew that if the Attorney-General were removed, it would be necessary to offer the post to Sir N. Tindal, who represented the University of Cambridge, and who might very probably lose his seat there, if he accepted office, which would require him to vacate it; and thus the administration would receive a blow which, at such a moment, it could ill sustain. Sir C. Wetherell was therefore permitted to remain in office; and when the bill was introduced, it found in the Attorney-General of the government by which it was proposed its ablest and most bitter opponent.

When it was brought in, he broke forth into vehement vituperation of his ministerial superiors, and especially Lord Chancellor Lyndhurst. "Am I, then," he exclaimed, "to blame for refusing to do that, in the subordinate office of Attorney-General, which a more eminent adviser of the Crown, only two years ago, declared he would not consent to do? Am I, then, to be twitted, taunted, and attacked? I dare them to attack me! I have no speech to eat up. I have no apostasy disgracefully to explain. I have no paltry subterfuge to resort to. I have not to say that a thing is black one day and white another. I have not been in one year a Protestant Master of the Rolls, and in the next a Catholic Lord Chancellor. I would rather remain as I am, the humble member for Plympton, than be guilty of such treachery, such contradiction, such unexplained conversion, such miserable and contemptible apostasy. . . . They might have turned me out of office, but I would not be made such a dirty tool as to draw *that* bill. Let who would do it, I would not defile pen or waste paper by such an act of folly, and so forfeit my character for sense and honesty. I have therefore declined to have anything to do with it." Of course, whatever the dangers or embarrassments of government, the man who delivered this tirade could not be allowed to retain his office, and he was at once dismissed.

If such sentiments were expressed in the ministry itself, and by one whose official position afforded him the means of judging the crisis, and the motives by which his chiefs were actuated, we may easily conceive what were the feelings and what the language of those outside, especially among the ignorant, whose prejudices against the Roman Catholics had been industriously fostered and fomented by one-sided histories and speeches,—who saw nothing in that religion but a hellish conspiracy against the happiness and liberties of mankind, for the benefit of the priesthood, and who believed that this measure would be the means of restoring their old ascendancy, and delivering England, bound hand and foot, into their power. An opportunity for the display of these prejudices was soon afforded. Mr. Peel, though prevented by the peculiar circumstances in which he was placed from withdrawing from the ministry, felt that he was bound in honour to resign his seat at Oxford. Some of his friends resolved to propose him again. The Protestant party put forward in opposition to him Sir R. Inglis; an upright and honourable country gentleman, deeply imbued with the prejudices of the party whose chosen champion he was, and in every respect greatly inferior to Mr. Peel. He was returned by a triumphant majority.

The alienation of their old Tory friends was compensated by the support generously given to the ministry by the Whig party. By their aid the bill was rapidly and triumphantly carried through all its stages in both Houses of Parliament. Mr. O'Connell, after the passing of the measure, claimed his seat; but the House of Commons, influenced by the ministry, rejected his claim, and declared, that as his return had taken place before the passing of the Emancipation Act, he was not duly elected; he was, however, re-elected by the county of Clare, and took his seat without opposition.

The ministry got through the rest of the session without farther difficulty; but they had alienated the old Protestant Tory party, who anxiously waited for an opportunity of wreaking their vengeance on their former leaders for what they regarded as an act of the blackest treachery. Actuated by this feeling, many of them became strong reformers, and in the transient ardour of their new-born zeal outran most of those who had hitherto taken charge of this question. On the other hand, the Whig and Catholic parties were but half satisfied. The former saw that the ministry, while it depended on them for its existence, entirely excluded them from all participation in the framing of their measures or the emoluments of office. Their discontent was increased as they saw that the government tried every means of reconciling its old supporters, and of rendering itself independent of those by whose aid it had recently triumphed. In Ireland the agitation still continued. The Catholic Association, though suppressed by the recent act, still carried on its operations under a new name. Meanwhile all interests in all parts of the kingdom seemed to suffer. Trade, manufactures, agriculture,—all stagnated. Many parishes were reduced to such a state of pauperism that the whole property within their limits was insufficient for the maintenance of their poor; and assistance had to be sought from neighbouring parishes already over-burdened with the expense of supporting their own paupers. Landlords could not obtain their rents; farmers were impoverished; the agricultural labourer, whose wages were often eked out from the poor-rates, received just enough to enable him to procure for his family and himself the barest necessaries of life. The manufacturing operatives of Lancashire and Yorkshire were, in many instances, receiving only threepence and fourpence a day for more than twelve hours' labour. O'Connell stated in the House of Commons that in Ireland 7,000 persons were subsisting on three-halfpence a day; and though this statement was perhaps exaggerated, there can be no doubt that great distress prevailed in that unhappy country, and that the peasantry were reduced to the smallest allowance of the lowest kind of food.

Such was the state of things throughout the United Kingdom at the commencement of the year 1830. Parliament was again opened by commission. In the King's speech the prevailing distress was indeed mentioned, but in terms which were justly regarded as evincing a very inadequate sense of its fearful intensity, and which did not disclose any intention on the part of the ministry to introduce measures with a view to its mitigation or removal. Amendments were accordingly moved to the address in both Houses of Parliament, the object of which were to pledge the legislature to take the distress and means of alleviating it into their serious consideration; but in both ministers triumphed, though the minority of 105 in the Lower House—composed chiefly of old adherents of the administration—showed how unsuccessful had been their efforts to win back those who had been alienated from them by their conduct in respect to Catholic emancipation.

One of those, the Marquis of Blandford, eldest son of the Duke of Marlborough, moved that what he termed 'a wholesome admonition' should be appended to the address from the House of Commons. In this admonition, after referring to the 'awful and alarming state of universal distress in which the landed, commercial, and all the great productive interests of the country' were at that moment involved, he ascribed it to the fact, already too notorious, that the House was nominated for the greater part by certain proprietors of close and decaying boroughs, and by a few other individuals, who, by the mere power of money, employed in means absolutely and positively forbidden by the laws, had obtained a 'domination,' also expressly forbidden by Act of Parliament, over certain other cities and boroughs of the United Kingdom.

The majority of the reformers in the House refused to support a motion which was evidently intended to entrap the government; and only 11 members voted for it, while 96 voted against it. It was, however, intimated by Sir F. Burdett, and other speakers, that if the ministers expected to be maintained against their late supporters, now become their bitterest foes, they must enter into a close connection with the Whig party. The marquis, however, was not deterred, by the defeat he had undergone, from bringing in a bill in accordance with the indications of his rejected motion. He proposed to transfer the franchises of decayed or corrupt boroughs to large unrepresented towns, to give all payers of scot and lot, and all copyholders and leaseholders, the right of voting. County members were to be paid 4*l.*, and borough members 2*l.* a day. In Scotland the representation was to be placed on the same footing as that of England. Members were to be chosen from the inhabitants of the places they represented. This measure of course shared the fate of the 'wholesome admonition.' Lord Althorp, as the leader of the Whig party in the House, moved, as an amendment to the motion for leave to bring in the bill, 'That it is the opinion of this House that a reform in the representation of the people is necessary.' The amendment and the original motion were both negatived. The East Retford case was brought up again, and decided in accordance with the views of the Wellington administration. The same fate also befell motions by Lord Howick for checking bribery; a petition from Newark complaining of the manner in which the Duke of Newcastle had exercised his influence in that borough; a bill proposed by Lord J. Russell for giving members to Manchester, Birmingham, and Leeds; and a bill proposed by Mr. O'Connell for the introduction of triennial parliaments, vote by ballot, and universal suffrage.

On the whole, then, the reform question, though decidedly making way, did not wear a very promising aspect. While the more extreme or crotchety propositions were rejected by overwhelming majorities, even the most moderate were in a decided minority; and it was little expected on any side of the House, that within less than a year from the time that Lord J. Russell failed to obtain leave to bring in a bill for the very moderate measure of reform which he proposed, he would, as a minister of the Crown—without a division, and almost without a negative voice—obtain leave to bring in a bill to make a great and sweeping change in the national representation. But two events which occurred in the course of this year placed the question of reform and its advocates in a much more favourable position than they had hitherto occupied.

The first of these events was the death of George IV. While young he had manifested a sympathy for liberal opinions, and had attached himself to the Whig party, who entertained great hopes that when he became regent he would put the administration of affairs into their hands. But these expectations were completely disappointed. From that moment he gradually detached himself from them; and during the later years of his life he manifested a deep-rooted aversion both to their principles and their persons, and especially to Earl Grey, who had become their leader. We have already seen with what reluctance he yielded to an imperious necessity, in consenting to the introduction of the Catholic Emancipation Bill; and there can be no doubt that his opposition to any measure of parliamentary reform would have been even more obstinate and decided.

His brother, William IV., who succeeded him on the throne, was supposed to be not unfavourable to the Whigs, and was known to dislike the Duke of Wellington, who, greatly to his honour, had refused to sacrifice a respectable officer, Sir G. Cockburn, who had incurred the displeasure of the new monarch when Duke of Clarence and Lord High Admiral, by a refusal to obey orders from his royal highness that were inconsistent with his duty. The consequence of the Duke of Wellington's firmness on this occasion was, that the Duke of Clarence resigned the office of high admiral, for which he was ill qualified, and in which he was doing great mischief. Nevertheless, on his accession, the new monarch declared to his ministers that he approved their policy, and would give them his support. He was probably sincere in making this declaration; but his feeling towards them could hardly have been very cordial. The Whigs were now in high spirits, and no longer disposed to continue the aid they had hitherto given to the government. They knew that, if not actually favoured by the new sovereign, they were, at all events, not personally obnoxious to him. They were confident that a general election, which must shortly take place, would give them great additional strength; for they were highly popular in the country, and the government very unpopular. They saw that the ministry were determined to recover, if possible, the confidence of their old supporters, and to estrange themselves more and more from those by whose aid they had carried the Catholic relief bill, and maintained themselves in office since the passing of that measure. The Whigs now began to exchange their position of independent support to the ministry for an attitude of determined and uncompromising opposition. They took every opportunity of contrasting them with their new sovereign, speaking of the latter in highly adulatory terms, while they declaimed strongly against the former. The Duke of Wellington, seeing that the approach of the dissolution of Parliament diverted the attention of the members of the House of Commons from the measures of the government, resolved to dissolve as speedily as possible. The opposition, on the other hand, sought by all means in their power to delay the dissolution, and insisted on first settling the appointment of a regency, in case of the king's decease before the re-assembling of Parliament. On this question they divided both Houses against the government; but in both they were defeated by large majorities. On the 23rd of July Parliament was prorogued with the usual formalities, and on the following day dissolved by proclamation.

Thus the administration found themselves on the eve of the general election in the presence of two powerful and bitterly hostile parties—the Tories, who were still exasperated against them on account of their conduct in reference to the Catholic question; and the Whigs, who hoped to replace them in the government of the country. The former were strong for electioneering purposes in their wealth, their property, the number of boroughs which were under their control, and the violent prejudices against the Roman Catholic religion, which had long prevailed in this country, and which were carefully fostered by the ultra-Protestant party. The Whigs, on the other hand, besides having at their disposal a large amount of property and borough influence, enjoyed the support of the great majority of the people, who looked to them as the party by whose aid their political redemption was to be wrought out, and who, though at that time very inadequately represented, were by no means altogether without a voice in the choice of members of the House of Commons; for there were at that time some places, such as Preston, in which the suffrage was more nearly universal than it is at present. It is true that there was an immense amount of bribery, corruption, and intimidation; but these practices were resorted to by the opponents of the ministry as well as by their supporters, and they were less influential in times of great popular excitement, such as those during which the present election was carried on. Thus the anti-reform influence of the immense number of close boroughs was to some extent neutralised, and an anti-reform ministry was assailed by means of the very system of which they were the last possible upholders.

Such was the state of things and such the aspect of affairs when an event occurred which resounded throughout the world, and exercised on the elections, which were just on the eve of their commencement, an influence which proved fatal to the Wellington administration. The French ministry, finding that each successive election produced a Chamber of Deputies more unfavourable to their views, and more opposed to the royal authority—that the press was becoming more and more violent and audacious in its assaults on the government—and that changes of great importance, and in their eyes likely to lead to its entire subversion, were otherwise inevitable, issued a body of ordinances, which fundamentally changed the then existing constitution of the country, and destroyed the liberty of the press. The publication of these ordinances produced an insurrection, for which the French Government had made no adequate preparation; and after three days' fighting in the streets of Paris, during which the troops were almost without food, the city was evacuated and left in the hands of the populace. The king abdicated in favour of his grandson; but the condition was disregarded. The dethroned monarch fled to England; and it was for some days doubtful whether the monarchical form of government would be preserved in France, or a republic established. The white flag, the symbol of French royalty, was discarded, and the tricolor flag, then regarded as the emblem of revolution and republicanism, was substituted for it. However, the Duke of Orleans was appointed first Lieutenant-General of the Kingdom, and afterwards King of the French.

This event produced an immense sensation throughout Europe. In Brussels the popular enthusiasm issued in an insurrection, which ended in the separation of Belgium from Holland, and its erection into an independent kingdom. But nowhere was sympathy with the popular victory in France more warmly felt and manifested than in England, where, as we have seen, the general election was just on the point of commencing, under circumstances of peculiar gravity. Had the monarch been at that moment unpopular, he would probably, like Charles X., have been hurled from his throne. Fortunately, however, the new king, by his affable demeanour, his sailor-like bluntness, his dislike of ostentation, and his supposed liberal leanings, was highly popular throughout the nation, and especially in the metropolis. Therefore the feelings which might under other circumstances have been directed against the sovereign were turned against his ministers, who were not supposed to stand very high in his favour; and these feelings found a ready vent in the electoral struggle. The result was, that the elections—which before the Reform Bill were almost invariably carried on amidst tumult and disorder, especially in the large towns—were scenes of greater confusion than ever, and resulted, almost in every place where the constituency was really free to elect its own representatives, in the triumph of the advocates of parliamentary reform over the ministerial candidates. In county after county the latter were defeated; in some cases by ultra-Tories, bent on avenging themselves on the government for its supposed treachery in conceding Catholic emancipation; in others, by their Whig opponents. Of the defeats which the ministry thus sustained, the most remarkable and the most damaging was that which they experienced in Yorkshire, where their great opponent, Mr. Brougham, though entirely unconnected with the county, was returned without serious opposition. The government, greatly to its credit, abstained from using the means for influencing the election, which had usually been employed by preceding administrations. The result of the general election was, that the ministry was weakened by about fifty votes in the House of Commons, besides the damaging moral effect produced by the number, and still more by the character, of these defeats.

The new Parliament assembled on the 26th of October; but the session was not opened till the 2nd of November, the interval having been occupied in swearing-in the members. On the last-mentioned day the king came to the House with great pomp, and delivered his speech in person. The address in reply passed both Houses without a division; but in the upper chamber a debate arose upon it, which was remarkable on account of the following declaration of the prime minister against reform, which is supposed to have been the immediate cause of the fall of the administration, and of the consequences to which that event led. Referring to some remarks on the subject of reform which had been made by Earl Grey, the duke said:

'The noble earl has alluded to something in the shape of a parliamentary reform; but he has been candid enough to acknowledge that he is not prepared with any measure of reform; and I have as little scruple to say that his majesty's government is as totally unprepared as the noble lord. Nay, on my own part, I will go farther, and say, that I have never read or heard of any measure up to the present moment which could in any degree satisfy my mind that the state of the representation could be improved, or be rendered more satisfactory to the country at large than at the present moment. I will not, however, at such an unseasonable time, enter upon the subject or invite discussion; but I shall not hesitate to declare unequivocally what are my sentiments upon it. I am fully convinced that the country possesses at the present moment a legislature which answers all the good purposes of legislation, and this to a greater degree than any legislature ever has answered in any country whatever. I will go farther, and say, that the legislature and the system of representation possess the full and entire confidence of the country, deservedly possess that confidence, and the discussions in the legislature have a very great influence over the opinions of the country. I will go still farther, and say, that if at the present moment I had imposed upon me the duty of forming a legislature for any country, and particularly for a country like this, in possession of great property of various descriptions, I do not mean to assert that I would form such a legislature as we possess now—for the nature of man was incapable of reaching it at once—but my great endeavour would be, to form some description of legislature which would produce the same results. The representation of the people at present contains a large body of the property of the country, in which the landed interests have a preponderating influence. Under these circumstances, I am not prepared to bring forward any measure of the description alluded to by the noble lord. I am not only not prepared to bring forward any measure of this nature, but I will at once declare that, as far as I am concerned, as long as I hold any station in the government of the country, I shall always feel it my duty to resist such a measure when proposed by others.'

The wisdom of this declaration has often been assailed; and certainly not without reason. But when its impugners add, as they generally have done, that if the duke had at this time conceded the transfer of the franchises of a few corrupt nomination boroughs, such as Penryn and East Retford, the people would have been satisfied, and the changes which form the subject of this work might have been deferred for a long time, we must demur to the statement. Believing, as we do, that the diminution of the predominance of the landed interest, through the reform of the House of Commons, was a moral and political necessity, that it was rapidly becoming to a large portion of the nation a question of bread or no bread, we also believe that changes which had no tendency to remove the evils which were felt, and which would have produced no visible alleviation of them, would not have satisfied a demand for reform which owed its force to far other causes than a mere sentimental disapproval of abuses; and therefore it seems to us that, viewing the matter from the duke's standpoint, he was quite right in resisting changes which were not likely to prevent, but rather to produce, a demand for farther changes in the same direction. But in every point of view this frank and uncompromising declaration was highly impolitic. It proved that reform was more than ever hopeless under the Wellington administration, and showed the Whigs, if they were not already convinced of the fact, that they could not obtain office in any other way than by overturning it. The duke was now fairly at bay; he turned on his assailants with the same steady tenacity which he had displayed at Torres Vedras and Waterloo; but he took up his ground with far less skill and with very different fortune.

Closely on this declaration there followed another event, of very little importance in itself, but which greatly increased the unpopularity of the ministry, and encouraged its opponents in their assaults on it. Their majesties had been invited to dine at the Guildhall on the 9th of November, and the invitation had been accepted. A few days before the intended dinner, Mr. Peel, the home secretary, received information from various quarters, and particularly a communication from Mr. Key, the Lord Mayor elect, warning him that some ill-disposed persons were likely to take advantage of the occasion to create a disturbance; and though the Duke of Wellington was the person against whom these designs were alleged more particularly directed, it was thought that even if he absented himself on the occasion some disturbance might take place, which, in the crowded state of the streets that the king's visit was certain to produce, might cause terrible confusion and even loss of life. Under these circumstances ministers advised the king to postpone his visit to the City. The announcement of this resolution produced great disappointment in the metropolis and consternation throughout the country. As the visit was countermanded at the last moment, expensive preparations had been made. The most sinister rumours were in circulation. In the first moments of panic it was thought that London was going to follow the example of Paris, and that a revolution was imminent. The funds, which the declaration of the Duke of Wellington had brought down from 84 to 80, now fell to 77. As these apprehensions were soon seen to be entirely groundless, terror was succeeded by ridicule and censure. Ministers were now accused of having allowed themselves to be alarmed, and of having terrified the country without any good reason, and having, through fears originating entirely in their own unpopularity, prevented the most popular monarch who had ever occupied the throne from receiving the homage of a loyal and enthusiastic people.

Never perhaps before or since had any administration become so odious to the people as was the government of the Duke of Wellington at this moment. Abuse, ridicule, argument, invective, calumny, in fact every species of assault, was directed against them from every quarter. The shops, not only of the booksellers, but of the linen-drapers, were filled with caricatures of them; in the case of the latter they were stamped on handkerchiefs and other articles of linen or calico. The duke was usually represented in the dress of an old hackney-coachman, while Sir R. Peel figured as a rat-catcher. The old Tories were entirely alienated, and though most of them dreaded reform, they distrusted a ministry which in their opinion had already betrayed them, and might betray them again. They remembered that if the duke now declared strongly against reform, he had formerly declared as strongly against Catholic emancipation. Besides, they were so blinded by passion and indignation, that they were ready to run any risks in order to take vengeance on the supposed treachery of their old leaders. Little did they dream of such a measure of reform as we shall speedily see proposed, and ultimately carried, or of the utter shipwreck of their party which was close at hand. Others again, as we have already seen, like the Marquis of Blandford, had become reformers, hoping that the people, who were strongly imbued with anti-catholic prejudices, might, if admitted to the franchise, elect men who would retract the concessions made to the Catholics, or at all events prevent any farther legislation in that direction, and punish the authors of the hated measure with political annihilation. The Whigs, who had now completely broken with the government, clearly saw that their only chance of power lay in its overthrow. The friends of the ministry supported it without enthusiasm; its enemies were open and vehement in their attacks on it; and many, foreseeing its approaching downfall, were preparing to desert it. The king, who was very fond of popularity, did not choose to sacrifice it by sustaining a ministry evidently odious to his people, and which he himself had no great reason to love. The Opposition encouraged these feelings by the most unbounded adulation of the patriot king, whom they took every opportunity of eulogising at the expense of his government. The ministers themselves began to see that their fall from power was inevitable, and to pave the way for a future return to it.

Nor was that fall long deferred. On the 14th of November a motion was made by Sir H. Parnell 'for the appointment of a select committee to take into consideration the estimates and amounts proposed by command of his majesty regarding the civil list.' This motion was carried by a majority of 29, in spite of the strenuous opposition of the government. The defeat was not of a nature to render a resignation absolutely necessary, according to constitutional usage, and the government might very probably have tried their fortune again, if they had not been prevented from doing so by the fear of placing themselves and the party they represented in a worse position. Mr. Brougham, during the Yorkshire election, had pledged himself to the electoral body of that county to take the earliest opportunity of bringing forward a bill for the reform of the representation. He had accordingly, as soon as the House assembled, and before the Speaker had even read the speech from the throne, given notice of his intention to carry out this pledge. His plan had been submitted to a large meeting of members, and had been approved by them. He proposed to give votes to all copyholders, leaseholders, and householders; to give members to Manchester, Glasgow,

Leeds, Sheffield, and other large towns; to deprive each nomination borough of one of its representatives; to disfranchise the out-voters in towns, but not in counties; to allow freemen in towns to vote if they had resided for six months; to reduce the time of elections to a single day; and perhaps to limit the number of members in the House to five hundred.

Such was the plan which Mr. Brougham had undertaken to introduce on the evening following that on which Sir H. Parnell's motion was carried. The success of that motion showed the ministers that they had lost the confidence of the House, and that their fall could not be much longer delayed. It was highly probable that they would suffer another defeat on Mr. Brougham's motion, which the Duke of Wellington's declaration pledged them to resist, and to which most if not all of them were strongly opposed. Should this prove to be the case, they would be compelled to resign on the question of reform, and this would necessitate the appointment of a ministry pledged either to carry Mr. Brougham's plan, or bring forward another. This danger they hoped to elude by resigning at once. Besides, by quitting office on the civil-list question, they placed their opponents in a very embarrassing position. The king strongly objected to any interference with the civil list, as an invasion of his prerogative as well as likely to lead to a reduction of his own appointments, or at least to unpleasant investigations. By resigning on this question, they placed their opponents in the position of assailants of the royal prerogative, and themselves in that of champions and almost martyrs of the interests and prerogatives of the crown. The ministry, therefore, resigned on the morning after their defeat on Sir H. Parnell's motion. Their resignation was accepted by the king, and communicated the same evening to both Houses. Mr. Brougham, though really unprepared to introduce his measure, professed great reluctance in consenting to its postponement at the earnest request of Lord Althorp and several other political friends, adding, at the same time, 'as no change that may take place in the administration can possibly affect me, I beg to be understood that, in putting off this motion, I will put it off to the 25th of this month, and no longer.'

It may be thought that a House of Commons, of which

the majority were, as we have seen, representatives of a few individuals or close corporations generally selling their right of nominations for a valuable consideration, would never be likely to admit a reform which remedied abuses so profitable. There were, however, two things which served to counteract, to a very great extent, the defects of the representation, and to give public opinion a very considerable influence over its measures. The first of these was the right of free speech, which was enjoyed by all its members; the second was the publicity given to its debates by the newspaper press.

The freedom of speech, which had from the earliest ages been enjoyed to a great extent by the members of the legislature, was now as fully admitted and as firmly established as could be desired. Every member, however unpopular his opinions might be, could command the attention to which his abilities entitled him. He might bring forward any proposal he thought fit, or introduce any arguments he pleased in supporting or opposing the propositions of other members, and might protest as strongly as he pleased against the conduct of the government and the measures of Parliament. And though he might be in a most insignificant minority, or even might stand alone, yet if he had truth and right on his side he generally, at length, found support; and if he did not himself witness the success of his endeavours, he bequeathed his cause to others, who took it up and carried it forward to victory.

But there was another principle which constituted an important and necessary supplement to the freedom of speech enjoyed by the House, and that was, the right, now fully accorded to the press, of reporting and commenting freely on the proceedings of Parliament, by which means the English people assisted, as it were, at the discussions of their representatives; and many members, whose views were scarcely listened to in the House, produced a great impression in the country. Thus, every man who could read the periodical press might form his own opinions on the questions brought before the legislature, and every one who could write might publish his thoughts, and might suggest new arguments in favour of, or in opposition to, the measures brought under discussion; and if his arguments were worthy of attention, they were pretty sure to find their way through some channel or other into the great legislative arena in which the decisive struggle was carried on. Hence everything that could be urged in favour of or against measures proposed was sure to be brought forward, and so the progress made was safe and well considered. Public opinion was long in getting itself recognised; yet when once fully and firmly formed, its success was only a question of time. Still, the process was extremely slow; and it often happened that while public and legislative attention was occupied with one class of questions, abuses grew up in other quarters, and multiplied unchecked. And this was necessarily and especially the case with regard to abuses inherent in the legislature itself, and which many of its members had a strong interest in perpetuating. Of the truth of this statement, the great struggle, on the history of which we are now entering, is the best illustration. The abuses which it ultimately removed had grown up almost unheeded during a long period; and when at last public opinion was directed to them, more than half a century of fruitless discussion—fruitless, at least, so far as any immediate result was concerned—was carried on before the final effort which we are now to record.

On receiving the resignation of the Duke of Wellington and his colleagues, the king sent for Earl Grey, who, from his age, his abilities, his constant advocacy of parliamentary reform, his high worth and integrity, occupied the foremost position in the Whig party, and was the man who was generally expected to take the place vacated by the duke's resignation. In accepting office he stipulated that the reform of Parliament should be made a cabinet measure. From that moment the question assumed a new position. Hitherto it had figured in the Whig programme as one among the many measures of improvement which they deemed necessary. At the late election it had appeared on the banners of the party side by side with 'retrenchment,' 'triennial parliaments,' 'civil and religious liberty,' and the 'abolition of colonial slavery;' and though it was supported by the masses, their want of education and direct political power prevented their wishes from having much influence; and their partiality for the measure was in some degree prejudicial to it, on account of the recollection of the excesses and atrocities which had been perpetrated in France in the years 1792 and 1793. But from the moment that it became known that the measure had been adopted by the government, it assumed a paramount importance; all other questions seemed to sink into insignificance; and the whole nation formed itself into two hostile parties of reformers and anti-reformers: the first composed of the great mass of the people, and especially of the youthful ardour and progressive spirit of the country; the other comprehending the aged, the wealthy, the cautious, and the interested, who all combined in organising resistance to an innovation which they feared would reproduce in this country the terrible scenes of the first French Revolution.

The support of the great majority of the nation facilitated the task which Earl Grey had undertaken, and enabled him to construct his ministry without much difficulty. The most serious impediment he encountered was that which was created by the position of Mr. Brougham. He was a man of transcendant ability, great diligence, extraordinary mental and physical energy, and indisputably the first orator of the day. Though not the nominal, he was the real leader of the Whig party in the House of Commons; and he had a number of followers large enough to make him the absolute arbiter of the fate of any ministry that Lord Grey might form. But what was much more than all this, he had in his hands the question of reform—the question on which the whole strength of the ministry must depend, and without which it could not hope to cope with the Tories, most of whom were now thoroughly alive to their danger, and ready to restore their allegiance to the leaders whom they had assisted to overthrow. The fate of the new government was evidently in his hands; he felt it, and so did all parties. We have already seen how he declared that under no circumstances could any change in the ministry affect him; and there is not the least ground for believing that he was insincere in this declaration, or that he made it, as was afterwards insinuated, in order to extort higher offers from his political associates. Throughout life he gloried in his election as member for Yorkshire, to which he had been chosen by the largest constituency in the empire, entirely on public grounds. The position he then occupied, both at the bar and in the House of Commons, seemed to render it certain that he must make a very large sacrifice of wealth and of real power in accepting office, which at that time seemed likely to be of very precarious and uncertain tenure. Earl Grey first offered him the office of Attorney-General, which he rejected, not, as was asserted at the time, rudely and peremptorily, but with a calm and courteous statement of the reasons of his refusal. Earl Grey next suggested that the Mastership of the Rolls should be offered to him, with the understanding that he would retain his seat for Yorkshire. This offer Mr. Brougham was prepared to accept; but it was objected to by the king, on the ground that, as member for Yorkshire and with the reform question in his hands, he would be too strong for the ministry and the king together.

'But,' rejoined the premier, 'how am I to carry on the government, if he remains in the House of Commons with the feeling that he has been slighted and ill-used by the party to whom he has rendered such great services, and to which his support is so essential?'

'Let him be Lord Chancellor,' replied the king.

'Your majesty has just objected to his appointment to the inferior office of Master of the Rolls, and therefore I should not have ventured to suggest his name for the higher office of Lord Chancellor; nevertheless, if such is your majesty's pleasure, I will offer him the office.'

That office was accordingly offered to Mr. Brougham, who, however, was in no haste to accept it. His professional income at the bar was much greater than that which he would derive from the chancellorship; an office which he might lose in a few months, and be compelled to retire with a pension of 4000*l*. per annum. Besides, having hitherto practised at the common-law bar, he was ill acquainted with the mode of procedure in Chancery, and could only hope to discharge creditably the duties of an equity judge by exertions from which even his gigantic energy and powers of application might well shrink. Moreover, if he gained in dignity, he would lose in real power; for he would relinquish the lead of a great party in the House of Commons for the more splendid but less influential position of Chancellor. These considerations disposed Mr. Brougham, in the first instance, to decline the chancellorship. Lord Grey, however, requested him, before giving a final answer, to talk the matter over with some of his proposed colleagues. At this meeting he stated to his political friends the reasons above assigned, and they agreed that they could not fairly expect him to make the sacrifices which the acceptance of the chancellorship would involve. When the rest had gone, Lord Althorp remained, and said to him, 'Remember that our party has been out of office for twenty-five years, and that your refusal to join us will, in all probability, prevent the formation of a ministry, and keep us in opposition for another quarter of a century.' Mr. Brougham yielded to this appeal; the new ministry was constituted, and the names were soon after announced.*

* The following is the list of the new ministry:—

Earl Grey	First Lord of the Treasury.
Mr. Brougham	Lord chancellor (created Lord Brougham and Vaux).
Viscount Althorp	Chancellor of the Exchequer.
Marquis of Lansdowne	President of the Council.
Lord Durham	Lord Privy Seal.
Viscount Melbourne	Secretary for the Home Department.
Viscount Palmerston	Secretary for the Foreign Department.
Viscount Goderich	Secretary for the Colonies.
Sir J. R. Graham	First Lord of the Admiralty.
Lord Auckland	Master of the Mint.
Mr. Charles Grant	President of the Board of Trade.
Duke of Richmond	Postmaster-general.
Lord Holland	Chancellor of the Duchy of Lancaster.
Earl of Carlisle	

(The above formed the cabinet.)

Mr. C. N. W. Wynn	Secretary at War.
Sir James Kempt	Master-general of the Ordnance.
Duke of Devonshire	Lord Chamberlain.
Marquis Wellesley	Lord Steward.
Earl of Albemarle	Master of the Horse.
Marquis of Winchester	Groom of the Stole.
Lord John Russell	Paymaster of the Forces.
Mr. G. J. W. Ellis	First Commissioner of Land Revenue.
Mr. C. P. Thompson	Treasurer of the Navy, and Vice-President of the Board of Trade.
Sir Thomas Denman	Attorney-general.
Sir W. Horne	Solicitor-general.

IRELAND.

Marquis of Anglesea	Lord-lieutenant.
Lord Plunket	Lord chancellor.
Sir J. Byng	Commander of the Forces.
Hon. E. G. Stanley	Chief Secretary.
Mr. E. Pennefather	Attorney-general.
Mr. P. Crampton	Solicitor-general.

Anti-reformers pointed out with triumph, and reformers observed with regret, that Lord Grey had placed six or seven relatives and connexions in his administration.

On the 22nd of November, Earl Grey, in his place in the House of Lords, briefly explained the policy of the new administration. He thought that government should at once consider the state of the representation, to correct those defects which had been occasioned by the operation of time; but he would not support universal suffrage, nor any of those fanciful and extensive plans which would lead not to reform but to confusion. Government had succeeded to the administration of affairs in a season of unparalleled difficulty; and he promised that the state of the nation should have the immediate, diligent, and unceasing attention of the cabinet. It was their intention to suppress outrages with severity, and to reduce all unnecessary expense with an unsparing hand. 'My lords,' he said in conclusion, 'the principles on which I stand are—amelioration of abuses, promotion of economy, and the endeavour to preserve peace consistently with the honour of the country. The administration stands before you and the public. You know the persons, you have heard our principles; for the maintenance of them we throw ourselves upon the confidence and support of our sovereign, the house, and the country.'

Some time necessarily elapsed before those members of the administration who were also members of the House of Commons could be re-elected. They were all, however, returned without difficulty, except Mr. Stanley (the late Earl of Derby), who was defeated at Preston by radical Hunt. This defeat was owing to the refusal of Mr. Stanley to support the ballot, a measure very popular at this time. After the dispatch of business requiring immediate attention, Parliament was prorogued on the 22nd of December to the 3rd of the following February.

Earl Grey assigned the task of framing the government plan of parliamentary reform to a committee composed of Lord Durham, Lord Duncannon, Lord J. Russell, and Sir J. Graham. To this committee Lord J. Russell brought an outline of the scheme which appeared to him best calculated to meet the expectations of the nation and the requirements of the times.* He proposed that fifty of the

* For fuller details, see the introduction to the now edition of Earl Russell's Essay on the *History of the English Government and Constitution*, p. xxxvi., &c.

smallest boroughs should be totally disfranchised; that fifty more should in future return one member instead of two; that the seats thus gained should be transferred to counties and large towns; that the qualification for voting should be the payment of a certain rental, the amount of which was left blank, in order that it might be the subject of future deliberation, and which, as we shall see, was subsequently fixed at 10*l*. Lord J. Russell's plan was adopted by the committee; but in deference to the opinion of Lord Durham, it was so far modified that, instead of the arbitrary number of fifty being selected for disfranchisement or semi-disfranchisement, it was determined that all towns which by the census of 1821 had fewer than 2000 inhabitants should be disfranchised entirely, and that all towns having a population of between 2000 and 4000 persons should be disfranchised partially. Finding that the amount of disfranchisement would be pretty nearly the same on this system as on his own original plan, Lord J. Russell assented to this modification, not, however, without some misgivings, which were abundantly justified by the event. In the discussions which subsequently took place, he had repeated reason to repent that he had not more strongly resisted this suggestion, which was eventually set aside in favour of one nearly identical with that which he originally suggested. The plan agreed on by the committee was submitted to the cabinet by whom it was received not only with unanimity but with enthusiasm. Many of them, if we may judge by the opinions they had previously expressed on the subject, must have regarded the proposed measure as excessively violent and pregnant with danger. But they probably felt that there was quite as much peril, under existing circumstances, in not going far enough as in going too far; that it was desirable that the subject should be dealt with broadly, boldly, and, for the time being, finally, and that consequently they must be prepared to yield and even to risk a good deal, rather than disappoint the highly-raised expectations of the people. Besides, the state of the nation at that moment was such as required strong measures of some sort. The popular discontent had for the moment been allayed; but a disappointment of the hopes that had been raised would soon cause it to revive, and therefore it was evident that either the causes of their dissatisfaction must be removed, or a lamentable and continually widening estrangement must take place between the government and the governed.

Nor were these discontents without reason. The people of this country had for some time past been suffering cruelly, and had been forcing themselves on the attention of their lawgivers in an altogether unpleasant and unsatisfactory manner. Statements of agricultural distress, mining distress, and manufacturing distress were made, echoed, and re-echoed. Sometimes they were met by qualified assent, sometimes by vehement contradiction; but they still continued to be made. But let governments and members of Parliament say what they would, there *was* distress, and very serious and terrible distress too. Agricultural labourers were found starved to death, having tried in vain to support nature with sorrel and other suchlike food. In vain did landlords abate their rents, and clergymen their tithes; wages continued to fall, and had at length reached such a point of depression that they did not suffice to support existence. Nay, we find that in the division of Stourbridge, in the county of Dorset, the magistrates published the following scale, according to which relief was to be given:—

When the standard quartern wheaten loaf is sold at	s. d.	s. d.	s. d.	s. d.	s. d.	s. d.
	1 0	0 11	0 10	0 9	0 8	0 7
The weekly allowance, including earnings, is to be made up to—						
For a labouring man	3 1	2 10	2 7	2 4	2 1	1 10
For a woman, boy, or girl, above 14 years old	2 4	2 2	2 0	1 10	1 8	1 6
For a boy or girl of 14, 13, or 12	1 11	1 9	1 7	1 5	1 3	1 1
,, ,, of 11, 10, or 9	1 7	1 6	1 4	1 3	1 2	1 0
,, ,, under 9	1 5	1 5	1 3	1 2	1 1	1 0

At the time to which we refer, the quartern loaf cost 10d. Let us suppose a family consisting of a man, his wife, one boy or girl of fourteen, one boy or girl of eleven, and one little child. For these five persons there are eight shillings and ninepence altogether; that is to say, there are ten and a half quartern loaves, or forty-three pounds of bread to divide among the five, which gives a little more than eight pounds of bread for each to live on for a week, or rather more than a pound of bread per day for each to live and work on, and that without allowing anything at all for rent, fuel, drink, clothing, or washing. And to this condition the agricultural labourer was rapidly sinking everywhere; for if in some counties the allowance was on a somewhat more liberal scale, in others it was even lower than in Dorsetshire. It was clear that such a state of things could not be allowed to continue. Something must be done, and that speedily. Political economists might demonstrate that it was unavoidable; but flesh and blood will rebel. It is not therefore very surprising, though it puzzled legislators and justices of the peace a good deal, that agricultural labourers who were thus provided for took the matter into their own hands; that they assembled in an altogether unlawful manner, nay compelled others, though not very much against their own will, to join them, and go about tumultuously demanding increased wages; and when this demand was refused, that they began to break threshing and other agricultural machinery, which they believed to be the chief cause of their distress. The farmers, thoroughly frightened, referred their labourers to the clergyman or landlord to ask for a reduction of tithe or rent, and thus to enable them to pay better wages. However, these violences, as might be expected, produced little or no benefit, and things were rapidly going from bad to worse. The peasantry, finding no more machines to break, or forcibly prevented from breaking them, began secretly to set fire to stacks of corn or hay; and soon through twenty-six counties, night after night, the sky was reddened with the blaze of the nation's food going up in flame and smoke skywards. The peasantry who beheld these sad scenes often stood with folded arms grimly smiling at the work of destruction; nay, they sometimes cut the hose of the fire-engines brought to extinguish the conflagration, and in other ways obstructed the firemen. Never perhaps had this country been in a more deplorable condition; never had so deep a sadness weighed on the minds of all classes of the population as towards the close of this year 1830. Terrible imaginations magnified tenfold the terrible reality. The political atmosphere seemed to be charged with electricity. Members of the government, members of the legislature, well-to-do country gentlemen, substantial and unsubstantial farmers, were all sorely distressed, puzzled, bewildered, and affrighted. All sorts of reports were in circulation; all sorts of explanations were given of the supposed causes of these fires. There were stories of foreigners, of elegantly-dressed gentlemen riding on horses or in post-chaises, who had come down to instigate the peasants to fire the ricks, or who fired them with their own hands. Cobbett also, who often employed very unmeasured language in his efforts to draw attention to the sufferings of the labouring classes and the causes of their distress, and who, notwithstanding a great deal of violence, and a great deal of crotchety nonsense about bank paper, saw clearly and told plainly what required to be done, was accused most unjustly of being the instigator of the outrages committed by the labourers. Then, again, there was a mysterious "Swing," with whose name many threatening letters were signed, who was generally supposed to be at the bottom of all the mischief. Old Lord Eldon assured the House of Lords that he was informed that the gaols contained great numbers of persons who were not natives of this country; and Lord Sidney, in a long and intemperate letter, repeated the statement. But there was no shadow of foundation for these assertions. The simple fact was, that wars, national debt, increase of population, corn-laws, mal-administration of the poor-laws, and other legislation or hindrance of legislation, had reduced the great mass of the people, and especially the agricultural labourers, to the verge of starvation and despair. They were going mad with misery; and in their madness they did mischief by which they themselves were sure to be the first and greatest sufferers. We know that it has been maintained that the condition of the people at this period was grossly misrepresented for party purposes both by Whigs and Tories, and that, in spite of partial distress, the people were really well off. Now we hold this to be a capital error, and one which, if entertained, must not only lead to a very erroneous view of the nature of the reform struggle, but also prevent those who entertain it from doing justice to the government by which the Reform Bill was proposed, and the House of Commons by which it was carried. Were the people goaded on by suffering to demand reform, or were they incited to it by the arts of a party? That the former is the true explanation of the matter is proved by innumerable petitions, from every county of England, presented to the House of Commons in the course of this year, 1830, one hundred and eighty-five of which the author of this work has examined, and which distinctly show the distress that then prevailed in every part of the kingdom and in every branch of industry.* These petitions, with scarcely a single exception, breathe an ardent spirit of loyalty and attachment to the institutions of the country. Agreeing in the existence and the extremity of the distress, they ascribed it to different causes; some to excessive taxation, some to the malt-tax, some to the East India Company, some to the state of the currency, to paper money, machinery, or the corn-laws; and the prayers of the petitioners are as various as their opinions.

The French Revolution, and the events which followed it both in France and England, impressed a new direction on the feelings of the working classes, and especially on the more ignorant portion of the agricultural labourers. Finding that a neighbouring people had risen in insurrection and overthrown their government; having discovered that the ruling few with all their politics are no match for the misgoverned many when they combine in their fury and despair, they resolve that they will have bread, or that none else shall have it. If they cannot raise themselves out of the pit of misery in which they are sunk, they will at least pull down into it those whom they regard as the authors of their calamities. Such were the feelings and such the designs which distress and misery have engendered; and we have already seen the crimes and follies to which they have led. But now a new light has come to those sufferers. The hated government of the Duke of Wellington has been overthrown, and has been succeeded by a new government composed of 'friends of the people.' They are told that the changes from which they have been taught to expect the removal, or at least the alleviation, of their miseries are to be speedily made, and especially that the great measure of reform, which they have come to regard as the grand panacea for all their sufferings, is about to be carried; above all, that they have a 'PATRIOT KING' devoted to the welfare of his people, who has chosen

* For full proof of this allegation, see my *History of the Reform Bill of 1832*, pp. 78-95.

reform ministers, and is determined to give them every kind of support. From that moment hope sprang up again; the tumultuous assemblages ceased; the incendiary fires became less frequent; trade revived and distress diminished; and a proclamation issued by the government condemning the outrages and directing that they should be promptly repressed, found the people already contrite and submissive. The reform government, however, were determined to show that, though friends of the people, they were no friends of their excesses. Special commissions were issued for the trial of the rick-burners and machine-breakers, who had been apprehended in great numbers; and by a mixture of judicious lenity and judicious severity, the last remnants of insubordination were almost entirely trampled out.

The distress of the manufacturing districts, though less severe, was far from being inconsiderable, and manifested itself in strikes, disturbances, and assassinations. But in this case the suffering was less and the situation better understood. The manufacturing population too, on the whole, were more patient, because they had more hope of the speedy removal of their distresses, and saw more clearly how it was to be achieved.

In Ireland, as has been already mentioned, a very extensive failure of the potato crop had brought the western districts of that country, almost always close down upon the starvation point, to actual famine. The consequence was, a fearful increase of those outrages and assassinations which were so common at all times as to be regarded by English statesmen as the chronic and irremediable malady of that unhappy country.

In all these cases the ministers, feeling themselves strong in the confidence of the people, acted vigorously and wisely, and their bitterest opponents were obliged to confess that they manifested more firmness than their predecessors in office. They did what they could, which was but little, to mitigate the immediate sufferings of that unhappy and long misgoverned people; they vindicated the majesty of the law by putting down and punishing crime as far as it was possible to do so. O'Connell, who had now commenced an agitation for the repeal of the union with

England, was prosecuted and convicted, though he was ultimately allowed to escape punishment; and all that the state of law and the state of society in that country admitted of being done to repress violence and restore order was done by the government.

CHAPTER II.

FIRST INTRODUCTION OF THE REFORM BILL.

Such was the aspect of affairs when Parliament reassembled on the 3rd of February, 1831, the day to which they had adjourned before Christmas. Earl Grey, after presenting numerous petitions in favour of reform, announced that a measure on that subject had been framed, which would be effective without exceeding the bounds of a just and well-advised moderation. He added, that it had received the unanimous consent of the whole government, and would be submitted to the other House of Parliament at as early a period as possible.

In the Lower House a similar announcement was made by Lord Althorp, who added that the bill would be introduced on Tuesday, the 1st of March, by Lord J. Russell, who had been selected by the government for the discharge of this important duty, in consequence of the ability and perseverance he had displayed in advocating parliamentary reform in days when it was unpopular. 'Now, therefore,' said Lord Althorp, 'that the cause is prosperous, the government think that, on account of his perseverance and ability, the noble lord should be selected to bring forward a measure of full and efficient reform, instead of the partial measures he has hitherto proposed.' This intimation was received with lively satisfaction by a large party in the House, and by an overwhelming majority out of the House, who evidently desired a strong and sweeping reform.

The selection of Lord John Russell to introduce the bill was not only a wise, but an almost necessary choice on the part of the government. Lord Althorp—good-natured, courteous, thoroughly honest, a sincere, tried, and enthusiastic reformer, but feeble and incapable as a legislator, and as a speaker so hesitating, tedious, and embarrassed, that it was painful to listen to him—was no match for such antagonists as Sir Robert Peel, Sir C. Wetherell, Mr. Croker, and other able debaters, who sat on the opposite side of the House, and were sure to offer the most pertinacious opposition to the intended measure. Other members of the cabinet rather accepted the bill as a concession to the demands of the people that could no longer be safely denied than as a measure desirable on its own account. Others, again, had not the weight and the moderation which the task required. It therefore devolved almost inevitably on Lord John Russell, whose connection with the house of Bedford—identified with most of the great struggles for English liberty in modern times—gave him great weight; whose known courage, patience, and perseverance, and tried attachment to the cause of reform, but above all, whose virtuous and noble character pointed him out as pre-eminently fitted to take charge of the measure on which the government deliberately staked its existence, and on the strength of which it claimed and received the support of the great body of the nation. The result proved the propriety of the selection. Probably no other member of the ministry would have exhibited the same combination of firmness and tact throughout the whole of the long and vexatious struggle which ensued, or would have steered his way through the two great dangers that were continually impending—that of a serious mutilation of the measure on the one hand, or of a violent popular outbreak on the other.

This selection of Lord J. Russell was not, however, allowed by the Opposition to pass unchallenged. In referring to it, Sir C. Wetherell fastened on the fact that Lord J. Russell was not a member of the cabinet, and insinuated that the measure was committed to him because it had not the support of the whole government. This insinuation Lord Althorp vigorously repelled, declaring that every member of the cabinet was favourable to the bill, and that it would be regarded as a government measure. In justification of the arrangement, he reminded the House that the celebrated East India bill was brought forward by Mr. Burke, who, like Lord J. Russell, was paymaster of the forces, and not a member of the cabinet.*

* On the precedent thus adduced Mr. Roebuck remarks, "The plan proposed by Burke was his own, and Lord J. Russell was not Mr. Burke." But as we have already stated, the Reform Bill in all its principal outlines was Lord J. Russell's plan, just as much as the India Bill was Mr. Burke's: and to say that Lord J. Russell was not Mr. Burke, is quite irrelevant to the question at issue, which did not relate to his competence, or want of

The most serious difficulties and the greatest perils which the new ministry encountered arose out of their financial measures. On this subject the expectations of their followers had been highly raised. At the last general election 'reform' and 'retrenchment' had figured together on their banners. On every hustings their candidates had exaggerated and inveighed against the extravagance of preceding administrations, and had led the people to expect that the accession of the Whig party to power would be at once followed by an enormous reduction in the expenditure of the government and the burdens of the people. Moreover, the new government had come into office through the success of Sir H. Parnell's motion on the civil list. It was therefore confidently expected by the supporters of the ministry both in and out of Parliament, that very considerable reductions would be made; that the civil list, in particular, would be at once brought under the control and supervision of the House, and many items of expenditure which it contained would be struck out. The government, however, found themselves very much embarrassed by these expectations, which had certainly contributed in no small degree to place them in office. William IV. was quite as tenacious of his supposed right to control the civil-list expenditure, and quite as much opposed to any parliamentary interference with that fund, or any reduction of it, as the most unreforming of his predecessors. This probably laid the first foundation of that gradual estrangement of the king from the new ministry, which began to be manifested at a very early period of the reform struggle, and which led at length to the recall of the Duke of Wellington. The new government were most anxious to propitiate the sovereign, but they could not altogether ignore the pledges they had given, nor the circumstances under which they had obtained office. Again, when they turned their eyes from the civil list to the general expenditure of the country, they found that they succeeded a very frugal administration, which had already made great reductions, and in some respects had

competence, but simply to the fact of his not being a member of the cabinet. One thing at least must be admitted, which is, that Lord J. Russell succeeded in carrying through the measure entrusted to him; while Mr. Burke, with all his transcendent abilities, signally failed.

carried them farther than, under the present circumstances of the country, ministers considered safe or prudent. They were almost, or altogether, new to office, and were to a great extent in the hands of subordinate officials appointed by preceding governments, who hated the names of reform and retrenchment, and who, though obliged to work under the government, were little disposed to suggest reductions, or to assist in carrying them out. Besides, Lord Althorp, with all his amiability and personal popularity, was a wretched chancellor of the exchequer. The consequence was, that the financial measures of the government signally failed; and great was the disappointment of the nation when the budget was brought forward. The only important changes the ministry effected were to wring from the reluctant monarch his consent to waive a claim for an outfit for the queen, and to make some portions of the civil list, in which the sovereign had no direct interest, a little more subject than before to the control of Parliament. They also proposed some unimportant reductions and a few changes in the incidence of taxation, most of which were afterwards withdrawn, as being admitted on all hands to be undesirable; but nothing was attempted at all commensurate with the expectations that had been raised. The nation saw, with surprise and displeasure, that the pension-list was untouched; the army increased by 7,000 men, and the navy by 3,000; that an annuity of 100,000*l*. was voted to the queen in case she should survive her husband. Had the reform measures of the government disappointed the expectations of the nation nearly as much as their measures of retrenchment, the fate of the Whig party would have been sealed; but the disappointment was soon forgotten in the general joy and enthusiasm which the provisions of the ministerial measure of reform excited. In the mean time the press did great service to the government. It pointed out the difficulties in which the ministry were placed in a Parliament filled with the nominees of boroughmongers. It asked whether a patriotic and reforming king was to be treated less liberally than his unreforming predecessors. And it reminded the country that a reformed House of Commons would speedily enable the ministry to deal with financial questions more vigorously and unsparingly. By these and other arguments it palliated, if it could not altogether cover, the financial failure of the ministry.

But had matters been even worse than they were, the country was not disposed to brood over the budget. All men were now looking forward with excited curiosity to the appearance of the coming measure of reform. Meetings were being held in such numbers that the newspapers could scarcely find space for the enumeration of them; and from all parts of the country petitions for reform came pouring into the two Houses, and gave rise to frequent discussions, which tended to keep alive the feverish excitement that prevailed on the subject. Great numbers of these petitions asked for the ballot, universal suffrage, and annual or triennial parliaments. Still there was a general disposition to wait for the promised measure of the government, and to give it a fair and candid consideration.

At length the long-expected first of March arrived. The state of the House and of all its approaches testified to the intensity of the public feeling. Never before had there been so great a desire to witness the proceedings; never had the avenues leading to the House been so thronged with persons anxious to obtain admission. The lobbies, the staircases leading to the galleries, were all crowded. The business on which the House was engaged caused the opening of the doors, by which the public were admitted, to be delayed till nearly five o'clock. No sooner were they thrown open than a tremendous struggle for admission took place, attended by so much noise and violence, that the speaker threatened to order the galleries to be cleared, if the tumult were not at once suppressed. This menace put a stop to the disorder, and the fortunate few who had succeeded in fighting their way into the gallery had leisure to look around them. Only about a hundred members were present at the time, but every bench in the body of the House and in the side galleries had its back labelled with the name of some member, who had adopted this means of securing a seat for the debate. As the hour of six approached, the House filled rapidly, and before it arrived, scarcely a single unoccupied place was discernible. The clock was on the stroke of six when Lord J. Russell entered, and was welcomed with a tremendous cheer.

And now we have reached the commencement of that unparalleled war of tongues, which continued with some intervals, night after night, from this 1st of March 1831 to the 5th of June 1832. Its word-battles, intensely interesting to a nation in a state of violent political ebullition, would be insupportably tedious to the cool and unexcited reader, even in the most condensed form. Nevertheless they must ever constitute the surface of our history, nay to some considerable extent its pith and substance, affording, as they do, insight into the great conflict of social forces that was going on behind them, and of which these debates were the parliamentary outcome. Our undertaking therefore imposes on us the necessity of giving the reader some account of them, and particularly of this first discussion, more notable than any of those that succeeded it, because it was the first, and because, though it led to no decisive result, it pretty nearly exhausted all the arguments for and against the leading features of the measure. We shall therefore try to put before the reader not the speeches themselves, but their distilled essence. We shall first allow Lord J. Russell to unfold and explain his plan at some length, though still in a considerably condensed form; then we shall give, with much more condensation, portions of the speeches of some of those who delivered their reasons for supporting or opposing the bill. We have selected only those who are representative men, that is to say, men who expressed not only their own feelings and opinions, or those of a select circle of friends, but who also spoke the sentiments and views of large bodies of their countrymen. In every case we shall preserve the style, and, as far as the exigencies of great abbreviation will allow, the very words of the different orators. In this way we hope to give the reader as good a notion as we can, in the smallest possible compass, of the nature and extent of the proposed changes, and of the manner in which they were regarded. Of the subsequent debates our account will be much more brief, though probably quite full enough for the reader's patience.

After a short interruption, arising from its crowded state, Lord J. Russell, amidst breathless and expectant silence, but in a low voice and somewhat deprecatory manner, thus unfolded his plan.

'The object of ministers has been to produce a measure with which every reasonable man in the country will be satisfied. We wish to take our stand between the two hostile parties, neither agreeing with the bigotry of those who would reject all reform, nor with the fanaticism of those who contend that only one plan of reform would be wholesome or satisfactory, but placing ourselves between both, and between the abuses we intend to amend and the convulsion we hope to avert.

'The ancient constitution of our country declares that no man should be taxed for the support of the state who has not consented, by himself or his representative, to the imposition of these taxes. The well-known statute *de tallagio non comedendo* repeats the same language; and although some historical doubts have been thrown upon it, its legal meaning has never been disputed. It included "all the freemen of the land," and provided that each county should send to the Commons of the realm two knights, each city two burgesses, and each borough two members. Thus about a hundred places sent representatives, and some thirty or forty others occasionally enjoyed the privilege; but it was discontinued or revived as they rose or fell in the scale of wealth and importance. Thus, no doubt, at that early period the House of Commons did represent the people of England; there is no doubt likewise that the House of Commons, as it now subsists, does not represent the people of England. Therefore if we look at the question of right, the reformers have right in their favour. If we consider what is reasonable, we shall arrive at a similar result. A stranger who was told that this country is unparalleled in wealth and industry, and more civilised and more enlightened than any country was before it—that it is a country that prides itself on its freedom, and that once in every seven years it elects representatives from its population to act as the guardians and preservers of that freedom—would be anxious and curious to see how that representation is formed, and how the people choose their representatives, to whose faith and guardianship they entrust their free and liberal institutions. Such a person would be very much astonished if he were taken to a ruined mound, and told that that mound sent two representatives to Parliament; if he were taken to a stone wall and told that three niches in it sent two representatives to Parliament; if he were taken to a park where no houses were to be seen, and told that that park sent two representatives to Parliament. But if he were told all this, and were astonished at hearing it, he would be still more astonished if he were to see large and opulent towns, full of enterprise and industry and intelligence, containing vast magazines of every species of manufactures, and were then told that these towns sent no representatives to Parliament. Such a person would be still more astonished if he were taken to Liverpool, where there is a large constituency, and told, "Here you will have a fine specimen of a popular election." He would see bribery employed to the greatest extent and in the most unblushing manner; he would see every voter receiving a number of guineas in a box, as the price of his corruption; and after such a spectacle, he would no doubt be much astonished that a nation whose representatives are thus chosen could perform the functions of legislation at all, or enjoy respect in any degree. I say, then, that if the question before the House is a question of reason, the present state of representation is against reason.

'The confidence of the country in the construction and constitution of the House of Commons is gone. It would be easier to transfer the flourishing manufactures of Leeds and Manchester to Gatton and Old Sarum than to re-establish confidence and sympathy between this House and those whom it calls its constituents. If therefore the question is one of right, right is in favour of reform; if it be a question of reason, reason is in favour of reform; if it be a question of policy and expediency, policy and expediency are in favour of reform.

'I come now to the explanation of the measure which, representing the ministers of the king, I am about to propose to the House. Those ministers have thought, and in my opinion justly thought, that no half measures would be sufficient; that no trifling or paltering with reform could give stability to the Crown, strength to Parliament, or satisfaction to the country. The chief grievances of which the people complain are these: first the nomination of members by individuals; second, the election by close corporations; third, the expense of elections. With regard to the first, it may be exercised in two ways, either over a place containing scarcely any inhabitants, and with a very extensive right of election, or over a place of wide extent and numerous population, but where the franchise is confined to very few persons. Gatton is an example of the first, and Bath of the second. At Gatton, where the right of voting is by scot and lot, all householders have a vote; but there are only five persons to exercise the right. At Bath the inhabitants are numerous, but very few of them have any concern in the election. In the former case we propose to deprive the borough of the franchise altogether. In doing so we have taken for our guide the population-returns of 1821; and we propose that every borough which in that year had less than 2,000 inhabitants should altogether lose the right of sending members to Parliament; the effect of which will be to disfranchise sixty-two boroughs. But we do not stop here. As the honourable member for Boroughbridge (Sir C. Wetherell) would say, we go *plus ultra*: we find that there are forty-seven boroughs of only 4,000 inhabitants, and these we shall deprive of the right of sending more than one member to Parliament. We likewise intend that Weymouth, which at present sends four members to Parliament, should in future send only two. The total reduction thus effected in the number of the members of this House will be 168. This is the whole extent to which we are prepared to go in the way of disfranchisement.

'We do not, however, mean to allow that the remaining boroughs should be in the hands of a small number of persons, to the exclusion of the great body of the inhabitants who have property and interest in the place. It is a point of great difficulty to decide to whom the franchise should be extended. Though it is a point much disputed, I believe it will be found that in ancient times every inhabitant householder resident in a borough was competent to vote for members of Parliament. As, however, this arrangement excluded villeins and strangers, the franchise always belonged to a particular body in every town. That the voters were persons of property is obvious from the fact that they were called upon to pay subsidies and taxes. Two different courses seem to prevail in different places. In some, every person having a house and being free was admitted to a general participation in the privileges formerly possessed by burgesses; in others, the burgesses became a select body, and were converted into a kind of corporation, more or less exclusive. These differences, the House will be aware, lead to the most difficult, and at the same time the most useless, questions that men can be called upon to decide.* I contend that it is proper to get rid of these complicated rights, of these vexatious questions, and to give the real property and real respectability of the different cities and towns the right of voting for members of Parliament. Finding that a qualification of a house rated at £20 a year would confine the elective franchise instead of enlarging it, we propose that the right of voting should be given to householders paying rates for houses of the yearly value of £10 and upwards, upon certain conditions hereafter to be stated. At the same time, it is not intended to deprive the present electors of their privilege of voting, provided they are resident. With regard to non-residence, we are of opinion that it produces much expense, is the cause of a great deal of bribery, and occasions such manifest and manifold evils, that electors who do not live in a place ought not to be permitted to retain their votes. With regard to resident voters, we propose that they should retain their right during life, but that no vote should be allowed hereafter except to £10 householders.

'I shall now proceed to the manner in which we propose to extend the franchise in counties. The bill I wish to introduce will give all copyholders to the value of £10 a year, qualified to serve on juries, under the right hon. gentleman's (Sir R. Peel's) bill, a right to vote for the return of knights of the shire; also that leaseholders for not less than twenty-one years, whose annual rent is not less than £50, and whose leases have not been renewed within two years, shall enjoy the same privilege.

'It will be recollected that, when speaking of the numbers disfranchised, I said that 168 vacancies would be created. We are of opinion that it would not be wise or expedient to fill up the whole number of those vacancies.

* The author believes the following to be a tolerably complete list of the voting qualifications for boroughs before the passing of the Reform Bill; Householders, resident householders, householders paying scot and lot; inhabitants, resident inhabitants, inhabitants paying scot and lot; burgesses, capital burgesses, burgageholders; freeholders, freemen, resident freemen; corporations, potwallopers, payers of poor's rates.

After mature deliberation, we have arrived at the conclusion, that the number of members at present in the House is inconveniently large. Besides, when this House is reformed, as I trust it will be, there will not be such a number of members who spend their moneys in foreign countries, and never attend the House at all. We propose, therefore, to fill-up a certain number of the vacancies, but not the whole of them. We intend that seven large towns should send two members each, and that twenty other towns should send one member each. The seven towns which are to send two members each are as follows:

Manchester and Salford.
Birmingham and Aston.
Leeds.
Greenwich, Deptford, and Woolwich.
Wolverhampton, Bilston, and Sedgley.
Sheffield.
Sunderland and the Wearmouths.

The following are the names of the towns which it is proposed should send one member each to Parliament:

Brighton.
Blackburn.
Wolverhampton.
South Shields and Westoe.
Warrington.
Huddersfield.
Halifax.
Gateshead.
Whitehaven, Workington, and Harrington.
Bolton.
Stockport.
Dudley.
Kendal.
Tynemouth and North Shields.
Cheltenham.
Bradford.
Frome.
Wakefield.
Kidderminster.

It is well known that a great portion of the metropolis and its neighbourhood, amounting in population to 800,000 or 900,000, is scarcely represented at all; and we propose to give eight members to those who are thus unrepresented, by dividing them into the following districts:

	Population.
Tower Hamlets	293,000
Holborn	218,000
Finsbury	162,000
Lambeth	128,000

Next, we propose an addition to the members of the larger counties; a species of reform always recommended, and which, I believe, Lord Chatham was almost the first to advocate. The bill I shall beg leave to introduce will give two members to each of the three ridings into which Yorkshire is divided—the east, west, and north—and two additional members to each of the following twenty-six counties, of which the inhabitants exceed 150,000:

Chester.	Warwick.	Stafford.
Derby.	Cumberland.	Sussex.
Durham.	Northampton.	Nottingham.
Gloucester.	Cornwall.	Surrey.
Lancaster.	Devon.	Northumberland.
Norfolk.	Essex.	Leicester.
Somerset.	Kent.	Southampton.
Suffolk.	Lincoln.	Worcester.
Wilts.	Salop.	

'I now beg leave to direct the attention of the House to that part of the plan which relates to the expense of long-protracted polls, and which, while it removes that evil, also greatly facilitates the collection of the sense of the elective body. We propose that all electors in counties, cities, towns, or boroughs shall be registered; and for this purpose machinery will be put in motion similar to that of the Jury Act—that is to say, at a certain period of the year (I now speak of boroughs) the parish officers and churchwardens are to make a list of persons who occupy houses of the yearly value of £10. This list of names will be placed on the church doors, we will suppose in September; and in October the returning officer will hold a sort of trial of votes, where claims made and objections stated will be considered and decided. On the 1st of December the list will be published; every person who chooses may obtain a copy of it; and it will be the rule to govern electors and elections for the ensuing year. The means of ascertaining who are the electors being thus easy, there is no reason why the poll should be kept open for eight days, or, as in some places, for a longer period; and it is proposed that, nearly according to the present law, booths shall be erected in the different parishes, so that the whole poll may be taken in two days. For my own part, I may say that I expect the time will come when the machinery will be found so simple, that every vote may be given in a single day; but in introducing a new measure, it is necessary to allow for possible defects. Attempts might be made to obstruct the polling; and I therefore recommend two days, in order that no voter may be deprived of the opportunity of offering his suffrage.

'As to the counties, the matter may be somewhat more difficult. We propose that the churchwardens should make out a list of all persons claiming the right to vote in the several parishes, and that these lists shall be affixed to the church doors; a person to be appointed (say a barrister of a certain standing) by the judge of assize shall go an annual circuit within a certain time after the lists have been published, and he will hear all claims to vote and objections to voters. Having decided who are entitled to exercise the privilege, he will sign his name at the bottom of the list, and will transmit it to the clerk of the peace, and it will then be enrolled as the list of the freeholders of the county for the ensuing year.

'Everybody knows and must have lamented the enormous expense to which candidates are put in bringing voters to the poll. In Yorkshire, without a contest, it costs nearly 150,000*l.*; and in Devonshire the electors are obliged to travel forty miles, over hard cross roads, which occupies one day, the next is consumed in polling, and the third in returning home; the whole a manifest source of vast expense and most inconvenient delay. We propose, therefore, that the poll shall be taken in separate districts, those districts to be arranged according to circumstances by the magistrates in quarter sessions, and not changed for two years. The sheriffs will hold the election on a certain day; if a poll is demanded, they will adjourn the election to the next day but one, and the poll will be kept open for two days. On the third day the poll will be closed, and on the sixth day an account of the number of votes will be published. It shall be so arranged, that no voter shall have to travel more than fifteen miles to give his vote. It is also proposed that the number of polling places in each county shall not exceed fifteen, as the multiplication of places for receiving the votes would give rise to great inconvenience. We propose that each county should be divided into two districts, returning each two members to Parliament. There will be some difficulty in adjusting these districts;

but I propose that his Majesty shall nominate a committee of the Privy Council to determine their extent and direction. In some of the boroughs to which the right of representation will be continued, the number of electors is exceedingly small. We shall therefore insert in the bill a clause, giving power to the commissioners nominated under that bill to enable the inhabitants of the adjoining parishes and chapelries to take part in the elections, when the number of electors in such borough shall be below 300. That these are extensive powers, I shall not attempt to deny; and if any gentleman in the House will suggest a better, safer, and more constitutional mode of effecting the object, his Majesty's ministers will have no hesitation in adopting that mode, and waiving their own.

'I have now only one thing more to say with regard to the representation of England. In all those new towns to which we propose to give the right of sending members to Parliament, all persons who are entitled by their property to vote shall be excluded from the right to vote for the representatives of the county; but it is not intended to interfere with the franchise of those freeholders who are at present entitled to vote. With respect to the right of the forty-shilling freeholders, I do not think that there should be any alteration.'

In obedience to the loudly-expressed wish of the House, Lord J. Russell then read, amidst great laughter and much cheering, the list of the boroughs which the bill proposed to disfranchise, as having fewer than 2000 inhabitants, according to the population returns of 1821; as well as that of the boroughs to be semi-disfranchised, as having a population under 4000, according to the same census.* He then proceeded as follows:

* Subjoined is the list read by Lord J. Russell, to which we have added the prevailing influence in each borough, and the number of the constituency:—

Place.	Prevailing Influence.	No. of Constituency.
Aldborough	Duke of Newcastle	60
Aldeburgh	Marquis of Hertford	80
Appleby	Earl of Thanet and Earl Lonsdale	100
Bedwin	Marquis of Aylesbury	80
Beeralston	Earl of Beverley	100
Bishop's Castle	Earl Powis	60
Bletchingley	Mr. M. Russell	80

'Scotland needs reform even more than England, as in that country no such thing as popular representation is known. There we intend to give the suffrage to every copyholder to the annual value of 10*l.*, and to holders of leases for ten years, not renewed within two years previous to the election, and paying 50*l.* a-year rent. The counties

Place.	Prevailing Influence.	No. of Constituency.
Boroughbridge	Duke of Newcastle	50
Bossiney	Lord Wharncliffe and Mr. Turno	35
Brackley	R. H. and J. Bradshaw	33
Bramber	Lord Calthorpe and the Duke of Rutland	20
Buckingham	Duke of Buckingham	13
Callington	Mr. A. Baring	50
Camelford	Marquis of Cleveland	25
Castle Rising	Marquis of Cholmondeley and Hon. F. G. Howard	30
Corfe Castle	Mr. H. Bankes	60
Dunwich	Lord Huntingfield and Mr. Barne	18
East Looe	Mr. Hope	50
Eye	Sir E. Kerrison	100
Fowey	Mr. Austin and Mr. Livey	70
Gatton	Lord Monson	5
Haslemere	Earl of Lonsdale	60
Hedon	Money	830
Heytesbury	Lord Heytesbury	50
Higham Ferrers	Lord Fitzwilliam	145
Hindon	Lord Grosvenor and Lord Calthorpe	240
Ilchester	Disputed between Lord Cleveland and Lord Huntingtower	70
Lostwithiel	Earl of Mount Edgcumbe	94
Ludgershall	Sir G. Graham and Mr. Everett	70
Malmesbury	Mr. Pitt	13
Maw's, St.	Duke of Buckingham	20
Michael, St.	Lord Falmouth and Mr. J. H. Hawkins	32
Midhurst	Mr. John Smith	18
Milborne Port	Marquis of Anglesea	90
Minehead	Mr. Luttrell	10
Newport, Cornwall	Duke of Northumberland	62
Newton, Lancashire	Mr. Legh	60
Newton, Isle of Wight	Lord Yarborough and Sir F. Barrington	40
Okehampton	Money	250
Orford	Marquis of Hertford	20
Petersfield	Colonel Jolliffe	140
Plympton	Mr. Trehy and the Earl of Mount Edgcumbe	210
Queenborough	Money *versus* Ordnance	270
Romney, New	Sir E. Dering	150
Reigate	Earl of Hardwicke and Lord Somers	200
Saltash	Mr. Buller	36
Seaford	Lord Seaford and Mr. J. Fitzgerald	—
Steyning	Duke of Norfolk	110
Stockbridge	Lord Grosvenor	106
Tregony	Mr. J. A. Gordon	180
Wareham	Right Hon. J. Calcraft	21

72   THE REFORM BILL.   [CHAP. II.

are to be settled as follows: Peebles and Selkirk to be joined, and to elect one member together; Dumbarton and Bute, Elgin and Nairn, Ross and Cromarty, Orkney and Shetland, Clackmannan and Kinross, with certain additions, to do the same. The remaining twenty-two counties are each singly to return one member. The burghs are to be as follows: Edinburgh to have two members; Glasgow

Place.	Prevailing Influence.	No. of Constituency.
Wendover	Lord Carrington	140
Wenbly	Marquis of Bath	90
West Looe	Mr. Buller	55
Whitchurch	Lord Sidney and Sir S. Scott	70
Winchelsea	Marquis of Cleveland	40
Woodstock	Duke of Marlborough	400
Woolton Bassett	Earl of Clarendon and Mr. Pitt	100
Yarmouth	The Holmes Family	50

The following was the list of boroughs which would return one member of Parliament each:—

Place.	Prevailing Influence.	No. of Constituency.
Amersham	Mr. W. Drake	125
Arundel	Money	450
Ashburton	Lord Clinton and Sir L. V. Palk	170
Bewdley	Lord Littelton	13
Bodmin	Marquis of Hertford and Mr. D. G. Gilbert	36
Bridport	Money	340
Chippenham	Mr. Neald	135
Clitheroe	Earls Howe and Brownlow	45
Cockermouth	Earl of Lonsdale	180
Dorchester	Earl of Shaftesbury and Mr. R. Williams	200
Downton	Earl of Radnor	60
Droitwich	Lord Foley	12
Evesham	Bribery	600
Grimsby	Money	300
East Grinstead	Earl de la Warr	30
Guildford	Lord Grantley	250
Helston	Duke of Leeds	36
Honiton	Money	350
Huntingdon	Earl of Sandwich	240
Hythe	Corporation and patronage	150
Launceston	Duke of Northumberland	15
Leominster	Money	700
Liskeard	Earl St. Germains	105
Lyme Regis	Earl of Westmorland	30
Lymington	Sir H. B. Neale	70
Maldon		2000
Marlborough	Marquis of Aylesbury	21
Marlow	Mr. O. Williams	285
Morpeth	Earl of Carlyle and Mr. W. Ord	240
Northallerton	Earl of Harewood	200

to have two; Aberdeen, Paisley, Dundee, Greenock, and Leith (with the addition of Portobello, Musselburgh, and Fisherow), each singly to return one member. Thirteen districts of burghs to return one member. By the proposed alterations there will be an addition of five new members to the representation of Scotland, making the total number fifty, instead of forty-five, as at present.

'In Ireland we propose to give the right of voting to all holders of houses or land to the value of 10l. a year. There are some places in that country which have not their due share in the representation; of those the principal are Belfast, Limerick, and Waterford, to which we propose to give representatives so as to add three to the whole number of members for Ireland. The arrangement which I now propose will be eminently favourable both to Ireland and Scotland, and to Ireland particularly so; for as the number of the present members in the House representing places in England is to be reduced, and their places are not to be supplied, the Irish members will become of greater relative importance.

'The result of all the measures comprehended in this bill, as affecting the number of members in this House, will

Place.	Prevailing Influence.	No of Constituency.
Penryn	Money	400
Richmond	Lord Dundas	270
Rye	Dr. Lamb	25
St. Germains	Earl St. Germains	70
St. Ives	Mr. Wellesley	200
Sandwich	Money	855
Shaftesbury	Lord Grosvenor	300
Sudbury	Money	600
Tamworth	Lord Townshend and Sir R. Peel	300
Thetford	Duke of Grafton and Mr. A. Baring	31
Thirsk	Sir F. Frankland	60
Totnes	Corporation	68
Truro	Earl of Falmouth	26
Wallingford	Money	180
Westbury	Sir E. A. Lopes	70
Wilton	Earl of Pembroke	20
Wycombe	Corporation and Sir J. D. King	68

In most of these boroughs the seats were sold by the proprietors. Sometimes they themselves, or some of their relatives or dependants, were nominated to represent them. Bribery was also practised with little or no reserve or concealment, where it was necessary; but in many instances the constituency was so dependent on the proprietor, that no expenditure of this kind was requisite.

be, that of the present number of 658—168 being taken off by disfranchisement—490 will remain. To that number five being added as the increase of members for Scotland, three for Ireland, one for Wales, eight for London, 34 for large towns, and 55 for counties, in England; making the future number of members of the united Parliament 596, the decrease of the present number will accordingly be 62. The number of persons who will be entitled to the suffrage under this bill, not previously possessing that right, will, I suppose, be in the counties 110,000; in the towns, 50,000; in London, 95,000; in Scotland, 50,000; in Ireland about 40,000; and it is my opinion that the measure will add to the constituency of the Commons House of Parliament about half a million of persons, all connected with the property of the country, having a valuable stake amongst us, and deeply interested in our institutions. They are persons on whom we may depend in any future struggle in which the nation may be engaged, and who will maintain and support Parliament and the throne in carrying that struggle to a successful termination. I think this measure will farther benefit the people by inciting them to industry and good conduct. For when a man finds that by industry and attention to his business he will entitle himself to a place in the list of voters, he will have an additional motive to improve his circumstances and preserve his character. I think, therefore, that in thus adding to the constituency, we are providing for the moral as well as for the political improvement of the country.

'Language has been held as if I had said that the institutions of the country could by their own indirect strength defend every attempt at sedition, if no reform were adopted. In my opinion, the question has little to do with sedition or rebellion. The question is, whether, without some large measure of reform, the government, or any government, can carry on the affairs of the country with the confidence and support of the nation. If this cannot be done, then it may become a question whether reform can be resisted; but there can be no question that in such a case the British constitution must perish. The House of Commons in its unreformed state has nothing to look to but public confidence and the sympathy of the nation for its support. It appears to me that if reform is refused, all such sympathy and confidence will soon be withheld. I ask whether, when the ministers of the Crown consider that reform is necessary, when the sovereign has permitted them to lay before the House their proposition, and when they come with that proposition to declare in the most unequivocal manner that they consider reform to be indispensable; and when people out of doors, by multitudes of petitions and millions of voices, are calling for the same thing, is it for the House of Commons to say, " We are the judges of our own purity; we equally despise the ministers of the Crown and the voice of the people; we will keep our power against all remonstrances and all petitions; and we will take our chance of the dreadful consequences?" I appeal to the gentry and the aristocracy of England. In my opinion, they were never found wanting in any great crisis of the country. When war was carrying on against the national enemy, they were always the foremost to assert the national honour; and when great sacrifices were to be made and great burdens to be supported, they were as ready to bear their proportion as the rest of their fellow-subjects. I ask them now—now that a great sacrifice is to be made for the public safety and the general good—will they not show their generosity, will they not evince their public spirit, and identify themselves in future with the people? I ask them to come forward under these circumstances and give stability, political strength, and peace to the country. Whatever may be the result of the proposition I have made to the House, I must say that his Majesty's ministers will feel that they have thoroughly done their duty in bringing the measure forward; neither seeking for the support of particular classes nor the applause of the multitude. When they have felt it their duty to resist popular feelings, they have not hesitated to encounter and withstand them by a firm and vigorous enforcement of the law, by which many disturbances have been prevented or suppressed, I trust permanently. By their vigorous enforcement of laws passed before they entered office, agitation has been made to subside, and peace has been reëstablished. In no case could it be said that ministers have wavered in their duty by bending to popular clamour, or by seeking to ingratiate themselves in popular and transient favour. I have a right to say that, in submitting the present proposition to the House, they have evinced an interest in the future welfare of the country. They think that what they propose is the only thing calculated to give permanence to the constitution, which has so long been the admiration of foreign nations on account of its free and popular spirit, but which cannot exist much longer except by an infusion of new popular spirit. By these means the House will show to the world that it is determined no longer to be an assembly of the representatives of small classes and particular interests, but that it is resolved to form a body of men who represent the people, who spring from the people, who have sympathies with the people, and who can fairly call upon the people to support their burdens in the future struggles and difficulties of the country, on the ground that they who ask them for that support are joining hand and heart with them, and, like themselves, are seeking only the glory and welfare of England.'

Lord J. Russell then sat down, amidst loud and prolonged cheering from all sides.

The motion which he made for leave to bring in the bill was briefly seconded by Sir J. Sebright.

The first man who rose to oppose the motion was Sir R. H. Inglis, member for the University of Oxford; an elegant scholar, a thorough gentleman, a worthy and honest man. He admirably represented the opinions and prejudices of the country gentlemen and clergy of the day. Nobody in the House was more deservedly popular and respected, none more strongly resisted every proposed alteration of the existing institutions of the country. His opposition to the measure might certainly be reckoned on, and his opinion on it was all the more important because it was sure to be the opinion of the two great classes of which he was at once the representative and the *beau idéal*. After some preliminary observations, he thus proceeded to deal with the arguments which the proposer of the motion had advanced in favour of the bill:—

'We are not sent here for the particular spot which we represent, but to consider the affairs of the country and the good of the church. When a member is returned to this House, he ceases to be responsible to his constituency. It is at the end of the period when he has to serve them in Parliament that he again comes before them, and it is then only that he is accountable to them. In the United States, in France, or in Belgium, where there are changes from day to day, the proposition of the noble lord might find favour; but in England the case is very different. I know there are such men as Delolme and Montesquieu, who have taken on themselves to talk of representation being founded on the basis of population and taxation; but I can find no trace of such a principle in any of the ancient times of our constitution. If it can be shown that places were returned to send members which were neither parishes nor market towns, I presume it will be admitted that those places could not be very considerable. Now, there are Haslemere and West Looe, which have never been one or the other, and yet they have been called on to send representatives to Parliament. And not only have small towns been called on to send representatives, but large towns have been left unrepresented; and this is a most important point in answer to those who pretend that they only ask for the restoration of the constitution. Can the noble lord show that any town or borough has been called into parliamentary existence because it was large or populous, or excluded from it because it was small? The noble lord has tried to make much of the instance of Old Sarum. In one and the same year, the 23rd Edward I., a writ was issued to both Old and New Sarum, and in neither case was it conferred on account of population or taxation. On the contrary, I believe it was given, in the first instance, to oblige some Earl of Salisbury, by putting his friends into the House. And in an account of the borough, it was stated that it had lately been purchased by Mr. Pitt, the possessor of the celebrated diamond of that name, who has obtained an hereditary seat in the House of Commons, as much as the Earl of Arundel possessed one in the House of Peers by being the owner of Arundel Castle. How, then, can it be said that, according to the constitution of the country, noblemen are not to be represented and their interests regarded in this House? The cause of the creation of many boroughs is, I believe, obscure; but, on the other hand, some were as clear and as well ascertained as possible. It is known that two writs to return members were issued by Elizabeth at the desire of one of her favourites, Sir Christopher Hatton; and Newport in the Isle of Wight had received its franchise to please Sir George Carew.

This is the history of many of the small boroughs; and all the Cornish boroughs were formed in that manner. Fifteen Cornish boroughs had at one time received the right of representation, some of which were small villages, and none of them entitled to rank as considerable among the towns of England. It is in vain after this to talk of the purity of representation in former times. I defy the noble lord to point out at any time when the representation was better than it is at present. I say, therefore, that what is proposed is not restorative. The House and the country may judge what it is; but I will state, in one word, that it is REVOLUTION—a revolution that will overturn all the natural influence of rank and property.

'I have omitted to observe in the proper place, that many of the towns to which the noble lord proposes to give the elective franchise were considerable places at the period when the right of representation was given to other places, and yet they were omitted. Halifax three hundred years ago was known to have a population of 8400; Wakefield was a most considerable town at the same time; and Manchester, according to tradition, had not less than 5400 inhabitants for two hundred years before the year 1580; and, at all events, it is certain that at the latter period it possessed the amount of population I have just mentioned. But can it be said in answer to this that no boroughs have been created after that time, and that therefore it had not been possible to do justice to such considerable places? Just the reverse of this is the fact; for after the date to which I have referred with respect to Halifax, fifty-one boroughs have been summoned to send representatives to Parliament; and after the date with respect to Manchester, fourteen boroughs have received writs. But I have another objection to that part of the proposition of the noble lord in which he would have taxation and representation go hand in hand. There are individuals who only come into this House by a casting vote. In such cases, the minority is all but equal to the majority; and yet they are to have no representation. If this principle of the noble lord is worth anything, it is worth this: that no person of such minority would be bound to pay the taxes or obey the laws that were enacted, as his representative had no share in their formation.

'The great benefit of the constitution of the House of Commons as it now exists (though if the noble lord's plan is adopted, that benefit will cease) is, that it represents all interests, and admits all talents. If the proposed change takes place, it will be almost entirely confined to one interest, and no talent will be admitted but the single one of mob oratory. Many of those who sat for " close and rotten boroughs," as they have been designated for the first time by a member of the government, have constituted the chief ornaments of the House and the support of the country; but would, if this plan had been adopted in their days, never have been received into the House. I ask the noble lord by what means the great Lord Chatham came into Parliament? By the bye, the first borough for which that great man sat was Old Sarum itself. Mr. Pitt sat for Appleby. Mr. Fox came in for a close borough; and when rejected for a populous place, he again took refuge in a close borough. Mr. Burke first sat for Wendover; and when by that means he became known, he was transposed in his glory to Bristol, as Mr. Canning, who also first sat for Wendover, was transposed to Liverpool. When their talents became known, they were the honoured representatives of large towns; but would such places ever have thought of selecting Mr. Canning, Mr. Burke, or Lord Chatham, if they had not previously had an opportunity of showing their talents in the House? It is only by this means that young men who are unconnected by birth or residence with large towns can ever hope to enter this House, unless they are cursed—I will call it cursed—with that talent of mob oratory which is used for the purpose of influencing the lowest and most debasing passions of the people.'

Passing by Mr. Twiss and Lord Althorp, we come to Mr. Hume, the member for Middlesex, and the leader of the more moderate portion of the radical party. He frankly declared that, 'radical reformer as he was, the plan proposed much exceeded his expectations, and that, with all his disposition to put confidence in ministers, he was not prepared to find them come forward with so manly a measure.' 'They have,' said he, 'fully redeemed their pledge; and though, in my opinion, the omission to shorten the duration of Parliament and to introduce the ballot are deficiencies, yet as they are points on which a large number

of members have not made up their minds, ministers have
acted wisely is not encumbering the present measure with
them, as they can be brought forward at any time as
separate questions. . . . I can assure the House, that all
those with whom I have conversed are satisfied with the
measure. Many whom I know to be the strongest reformers
in England allowed that they have the utmost reason to be
delighted. . . . I have no doubt that many think the
qualification too high; but there is too much sense in the
British community not to feel that vast good will result
from this measure, though some may not immediately
participate in its benefits.' *

The next speaker we shall select will be our old acquaintance, Orator Hunt, now sitting, as we have seen, for the town of Preston. His approbation of the measure was much less warm than Mr. Hume's, and as the discussion proceeded, it became icy cold; in fact, was changed into something very closely approximating to opposition. He acknowledged that the measure went beyond his expectations, but declared that he had not heard a single word in the course of the debate that was new to him. 'All,' said he, 'that has been said in this House has been said twenty years ago by the weavers of Lancashire. As the bill does not touch the rights of my constituents, I will give it my support; but I am sorry that so little is said about the ballot and the duration of Parliaments. The suffrage is not widely enough extended, if the rabble, as they are called, are not to have votes. My opinions are well known to the country. I have fearlessly and manfully advocated the rights of the people, and I should be unworthy of a seat in this House, if on an occasion like the present I did not advocate the same sentiments here. I have always contended for the right of every one to have a share in the elective franchise, because I have been taught that, according to the constitution of England, representation and taxation go hand in hand, and that no man ought to pay taxes unless he has a share in the representation. Am I to be told that the people who have fought the battles of the country, the lower orders, whom I call the useful classes of society, are to be called on to pay taxes on every article of human subsist-

* Mr. Macaulay's speech is omitted, because it has been published in the collection of his speeches.

rnce, and afterwards denied the right of choosing representatives? I plainly tell the House, and I speak the voice of millions, that such an exclusive doctrine will give no satisfaction out of doors. I am delighted to hear that the rotten boroughs are to be sacrificed. Some honourable members have called the measure proposed by the noble lord not reform but revolution, and an alteration in the constitution. Now, I will admit that statement to be correct, the moment it is proved that rotten boroughs are a part of the constitution. When the honourable member for Calne (Mr. Macaulay) talked of the *rabble*, he looked very hard at me. (These words were received by the House with shouts of laughter.) I understand,' continued Mr. Hunt, ' the meaning of that laugh; and I am only sorry that the honourable and learned member has not remained in his place, that I might have looked in the same way at him. How is this House constituted? How are many honourable members elected? Look at the borough of Ilchester, and the boroughs of Lancashire and Cornwall, and see what classes of men return members to this House. I will tell the House a fact which has come to my knowledge, and which bears on that particular point. In the borough of Ilchester, where I was sent to gaol for two years and six months—(great laughter)—I understand the meaning of that laugh again—but I repeat, that in Ilchester many of the voters are of the most degraded and lowest class, who can neither read nor write, and who always take care to contract debts to the amount of 35*l*. previous to an election, because they know that those debts will be liquidated for them. Is that, then, the class of men which the House is told represents the property of the country? I am one who think that this House ought to be what it professes to be—the Commons House of Parliament, representing the feelings and interest of all the common people of England. I do not stand up to approve the disfranchisement of any persons, because I have always contended for the right of the whole people of England to have a share in the representation. I am fully convinced that the people of England are competent to choose proper representatives. I have been in the habit, for many years past, of attending large public meetings, composed of persons whom the honourable and learned member for Calne has chosen to call the rabble; but I will

undertake to say that they are a much more intelligent
rabble than the electors of Calne. That *Calne* is one of the
most degraded of rotten boroughs; and I wonder by what
chance the ministers have overlooked that most rotten and
stinking hole of corruption in their sweeping measure of
reform. We have been told by the honourable and learned
member for Calne, that if the present measure is not
conceded to the middle classes, we shall have revolution and
massacre. What sort of massacre is it that the hon.
member has alluded to? I remember that when the people
of Manchester assembled together in 1819, as legally and as
peaceably as the hon. members are now assembled in this
House, for the purpose of petitioning for a reform in Parliament and a repeal of the corn-laws—and their petitions were
couched in much more respectful and moderate language
than many petitions which have been lately presented to this
House—then, indeed, there was a massacre. (Cries of
'No, no.') I say yes. The meeting was constitutionally
and peaceably assembled, and what was the result? Why, a
drunken and infuriated yeomanry—('Order,' 'order,' 'question,' 'question,')—with newly-sharpened sabres—('question,' 'question')—rushed among the people and chopped
them to pieces. ('No, no,' 'order,' 'order.') They slaughtered
to death fourteen—('No, no,')—cut and badly wounded
six hundred and eighteen. (Here the excitement and outcries became so great, that Mr. Hunt was unable to proceed; nothing daunted, however, by the interruption, he
lifted up his powerful voice above the tumult, and exclaimed in his most stentorian tones:)—Where is the man
who says no? I repeat that this infuriated yeomanry
murdered fourteen, wounded and slaughtered six hundred
and eighteen, of as peaceable and well-disposed subjects of
his majesty as any I see around me at the present moment.
At that meeting I was advocating the cause of reform.
And I was astonished to hear the noble lord, the paymaster
of the forces, say, in bringing forward the present measure,
that the government had not taken up the question before,
because the people of England had not called upon them
in a manner to justify the interference of government.
The people of England have for many years past been
anxious for reform, and in the years 1816, 1817, 1818,
1819, loudly expressed their wishes for some measure to

amend the state of the representation. . . . I certainly
thought that the scene which was exhibited in the House
yesterday, when the noble lord brought forward the reform
measure, had never been equalled since the time of the
Revolution, when Cromwell came into the House and took
away the bauble of the mace. When I was tried, condemned, and sentenced to suffer two years and six months'
imprisonment in a dungeon—(Here Mr. Hunt was interrupted by laughter and loud cries of 'question')—I think
it is very hard, that while some members, in urging the
question of reform, have gone back to the time of Edward
III., I am not allowed to refer to transactions which have
taken place within the last twenty-nine years. (Here
renewed interruption occurred.) Well, then,' exclaimed
Mr. Hunt, ' I will tell the people of England, that the man
whom they have sent to this House to advocate their right
is not allowed to be heard. ('No, no.') But I say, yes,
yes! I repeat,' continued the imperturbable orator, ' when
I was condemned to suffer two years and six months'
imprisonment in a solitary dungeon, for advocating that
question which is now advocated by so many honourable
members in this House, I little expected to see a measure
of reform proposed by government; though I knew that
Lord Chatham had said, that if reform did not come from
within, it would come from without with a vengeance. The
honourable member for Calne has said that none but a few
crazy radicals in the street would ever dream of invading
the rights of the throne. I ask that honourable and learned
member where any of those radicals are to be met with?
I am as thorough-going a radical as ever paced the Strand;
but I defy the hon. and learned gentleman to prove that I
have ever proposed to attack the privileges of the crown,
though I have often enough protested against the extravagance of the family on the throne, and the misconduct of
that House which has brought the institutions of the country
into disrepute.'

He expressed his determination to support the bill. He
regretted that he had been compelled to address the House
before the hon. members for Tamworth and Boroughbridge.
Hitherto he had heard nothing in the course of debate that
he was not familiar with in the proceedings at the meetings
of the Lancashire weavers.

We next come to Sir C. Wetherell, the comical member of the House, and withal one of the ablest, the darling and champion of the high Tory party. He began by bespeaking, in those tones of mock solemnity which he could assume with a most powerful effect on the risible muscles of his fellow-members, the favour of the House, as he was now making his last dying speech as member for the condemned borough of Boroughbridge. Referring to Mr. Hunt's speech, he insinuated that Calne had been spared because it was a Whig borough, and called upon ministers to rise and defend themselves from the imputation of partiality, to which the preservation of this borough rendered them obnoxious. Coming then to the subject immediately before the House, he said: 'I am aware that in long debates elegance is too apt to run away with accuracy.' (Here a cry of 'hear' and 'question' was raised.) The hon. gentleman paused, and addressing himself directly to the interrupting member, exclaimed: 'Does the hon. member who cries "hear" and "question," and says nothing else, and never affords others an opportunity of reciprocating the same cries—does the hon. gentleman behind the chair ('O!') suppose—but I will not pursue the subject. It appears, then, by this bill of the military paymaster, sixty boroughs are to be deprived of their franchise, and of the right of sending one hundred and twenty members to Parliament; and that forty-seven are to lose one member each; and that in the whole, one hundred and sixty-eight members are to be ejected from this House. I do not wish to call this by an offensive term; but as a great man, Mr. Locke, has said that things should be called by their right names, I call this "corporation robbery." But then there is to be a sort of restitution made, "except that there will be sixty members less in the House than there are now." But does this make the robbery less? Is it less a measure of robbery and pillage, if you take from AB and CD, and give to EF, and if the House is to be composed of sixty members less than at present? The present cabinet of Althorp and Co. seem to have proceeded upon the precedent in the history of England which was given by Cromwell, Fairfax, Milborne, and Co. This plan of cutting off the boroughs and diminishing the number of members has not the merit of originality; for it is almost the same in form, in substance, and in principle, as the radical system of reform which was introduced by the regicides when they established a commonwealth in England.'

After proceeding in the same strain at great length, the honourable gentleman thus perorated:

'I have now performed, and I trust within reasonable limits, the duty which I owe to myself, to the British public, and the House of Commons, in making the observations on this bill which I have found myself compelled to make, and I have now but a few more words to utter. There existed in Cromwell's time a purge of the House of Commons. (Laughter.) That purge was called Colonel Pride's purge. (Laughter and cheering.) The gentlemen on the opposite side of the House are close imitators of the Cromwellian system; not only of his system of parliamentary reform, but also of his sanitary and purgative system; for they are prepared to expel, by one strong dose, no fewer than one hundred and sixty-eight members from the House. I do not know what name should be attached to this specific, for I did not conceive it possible that the country would see a repetition of such a process. Within the last three days, however, the House has been promised a purge, to which, as no name has been attached, I will attach the name of "Russell's purge." (Roars of laughter, and great cheering for some time.) I say that the principle of the bill is republican at the basis; I say that it is destructive of all property, of all right, of all privilege; and that the same arbitrary violence which expelled a majority of members from that House at the time of the Commonwealth, is now, after the lapse of a century from the Revolution, during which the population has enjoyed greater happiness than has been enjoyed by any population under heaven, proceeding to expose the House of Commons again to the nauseous experiment of a repetition of Pride's purge.' The cheering which followed the delivery of this speech was very loud, and lasted for several minutes.

The Opposition had already adopted that Fabian policy which we shall afterwards find them carrying to great lengths, and were seeking to prolong the debates as much as possible, in the hope that some contingency might arise which might diminish the popularity of the measure in the House or in the country, and enable them to get rid of it.

This was evident in many of the speeches already delivered
from the Opposition side of the House, and in none more so
than in that of Sir C. Wetherell, which, able as it was, contained a good deal of repetition, and was evidently intended
to occupy as much time as possible. When, therefore, the
attorney-general (Sir T. Denman) rose to reply on the part
of the government, although it was not yet half-past twelve
o'clock, and though he had been very pointedly alluded to,
and in some sort challenged, in the preceding speech, his
rising to reply was the signal for loud cries of 'adjourn'
from the Opposition, which were continued during a great
part of the honourable gentleman's address. He, however,
persevered, and spoke for an hour, replying to the various
points which had been raised by the preceding speaker.

The next speech which we shall notice is that of Lord
Palmerston, the representative of the party of the late Mr.
Huskisson and Mr. Canning—a party which had hitherto
been almost as strongly opposed to parliamentary reform as
the Duke of Wellington himself. A considerable part of his
speech was taken up with justifying and defending the policy
of the administration to which he belonged. Coming at
length to the question immediately before the House, he said:

'What is it which for years has produced so much misgovernment, so much disregard of public opinion? The
gross bribery practised at elections, by means of which
parties come into Parliament, and undue influence at elections for members of this House, by means of which so
many of them come in, either without constituents, or only
with those whom they have purchased and may sell again.
When, then, by such practices, the people were driven to
tear aside the veil of sanctity with which hereditary respect
had invested even the imperfections of the constitution, it
was impossible that they whose limited propositions of
reform had been rejected would not be led to demand
wider and more extensive changes. There are many men
in this House who wish things to remain as they are, and
who are willing to bear the faults of the constitution for
the sake of its many excellences. I will tell them, that if
they are now driven to the necessity of choosing between a
change which they fear and the evil consequences which
would arise from the refusal of that change, the blame
must rest on those who three years ago refused to make

even the smallest concession to public feeling. If, three years ago, advantage had been taken of the conviction of corrupt boroughs, to bring gradually into connection with this House the great unrepresented towns—if, instead of drawing nice equations between the manufacturing and agricultural interests, they had turned reformers on even a moderate scale—the House would not now have been discussing a plan of general reform, proposed by my noble friend, his majesty's paymaster of the forces. I supported all those plans of limited reform, because I thought them good in themselves, and because I saw that if they were refused, we should be obliged to have recourse to wider and more extensive changes. But my predictions were condemned and disregarded by the gentlemen opposite. For reasons similar to those for which I then supported those limited propositions of reform, I am now prepared to support the more extensive measure which has been proposed by my noble friend. Taunts were thrown out in the course of last night's debate against those who, like myself, were admirers of Mr. Canning. We have been taunted with abandoning the principles which that great man had adopted with respect to the important question of reform. I think that the events which have taken place in this House since the lamented death of that illustrious person might have taught those who indulged in such taunts, that public men might change their opinions on questions of national concernment without being influenced by any but honest and honourable motives. What Mr. Canning's opinions on the question of reform would now have been, had he lived to the present day, it is not for me to say; but they are bad expounders of Mr. Canning's opinions who look for them in the particular sentiments expressed at particular times, and do not scrutinise the principles by which his public life was guided. If any man took a great and enlarged view of human affairs, without doubt that eminent man did; and I venture to say, that had Mr. Canning lived in the present day, and stood in the circumstances in which I stand, his great genius would at once have comprehended the necessity on which the opinions of the government were founded, and would have stated to the House, in my belief, the sentiments which I am now expressing.'

The next speaker was Sir R. Peel. Admirable in tact, in talent, and in the management of details: he was unable to conceive or accept a great and organic change. His temper, cautious even to timidity, led him generally to yield before it was too late, but never to yield too soon. The reform bill, however, involved far too large a stride for his mind to take at once; and though he afterwards profited by the mistake he made on this occasion, he resisted it with all his power, and to the very last. He began his speech by declaring that he was not one of those who joined in taunting Lord Palmerston on account of the change of his opinions, and begged to assure him that his character, conduct, and views afforded a sufficient guarantee for the purity of his intentions. He replied to some charges which Lord Palmerston brought against the late administration. Referring to the manner in which the name of the king had been used in favour of the measure, he said:

'I thought the king had been the fountain of grace and favour; but it seems as if this plan of extreme disfranchisement is to be received by the House, and not dissented from, under the terror of its being introduced with the king's express sanction, if not at the king's suggestion. Then the House is menaced with dissolution. The chances of dissolution are as strong if the measure is carried as if it fails. I care not if the House is dissolved, or not; nor should I be fit for the performance of a single legislative duty if I permitted such a menace to influence me. I care not whether I am returned again or not; but if I felt any anxiety on that head, I would go to my constituents with the bill in my hand, and would place my special ground to their renewed confidence on my determined opposition to it. I will go to a community, whose numbers by the returns of 1821 were not more than 4000, and I would tell them that this bill had been brought in without any allegation of necessity, or without any case being made out against them, and that I opposed it. I know that they have never abused their right, that the humblest man amongst them never obtained or asked a bribe for the vote he gave. They received me when I had been subjected to the indignity of expulsion for what I conceived to be a special act of duty, even to the church of which I am a humble member. They then returned me as

their representative; and till the necessity of the measure
is established by more cogent arguments than I have yet
heard, I will not consent to deprive them of their right.
But I am told that I must adopt this measure, as the
alternative is civil commotion. I at least have not been
one who industriously excited the stormy wave of the
multitude,—who employed all my faculties to create dissatisfaction and discontent. I at least never uttered the
language of the noble lord in 1827, who found the people
peaceful, quiet, and contented, and complained that he
could not rouse their indignation against the constitution
of the House of Commons,—who grieved that they were so
apathetic, as to "prove deaf to the voice of the charmer,
charm he never so wisely." I at least never called for a
list of the names of 113 privy councillors, in order to direct
against them the full torrent of popular displeasure and
resentment, on account of the remuneration afforded to
their services. Neither have I ever instituted any invidious comparison between great naval commanders and the
civilians who presided over the Admiralty. Neither have
I instigated or encouraged any body of men to display,
under the very window of the seat of government, a foreign
emblem of revolution. I have never been the person to
excite the people to a pitch of frenzy, to spur their lazy
indifference to an emulation of revolutionary clamour. If
therefore this extraordinary measure (which common prudence would have forborne introducing at such a crisis in
our foreign and domestic relations, when fresh causes of
excitement ought to have been avoided)—if, I say, this
extraordinary measure should be defeated, I can never
allow that the responsibility of the disappointment could
attach to me, or to any other individual member of this
House. It is the inevitable tendency of this bill to sever
every link of connection between the poorer classes and
that class from which their representatives are usually
chosen. Now this severing of the ties which connect the
highest and the lowest class is opposed to the practical
workings of the present system of representation—a great
characteristic recommendatory feature of which is, that it
enables every class in the community, in some way or
other, to have a voice in the election of the members of
this House. Now, I do not mean by this to say that the

franchise should be extended to all the members of all the classes of the community, but that the constitution works well, from having here and there an entrance channel for the broadest principle of popular representation. If, to make myself better understood, it was proposed to me to make a selection between the franchise in force in Windsor and that in force in Preston, I should not hesitate to prefer the former; but I would not therefore abolish the Preston franchise, and assimilate it to that in Windsor. All that I would do would be, to take care not to take it as the model of my plan of extending the franchise to other places. But not so the noble lord's bill. It would disfranchise all those open boroughs the voters of which are not rated at 10*l*.— though no reason had been or could be adduced for depriving the freemen of Coventry or the potwallopers of Preston of their franchise. I put it to the noble lord and the House, to consider whether the effect of this disqualifying principle would not be, the affixing a political stigma on those not eligible to vote under the 10*l*. qualification? I could not consent to the measure, were it only on this ground; for I could not consent to a stigma on from 200 to 300, which this bill would disfranchise.'

Applying himself to the arguments which had been employed against the close-borough system, Sir Robert then proceeded:

'It is usually, and as it appears to me most convincingly, argued, that these boroughs are advantageous, by affording the means of access to the House to men who have no claims beyond their ability. Two objections have, in the course of this debate, been urged against that argument. The one—which, I must say, came with a very bad grace from the hon. member for Westminster (Mr. Hobhouse), himself a man of great ability—was, that it is by no means desirable that men of splendid talents should be members of this House,—that in a reformed Parliament, solid sense and integrity will be more highly valued. Now I, on the other hand, maintain that nothing tends more to foster the public respect for this House than its being the great arena of talent and eloquence, and that nothing would lower it more in public estimation than that it should be below the average ability of educated gentlemen. But, says the hon. member for Calne, "Yes, let us have men of ability by all

means, but let us select other means for their obtaining
seats than close boroughs; give us a purer and more extensive franchise, and they will get at least as much as
they do at present. But what," said he, "is your test of
ability? Take every hundred men you meet in the street,
and one of them will be a man of ability—take one hundred
names in the Red Book, and one may be a man of ability
—and so of one hundred men of tawny complexion; but
are these men to get in by the accident of close boroughs?"
And then the hon. member asked, "Was it fair to judge
by the accident instead of the general tendency of a system?"
Now I am content to judge by the tendency, and not by the
accident of the close-borough system, and I maintain that
that tendency is essentially favourable to the entrance of
men of ability into this House. I have this morning turned
over a list of from twenty to twenty-five of the most distinguished men that have graced this House for the last
thirty or forty years,—men of whom it might be said, in
the glowing language of Lord Plunkett, that they were
possessed of that "buoyancy of genius which would float
them down the stream of posterity;" and I found that,
with three exceptions, they were all returned for boroughs
which the noble lord's bill would wholly disfranchise.
There was Mr. Gunning, Lord North, Mr. Townshend, Mr.
Burke, Mr. Flood, Mr. Pitt, Mr. Fox, Lord Grenville, the
Marquis Wellesley, Mr. Perceval, Lord Plunkett, Mr. Canning, Mr. Wyndham, Mr. Horne, Mr. Huskisson, Mr.
Brougham, Sir S. Romilly, Lord Castlereagh, Mr. Tierney,
Sir W. Grant, Lord Grey, and the late Lord Liverpool, all
first returned for close boroughs, and but three of them
ever members for counties. Nor is the mere facility of
admission the only benefit. The introduction, by affording
them an opportunity—the essential condition of successful
talent—for displaying their legislative ability on a larger
scale, recommended them to more extended franchise at
a more mature age; and again, when they, by caprice, or
want of money, or otherwise, were deprived of their larger
seats, those close boroughs, which the noble lord's bill
would destroy altogether, received them, and secured their
invaluable labours to their country. Such was the case
when Mr. Sheridan was defeated at Stafford. He found
shelter at Ilchester. Mr. Wyndham, having failed at

Norwich, took refuge at Higham Ferrers; and Lord Castlereagh, in like manner, having lost his election in the county of Down, was returned for Oxford. Mr. Tierney also, when he lost Southwark, was returned for Knaresborough; and Lord Grey for Tavistock, when defeated in Northumberland. All this proves that the tendency, and not the mere accident, of the close-borough system, is to facilitate the entrance of men of ability, who otherwise could not obtain a seat in this House. And is this system, thus working so advantageously for the general weal,—so fostering of talent and statesmanlike ability,—to be destroyed, in obedience to the noble lord's plan? During 150 years the constitution, in its present form, has been in force; and I would ask any man who hears me to declare whether the experience of history has produced any form of government so calculated to promote the happiness and secure the rights and liberties of a free and enlightened people? Many other experiments have been tried to engraft democratical on monarchical institutions, but how have they succeeded? In France, in Spain, in Portugal, in the Netherlands, in every country on the face of the earth, with the exception of the United States, has the experiment of forming a popular government, and of uniting it with monarchy, been tried; and how, I will again ask, has it succeeded? In America, the House has been told that the most beneficent effects of a representative form of Government are plainly visible. But I beg to remind the House that there is a wide difference indeed between the circumstances of this country and of America. In the United States the constitution has not been in existence more than forty years. It was not till the year 1779 that the representative part of the American system of government was established, and since that time many important changes, as everybody knows, have been made respecting the mode of electing their president. As yet, everything is in uncertainty, for ever since the first establishment of the government of the United States it has been undergoing a change. I will not say it has been deteriorating, for I wish to avoid all invidious phrases; but it has been rapidly undergoing a change from a republic to a mere democracy. The influence of the executive—the influence of the government—has been daily becoming less, and more power has consequently been vested in the hands of the people. And yet, in that country, there is land uncultivated to an extent almost incalculable,—there is no established church, no privileged orders,—property exists on a very different tenure from that on which it is held in this country; therefore let not the people of England be deceived, let them not imagine, from the example of the United States, that because democracy has succeeded and triumphed there, it will also succeed and triumph here.'

He next pointed to the failure of democracy in the States of South America, and maintained that the question of reform always flourished when there was either the pressure of some great difficulty in the country, or a revolution on the Continent. In support of this assertion, he instanced its being brought forward in 1745, during the American war; in 1817, 1819, and 1822,—in a word, in every period when there was great commercial and agricultural distress in this country; and again in 1780, on the establishment of American independence; in 1790, at the commencement of the great French revolution; and now, again, when a new revolution had occurred in France. He concluded as follows:

'I lament exceedingly that government should have determined to agitate such a question as that of reform at this particular crisis: it would have been wiser, in my opinion, to have avoided these new causes of excitement; for, depend upon it, that by this process throughout the land the first seeds of discontent and disunion are sown. In every town there will be a conflict—a moral conflict, I mean—between the possessors of existing privileges and those to whom the existing authority and existing privileges are to be transferred. O, sir, I lament beyond measure, that government had not the prudence to adhere to that temperate course of policy that they had pursued elsewhere. I lament that, if they did think it necessary to propose a plan of reform in this excited state of the public mind, they did not confine it within those narrow limits which are consistent with the safety of the country and the dignity of their own characters. They have thought proper, however, to adopt another course; they have sent through the land the firebrand of agitation, and it is easy so far to imitate the giant enemy of the Philistines, as to send three hundred firebrands through the country, carrying danger and dismay in all quarters; but it is not easy, when the mischief is done, to find a remedy for it. In the present difficulties of your situation, you should have the power of summoning all the energies of life, and should take care that you do not signalise your own destruction by bowing down the pillars of the edifice of your liberty, which, with all its imperfections, still contains the noblest society of freemen known to the habitable world.'

This speech was answered by Mr. Stanley,* the brilliant and fiery scion of the house of Derby. Referring to the passage in which Sir Robert Peel said that he would take the bill in his hand, and go with it to his constituents, and appeal to them on the ground of his opposition to it, Mr. Stanley observed:

'I suppose that every gentleman opposed to this measure will make his appeal where he has constituents; and those who are so fortunate as not to have any constituents— I mean individuals who are returned by patrons of boroughs —will doubtless make the same representation in the proper quarter. It is therefore evident, that those gentlemen look more to the private interests, passions, and feelings of a large portion of the people, than to the welfare of the country at large. But the right hon. baronet said, "If any danger arises from this measure, impute it not to those who oppose it. I throw the responsibility on your own shoulders." I however will contend, that the responsibility must rest with those gentlemen on the other side of the House, who could not go on with the government because they were prepared to resist all reform, and went out when they could not prevent it from being carried, though it was loudly called for by the people. If they afterwards endeavour to baffle the efforts of those who have succeeded them, they must take upon themselves the responsibility that will attach to the loss and defeat of that great measure.

'I was in hopes that a gradual reform would have been effected in Parliament, by selecting, one after another, the most notorious cases of delinquency. If a determined desire to reform by degrees the abuses of the present system had been manifested, then the public would have been satisfied with a less sudden change than that which is now contemplated. But let the House look back for the last few years,

* The late Lord Derby.

and mark the time, the money, and the talents, which have been wasted in discussing useless questions respecting boroughs charged with malpractices; inquiring, for instance, whether one voter received one guinea and another five, when it is as notorious as the sun at noonday, that boroughs are commonly bought and sold in the market by the proprietors. And after all this labour, after all this investigation, after all this minute inquiry, what has been gained for the cause of reform? Not one great town—not one great district—has been added to those represented in this House. Not one corrupt borough has been deprived of the means of corruption.

'My honourable friend (Sir R. Peel) talked of the advantages to be derived from nomination—he contended that it afforded an opportunity of admitting very clever men into the House, who might not be able to find a seat in any other way. Whatever advantage might be derived from this mode of admission would be more than balanced by this disadvantage—that the class of persons thus introduced would, whatever may be their talents and acquirements, not be looked upon by the people as representatives.

'We were told last night that this measure would admit 500,000 persons to the councils of the nation. In my opinion it will do no such thing. It will admit them to the possession of rights which belong to them from their wealth and intelligence, and consequent importance in the political scale. By this means we shall attach them to the institutions of the country, and gain more from their affection than we could by keeping them unconnected with and at a distance from the benefits of the constitution. But then it is said that the measure is revolutionary. To this it is scarcely necessary that I should urge more in reply than a mere denial of any such object on the part of those who introduced it. Is my noble friend who introduced the measure into this House a man without any stake in the country? Is not the name he bears in itself a guarantee against any such intention? Is my noble friend at the head of the government, who is said to be strenuously attached to the privileges of his order,—who has on more than one occasion been made the subject of attack on that ground, —likely to advocate a measure which is to involve those

privileges and the monarchy in one common ruin? Look
round at the other members of his majesty's government,
and at those who come forward to support them on this
occasion,—are they men of no fortune, mere adventurers,
who would have everything to gain, and nothing to lose,
by a revolution? Are they not men who have large stakes
in the country, and whose individual interests are bound
up with the permanent peace and security of the state?
What, then, could they gain by a revolution? They
conceive that they cannot more effectually secure the true
interests of the country, and render its institutions permanent, than by basing them on the affections of the people.
For my own part, I feel no alarm of the kind for the results
of the bill. By that bill the influence of the aristocracy will
be upheld—I mean the influence which they ought to possess; not the influence of bribery and corruption, not the
influence of direct or indirect nomination.

'Ministers came into office pledged to economy, reduction, and reform. These pledges they have redeemed. They
have cut off from themselves and their successors, for
ever, that corrupt patronage on which heretofore so much
of the influence of government depended. With these
views of the measure before the House, I earnestly implore honourable members, by their sense of justice to the
country,—by their respect of what is due to the people,—
by their regard for that glorious constitution which has
been handed down to them from their ancestors—(great
cheering from the Opposition)—I repeat,' said the hon.
member, raising his voice, and looking his opponents full
in the face, 'I repeat, that constitution which ministers are
now endeavouring not to violate, but to amend,—by their
regard for the permanency of our institutions, and the peace
and security of the state,—I call on them, by all these considerations,—by their respect for the petitions of the people
for what may be lawfully asked, and cannot be constitutionally refused,—to support his majesty's ministers in their
endeavour to uphold and cement the legitimate rights of
the crown, the aristocracy, and the people,—and by so
doing, to fix the whole, as well as their own fame, on the
imperishable basis of the affections of the people.'

Mr. C. W. Wynn, the secretary at war, but without a
seat in the cabinet, stated that unless the proposition of

the noble lord underwent a modification greater than he had reason to expect, he could not give it his support.

Mr. Croker: 'I challenge the other side, out of the whole mass of petitions which they have wielded as weapons against my side of the House, to produce one solitary petition in which the petitioners state that they will be satisfied with this extent of parliamentary reform. (Cries of 'Hear, hear,' from Mr. O'Connell and Mr. Hunt.) In the many thousand petitions which I have recently read, there were only two or three worded with that happy generality that led the reader to expect everything or nothing from them. The rest were unanimous in their language and their prayers.

'The lord advocate has told us that discontent is mischievous when it arises from the denial of sacred rights; and he then asked what occasioned the discontent that prevails? I will leave the noble lord opposite to reply to the question of his learned colleague. In the year 1821, 19 petitions only were presented in favour of reform. In the year 1822 the number was reduced to 12. In the year 1823 the number was 29. In the year 1824 there was no petition at all in favour of reform. The same was the case in the years 1825, 1826, 1827, 1828, 1829. (Loud cries of 'Hear.') In the session of 1830 there were 14 petitions presented in favour of reform. Then came the dissolution of Parliament. The noble lord and his friends looked about for a political leader to move the government of the day from its place, and then from hustings and bay-windows, and their different places of abode, they made addresses about reform to the people. The country at length responded to their call, and 650 petitions were the result of that appeal. Now, I venture to affirm, that in the vast majority of these petitions the most prominent demand of the petitioners was for the abolition of tithes, the second was the reduction of taxation, and reform occupied only the third place in the prayers of the petitioners. There is hardly one instance in which reform is not asked for as a means of getting rid of tithes and taxation. In this crusade of petitions for reform, a noble lord opposite was anxious that the respectable inhabitants of Cockermouth should bear their part in expressing their opinions on this important subject; and straightway there came from Cockermouth a petition which, for the

moderation of its language and of its desires,* is most
worthy of the attention of the House. (Here the honourable
member read the petition from Cockermouth, which,
complaining of distress and misery, asked for reform, for
the abolition of the East-India monopoly, the abolition of
slavery and of the corn-laws, which the petitioners said had
acted so prejudicially, that a pestiferous demon of hunger
stalked through the land, carrying with it interminable
ruin, and by its baneful influence bringing many to an
untimely end.) But the noble and learned lord advocate
has acted more prudently than to rest his case on such
petitions as these.'

On Tuesday, March 8th, Mr. O'Connell resumed the adjourned
debate. We have already seen the effect produced
by his eloquence on the Irish peasantry; it proved to be
hardly less successful in the House of Commons. He
played on the passions of that highly cultivated assembly
with the same ease and success as on those of his ignorant
countrymen, now convulsing them with laughter, now
almost melting them to tears, now firing them with indignation.
On this occasion he gave the bill his most decided
and anxious support, as a large, liberal, wise, and
even generous measure. 'There are, however,' he added,
'objections to the measure. I am, upon conviction, a
radical reformer, and this is not a measure of radical reform.
I am of opinion that, in every practicable mode,
universal suffrage should be adopted as a matter of right;
that the duration of Parliaments should be shortened to the
time stipulated in the glorious revolution of 1688; and,
above all, that votes should be taken by ballot. As a
radical reformer, I accept this measure heartily. But there
is another point of view in which I have a right to object
to it. It will not carry its own principle into effect in
Ireland. I think Ireland has been badly treated by it.
The measure is, however, too advantageous to be cavilled
at, and this consideration makes me waive all paltry objections
to a measure which I believe will be highly advantageous
to the people of England.'

After dealing in detail and at great length with various

* It is necessary to inform the present generation that the honourable
gentleman was here speaking ironically.

objections which had been urged against the bill, the hon. member proceeded as follows:

'The charge of inconsistency and of creating anomalies comes with a very bad grace from honourable gentlemen who contended for the beauty of that system which gave Gatton as many members as Westminster. The truth is, that the ancient system has been dilapidated and disfigured by those who now pretend to venerate it, and the government is endeavouring to build up again the old and simple fabric of the constitution. The gentlemen on the other side have in some cases destroyed the very foundations of that fabric, and have left no basis whereon a structure could be raised; but, wherever they have left even the ruins of the ancient edifice, the government has endeavoured to build up again on such remnants, scanty as they are, which have escaped the lawless hands of the spoliators. We have next been told that this bill is a corporation robbery, and we have had that assertion sounded in every tone except a low tone, and every key except a minor key. But being a lawyer, and having a little of the curiosity which belongs to my profession, I have gone through the boroughs, with the view of ascertaining how many of them are corporations; and I have found that only sixteen out of sixty are so. Then, again, we have been told that this bill is a seizure of franchises and of the rights of the people. Now I should be glad to know if the gentlemen who hold this language mean to assist me in my endeavours to carry the repeal of the Union. For if they think that the legislature has no right to take away franchises, what do they think of two hundred boroughs being disfranchised by one single Act of Parliament? Yet this was done by the union. And were the voters tried and convicted? Oh no; so far from it, that forty of them were so innocent, that it was thought right to give 13,000*l.* apiece of the public money to each of the forty. It was acknowledged that the people so disfranchised were innocent and guiltless; and I would ask the honourable member for Tamworth, who has called the present bill atrocious, and the noble lord who has called it iniquitous, whether they mean to join with me in repairing those acts of greater iniquity and greater atrocity which were committed at the time of the union.'

After dwelling at some length on the advantages which

the bill would confer on Scotland, and at still greater length on the injustice with which, as he alleged, Ireland was treated, he thus concluded:

'It is said that the system has worked well. I would ask you to inquire from your agricultural population whether such is the case—whether such a fact is reflected from the fires which lately blazed through the counties— and whether such would be the statement we should receive if we inquired from the unfortunate men who fill our gaols, on account of the late disturbances in the country.  Does the Wilful Trespass Act, which gives the magistrates such dominion over the poor, evidence the well-working of the system? Are the game-laws a proof of such a fact? Has the House listened to the complaints of the people? I will give specimens to show how the boroughmongering representatives have voted upon questions of retrenchment, as an exemplification of the working of the close-borough system. From returns which have been made with regard to divisions on questions of retrenchment in 1822, it appears that of nineteen representatives for boroughs with a population under five hundred, all voted against retrenchment; that of the representatives of boroughs with a population above five hundred, and not exceeding one thousand, twelve voted for retrenchment, and thirty-three against it; that of the representatives of boroughs with four thousand inhabitants, seventeen were for retrenchment, and forty-four against it; and that of the representatives of boroughs with a population beyond five thousand, sixty-six voted for retrenchment, and sixty-seven against it. It was the boroughmongering Parliament which saddled the country with a debt of 800,000,000l. or 900,000,000l. It is said that the country has enjoyed prosperity under this system. True, it has; but why has it been prosperous? On account of its great resources, and in spite of the evil effects of the boroughmongering system. Is there a heart in a true British bosom that does not wish success to the brave and generous Poles? But if the despot of Russia should trample them in the dust, could this country interfere? No, for the debt at once prevents her from doing so. The aristocracy and their dependents have fattened upon the public plunder; and the consequence is, that the country is bound up in the manner

I have described, and the only way for extricating it consists in calling the universal people of England around us. When I hear such triumphant assertions made as to the working well of the system, I would refer you to Ireland for the illustration. We have had a complete trial of it for thirty years at least, and yet Ireland is one of the most miserable countries on the earth, with wretchedness and starvation spreading desolation through the land. I call upon you, in the name of that God of charity whose spirit inhabits your bosoms, to do this great act of justice to Ireland, in the spirit in which it is intended, for the benefit of the people of England, and of the people of Scotland; and by so doing to secure us against a revolution, the consequences of which no man can foretell.'

Thus during seven nights did this debate drag on its weary length to a late hour of the 9th, or rather an early hour of the 10th of March, when Lord J. Russell at length rose to reply. The number of those who had addressed the House in the course of this debate was seventy-one. Of these, thirty-four spoke in favour of the measure, and thirty-seven against it. Of the former, three sat for boroughs which the bill proposed to disfranchise, and two for boroughs which it deprived of one member. Of the thirty-seven adverse speakers, thirteen were members for boroughs which were to be disfranchised, and seven for boroughs which were to be reduced to one representative. Lord J. Russell, in his reply, briefly and temperately answered some of the chief objections which had been urged against the measure. The Speaker then put the question, 'That leave be given to bring in a bill to amend the representation of the people in England and Wales.' This motion, in accordance with an understanding between the leaders on both sides of the House, was agreed to without a division. The ayes were shouted with a vehemence that made the old walls of St. Stephen's ring; while the noes proceeded from only three members; one of them was uttered in a loud and defiant tone, the other two in a weak and dispirited manner, like faint echoes of the first. Leave was subsequently granted, after some discussion, to introduce reform bills for Scotland and Ireland. The bill was read a first time on the 14th, without opposition.

The plan thus brought forward was received by the

radical party with delight, by the Whigs with doubt, by the Tories with terror. It surprised all; for though it did not come up to the wishes of the radicals—who desired the ballot, more frequent parliaments, and universal suffrage—it surpassed the expectations of all parties. By the great body of the people it was hailed with enthusiasm. From the moment of its first announcement they seemed to forget all the other measures which had been prayed for in their petitions, and adopted the cry of 'The bill, the whole bill, and nothing but the bill;' which they sustained under all the changes and vicissitudes it underwent, till it finally became the law of the land. On the other hand, the higher and better-educated classes generally regarded the measure with great alarm, as the commencement of the overthrow of all the established institutions of the country. They had not forgotten that, under the first French revolution, the landed proprietors had been stripped of their property and driven into exile or put to death; and they dreaded that what they regarded as similar beginnings would lead to similar results. The clergy especially, remembering the fate of the French priesthood and the spoliation of the French Church, were almost unanimous in their hatred of the proposed innovation. Already highly unpopular, partly on account of the determined opposition which as a body they had offered to every proposal for the extension of civil and religious liberty, and partly on account of the vexations and disputes attendant on the collection of tithes, they rendered themselves still more odious by their undisguised detestation of the new measure. Their growing unpopularity increased their fears, and presented yet another feature of resemblance in the parallel they drew between the England of 1831 and the France of 1793. And it must be admitted, that the danger was not wholly imaginary. There can be no doubt that if, during the reform struggle, or immediately after its conclusion, the government had introduced a measure for the secularisation of church property, the proposal would have been welcomed by the nation with an enthusiasm which would have borne down all resistance. But the danger which they had so much reason to apprehend was of their own creation. They allowed themselves to be frightened by the declamations of a few violent demagogues, who themselves probably would not, in their cooler moments, have supported the measures which they advocated in a season of national exultation and excitement, whose followers would not have gone along with them, and who would have been controlled by the good sense and moderation of the overwhelming majority of the nation. Under the influence of terrors thus excited, the clergy set themselves to oppose that which the people fondly and almost unanimously desired. Had they yielded to the movement, or even preserved as a body an honest neutrality, they might have rendered the change less violent, and have retained the affection and respect of their flocks. The consequence of their grievous but very intelligible error was, that for many long years after the termination of the struggle, the Church was endangered in her stability, crippled in her usefulness, and greatly diminished in the number of her children; while the government, which was sincerely anxious to aid her in her difficulties, and which, being the only strong government that had existed for many years, was able effectually to befriend her, was alienated by the impolitic opposition of the clergy, and hindered by the hostility it excited in their supporters. The moneyed interest too, as a whole, and of course the proprietors of the nomination boroughs, and the holders of places and pensions, were, with few exceptions, arrayed against the bill. The mercantile interest was also, though not so unanimously, hostile to it. On the other hand, a class rapidly rising in importance, the manufacturers of Lancashire and Yorkshire, were generally and strongly in favour of the measure. They felt that they did not enjoy the influence in the legislation of the country which their rapidly increasing wealth and intelligence fairly entitled them to claim, and that their trading operations were shackled and fettered, through the want of representation in the House of Commons. But the chief strength of the ministry lay in the shopkeepers and in the labouring class, whatever the nature of their employment, who, though as a class they were not admitted to the franchise by the bill, and were apparently not gainers by it, felt, and rightly felt, that it would benefit them indirectly by giving legislative influence to classes whose interests were in many respects identical with their own, and who were much more likely to attend to their representations than the present monopolists of political power. Thus was the country divided into two hostile camps, regarding each other with feelings of increasing exasperation. On the one hand, the anti-reformers, though comparatively few, were immensely strong in position and prestige: they had the court, the House of Lords, the clergy, the army, the navy, the magistracy, the gentry, the old functionaries in all the public departments, the universities, the inns of court, and the influence belonging to the collection of the greater part of the revenue. On the other hand, the reformers could count upon the support of the great mass of the people. On the one side were the wealthy and educated portion of the community, with those whom they were able to command; on the other the distressed and the suffering classes, but with them the vigorous, robust, and progressive, though generally untrained, thought of the country. On the one side, they who lived in the past; on the other, they who lived in the future. On the one side, they who recoiled under the influence of fear; on the other, they who marched onward under the inspiration of hope. On the one side the old and middle-aged; on the other, the young. All took their part; none could stand aloof. The very children were carried away by the pervading party feeling, and often outdid their parents in enthusiasm for or against 'The Bill,' as it was now emphatically denominated.

It may seem strange that a change, which all men now admit to have been a great and necessary improvement, should have been resisted by the wealthy and educated few, and carried mainly through the exertions of the poor and uneducated many; but there is really nothing very surprising in this circumstance. The same may be said with regard to almost every great improvement that has been effected in this or in any other country. The leaders of the movement have usually been men of rank and intelligence, and there have been found amongst their followers many men of liberal and highly cultivated minds—nay, sometimes, whole classes of such persons, on whom the existing abuses have pressed with unfair severity, may have joined them; yet, as a general rule, the rank-and-file of the army of progress has been composed of the classes which constituted the chief strength of the reform party. But perhaps this truth was never more strikingly exemplified than in the instance now before us; for if we would put our hands on the men who brought the reform struggle to its triumphant conclusion, we must not seek them in the ministry, 'in the leading bankers, manufacturers, and tradesmen,' who in various parts of the kingdom petitioned for reform, but in the London mob, in the two or three hundred thousand members of the Birmingham political union, in the determination of the great mass of the people in all parts of the kingdom to march on London at the first signal given by their leaders; and if, on the other hand, we are asked to put our hands on the quarters from which the most formidable and pertinacious resistance to the bill proceeded, we must fix on the court, the two universities, the inns of court, and the other ancient seats of learning. The true explanation of this seeming paradox is, that in political questions the belly is generally much more logical than the head. They who are well off deprecate change, because, if it does not bring with it peril to their fortune and position, it at least renders necessary efforts for the preservation of the one or the other, and that often of a character to which they are unaccustomed, and which perhaps they are unable or unwilling to put forth. But truth and right must ultimately prevail;—the resistance thus offered may indeed defer the dreaded change, but cannot prevent its advent, and is certain to render it more violent when at last it does come. On the other hand, the very poor are the first to feel the evils which result from a vicious state of things acutely, and their demand for the remedy is sure to cause its production, which they, guided by a blind but sure instinct, readily recognise and earnestly demand. And this is perhaps the true explanation of the old maxim—*Vox populi, vox Dei*; a maxim which certainly rests on a foundation of facts very far from contemptible. It is not, of course, meant to be asserted that everything the people clamour for ought to be granted; but it is a truth, confirmed in each case by the verdict of posterity, that they have almost invariably been right in their demands when they have generally and persistently supported any measure of alleged improvement. The opinion of the rabble, as they are sometimes called, is by no means to be despised; for it has often proved to be more correct than the judgment of men who have enjoyed a high reputation for statesmanship. Unquestionably, in the reform struggle the mob were right, and their learned, wealthy, and aristocratic opponents altogether mistaken.

The government, encouraged by the feeling in favour of the bill, manifested by an overwhelming and rapidly increasing majority of the people, gradually assumed a bolder attitude, and openly declared their intention not to consent to any serious modification of its provisions. In fact, there was now no drawing back. The nation was determined to be satisfied with nothing short of it, and if the government had faltered in their adhesion to it, men prepared to go farther still would speedily have occupied their places. In the temper of the English people at that time, no ministry of a less decidedly liberal character could have stood its ground. From the moment that the Reform Bill was proposed, there could be no safety for the country until it was carried. And the wisest course would have been to have allowed it to pass without exasperating the popular passions by protracted resistance. Many of those who thought the proposed change far too violent supported it, justly deeming that the dangers of delay or rejection were far greater than any which could arise from the adoption of the measure. Others did not see this—indeed, from their position and habits of thought, could not possibly see it; and so they continued to obstruct and delay the passage of the bill until it had become too evident to almost all men, that the country was on the verge of revolution, and that concession was indispensable and inevitable.

Among the expedients to which reformers at this time had recourse, in order to insure the success of the bill, was the formation or extension of societies called political unions. These societies, which were now established in all the chief towns of the empire, had a kind of military organisation, with the avowed design of 'defending the king and his ministers against the boroughmongers;' a name which now began to be applied not only to those who trafficked in seats, but indiscriminately to all the opponents of the bill. The chairman of the Birmingham union publicly boasted that it would supply two armies, each of them as numerous and brave as that which had conquered at Waterloo, if the king and his ministers required them in their contest with the boroughmongers. Colonel Evans, at a reform meeting held in London, stated that he had just arrived from the county of Sussex, where two reform meetings had been held, and he knew that ten thousand men were ready to march from Reigate, if the measure before the House should be defeated. Almost every town was paraded by large bodies of men, marching in procession with banners and bands of music, and in semi-military array, evidently for the purpose of intimidating the opponents of the bill by a display of physical force. They were still tolerably good-humoured, for they were confident of speedy success. Though the whole country was at the mercy of these reform volunteers, no breach of the peace was committed, but threats were openly uttered, and it was evident that if the measure could not be carried by regular constitutional means, it would be carried by force. As for the poor anti-reformers, it was clear enough that they were not likely to take arms, and that the king and his ministers could not require the irregular assistance of these unions in order to resist them. The true object of these demonstrations was to strike terror into the hearts of the opponents of the bill, and to deter the government and the king from faltering in their adherence to it. The latter accordingly regarded these movements, and especially the political unions, with great uneasiness; frequently urged his ministers to take measures for their suppression; and there can be no doubt that the terror which these organisations inspired caused him to waver in his support of the measure, and induced him to yield at several important crises of the struggle.

The press, as a whole, headed by the *Times*, rendered great assistance to the reform cause by keeping alive the enthusiasm for the bill, by directing public opinion against its foremost opponents both in and out of Parliament, and terrifying the more timid of them into silence. Many newspapers which had hitherto supported the Tories now yielded to the torrent and joined their opponents, whilst others ceased to appear. Many new journals and penny sheets came into existence at this period, and largely contributed to swell the demand for reform, to which they owed their existence. The anti-reformers, on the other hand, started a few papers, and purchased others. Many of these were edited with great ability; but their circulation was almost confined to the small minority whose opinions they represented, and they had little or no success in their endeavours to stem the tide of popular feeling which was running so strong in favour of the bill.

We have already mentioned the large number of public meetings that were held and petitions sent up in favour of parliamentary reform, while the character of the ministerial measure was yet a secret. These demonstrations became far more numerous after the provisions of the bill had been announced, and they now, almost without exception, urged on the legislature to adopt the measure as it stood as speedily as possible. On the other hand meetings of a more private character, less numerous and less numerously attended, and petitions with fewer signatures, were diligently got up by the anti-reformers, to counteract, in some degree, the impression made by those in favour of the bill, and to encourage its parliamentary opponents in their resistance. These proceedings, however, only served to render yet more strikingly manifest the generality of the feeling in favour of reform, and the numerical weakness of the party by whom they were promoted. The grounds on which this opposition was based, and the manner in which the bill was regarded at this time by some of its ablest and most reasonable opponents, are well stated in a declaration drawn up soon after its first introduction, and signed by several hundred merchants, bankers, and other influential citizens of London.

'While we should have been far from opposing ourselves to the adoption of any proposition so recommended of a temperate character, gradual in its operations, consistent with justice and the ancient usages of this realm, and having for its object the correction of acknowledged abuses, or any amelioration in the administration of public affairs, which might seem to be called for by the changes or necessities of the times, we feel it impossible to regard in that light a measure which, by its unprecedented and unnecessary infringements on the rights and privileges of large and wealthy bodies of the people, would go far to shake the foundations of that constitution under which our sovereign holds his title to the throne, his nobles to their estates, and ourselves and the rest of our fellow-subjects to the various possessions and immunities which we enjoy by law: a measure which, while it professes to enlarge the representation of the kingdom on the broad basis of property, would in its practical operation have the effect of closing the principal avenues through which the moneyed, the funded, the commercial, the shipping, and the colonial interests, together with all their connected and dependent interests throughout the country, or dispersed throughout our vast empire abroad, have hitherto been represented in the legislature, and would thus, in reality, exclude the possessors of a very large portion of the national wealth from all effectual voice and influence in the regulation of the national affairs.'

Never probably, in the whole previous history of this country, had the public feeling been so strongly and rapidly excited, as at the moment when the bill was brought before the House of Commons for a second reading. In every town of the empire thousands each day were waiting with eagerness the arrival of the coach which brought down from London the reports of the parliamentary debates. They were read with the utmost avidity, every argument was warmly discussed in the streets, and in every public place to which newspapers came. Men who are accustomed to the calm and almost careless manner in which the proceedings of Parliament are read in the present day can hardly realise the fiery excitement with which they were expected and discussed during the debates on the Reform Bill. And this excitement became more and more intense as the time approached when the great trial of strength was to take place between the supporters and opponents of the bill, on the division at the second reading, by which the general principle of the bill would be affirmed or rejected.

On the evening of the 21st of March, Lord J. Russell, without any preliminary observations, moved the second reading of the bill. He was followed by Sir R. Vyvyan, member for the county of Cornwall, who moved that it should be read a second time that day six months, promising at the same time that if his motion should be adopted, he would follow it up by another, which should pledge the House to a bill of a more moderate character. His speech, like many others delivered on the same side of the House throughout the discussions on the bill, related much more to the first French Revolution than to the question of English parliamentary reform. One remark, however, which fell from him is worthy of attention, for it bore on a subject respecting which he was a very competent witness. He attributed the cry for reform mainly to the denial of the distress under which the country was suffering by the late House of Commons. This amendment was seconded by Mr. Cartwright, and a debate ensued, which was adjourned to the following evening. Both parties were thoroughly wearied with the preliminary skirmishing in which they had been so long engaged, and both were anxious to test their respective strength by a division. Accordingly, at the conclusion of the second night of the debate, the House divided, when the numbers were:

For the amendment 301
For the second reading 302
                                     ———
        Majority in favour of the second reading . . . 1*

The announcement of these numbers was received with a perfect storm of cheers from both sides of the House. Nominally the victory was with the government, and their partisans felt that they must make the most of their triumph. But the real advantage was on the side of the opposition, who, as the principle of the bill was only affirmed by the balance of one single vote, would be able to do what they pleased with it in the committee, and to mutilate it in such a manner as to compel the ministry to abandon it altogether. It was true that the government might resort to a dissolution; but it was known that the king was averse to this step, and as the Parliament had so recently been elected, it was thought that the ministry would not be able to overcome an objection which rested on very plausible grounds. At all events, the state of public business, and especially of the estimates, seemed to

* This result was gained by the defection from the Opposition of the Right Hon. John Calcraft, who had been Paymaster of the Forces in the Wellington administration. In consequence of this one vote he was elected member for the county of Dorset instead of for Wareham, which he represented in this Parliament; but he lost the confidence of his former friends without gaining that of his opponents, sank into a profound melancholy, and committed suicide September 11th of the same year.

render it absolutely necessary that the sitting should be continued for some time longer; so that in any case the Opposition thought themselves secure of a considerable interval, and they hoped that before a dissolution could be effected, the popular excitement in favour of the measure would abate, and those portions of it which they deemed most objectionable might be removed from it, or that another bill of a less extensive character might be substituted for it. As the Easter vacation was now approaching, the bill was committed for Thursday, the 14th of April.

On the 12th of April the House re-assembled, and on the same evening Lord J. Russell, in reply to a question from Lord Encombe, made a statement of the modifications which ministers proposed to introduce into their measure; and when the bill was brought into committee on the 18th of April, Lord J. Russell specified the alterations which the government proposed to make in the provisions of the bill.

1. Five boroughs, viz., Aldborough, Buckingham, Okehampton, Malmesbury, and Reigate, to be taken out of Schedule A and added to Schedule B.

2. Eight to be taken out of Schedule B, viz., Chippenham, Leominster, Northallerton, Tamworth, Truro, Morpeth, Westbury, and Wycombe.

These boroughs had established their right to exemption in accordance with the principles laid down in the speech of Lord J. Russell, delivered on the 12th of April.

Eight members to be added to the following counties, having a population of from 100,000 to 150,000 inhabitants: Bucks, Berks, Cambridge, Dorset, Hereford, Hertford, Oxford, Glamorgan.

Seven members to be given to the following large towns: Oldham, Bury, Rochdale, Whitby, Wakefield, Salford, Stoke-on-Trent.

The borough of Halifax, situated in the parish of the same name, which is of enormous extent, to be restricted to the township, and to return only one member.

The bill provided that the rights of persons who already enjoyed the franchise should be preserved in places which sent members to Parliament. It was now announced, that the same privilege would be extended to their sons on coming of age, provided they were born before the introduction of the bill: and to apprentices, having entered into indentures before that time, who were to retain their right of voting on taking out their freedom, provided they were resident and were registered under the provisions of the bill.

After these changes in the government measure were announced, General Gascoyne moved that the following instruction should be given to the committee: 'That it is the opinion of this House that the total number of knights, citizens, and burgesses returned to Parliament, for that part of the United Kingdom called England and Wales, ought not to be diminished.'

After urging Lord J. Russell to withdraw the bill for the present, he said: 'My motion is directed against the proposed reduction of the members of this House, and is not founded on any superstitious attachment to a particular number, but on an anxiety to prevent the aggrandisement of the Irish and Scotch at the expense of the English representation. The proposed spoliation of the English representation is indefensible on any ground of justice or expediency. It cannot be defended on the ground of the population of Ireland having increased so much as to warrant an increase in the relative number of its representatives in this House. At the time of the legislative union, the population of Ireland amounted to 4,200,000 persons, and the taxation to 4,600,000*l.*; while the population of England was 10,700,000, and the taxation 27,700,000*l*. At present Ireland does not contribute more than one-tenth of the taxes in proportion to its population, as compared with this country; so that if the population is to be taken as the ground for adding to the representatives of the country, it ought also to be made the basis of a more equal taxation. Ireland may obtain her five additional members, and Scotland hers; but let it not be at the expense of the people of England. What would be the feelings of those countries, if the bill proposed to add to the English representation at the expense of the representation of Ireland and Scotland? Are you blind to the unanimity with which the representatives of Ireland and Scotland resist every plan, emanate from what quarter it may, which tends to equalise the burdens of the state in all parts of the United Kingdom? In the division on the property tax, on the assessed taxes, on the spirit duties—in fact, on every new impost whatever—the Irish and Scotch members always vote in such a way as to throw the weight of the taxes off their own shoulders on to the people of England; and yet the noble lord comes forward with a proposition which takes from the English representation, and adds to that of Scotland and Ireland. Do you forget that ministers were compelled to exempt Scotland and Ireland from the operation of the Metallic Currency Bill, in consequence of the opposition of the members of those countries?—that 83 out of 100 Irish members came to the resolution to oppose ministers altogether, if they persisted in depriving Ireland of her small-note currency, and that they succeeded in their object? Look how the Irish members contrive to throw the burden of supporting their own poor on this country, as indeed they will every other burden, if the relative superiority of the representation of this country is destroyed as the bill intends. On the other hand, consider the dangerous influence which the Irish representation places in the hands of any minister who chooses to court it at the expense of this country. By conciliating it he might carry any measure he pleased, no matter how it might affect the interests of the people of England. If the bill is altered, so as to transfer the franchise of the boroughs in Schedule A to places in England, I shall not object to it; but if it is retained in its present form, I will offer it every opposition in my power.'

Lord Althorp said: 'This motion is the first of a series of motions by which it is intended to interfere with the progress of the committee, and which, if agreed to, will be fatal to the bill—at least so detrimental to it as to render it impossible that it should be proceeded with. We have heard a good deal about the injustice of spoliating England for the sake of Scotland and Ireland; but the honourable member who introduced that topic might as well have talked of the injustice of spoliating Cornwall for the sake of the United Kingdom. The honourable member next made an appeal to the feelings of the English representatives, and endeavoured to persuade them that their interests and the interest of their constituents would be endangered by the proposed arrangement. But what was the fact? Why, the members for Great Britain would be as five to one to the members for Ireland, and yet this is the proportion which the honourable member pretends will endanger Great Britain. I beg all those who are friendly to the measure not to be deceived as to the consequences of the proposition now submitted to the House. If it is carried, it will so damage the bill, that it must be fatal to its success. I appeal therefore to all who are friendly to the bill to join in opposing the proposition of the honourable member.'

Mr. Stanley, referring to the speech of Lord Stormont, who argued that the bill in its present shape would give too great a preponderance to Catholic Ireland, and contended that the proportion laid down at the Union should be preserved, spoke as follows:

'That proportion was not then determined as a matter that should not be interfered with, and in fact the amendment moved by the gallant member for Liverpool does not go to preserve that relative proportion between the three countries, for proposing to disturb which some supporters of this motion have attacked his majesty's government. For my part, I am not inclined to attach any great importance to the strict maintenance of the present relative proportion between the three countries, and as long as I find large, wealthy, and populous places unrepresented in any of those three countries, I care little whether those places are to be found in England, Scotland, or Ireland. I thank God that this is now a united empire, and I am for meting out the same measure with strict impartiality to all. I caution honourable members, who stickle so pertinaciously for the maintenance of the proportion of members between the three countries, and who grudge to Ireland any increase of representatives beyond the number given to her at the period of the Union, to consider well the arguments which they are thus putting into the hands of those who are contending for a measure which I conceive would be most mischievous both to England and Ireland—I mean the repeal of the Union—and who put forward the doctrine that Ireland is not adequately represented in this House, and is therefore entitled to have a domestic legislature of her own. Where, I would ask, is the danger of giving the proposed additional members to Ireland? Surely they are not afraid that the half-stifled ashes of religious dissension will break forth again? Surely they are not afraid that religious feelings and religious prejudices will be brought into play? Or, if they do entertain such unfounded apprehensions, if they do fear to give any more members to "Catholic Ireland," as it is called, why did they pass the Relief Bill? why did they grant Catholic emancipation?'

Referring to the argument, that the increase of the business of the country necessitated an augmentation in the number of the representatives in the House of Commons—

'The utter and complete fallacy of such an argument as that,' he exclaimed, 'is proved by the experience of committees upstairs, where it is invariably found, that in proportion to the smallness of their numbers, the business they have to do is more expeditiously performed. I maintain that the business of this House would be better done by a smaller number of representatives, who really represented constituents here, than it would be by a larger number of representatives, a great number of whom have no constituents at all. I will appeal to the experience of honourable members, whether it is the members for the nomination boroughs who perform the business of the country in this House? With the exception of the great leading questions, on which the members of nomination boroughs are made to come down to the House, is it not done by the county members alone?

'It is said that we propose to diminish far too much the proportion, as it already exists, in favour of England. Now, the boroughs which it is proposed to disfranchise do not, in fact, form a portion of the real representation of England,—they are the property of the first man who chooses to buy them; and the members who are sent to this House from them are subject either to the man who has bought the borough, or to the patron of the borough. It is expected that the disfranchisement of such boroughs will take from England its just proportion of representatives. But what is the fact? That in many instances the boroughs are represented by Scotchmen and Irishmen. The boroughs, therefore, at present can be employed to incline the balance in favour of Scotland and Ireland, and if we are to have a united Parliament, we ought not to adhere too strictly to the existing scale of proportion between the representatives of the three kingdoms.'

Our account of this debate would be very imperfect if it did not include some portion of the speech of Mr. O'Connell, the member for Ireland, as he was sometimes called, and whose opinions, on a question which so greatly affected the country of which he was regarded as the representative, were naturally looked for with no ordinary expectation.

'One great objection to the Union is the gross partiality of the arrangement by which Ireland has only 100 members to watch over her interests, whilst England, with only twice its population, has five times the number of representatives. England, Scotland, and Wales are combined in an attempt to prevent an addition of members in Ireland. The honourable member for Liverpool, in calling on the House to retain all the English members in the House, told them that Irishmen could get seats for places in England and Scotland. Do those who say this believe it themselves? There is not an individual in Ireland who will believe it. I will remind the House of another thing. No person has pointed out a place in England fit to have representatives, which is not found on the ministerial list; but has any one place in Ireland been so treated? It is always so carried against Ireland. The Scotch members have, with few exceptions, joined the gallant general, and not even an Irish member, before I rose, has advocated Ireland. The Union is a measure, the professed object of which is to give good government to Ireland. Has it done so? Is there a country worse governed? It is not political feeling which has produced its present disorders, but distress and misery. I want adequate protection for Ireland. I call on the House to give me that adequate protection which is to be found in a domestic legislature; and while my tongue can utter and my heart throb, I will look for that domestic legislation. The gallant general has called reduction of the representation a monstrous thing; but look at Ireland—look at her 300 members reduced to 100. The honourable member said that "there might be a combination of Irish members against the interests of England," and he referred to a recent instance; but he gave a credit to Irishmen which they do not deserve.

I proposed it, but it was declined. The next charge of the honourable member was, that Irish members would resist anything for the improvement of England. What improvement have they opposed? It is said that Ireland does not pay the same proportion of taxation as England, but Ireland does pay the same proportion. (A laugh.) I thank you for that laugh. It shows how ignorant you are of Ireland. Do those gentlemen who laughed know that the taxes of the customs are never brought into the Irish treasury? that half a million for teas is all paid in London? that the duties on rum and wine are paid in England, and not one farthing from those taxes finds its way into the Irish treasury? But what do you say to the sums taken by absentees? Take a single estate, that of the Marquis of Hertford; he takes 42,000*l.* a year from Ireland. Is not that taxation? It is said that taxation is like the moisture absorbed by the solar ray, which falls in refreshing dews; but in Ireland there is a scorching sun, but no dew descends again. In Ireland there are thirty-two counties, and if there was a real union between England and Ireland, there would be an increase of thirty-two members for Ireland. Only two of the counties have less than 100,000 inhabitants; twenty counties have above 150,000; twelve have above 200,000; four above 300,000; and one about 600,000. Why should not Tyrone with 200,000 inhabitants be equally represented with Glamorgan? And Down with 313,000, with Oxford having only 100,000? Talk not, then, of agitation. The honourable members for Liverpool and Drogheda are the agitators. The first object in this proposition is to raise English prejudices; the next to excite Irish prejudices. But it is a base calumny to say that the Catholics of Ireland would prefer a Catholic to a Protestant, if their merits were equal. Show me any instance of it. I call on the honourable member for Drogheda, who is the chief calumniator of Ireland.' These words, spoken in a most excited and passionate manner, naturally produced a loud cry of 'order,' and the Speaker called upon Mr. O'Connell to abstain from such observations, remarking at the same time that his manner was as objectionable as his language.

Mr. O'Connell continued: 'I have not stated half the

case of Ireland; I have not referred to the towns. There
are fourteen towns in Ireland which, if they had been in
England, would have had representatives. I believe, however, that the bill is for the benefit of England, and no
mean rivalry shall prevent me from supporting it. I call
upon the gallant gentleman to give his motion to the winds,
that Ireland may have some benefit from the measure.
This apostrophe called forth a loud shout of derisive
laughter, whereupon Mr. O'Connell at once resumed his
seat, exclaiming, in a tone of great bitterness, 'O, I am
laughed at; I have my answer.'

The rest of the speeches were made up of criminations
and recriminations, and of arguments applicable rather to
the general question of reform than to the particular motion
before the House. It was past four o'clock in the morning
when the House divided, when there were—

For General Gascoyne's motion 299
Against 291

Majority against ministers 8

The effect of this victory of the Opposition was to keep
the House of Commons at its existing number, and thus to
place at the disposal of ministers a larger number of seats
for enfranchisement than they had asked for; and as,
according to the principles of the bill, they would unquestionably propose to give the seats thus gained to
populous towns and counties, the result would be, that
the popular, or, as the Opposition termed it, the democratic
element would receive a farther reinforcement. To use
the language of the *Times*, in its remarks on the decision,
it gave the reformers more of a good thing than they
wanted. But this circumstance only showed more clearly
the determination of the anti-reformers to offer a thoroughly
vexatious opposition to the progress of the bill, and to
avail themselves of every opportunity for mutilating
the measure and defeating its authors. It was quite
evident that the motive which actuated the great majority
of them was not a desire to strengthen the popular element
in the House, but a wish to embarrass the ministry.
Therefore, to prolong the struggle would have been a
manifest waste of time and energy, and would only have

served to help the Opposition in the game of delay which they were playing. The ministers had already hinted that an adverse decision on this question would in all probability lead to an appeal to the people. It was now resolved that the appeal should be made as speedily as the state of public business would allow.

There were, however, two great difficulties to be overcome before this resolution could be carried into effect. In the first place the king was adverse to a dissolution, and had distinctly intimated to his ministers, on their accession to office, that he was not prepared to dissolve the newly-elected Parliament in order to enable them to carry their Reform Bill. They therefore had no right to claim the consent of the sovereign to a dissolution, and it was doubtful whether they could extort his compliance by the threat of a resignation. In the next place, the supplies had not yet been passed; and many who were bitterly hostile to the ministerial measure, though they did not dare to vote against it, were willing to join the avowed opponents of the bill in throwing impediments in the way of a dissolution. It was probably owing to the embarrassment produced by these difficulties that ministers, on the evening which followed their defeat, abstained from giving any explanation of the course they intended to take. Nevertheless, rumours of an intended dissolution were very rife; and Mr. Hume, who was generally the chief advocate of retrenchment, and who was not unnaturally dissatisfied with the ministerial financial proposals, declared that he would withdraw from all opposition to the ordnance estimates that were then before the House, and would do everything in his power to facilitate their adoption, in order that a dissolution might take place without delay.

This was the event which, of all others, reformers desired, and anti-reformers dreaded and deprecated. The leaders of the opposition knew that on this question the king was with them, and they hoped that, if properly backed, he would be firm. If so, either the ministry and their bill would be got rid of, or a compromise would be effected which would render the obnoxious measure comparatively harmless. In this hope the question of the dissolution was brought before both Houses of Parliament on the 21st of April.

In the upper House the following conversation took place:

Lord Wharncliffe: 'As allusion has been made by the noble lord (Farnham) to certain reports that are in circulation on the subject of the dissolution of Parliament, I wish to ask his majesty's ministers whether there is any truth in the statement that they have advised his majesty to dissolve Parliament, and that it has been resolved to adopt that course. I ask this question, because, if I should receive an answer in the affirmative, it is my intention speedily to adopt some measure on the subject.'

Lord Grey: 'I believe the noble lord's question will be admitted to be one of a very unusual nature, and I can hardly bring myself to believe that when he put it, he expected an answer. But, whatever the noble lord's expectation may have been, I have only to say I must decline answering his question. As to any measure which he may think it necessary to propose, he will consult his own discretion, and take whatever course he sees fit. I can offer him no advice whatever.'

Lord Wharncliffe: 'My lords, I now give notice that I shall to-morrow move your lordships that an humble address be presented to his majesty, praying that his majesty will be graciously pleased not to exercise his undoubted prerogative of dissolving Parliament.'

In the lower House Sir R. Vyvyan asked Lord Althorp, 'whether it is the intention of ministers to proceed with the Reform Bill, or whether they would advise his majesty to dissolve Parliament because the House of Commons will not consent to reduce the number of the English members.' In the observations with which Sir Richard prefaced this question he appealed to the Protestant feeling of the House and the country, representing the issue on which the appeal was to be made to the country as being virtually a question between Popery and Protestantism.

The Chancellor of the Exchequer made the following reply: 'I have no hesitation in saying that ministers, having considered the necessary consequence of the division of the House the other evening on the bill, it is not their intention to proceed farther with it. It would not be consistent with my duty to answer the honourable baronet's second question.'

This reply was regarded by the House as an intimation that a dissolution had been resolved on; and a long and irregular debate followed, in which the policy and propriety of that measure were very freely discussed. An adjournment of the House was moved by Mr. Bankes, on the ground that several other gentlemen wished to express their opinions on the subject, but for the real purpose of preventing the consideration of the supplies, and, as it was hoped, of rendering an immediate dissolution impossible. Lord Althorp earnestly resisted the motion, urging that, if adopted, it would hinder the House from proceeding with the report of the committee of supply on the ordnance estimates, which had been ordered to be brought up this evening. This was precisely what the opposition desired. They thought that if they succeeded, they should at least delay the prorogation of Parliament over the following afternoon, when Lord Wharncliffe's address to the king, praying him to refuse his consent to a dissolution, would be brought forward in the upper House, and no doubt carried. It was hoped that the king, thus encouraged, would accept the resignation of ministers rather than allow them to dissolve, or at all events would urge them to avoid the necessity for a dissolution by making such concessions with regard to the Reform Bill as the Opposition desired to extort from the government. Moved by these considerations, Mr. Bankes and his friends pressed their motion to a division, and carried it by a majority of twenty-two.

The position of the ministers was now highly critical. The King was hostile, the Lords were hostile, the Commons were hostile. The old Tory party had by this time discovered the mistake they had committed in assisting to overthrow the Wellington administration, and were ready to give a steady support to their old leaders. The Parliament had still six years to run before the legal term of its existence expired, and during that time it was hoped that the duke might rally the Tories, pass a bill giving the representation to a few large towns, and the Whigs and their projects might be got rid of for the present.

Meanwhile, the question of a dissolution had already been discussed in the cabinet, and had formed the subject of frequent letters between Earl Grey and the king, who had at length very reluctantly assented to it; but no time

was fixed. The necessity for that measure had now become
urgent. Mr. Dankos's motion was carried on the morning
of the 22d. On the same day Lord Wharncliffe's address,
which in the opinion of the chancellor would have rendered
a dissolution constitutionally impossible, was to be brought
forward, and was sure to obtain the support of the majority
of the peers. It must be anticipated. The dissolution must
take place that very day, and the king, if possible, be persuaded to go down in person; for if the Parliament were
dissolved by commission, the motion might be passed,
though it would come too late to prevent the dissolution.
But the same motives which induced the ministry to wish
the king to go down and dissolve at once led the anti-
reformers, who filled the court, to strain every nerve to
persuade the king to refuse, and he was not unlikely to lend
a willing ear to their persuasions, and to object very strongly
to carry out with such unusual precipitation a measure to
which he had all along been opposed. Under these circumstances, Lord Grey with Lord Brougham, who by the king's
directions accompanied the premier on all important occasions, waited on the king at half-past eleven o'clock on the
morning of April 22d, to urge his majesty to go down and
dissolve Parliament that very afternoon.

Earl Grey, the pink and pattern of loyalty and chivalrous courtesy, shrunk from the disagreeable errand, and
requested his bolder and less courtly colleague to introduce
the subject, begging him at the same time to manage the
susceptibility of the king as much as possible.

The chancellor accordingly approached the subject very
carefully, prefacing the disagreeable message with which
he was charged with a compliment on the king's desire to
promote the welfare of his people. He then proceeded to
communicate the advice of the cabinet, adding, that they
were unanimous in offering it.

'What!' exclaimed the king, 'would you have me dismiss in this summary manner a Parliament which has
granted me so splendid a civil list, and given my queen so
liberal an annuity in case she survives me?'

'No doubt, sire,' Lord Brougham replied, ' in these
respects they have acted wisely and honourably; but your
majesty's advisers are all of opinion, that in the present
state of affairs, every hour that this Parliament continues to

"it is pregnant with danger to the peace and security of your kingdom, and they humbly beseech your majesty to go down this very day and prorogue it. If you do not, they cannot be answerable for the consequences.'

The king was greatly embarrassed: he evidently entertained the strongest objection to the proposed measure, but he also felt the danger which would result from the resignation of his ministers at the present crisis. He therefore shifted his ground, and asked, 'Who is to carry the sword of state and the cap of maintenance?'

'Sire, knowing the urgency of the crisis and the imminent peril in which the country at this moment stands, we have ventured to direct those whose duty it is to perform those and other similar offices, to hold themselves in readiness.'

'But the troops, the Life-guards, I have given no orders for them to be called out, and now it is too late.'

This was indeed a serious objection; for to call out the Guards was the special prerogative of the monarch himself, and no minister had any right to order their attendance without his express command.

'Sire,' replied the chancellor, with some hesitation, 'we must throw ourselves on your indulgence. Deeply feeling the gravity of the crisis, and knowing your love for your people, we have taken a liberty which nothing but the most imperious necessity could warrant; we have ordered out the troops, and we humbly throw ourselves on your majesty's indulgence.'

The king's eye flashed and his cheek became crimson. He was evidently on the point of dismissing the ministry in an explosion of anger. 'Why, my lords,' he exclaimed, 'this is treason! *high* treason; and you, my lord chancellor, ought to know that it is.'

'Yes, sire, I do know it: and nothing but the strongest conviction that your majesty's crown and the interests of the nation are at stake, could have induced us to take such a step, or to tender the advice we are now giving.'

This submissive reply had the desired effect. The king cooled, his prudence and better genius prevailed; and having once made up his mind to yield, he yielded with a good grace. He accepted, without any objection, the speech which had been prepared for him, and which the prevent it from being passed. The firing of the park guns announced that the king was already on his way to the House, and told the Opposition they had no time to lose. On the motion of Lord Mansfield, the Earl of Shaftesbury, presided, in the absence of the lord chancellor.

The Duke of Richmond, in order to baffle the Opposition, moved that the standing order which required their lordships to take their places should be enforced. The Opposition saw at once that this motion was made for the sake of delay, and angrily protested against it; whereupon the duke threatened to call for the enforcement of two other standing orders, which prohibited the use of intemperate and threatening language in the House. Lord Londonderry, furious with indignation, broke out into a vehement tirade against the conduct of the ministry, and thus effectually played the game of his opponents. So violent was the excitement which prevailed at this time in the House, that the ladies present were terrified, thinking that the peers would actually come to blows. At length Lord Londonderry was persuaded to sit down, and Lord Wharncliffe obtained a hearing. But it was too late to press his motion, and he contented himself with reading it, in order that it might be entered on the journals of the House. At this conjuncture the lord chancellor returned, and exclaimed, in a vehement and emphatic tone, 'My lords, I have never yet heard it doubted that the king possessed the prerogative of dissolving Parliament at pleasure, still less have I ever known a doubt to exist on the subject at a moment when the lower House have thought fit to refuse the supplies.' He had scarcely uttered these words when he was summoned to meet the king, who had just arrived and was in the robing room; he at once quitted the House, which resounded on all sides with cries of 'hear' and 'the king.'

This tumult having in some degree subsided, Lord Mansfield addressed the House, regretting the scene which had just occurred, and condemning the dissolution, which he qualified as an act by which the ministers were making the sovereign the instrument of his own destruction.

He was interrupted by another storm of violence and confusion, which was at length appeased by the announcement that the king was at hand. When he entered, the assembly had recovered its usual calm and decorous tranquillity. The members of the House of Commons having been summoned to the bar, the king, in a loud and firm voice, pronounced his speech, which commenced with the following words:

'My lords and gentlemen, I have come to meet you for the purpose of proroguing this Parliament, with a view to its immediate dissolution.

'I have been induced to resort to this measure for the purpose of ascertaining the sense of my people, in the way in which it can be most constitutionally and authentically expressed, on the expediency of making such changes in the representation as circumstances may appear to require, and which, founded on the acknowledged principles of the constitution, may tend at once to uphold the just rights and prerogatives of the crown, and to give security to the liberties of the people.'

While the House of Lords was agitated in the manner we have just described, a scene of scarcely less violence was occurring in the House of Commons. As the approaching dissolution had become pretty generally known, the House was crowded with members at half-past two o'clock, when the Speaker, attired in his state robes, took the chair.

Mr. Hodges rose to present a petition from Hythe, in the county of Kent, in favour of parliamentary reform.

On the question being put, that the petition be now read, Sir R. Vyvyan rose and made a long rambling speech, in which he asserted that the country was on the eve of a revolution, denounced the Reform Bill, censured the ministers, and especially condemned their resolution to dissolve; and at length exclaimed, 'The question before the House is whether we shall be dissolved or not, because we have voted that the number of the English representatives shall not be reduced.'

Sir F. Burdett called him to order.

The Speaker: 'The question before the House is, the reading of a petition, opened by the honourable member for Kent, on the subject of parliamentary reform. The point of dispute then comes to this—whether, when the honourable baronet speaks of the dissolution of parliament, he does not touch on matters applicable to the question of parliamentary reform. I cannot say it is not applicable to the question.'

Mr. Tennyson endeavoured, amidst indescribable uproar, to address the House, in support of Sir F. Burdett's call to order.

The Speaker again rose and said: 'This is not a question of order, as to whether an honourable member is to confine himself to the matter contained within the four corners of a petition, but whether the general scope and tenor of his speech has or has not reference to the subject-matter of the petition, that subject-matter being parliamentary reform.'

Mr. Tennyson: 'I entirely agree with what has fallen from the Speaker, who has drawn the line very clearly. But I will contend, that the course taken by the honourable baronet is disorderly, and, even though the Speaker should gainsay it, I will maintain that the honourable baronet is out of order.' Here the honourable member was interrupted by tremendous shouts of 'chair.' 'It is, I repeat, most disorderly and most unconstitutional for any honourable member of this House, be he who he may, to discuss before the House of Commons the question whether Parliament should be dissolved or not.' The cries of 'chair' were again repeated in the most tumultuous manner, as before.

At length Sir R. Vyvyan was enabled to continue his speech, and was still proceeding in a very excited strain, when the report of the first piece of artillery announced the approach of the king. It was received by the ministerial party with triumphant cheers and loud laughter, and cries of 'The king!' 'The king!' Each successive discharge increased the excitement and enthusiasm that prevailed within the House.

Sir F. Burdett and Sir R. Peel rose at the same moment, but the Speaker decided that the latter had possession of the House. Having given his decision, he farther observed: 'When honourable members call upon me to decide on questions of order, and I have endeavoured to give my opinion impartially, it is not perfectly consistent with the respect due to the chair to proceed farther with the matter.'

Sir R. Peel then began to address the House, which was now boiling with excitement; he himself too, for the first and perhaps the only time in his parliamentary life, was carried away by strong irritation, which strikingly contrasted with his usual self-possessed and impassive demeanour. An eye-witness of the scene told the author that he had never seen a man in such a passion in his life.

'The rules which the Speaker has laid down,' he exclaimed, 'are the rules under which this House has hitherto acted, though they may not be the rules that will suit a reformed Parliament. I for one, however, can never agree to set at defiance, as has this day been done, that authority to which the House of Commons has been accustomed to bow. I do not, I am happy to say, share the desponding feelings of my honourable friend the member for Cornwall. I do not desire the people of England to sit quietly, with their hands before them, patiently expecting the confiscation of the funds and the destruction of tithes. I have confidence in the power of the property and the intelligence of this country, that if they will unite in support of a just and honest cause, I do not despair of a successful and prosperous issue to their joint exertions. Is it decent, I ask,' said the honourable member, his excitement increasing with each manifestation of triumph made by his opponents —' is it decent that I should be interrupted, as I have been, contrary to order, when I am invading no rule of the House, and have regularly risen to address it? If that is the way in which we are to proceed in future, let the people of England beware of the consequences. If your reformed Parliament is to be elected, if the bill and the whole bill is to be passed, it does appear to me that there will be established one of the worst despotisms that ever existed. We shall have a Parliament of mob demagogues—not a Parliament of wise and prudent men. Such a Parliament, and "the spirit of journalism," to use a foreign phrase, has brought happy countries to the brink of destruction. At this moment society is wholly disorganised in the west of Ireland; and the disorganisation, I am grieved to say, is rapidly extending elsewhere. Landed proprietors, well affected to the state and loyal to the king, anxious to enjoy their property in security, are leaving their homes to take refuge in towns, and abandoning the country parts as no longer affording a safe residence. At this critical conjuncture, instead of doing their duty and calling for measures to vindicate, from the visitation of lawless and sanguinary barbarians, the security of life and the safety of property, his majesty's ministers—anxious only to protect themselves, and fearful of the loss of power—are demanding a dissolution of Parliament. Alas, I already perceive that the power of the crown has ceased! I feel that it has ceased to be an object of fair ambition with any man of equal and consistent mind to enter into the service of the crown. Ministers have come down here and have called on the sovereign to dissolve Parliament in order to protect themselves. But they have first established the character of having shown, during their short reign of power, more incapacity, more unfitness for office, more ignorance of their duties, than ever was exhibited by any set of men who have, at any time, been called on to rule the proud destinies of this country. After having assured their predecessors, during the last two years, of having done nothing—of having expended much time in useless debates —not one single measure have they themselves perfected. What have they done in the last six months? They have laid on the table certain bills—the Emigration and the Game bills, for instance—founded on their so much boasted Liberal principles. And what then? Why, there they have left them—'

At this moment the sergeant-at-arms knocked at the door of the House, and, though Sir Robert continued to speak for some minutes longer in the same excited tone as before, the noise and confusion prevented his remarks from being heard. The sergeant-at-arms summoned the Commons to attend the House of Peers to hear the prorogation of Parliament. Thereupon the speaker, followed by a great number of members, proceeded to the House of Lords; and after his return, read the king's speech to the House, which then broke up. A great number of members from both sides of the House shook hands warmly with the speaker. Let us hope that Mr. Tennyson was one of them.' On the following day Parliament was dissolved by proclamation.

CHAPTER III.

SECOND INTRODUCTION OF THE REFORM BILL.

The dissolution of the Parliament was a signal for general rejoicing. It was celebrated by illuminations throughout the country. In London, the lord mayor, finding that he could not prevent the demonstration, wisely put himself at the head of it, and issued a notice regulating the manner in which it was to be carried out. Some evil-disposed person caused another notice to be printed and posted, purporting to emanate from the chief magistrate, in which it was stated that the protection of the police would not be afforded to those who refused to illuminate. Fortunately, little or no mischief resulted from this forgery. Almost every house in the city was lighted up, and in the few exceptions that occurred little damage was done by the mob. At the West-end, however, the houses of several leading anti-reformers, who naturally refused to illuminate, were attacked, and their windows demolished, especially those of the Duke of Wellington and Mr. Baring.

And now the election struggle commenced,—the last that took place under the old system, which allowed the poll to be kept open for fourteen days, during the whole or a part of which drunkenness, rioting, bribery, and every kind of excess prevailed. On this occasion, the cry of 'The bill, the whole bill, and nothing but the bill,' rang from one extremity of the country to the other. The one question put to all candidates was, 'Will you support or oppose the bill?' The nation was now thoroughly aroused; and there could be no doubt in the mind of any impartial person, that nine-tenths of the population were zealously and enthusiastically in favour of the measure, and firmly resolved to put forth every effort to secure its success. But the other tenth—composed, as we have seen, of the great majority of the educated and moneyed classes, and of those under their influence—were determined, partly through interest, partly through panic fear, to strain every nerve in order to defeat it. By each party large sums of money were subscribed to defray the enormous expense of the contests. Bribery and improper influence were resorted to on both sides, but chiefly on that which had most to spend and most to lose. On the other side, popular violence and intimidation was too often employed. A society called the Parliamentary Candidate Society interfered everywhere, by recommending candidates supposed to be favourable to the bill, and denouncing others who were believed to be opposed to it. The boroughs destined to be disfranchised by the bill, or rather their proprietors, with a few honourable exceptions, returned men resolved to defend their franchises. But in the great towns, and in all places in which the election really rested with any large portion of the inhabitants, the public opinion in favour of the bill made itself felt. General Gascoyne, after having represented Liverpool for more than thirty years, could hardly muster the third part of the numbers polled by his reforming opponent. Michael Saddler, who seconded his motion, was driven from Newark, in spite of the hitherto irresistible influence of the Duke of Newcastle, strongly exerted in his favour. Sir R. Vyvyan was rejected at Cornwall. Sir E. Knatchbull did not even venture to contest Kent.* Mr. Ward retired from the representation of London, which sent four reformers. All Sir R. Wilson's professions of radicalism, all his promises of a general support to the bill, could not cover the sin of having supported General Gascoyne's motion, and Southwark rejected him in favour of Mr. Brougham, the chancellor's brother. Sir W. Heathcote and Mr. Fleming were beaten in Hampshire. Mr. Duncombe, Sir T. D. Acland, and Mr. Bankes were driven from Yorkshire, Devonshire, and Dorsetshire; Sir Edward Sugden was defeated at Weymouth. Newport rejected Mr. Twiss, and Malton refused Sir J. Scarlett. Sir J. R. Reid, though backed by all the influence of the Duke of Wellington—the warden of the Cinque Ports—was obliged to yield at Dover, which had hitherto been regarded as the nomination borough of the lord warden. Mr. Sturges Bourne, a personage of

* It may be mentioned, as illustrative of the popular spirit, that a large number of East Kentish reformers had arranged to march to Maidstone, where the poll for the county was then taken, and to bivouac in a barn on the road, in order to save all expense to their candidate.

no small account in those days, ceased to represent Mil-
bourne Port. Viscounts Ingestre and Grimstone lost their
seats. In a word, in England alone upwards of one hundred
of those who voted against ministers on one or both of the
two great divisions on the Reform Bill ceased to sit in the
House of Commons, and in almost every case made way for
thorough-going supporters of 'the bill, the whole bill, and
nothing but the bill.' On the other hand, the anti-reformers obtained a few triumphs, to console them in some
degree for these numerous defeats. The University of
Cambridge, chiefly through the votes of the county clergy,
substituted Messrs. Goulburn and Yates for Lord Palmerston and Mr. Cavendish. Harwich — mindful of past
favours, in spite of the influence of the government—again
returned Messrs. Herries and Dawson. Lymington sent
Mr. Mackinnon. Of the eighty-two county members for
England, all—with the exception of about half a dozen representatives of some of the smallest—were pledged to the
bill. Devonshire sent Lord J. Russell and Lord Ebrington;
Lancashire, Mr. Stanley; Middlesex, Messrs. Hume and
Byng; Cumberland, Sir J. Graham. In Ireland and Scotland the elections were, in the counties and open boroughs,
equally favourable to the cause of reform. In the latter
country the reform cause was disgraced by the ruffianly
violence of some of its partisans.

Never perhaps had any election worked so complete a
transformation. The reformers were now an overwhelming
majority. The survivors of the great party which had
carried General Gascoyne's motion came back a beaten and
dispirited minority, but nevertheless resolved to strain every
nerve to modify, if not defeat, a measure which they expected to overthrow the institutions of the country, and
effect their own political annihilation.

The first act of the House of Commons was to re-elect
Mr. Manners Sutton as speaker, although it was well known
that his opinions were at variance with those of the majority, especially on the great question which was destined
for some time to come to occupy their attention, as well as
that of the whole country. It was thought desirable that
an experienced president should occupy the chair of a house
which contained so many inexperienced members. He was
proposed by Mr. C. Wynn, who had been his competitor for

the office some fourteen years before, and was seconded by Sir M. W. Ridley, the gentleman who at that period seconded the nomination of Mr. Wynn. In the new Parliament, Lord J. Russell and Mr. Stanley appeared as members of the cabinet.

On Tuesday, June 21st, the Parliament was solemnly opened by the king in person. The intervening days had been spent in swearing-in the members and other customary preliminaries. The king went down to the House of Lords in the usual state. He was received with the wildest enthusiasm, not only by the populace, who attended in immense numbers along the line of procession, but also within the walls of Parliament by a well-dressed and fashionable crowd, which thronged the painted chambers and the lobbies through which his majesty passed on his way to the robing room, and thence to the House of Lords. The speech which he delivered on this occasion contained the following reference to the great question which engrossed the public attention: 'My lords and gentlemen,—I have availed myself of the earliest opportunity of resorting to your advice and assistance after the dissolution of Parliament. Having had recourse to that measure for the purpose of ascertaining the sense of my people on the expediency of a reform in the representation, I have now to recommend that question to your earliest and most attentive consideration, confident that in any measure which you may propose for its adjustment you will carefully adhere to the acknowledged principles of the constitution by which the prerogatives of the crown, the authority of both Houses of Parliament, and the rights and liberties of the subject are equally secured.'

The answer to the address was couched in terms calculated to disarm opposition, and was agreed to in both Houses without any amendment having been proposed, but not without a good deal of desultory and unimportant discussion, of which the mischief done at the illuminations and the words which fell from the chancellor during the scene in the House of Lords were the chief topics.

On June 24th the bill for the reform of Parliament was again introduced by Lord J. Russell. It was remarked that his bearing and manner on this occasion were very different from what they had been when he introduced the first bill.

Then he evidently felt that he was addressing an assembly
filled with hollow supporters or determined opponents. His
tone therefore was deprecatory, almost suppliant. It was
equally evident on the present occasion that he saw that the
game was now in his hands,—that he felt certain not only
of the House of Commons, but—what was more—of the
nation. His bearing betokened the confidence which this
feeling inspired, and when he turned to his opponents, he
spoke to them in tones of warning and almost of menace. 'I
now rise,' he said, 'for the purpose of proposing, in the
name of the government, a measure of reform which, in
their opinion, is calculated to maintain unimpaired the prerogatives of the crown, the authority of both Houses of
Parliament, and the rights and liberties of the people. In
rising to make this motion, I cannot but ask—recollecting
what took place in the last Parliament—that I may have
the benefit of a patient attention while I attempt to explain
the principles of the measure which ministers have thought
it expedient to propose. I trust now gentlemen will favour
me so far as not to repeat those gestures and those convul-
sions and that demeanour, from which it would seem they
thought the measure was not to be seriously entertained for
a moment, but that it was to be scouted out of the House
by jeers and taunts and ridicule. Whatever may be the
reception of the measure, hon. gentlemen may be assured
that government will not yield—as those gentlemen must
strongly feel) that government has not yielded nor abated—
one iota in consequence of the opposition that has been
raised against them. Neither the taunts nor the jeers
which marked the first reception of the measure, nor the
misrepresentations and the libels by which it had been
sought to disfigure it, nor the firm and able and manly
opposition which men of talent and honour had thought it
their duty to give it, nor those more dangerous weapons—
those unwarrantable and slanderous imputations that the
sovereign had an opinion on it different from his constitutional advisers;—none of these obstacles have prevented the
sovereign, the ministers, and the people from steadily pursuing an object which they considered ought to be dear at
once to all those who loved the ancient ways of the constitution, and to all those who are sincerely attached to the
liberties of the people. Of that sovereign and of those

ministers it does not become me to speak, but I cannot proceed farther in the discharge of the duty which at present devolves on me without saying that the sacrifices which have been made, and the devotedness which has been manifested even by the humbler classes of the people in pursuance of what they believed to be their duty to their country are facts of which Englishmen will have reason to be proud to the latest generation. It has been said that the late elections were governed not by reason but by passion.'

At those words, which expressed the sentiments of many of the anti-reformers in the House, a loud assenting cheer was raised by the Opposition, and was replied to by a still louder cheer from the ministerial side. 'That the electors,' continued the noble lord, as soon as the tumult had subsided, and looking the Opposition directly in the face—'that the electors had been moved by passion I will not deny.' At these words another loud cry went forth from the Opposition. 'Yes,' continued the speaker, 'love to one's country is a passion, and by that love the electors have indisputably been moved. This love, this passion, has kindled in them that noble degree of enthusiasm which makes men forget their own petty interests; and nothing but such a passion would induce men who could earn by their industry but a few shillings a week to refuse the bribes that were within their reach, to withstand the temptations that were thrown in their way, and to give up the prospect for themselves and their children of continuing to enjoy a valuable privilege. And for what have men done this? Why, for the sake of a measure which was not for their own personal benefit and advantage, but which I believe will be for the future benefit and advantage of the millions of these kingdoms.'

This manly preamble was very favourably received by the House, and was followed by a defence and explanation of the bill delivered in the same firm tone, and loudly cheered throughout its delivery. Coming to some objections which had been urged against it in many parts of the country and in various writings, during the interval between the dissolution of the late Parliament and the assembling of the present one, he said:

'The first and most general objection is, that the plan is far too extensive. The only answer I can make is, that it was on the conviction that it was the only plan which would satisfy the expectations of the people, that his majesty's ministers have proposed it. I think it but fair to state, that neither Lord Grey, nor the lord chancellor, nor any other member of the cabinet, who formerly advocated reform, have ever expressed themselves in favour of a reform so extensive as this. And in proposing what they do, they afford a proof of the conviction in their minds that it is absolutely necessary to introduce so extensive a measure, in order to satisfy the just expectations of the people, and to lay the foundation of a reform of this House, which will secure the permanent stability of the throne, and preserve the authority of both Houses of Parliament. I may have said at other times, that taking a member from each of these boroughs and giving them to large towns would satisfy the people; but I am now well convinced, that if a plan less extensive than the present were proposed, it would not be, like the present, calculated to be permanent and lasting.'

After considering other objections of less importance, and announcing some modifications he proposed to introduce into the details of the measure, particularly the addition of the boroughs of Downton and St. Germains to the list of those which were to be disfranchised, he concluded his speech amidst loud applause from all sides of the House.

After a short conversation, in which Sir R. Peel, as leader of the Opposition, took the principal share, it was agreed that the second reading of the bill, which ministers had proposed to bring forward on the following Thursday, should be deferred to Monday week, in order to allow time for the consideration of the Scotch and Irish Reform Bills, without which Sir R. Peel urged that it was impossible to discuss the English Bill. The motion for leave to bring in the bill was adopted without a division, there being a loud chorus of 'ayes' and only one solitary 'no.'

During the interval which elapsed between the first and second readings of the bill, the attention of reformers, both in the House and out of doors, was being directed to a clause in the new bill, which enacted that 10*l.* householders should have votes only in case they paid their rents half-yearly, so that those who paid them quarterly would not acquire the franchise. On the part of the ministry, it was explained that this provision was introduced to secure a *bonâ fide* yearly tenancy; and a promise was given that the clause should be amended in committee in such a way as to remove the objections which were made to it. On the 4th of July the question of the second reading was brought forward. Notwithstanding the thoroughness with which it had already been discussed, the interest taken in it by the members of the House, as evidenced by their attendance, had by no means diminished. Some of them had come down to the House at seven in the morning, while it was being swept, and had affixed to the seats they wished to secure cards bearing their own names or those of their friends. Mr. Hume, who arrived punctually at ten in the morning, the hour to which it had been adjourned, found some two or three hundred seats already ticketed, and among the rest that which he usually occupied. Thereupon he complained to the speaker; who could only recommend 'a spirit of general courtesy and accommodation on the part of the members.' This debate, deeply interesting as it was to the excited hearers and readers of the time when it occurred, is totally devoid of interest to the readers of the present day. Every argument that could be urged on either side of the great question had already been advanced. The discussion was carried on through three nights, until about five o'clock on the morning of Thursday, the 7th of July, when there was a division, which strikingly exhibited the change that had taken place in the composition of the House and the gain to the ministerial party, for the majority of one was now changed into a majority of 136; the numbers being—for the second reading 367, against 231, thus showing a ministerial gain of 135. It was remarked that the minority which voted against the measure equalled in numbers, as nearly as possible, the members returned by the boroughs which the bill proposed to disfranchise. A correspondent of the *Times*, under the signature of 'Radical,' went through the whole list of the minority, endeavouring to show that, whatever might be the motives of their opposition to the bill, every one of them had a direct personal interest to serve in opposing it.

There was small rest that morning for Mr. Attorney-General; his colleagues were all going homewards to their comfortable beds on the dawning daylight of that 7th of

July, but he had to make his appearance at an early hour of the same morning at the Guildhall, in order to prefer an indictment against the notorious William Cobbett, charging him with publishing, on the 11th of December last, a libel, with the intent to raise discontent in the minds of the labourers in husbandry, to incite them to acts of violence, and to destroy corn, machinery, and other property.

The present generation have nearly forgotten this extraordinary man, who in the beginning of this century, and particularly during the period which elapsed between the battle of Waterloo and the introduction of the Reform Bill, exercised a most powerful influence over the minds of the working classes of England, especially in reference to the question of reform, which by his writings and his lectures he had done more than any other man in England to promote, though the extreme violence of his language had made many enemies both to himself and the cause which he advocated. Born in a very humble position, and originally an unlettered private in the army, he had become by his own almost unaided efforts, one of the greatest masters of the English language that any age has produced. His pure, vigorous, racy, masculine Saxon, while it delighted the man of taste, was intelligible to the meanest capacity; and the violence of his language and the exaggeration of his opinions, of which we shall presently have a specimen, were highly acceptable to the more uneducated portion of his admirers. He was, moreover, one of the most prolific writers that ever lived; a man of untiring energy, a good lover, but a better hater; bold, ardent, and uncompromising. Like most men of a very fiery temperament, he was extremely intolerant, and almost unable to believe in the sincerity of any man whose views and opinions did not square exactly with his own. He often loaded those from whom he differed with the most unsparing abuse; and sometimes persons who had been his political associates and the objects of his warm eulogiums, for some trifling offence or difference of opinion were attacked by him with the greatest asperity. He was remarkably temperate, and abstained from intoxicating drinks at a time when such abstinence was almost unknown. His personal appearance was commanding. He was tall and erect, and the dress of an old English country gentleman of his day, which he usually wore, set off his person to great advantage. His speech, like his writings, was plain, forcible, and emphatic. Such was the man whom the government determined to prosecute. They were anxious to show that, while they defied the violence of those who would not go far enough, they were determined to repress the violence of those who went too far, and to prove that, while resolved to effect needful reforms, they would do more for the maintenance of public order than the feeble administrations which had preceded them. These motives would probably not have induced them to embark in this unpolitic proceeding, if they had not been urged to it by the king himself, who was much alarmed at the language and influence of Cobbett.

Cobbett, in his weekly *Register*, had given notice of the day of trial; and when he entered the court, the gallery, which was open to the public, was already crowded, chiefly by his admirers. On his entrance he was greeted by clapping of hands, which was followed by three loud rounds of cheering. These tokens of sympathy he acknowledged with evident satisfaction, and, addressing himself to his supporters, he exclaimed: 'If truth prevails, we shall beat them.'

The article for which he was indicted was one that had appeared in his *Political Register*. It was preceded by the following quotation from a paper published by him on the 20th of October, 1815: 'At last it will come to be a question of actual starvation or fighting for food; and when it comes to that point, I know that Englishmen will never lie down and die by hundreds by the wayside.'

The first paragraph in this article which was insisted on as being seditious was the following:

'In the meanwhile, however, the parsons are reducing their tithes with a tolerable degree of alacrity! It seems to come from them like drops of blood from the heart; but it comes and must all come now, or England will never again know even the appearance of peace. "Out of evil comes good." We are not, indeed, on that mere maxim, "to do evil that good may come from it." But without entering at present into the motives of the working-people, it is unquestionable that their acts have produced good, and great good too. They have been always told, and they are told now, and by the very parson I have quoted above, that their

acts of violence, and particularly their burnings, can do
them no good, but add to their wants by destroying the
food they would have to eat. Alas, they know better!
They know that one thrashing-machine takes wages from
ten men; and they also know that they should have none
of this food, and that potatoes and salt do not burn! Therefore,
this argument is not worth a straw. Besides, they
see and feel that the good comes, and comes instantly too.
They see that they get some bread in consequence of the
destruction of part of the corn; and while they see this, you
attempt in vain to persuade them that that which they do
is wrong. And as to one effect, that of making the parsons
reduce their tithes—it is hailed as a good by ninety-nine
hundredths, even of men of considerable property; while
there is not a single man in the country who does not
clearly trace the reduction to the acts of the labourers, and
especially to these fires; for it is the terror of these, and
not the bodily force, which has prevailed. To attempt to
persuade either farmers or labourers that the tithes do not
do them any harm, is to combat plain common sense. They
must know, and they do know, that whatever is received by
the parson is just so much taken from them, except that
part which he may lay out for the productive labour of the
parish; and that is a mere trifle compared with what he
gives to the East and West Indies, to the wine countries,
to the footman, and to other unproductive labourers. In
short, the tithe takes away from the agricultural parishes
a tenth part of the gross produce, which, in this present
state of the abuse of the institution, they apply to purposes
not only not beneficial, but generally mischievous to the
people of those parishes.'

The following was another of the passages on which the
indictment was founded. Speaking of the possibility that
some of those who were tried under the special commission
might lose their lives, he said: 'No, this will not be done.
The course of these ill-used men has been so free from
ferocity, so free from anything like bloody-mindedness.
They have not been cruel even to their most savage and
insolent persecutors. The most violent thing that they
have done to any person, has not amounted to an attempt on
the life or limb of the party; and in no case but in self-
defence, except in the cases of the two hired overseers in

Sussex, whom they merely trundled out of the carts which those hirelings had constructed for them to draw like cattle. Had they been bloody, had they been cruel, then it would have been another matter; had they burnt people in their beds, which they might securely have done; had they beaten people wantonly, which has always been in their power; had they done any of those things, then there would have been some plea for severity. But they have been guilty of none of these things; they have done desperate things, but they were driven to desperation; all men, except the infamous stock-jobbing race, say, and loudly say, that their object is just; that they ought to have that they are striving for; and all men, except that same hellish crew, say that they had no other means of obtaining it.'

The attorney-general urged, that the tendency of these passages was to excite the suffering people to a repetition of their crime. He treated Cobbett with much courtesy, speaking of him as 'one of the greatest masters of the English language who had ever composed in it.'

Cobbett, who was his own advocate, was not disarmed by the moderation or the compliments of his accuser. Not content with defending himself, he hurled wrath and defiance against his prosecutors, and especially the attorney-general. Indeed, his object seemed rather to be to assail the ministry than to defend himself; and he appeared to revel in the opportunity afforded him of pouring out the vials of his indignation upon them.

He said that the Tories had ruled the country with rods, but that the Whigs scourged it with scorpions; and he concluded a very long speech by the following declaration:

'Whatever may be the verdict of the jury, if I am doomed to spend my last breath in a dungeon, I will pray to God to bless my country; I will curse the Whigs, and leave my revenge to my children and the labourers of England.'

His address was frequently interrupted by applause from the gallery; and when he sat down, he was long and loudly cheered, in spite of the efforts of the officers of the court.

He then proceeded to call his witnesses. The first was Lord Brougham, who was summoned to prove that he had recently requested the publication of a paper by Mr.

Cobbett, addressed to the Luddites, dissuading them from breaking machinery, and which it was thought would be useful at the present time in dissuading the working classes from committing similar outrages. Lord Brougham testified that such was the case, but explained that the paper had not been published, on account of some objectionable expressions it contained, and which Mr. Cobbett would not consent to remove. Lords Grey, Melbourne, and Durham had also been subpœnaed, and appeared on the bench. The defendant had called them for the purpose of questioning them with respect to the pardon of a labourer of the name of Goodman, whom he supposed and asserted to have been spared because he attributed his crime of arson to Cobbett's lectures; but Lord Chief Justice Tenterden, the presiding judge, who throughout the proceedings had treated the defendant with marked courtesy, having decided that the questions were inadmissible, Mr. Cobbett intimated that he would not detain them, and they withdrew. Lord Radnor, who had known the defendant thirty years; Sir T. Beever, who had read his works fourteen or fifteen years, and knew him personally; Major Wyth, who had read his works thirty years, and several other persons who had been long acquainted with him, and had been readers of his *Register*, deposed that from what they knew of the defendant he was not likely to incite the labourers to destroy the property of farmers and others, but, on the contrary, to dissuade them from such violences. A letter from Lord Sydney, and some extracts from the defendant's publications, were also read. The jury, not being able to agree in their verdict, after having been locked up for fifteen hours, were discharged. Ten of them were for a conviction, and two for an acquittal.

About this time some papers were laid before Parliament which exhibited in a very striking manner the injustice and anomalies of the system which the Reform Bill proposed to abolish. From these papers it appeared that the boroughs of Beeralston, Bossiny, and St. Mawe's, each contained only one £10 householder; Dunwich, Dedwin, and Castle Rising, two; Aldborough, three; Ludgershall, four; Blotchingly, five; West Looe, and St. Michael's, eight. Of the boroughs in Schedule B, Amersham would have twenty-five; East Grinstead and Okehampton, forty-two each;

Ashburton, fifty-four.* On the other hand, it was shown that the large boroughs which were retained would have fewer voters under the proposed than under the old system, and that the constituencies of the new boroughs would not be unmanageably numerous. Thus, that of Preston would be reduced from several thousands to 976; Birmingham would have 6,532; Manchester, 12,639; Leeds, 6,683. Other returns presented striking contrasts between the revenues derived from the disfranchised and enfranchised boroughs. Thus, Booralston paid in assessed taxes 3$l.$ 9$s.$; Bramber, 16$l.$ 8$s.$ 9$d.$; Bishop's Castle, 40$l.$ 17$s.$ 1$d.$; while Marylebone paid 290,376$l.$ 3$s.$ 9$d.$; Tower Hamlets, 118,546$l.$; Finsbury, 205,948$l.$; Lambeth, 108,841$l.$; Leeds, 18,800$l.$; Manchester, 40,094$l.$; Birmingham, 26,986$l.$; Greenwich, 21,341$l.$

It was now evident that the only hope for the Opposition was in delay. Accordingly, when it was moved that the speaker do now leave the chair in order to go into committee, Lord Maitland, the member for Appleby, urged that there was a mistake in the population return of his borough, and moved that his constituents be heard in person or by counsel at the bar of the House. Lord J. Russell admitted the statement of the petitioner, that there had been a mistake, but thought that the present was an improper time to argue the case, and the House supported his opinion by a majority of 97. Still the question, that the speaker do now leave the chair, was before the House, and this question was met by the Opposition with repeated motions for adjournment, on each of which a discussion followed and a division took place. At length both parties agreed to go into committee *pro forma*, and the House adjourned at half-past seven o'clock in the morning, to meet again at three o'clock the following day. When Sir C. Wetherell, who led the Opposition on this occasion, came out of the House, he found that it was raining heavily. 'By G—,' he exclaimed in a tone of vexation to a friend who accompanied him, 'if I had known this, they should have had a few more divisions.' †

---

* It was intended that the boroughs in this schedule should have their constituency made up to at least three hundred by the annexation of adjoining districts.

† We cannot give a better idea of the history of this extraordinary night than by quoting the official statement of the divisions that occurred during

Thus the bill had at length got into committee with a
majority able and determined to carry it through unimpaired,
but with a minority equally resolved to dispute the
ground inch by inch, and if not to defeat, at all events to
delay to the very latest possible moment the passing of the
hated measure. They went on week after week quibbling,
wrangling, disputing, and speaking against time. Each
separate borough was warmly and unscrupulously defended,
sometimes two or three times over. The speakers eulogised
the purity of its electors, argued that its peculiar franchises
formed an essential part of the British constitution, gave
lists of the eminent men who had represented it; and when
all such topics were exhausted, they rang—over and over
again—the changes on anarchy, revolution, and military
despotism; every sentence, and almost every word of the
act was subjected to every imaginable criticism. To give

it: 'Reform of Parliament (England) Bill—Order for committee read;
petition of the burgesses and others of the borough of Appleby read;
motion made and question put: "That the said petition be referred to the
committee, and that the petitioners be heard by themselves, their counsel or
agents, and be permitted to produce evidence before the said committee in
respect of the facts stated in the said petition." The House divided: ayes,
187; noes, 284. Motion made and question proposed: "That Mr. Speaker
do now leave the chair." Debate arising thereupon.

Mercurii 13º Julii 1831.

Motion made and question put: "That the debate be now adjourned till this
day." The House divided: ayes, 102; noes, 329. Question again proposed:
"That Mr. Speaker do now leave the chair." Whereupon motion
made and question put: "That the House do now adjourn." The House
divided: ayes, 90; noes, 286. Question again proposed: "That Mr.
Speaker do now leave the chair." Debate arising thereupon, motion made
and question put: "That the debate be adjourned till Thursday." The
House divided: ayes, 63; noes, 235. Question again proposed: "That
Mr. Speaker do now leave the chair." Whereupon motion made and question
put: "That the House do now adjourn." Motion by leave withdrawn.
Question again proposed: "That Mr. Speaker do now leave the chair."
Debate arising thereupon, motion made and question put: "That the debate
be adjourned to this day." The House divided: ayes, 44; noes, 214.
Question again proposed: "That Mr. Speaker do now leave the chair.
Whereupon motion made and question put: "That the House do now
adjourn." The House divided: ayes, 37; noes, 203. Question again
proposed: "That Mr. Speaker do now leave the chair." Debate arising
thereupon, motion made and question put: "That the debate be adjourned
to Friday." The House divided: ayes, 25; noes, 187. Question again
proposed: "That Mr. Speaker do now leave the chair." Whereupon motion
made and question put: "That the House do now adjourn." The House
divided: ayes, 24; noes, 187. Question: "That Mr. Speaker do now
leave the chair," put and agreed to. Bill considered in committee; committee
to report progress; to sit again this day.'

an account of debates in which the work of two or three weeks was spread over as many months would be absurd. All that can be attempted is to furnish a general idea of the course which the discussions took, and to recount, here and there, some incident which illustrates the state of popular feeling, or which, for some other reason seems note-worthy. The House was chiefly occupied on the evening of July 13th with the proposal of Mr. Wynn, that the enfranchising clauses should be considered first, in order that the number of places to be enfranchised being previously settled, the House might gain the required number of seats, and avoid disfranchisement by uniting small boroughs. After a long debate this proposition was negatived by a majority of 118. On the following evening, July 14th, Sir Robert Peel proposed the omission of the word 'each' in the first clause, which enacted that each of the boroughs enumerated in Schedule A should cease to return any member or members to Parliament, under the consideration of the House. The adoption of his motion would have had the effect of destroying the sense of the clause, and thus either getting rid of it altogether, or of necessitating the substitution of a fresh clause. It was of course rejected; but a whole evening had been spent in discussing it, and reformers out of doors saw with apprehension and regret that the majority on this occasion had decreased to 97—not from the defection of reformers, but their absence. The tactics of the anti-reformers were clearly succeeding to a certain extent, and the friends of the bill out of doors began to manifest great impatience and alarm.

These feelings found a vent and manifestation in a manner which illustrates the prevailing spirit. It has been already mentioned that, on the night of divisions, Lord Maitland, who represented the borough of Appleby, asserted that it had been placed in Schedule A through a mistake in the population returns of 1821, which had been taken as the basis of the bill, and moved that his constituents should be heard at the bar of the House against the Reform Bill, so far as it affected their interests, and in support of the allegations contained in a petition which they had sent. Among those who spoke and voted in favour of the motion was Alderman Thompson, reforming member for the city of London, who was 'intimately acquainted' with Appleby,

and thought that its population was sufficiently large to
take it out of the list of proscribed boroughs. His constituents regarded a vote with the anti-reformers as an act
of treason against the reform party. A public meeting of
the livery of London—at that time a much more numerous
and important body than it is now—was called, and he
appeared before it. He received severe rebukes from
several speakers, and was distinctly told that he was sent
to Parliament to support the bill in all its parts and stages.
After listening very meekly to these lectures, he expressed
his contrition, and pleaded that such a prostration of body
and mind had seized him, owing to the fatigue arising from
his close attendance at the House of Commons, that he
had committed an 'inadvertence,' and in order to avoid
similar mistakes in future he would vote against every proposed alteration of the bill that was not sanctioned by the
government. The meeting, appeased by his protestations
and promises, administered some farther admonitions,
which were received with due submission, and concluded
by passing the following resolution: 'That the meeting of
the livery of London, after a full and complete inquiry into
the vote of Mr. Alderman Thompson relative to the borough
of Appleby, and his explanation of the same, are of opinion
that he acted therein inadvertently, and Mr. Alderman
Thompson having renewed his pledge to give entire support to the Reform Bill, this meeting feel themselves called
upon to continue their confidence in Mr. Alderman Thompson as one of the representatives of the city of London in
Parliament.' The *Times* and reformers generally thought
such a spirit as had been displayed on this occasion highly
creditable to the people. Anti-reformers, as the reader will
easily conceive, thought much otherwise, and took care that
neither the House nor the worthy alderman should soon
forget the inadvertence that had been committed, or the
severity with which it had been rebuked.

The hero of the evening of July 15th was Sir A. Agnew.
His object was the same as Mr. Wynn's—to save the
boroughs marked for disfranchisement—but he proposed
to effect this object by uniting several of them in the
election of representatives. This motion served as the
occasion of another long debate, which ended in its rejection
by a majority of 111. This evening, however, the com-

mittee at length took one forward step, and agreed to the disfranchisement of the borough of Aldeburgh, the first on the list contained in Schedule A.

On the 19th, the next day on which the committee sat, the House was again brought back to a general question, by the following motion from Mr. Mackinnon, member for Lymington: That it be an instruction to the committee, that the boroughs inserted in Schedules A and B (that is to say, the boroughs that were to be either entirely or partially disfranchised) be considered with regard to their population from the last census, and not from that taken in 1821, as proposed in the bill. As the census would not be ready to be laid on the table of the House for some time, it was clear that the adoption of this motion would cause great delay, and render necessary a reconstruction of some of the most important clauses of the bill; but it afforded some boroughs a prospect of escape from disfranchisement; hence it attracted a good deal of public attention, and not a few reformers were disposed to support it.

'The noble lord opposite,' said Mr. Mackinnon, 'has laid it down as a principle, that boroughs with a population under 4000 and above 2000 are to have one member; and those with a population above 4000 are to have two members. If that principle were acted on, and the census of the present year taken as a criterion of the population of boroughs, I believe that the result will be that six or eight boroughs will be taken out of Schedule A and transferred to Schedule B; that three or four boroughs now placed in Schedule B will be taken out; and that one or two boroughs will be transferred from Schedule B to Schedule A; and that one borough not at present in Schedule B will be placed there. I am aware of the argument which has been used against taking the census of 1831 as the criterion of population, namely, that it might be considered as not impartial. This argument, however, reflects but a poor compliment on those individuals who are employed to make up the returns.'

Lord J. Russell: ''The reason why I think that the census of 1821 ought to be used in preference to the census of 1831 is this: the House will remember that the reform measure was brought forward in the beginning of March last, and the latest census the government could make use of was the census of 1821. That document, therefore, is

the only sure document with respect to population which
we possessed. If the government had chosen to wait for a
new census, they might have taken that of 1831; but such
a course would only have led to an alteration of the time
of disfranchisement. I consider that much inconvenience
would result from acting on the census of 1831, and the
only advantage which the House could gain would be, to
see that while some boroughs had increased in population,
others had decreased. On the other hand, the census of
1821 was taken without any knowledge that it was to form
the test of disfranchisement, and might therefore be considered as an impartial document. But what would be the
result if the census of 1831 should be taken as the test?
Those boroughs in which no sort of fraud or mismanagement was practised would suffer; while those in which
mismanagement has prevailed, by sweeping a number of
persons into them, would be gainers, in consequence of the
statement which ministers have published, that 2000 is to
be the line of disfranchisement. I therefore think that the
House will be of opinion that it will be better to proceed
in the manner in which we have already begun.'

Mr. Mackinnon's proposition was rejected by a majority
of seventy-five—the smallest majority in favour of any
leading provision of the ministerial bill throughout the
whole progress of the struggle in the House of Commons.
It was subsequently adopted by ministers themselves, and
the measure which became law was based on the census of
1831.

The real business of the committee now fairly began, but
did not go forward very rapidly. The whole evening was
spent in a second wrangle over the borough of Appleby,
which was at length condemned to political extinction by
a majority of seventy-four.

On the following evening the progress was somewhat
more rapid; twelve boroughs were doomed to parliamentary extinction, notwithstanding all the efforts of the
Opposition to delay their fate. This rate of proceeding,
however, did not by any means satisfy the impatience of
reformers out of doors. They were beginning to complain
of the forbearance and courtesy with which the opponents
of the bill were treated by ministers, and to ask such
questions as, 'Why not (as Mr. Hobhouse has already

proposed) meet at ten o'clock in the morning?' 'Why not force the disfranchisement of nomination boroughs in the lump, instead of strangling the reptiles by the tedious and troublesome process of succession?' To all which questions ministers, heartily weary of the length to which the discussion had already gone, and contemplating with dismay the almost endless floods of talk that lay in prospect before them, lent a not inattentive or unwilling ear. On the 21st of July, the Chancellor of the Exchequer came forward with a plan, of which he had given notice the previous evening, 'to enable the House to make a more expeditious progress with the Reform Bill.' He proposed that the order for the day for the House resolving itself into a committee on the Reform Bill should precede all public business, and that the House should sit on Saturdays for the reception of petitions.

It was eventually agreed that the House should go into committee on the bill daily at five o'clock. Other business intervened, and it was late on this evening before the Reform Bill came before the House. However, some progress was made. Downton, Dunwich, Eye, Fowey, Gatton, and Haselmere were all disfranchised; and the Speaker, at the conclusion of the sitting, announced that, in accordance with what appeared to be the wish of the House, he would take the chair at three o'clock, whenever the attendance of members enabled him to do so. The only earnest contest took place in the case of the borough of Downton, which had not, in the first instance, been marked out for disfranchisement, and which had a population considerably exceeding 2000, but which had been placed in Schedule A at the suggestion of the patron, Lord Radnor, on the ground of the smallness of its constituency, and of its being a nomination borough. Lord J. Russell, after stating these circumstances, added, that the borough might be allowed to retain its right of sending a member without violation of any principle of the bill, and left it to the House to decide freely on its fate. Thus encouraged, Mr. Croker proposed its removal from Schedule A; and after considerable discussion, its retention in that clause was decided by a majority of 30 only, there being 244 for the motion, and 274 against it.

On the following day the new arrangement was carried

out. At five o'clock the House went into committee on the Reform Bill, and continued till about two o'clock, when it proceeded to the other orders of the day, which were very speedily disposed of. This first experience of its working was highly satisfactory to reformers, as eighteen more boroughs were condemned to disfranchisement.

But reformers outside, though glad to see this improvement, desired still greater rapidity. They complained that, after a discussion extending over several weeks, the *first* clause had not yet been disposed of, and there were *sixty* more, and the House of Lords after all. The division lists were carefully scanned, and absentees on the reforming side admonished to be at their posts, if they wished to preserve the favour and support of their constituents. On the other hand, the Tories were delighted at these delays. They were beginning to recover hope, and uttered very confident predictions that the bill would never be carried. Their vaunts increased the uneasiness and alarm of the reformers, and meetings began to be held in all parts of the country, for the purpose of petitioning the Houses to proceed with the measure more rapidly. Coventry took the lead in this movement, and in ten hours its petition, praying the House to be less dilatory in its proceedings, received 3,400 signatures.

These efforts were not altogether ineffectual. On the night of the 26th the remaining boroughs of Schedule A were disposed of, with the exception of Saltash, which was feebly condemned by the Chancellor of the Exchequer, defended by Lord J. Russell, and saved from disfranchisement by a majority of eighty-one. The borough of St. Germains was less fortunate. In this case the population of the town was considerably below 2000, but that of the parish to which it belonged was above that number. In the first bill it had been placed in Schedule B; it was now removed into Schedule A, because it was found that there were only thirteen houses in the town and parish that were assessed at 10*l.* and upwards. Mr. Ross moved that it should be reinstated in the position which it had originally occupied; but he, and a host of others who followed on the same side, failed to convince ministers; and after a long discussion the proposal to preserve its franchise was negatived by a majority of forty-eight.

At length, on the evening of July 27th, the committee reached the second clause of the bill, which enacted that for the future the boroughs named in Schedule B should return one member and no more to serve in Parliament. Sir Robert Peel at once rose, and proposed that the word *two* should be substituted for the word *one*. In contending for this change he developed more fully an argument urged by Mr. Croker on the 22nd, that the agricultural interest was very unfairly dealt with by the bill.

'I hold in my hand,' he said, 'a small map which has been lately published, entitled "A Map showing the places in England and Wales sending members to Parliament heretofore, with the alterations proposed to be made by the bill amending the representation." In this map I will draw a line, not exactly across the centre of the country, but from the indenture made in the coast by the Severn to the indenture made in the opposite coast by the Wash. This line would divide, with tolerable accuracy, the agricultural from the manufacturing districts. Taking this line for my guide, I will attempt to prove that the bill will give an immense preponderance to the northern or manufacturing districts. I will now show how this bill affects those two great divisions of the country. Schedule A comprises fifty-six boroughs, returning one hundred and eleven members. How are these boroughs situated with respect to the districts north and south of the line? The district north of the line loses only five boroughs out of the fifty-six; the district to the south of the line loses fifty-one; the district to the north of the line loses ten members and the district to the south loses one hundred and one. So much for Schedule A. I now come to Schedule B, in which forty-one boroughs are included. Out of these forty-one boroughs, eight are to the north of the line, and thirty-three to the south. By the combined operation of Schedules A and B, the manufacturing districts loses eighteen members, and the agricultural district loses one hundred and thirty-four. I now come to the constructive clauses. Here I find no compensation for the loss which the destructive clauses occasion to the agricultural division. Schedule C contains twelve new boroughs, each of which is to return two members. Every one of these new boroughs, with the exception of the metropolitan district

and the town of Devonport, is in the northern division.
It is clear that the return of members for the metropolitan
districts will be an injury instead of an advantage to the
agricultural interest. The bill creates twenty-six new
boroughs with one member each; and of these twenty-four
are to the north of the line and two to the south. I had
hoped that these two at least would be of some advantage
to the agricultural interest; but what was my disappointment when, in looking at the clause, I found that in these
instances the privilege of representation was conferred on
Cheltenham and Brighton? The result of my statement
is, that the southern division of the kingdom sustains a
loss of one hundred and thirty-four members, whilst the
northern division sustains a loss of only eighteen. On the
other hand, the southern district gains seven members,
and the northern district thirty-three. If the House will
accede to my proposition, and give two members to the
boroughs contained in Schedule B, the agricultural interest
will possess its due weight in the representative system.
At all times it is necessary to protect the agricultural
interest from the augmenting influence of the manufacturing districts. The constituencies of populous places
have greater power of combining than the scattered constituencies of agricultural districts. The influence of the
press and of clubs is much more powerful amongst the
former than amongst the latter body. I am aware that
there are anomalies in the present system of representation,
but they have existed for centuries. No such excuse can
be made for the anomalies that disfigure the new system. I
and others have argued that the destruction of nomination
boroughs would prevent the introduction of men of talent
into the House; but I do not mean to deny that men of
talent would find their way into the House under the new
system. On the contrary, I think it will bring into the
House men of tremendously active talent, who will feel too
strong a desire to recommend themselves to their constituents to allow them to interpose their reason between
the deliberations of Parliament and—I will not say popular
clamour—temporary popular feeling. I believe that, under
the system proposed by government, men of great experience in public life, but of retired habits, would shrink
from the election contests which this bill will produce.

Such are the combined considerations on which I most earnestly entreat the House to pause, and to inquire whether or no they might not consistently with the principle of the bill suffer those forty boroughs, which are included in Schedule B, to retain the right of sending two members to Parliament.'

Lord J. Russell followed; and, after some preliminary observations, thus replied to Sir Robert's arguments:

'The right honourable baronet ought to recollect that by the new system four additional members will be given to Cornwall, Dorsetshire, and Wiltshire, and to several other counties in the south and west of England. Cornwall, which is one of the counties which ministers have thought it necessary to despoil more than any other, having deprived it of thirty members, will still be in possession of twelve members; a very sufficient number, with which it will be better represented than it was when it sent forty-two members. Ministers have been accused of having unduly and unfairly enriched Durham in comparison with Cornwall. Now, how stands the fact? Cornwall contains 257,000 inhabitants, and Durham 205,000. The former returns twelve members, or, including Saltash, thirteen; the latter will send nine members to Parliament, being in fair and exact proportion with the population. I do not mean to assert that all these counties receive exactly all that their wealth and population might demand. But ministers, instead of taking the course which the right honourable baronet recommends—that of carrying their scale more to the south and west—looked rather to the great population of the northern counties. They found that Lancashire contains more than a million of inhabitants, while Dorsetshire had only a population of 140,000. Therefore, Lancashire is allowed nineteen members, while Dorsetshire will send nine; being little more, in the former instance, than two to one. I contend, therefore, that the last charge which ought to be made against ministers is that of neglecting the interests of the southern and western counties, or overlooking the agricultural districts. They wish to give to those vast dépôts of manufacturing wealth, which during the last thirty years have been constantly increasing, the importance to which they are entitled. The individuals connected with them are in the habit of

trading with every quarter of the world; they keep up the
relations of this country with every portion of the globe;
wherever they go they are admired for their mechanical
skill, and envied for their increasing and secure prosperity.
And yet, strange to say, they have never found admittance
into this House, where they ought to have been assisting in
the representation of the people of England, and legislating
for a great, mighty, powerful, and commercial country. In
proceeding as they have done, ministers feel that the representation should not be the representation of a particular class of men, strongly addicted to a specific set of
opinions. They think that if it were so, an impetus and a
velocity might be given to the machine of government not
consistent with the established state of things. Therefore
they have stopped their career at a particular point, and
laid down a line beyond which they will not go. There
are forty boroughs in this schedule which will send one
member each to Parliament, and there are thirty others
that will still return two members; these latter do not
contain any great body of constituents, but still they will
send members to Parliament, to represent certain portions
of the people who have as firm a right to be represented
as any other body. We have left the boroughs in this
schedule the right of sending one member to Parliament,
not from any personal or partial views, but because we
thought it right and just to stop where we conceived that
total disfranchisement is no longer necessary. The right
honourable baronet has argued, that under the new system
persons of very retired habits would not find their way into
this House, and he mentioned Mr. Sturges Bourne in
support of his argument. But really a person must be of
very retired habits, if he could not summon sufficient resolution to ask for the suffrages of the electors. I can see
no reason why Mr. Sturges Bourne could not ask for the
suffrages of the voters at Lymington, Christchurch, or
any other place in Hampshire.' The amendment was
rejected by a majority of 67; there being 115 for, and 182
against it.

Notwithstanding this adverse decision of the House on
the general question, the Opposition strenuously and at
great length defended each separate borough, and after each
successive defeat again renewed the hopeless struggle with

the same dogged and invincible obstinacy. Aldborough came first. Mr. Duncombe, who denominated it a rotten and stinking borough, proposed that it should be sent back to Schedule A, or in other words, entirely disfranchised. He was eventually persuaded to withdraw his motion, and it retained the place that had been assigned to it in the bill. The borough of Ashburton came next. Its two reforming members, Colonel Torrens and Mr. Poyntz, tried hard to avert its fate, but failed to convince the ministry or the House. An attempt to obtain an inquiry into the amount of the population of Chippenham, on the ground that there was a serious error in the population returns of the census of 1821 for that place, was equally unsuccessful. Eight boroughs, being a fifth part of the whole number designated by the bill for semi-disfranchisement, were disposed of this evening. The following evening six more were disposed of in nine hours. Never were procrastination and delay so systematically organised, or carried to such a pitch of perfection, as in these discussions. There was a regular division of labour in the work of obstruction, which was arranged and superintended by a committee, of which Sir R. Peel was the president.* Each borough had its own band of defenders, whose business was not so much to endeavour to save it—for of that there was no hope—but to consume time in advocating its retention. And in order to promote delay, the leaders of the Opposition stood up again and again every night, repeating the same stale statements and arguments, and often in almost the same words. The *Spectator* computed the number of speeches which had been delivered in committee between the 12th and the 27th of July, by some of the leading anti-reformers, and found that Sugden had spoken eighteen times, Praed twenty-two times, Pelham twenty-eight times, Peel forty-eight times, Croker fifty-seven times, and Wetherell fifty-eight times. It is needless to say that the greater part of these speeches were inexpressibly wearisome. Ministers, condemned to sit and listen, and sometimes obliged to reply, were taunted by their opponents for not answering their stale arguments, and severely lectured by their

* In justice to Sir R. Peel, it should be observed, that his opposition was much more candid and less vexatious than that of most of those with whom he was associated.

friends out of doors for their mildness, courtesy, and
forbearance. These reproofs were undeserved, for they
were really doing their very best to push the measure
forwards; but they had to do with men who, knowing the
facilities which the forms of Parliament afforded for
vexatious delay, were determined to take advantage of
them to the very uttermost. We have an instance of this
on July 29th, when more than two hours were spent in
higgling with the Opposition for a sitting on the day
following (Saturday, July 30.) The thermometer at this
time was ranging from 75° to 80°, and eight hours of each
evening were being given to the Reform Bill alone,
besides the time spent in other business. Ministers as
usual carried their point on a division; but the hours
consumed in this unprofitable discussion nearly counterbalanced the gain. However, on this evening, the rest of
the boroughs in Schedule B were disposed of according to
the intentions of the government, with the exception of
two, Sudbury and Totnes, which were postponed until the
next meeting of the House, which was fixed for the 2nd of
August—the 1st of that month being the day appointed
for the solemn opening of London Bridge by the king in
person.

Thus the anti-reformers went on night after night pro-
tracting the struggle by every possible artifice, suffering
defeat after defeat unchequered by any gleam of success
except the one solitary triumph achieved by the Marquis
of Chandos, who, with the aid of a few reformers, carried
an amendment, the object of which was, to give a vote to
any farmer occupying land on his own account at a rent of
not less than 50l. per annum, without any specific tenure.

On the 8th of September, the coronation was performed
as usual, but the cost was greatly reduced, and the ceremony shorn of much ancient pomp and time-honoured
absurdity. At the banquet which followed the ceremony
the king made a declaration which helped to increase his
popularity through the country: 'I do not agree with
those who consider the ceremony of coronation as indispensable, for the contract between the prince and the
people was as binding on my mind before. No member of
the House of Hanover can forget the conditions on which
I hold the crown; and'—added his majesty, striking an

energetic blow on the table—'I am not a whit more desirous now than before taking the oath to watch over the liberties and promote the welfare of my people.'

Although the Reform Bill had now passed through the committee, the contest was not ended, nor were the resources of obstruction and delay entirely exhausted. On Tuesday the 13th of September, Lord J. Russell brought up the report, and called the attention of the House to one or two alterations he proposed to make in the measure. The consideration of the report occupied the House during the evenings of Wednesday, Thursday, Friday, and Saturday; with no other result than that Derbyshire, Carnarvonshire, Ashton-under-Lyne, and Stroud in Gloucestershire, with which last borough Minchinhampton was incorporated, each gained a member.

At last, on the evening of September 19th, the third reading of the bill came on; and in order that every man might be at his post, a call of the House was proposed but not enforced. The attendance was by no means large. After the presentation of petitions, and some other routine business, Lord J. Russell moved that the order of the day be read for the third reading of the Reform Bill. This having been done accordingly, he rose again and said, 'I move that the bill be read a third time.'

The anti-reformers expected a long discussion on this motion, and very few of them were in their places. Sir J. Scarlett, the only leading member of the Opposition present, attempted to speak against time, in order to give his friends an opportunity of coming up to the division; but he quailed before the vehement shouts of 'divide' with which he was met, and, after persisting for a few minutes, during which his voice was drowned by the clamour, he gave way, and the House proceeded to the division, when the numbers were:

For the third reading 113
Against 58
                                    ———
Majority 55

These numbers sufficiently indicate that both sides of the House had been taken by surprise, and no sooner were the doors re-opened after the division, than the members who had been shut out came flocking in. Among them were

Sir R. Peel and Sir C. Wetherell, who were received by the exulting majority with peals of derisive laughter, which lasted for some minutes. It was the first time the majority had fairly stolen a march on their opponents, and they were naturally not a little triumphant.

After the discussion of a rider, providing against the contingency of the king's decease before the bill could come into operation, and the consideration and adoption of some unimportant ministerial amendments, Lord J. Russell once more rose, and said: 'Sir, I now move that this bill do pass.' The Opposition were not to be taken by surprise this time. They were now in full force; and so, on the motion thus laconically proposed, a discussion extending over the evenings of the 19th, 20th, and 21st of September, ensued. At length, at five o'clock in the morning of the 22nd of September, the House divided for the last time, when the numbers were:

For the question that the bill do now pass	345
Against	239
Majority	106

Thus at length the measure, on which the House of Commons had been almost continuously engaged during nearly three months of extraordinary labour and unusually protracted sittings, at last passed. And now the eyes of all men were turned towards the upper House. They had long been inquiring and were every day asking more anxiously as the critical moment approached, 'What will the Lords do?' Reformers asked the question, anti-reformers asked it, ministers asked it. There could be no doubt whatever, that if the peers consulted their own opinions and inclinations, the bill would be flung out by an overwhelming majority; but it was still fondly hoped by the administration and its supporters, that despair of ultimate success and dread of consequences would cause them to respect the wishes of the majority of the lower House and of the nation. In order to secure this result, the friends of the bill brought every possible influence to bear on the Lords. The press alternately soothed and threatened now the spiritual and now the temporal peers. Throughout the country, meetings were being held and resolutions adopted which would, it was hoped, convince the upper House that the people did not, as the enemies of the bill industriously asserted, waver in their attachment to it. At these meetings, which were both numerous and enthusiastic, petitions were adopted, praying the Lords, often in very outspoken language, to carry through the measure with all possible dispatch.

The people, thus up and doing, were not kept long in suspense. We have already related that the bill passed the Commons on the morning of the 22nd of September, and on the evening of the same day it was carried up to the House of Lords. The lord chancellor took his seat and opened the business precisely at five o'clock; but though it was well known that the proceedings of the evening would be only of a formal character, such was the interest felt in the bill, that long before that hour there was a very numerous attendance of peers, and the space before the throne was crowded with the members of the House of Commons who had been most active and determined in their opposition to the measure. No sooner had the chancellor taken his seat on the woolsack, than the deputy usher of the black rod appeared at the bar, and announced a message from the Commons. The Lords, who had hitherto been conversing in groups in different parts of the House, now took their seats, and perfect stillness prevailed, until the doors by which messages from the House of Commons are received were thrown open, and Lord Althorp and Lord J. Russell entered, followed by more than a hundred members, all staunch supporters of the bill.

The lord chancellor advanced to the bar with the usual formalities, and received the bill from the hands of Lord J. Russell, who said with a firm voice: 'This, my lord, is a bill to amend the representation of the people of England and Wales, which the House of Commons have agreed to, and to which they desire the concurrence of your lordships.' These words were followed by a loud cry of 'hear, hear,' from the deputation, which was met by a cry of 'order' from some of the peers. The deputation, instead of at once retiring, as is usual on such occasions, retained their position at the bar of the House.

The lord chancellor, having returned to the woolsack, communicated to their lordships the nature of the message in the usual form; but such was felt to be the solemnity of

the occasion, and such the deep feeling with which the
chancellor pronounced these words of course, that the
formula which usually passes unnoticed was listened to
with deep and breathless attention.

Earl Grey was not in the House at the moment when
the message was brought up, and, in consequence of his
absence, an embarrassing pause ensued. At length he
entered, and said: 'My lords, I was not present when the
bill for effecting reform in the representation of the people
was brought from the House of Commons; I beg, however,
to move, "That the bill be read a first time." Having
made this motion, it will be necessary to fix a day for the
second reading of this bill; and in doing this I have no
other wish than to consult the convenience of your lordships. I think the second reading of the bill should not be
taken sooner than Friday se'nnight, nor later than Monday
se'nnight. It will perhaps meet the convenience of all
parties if I fix the reading for Monday se'nnight.'

This proposal having been agreed to, the members of the
House of Commons retired.

It must not be supposed that the anti-reformers were idle
at this important crisis. They too, as has already been
intimated, had been eagerly asking the question, 'What
will the Lords do?' And they were straining every nerve
to induce them to throw out the bill. Already Lord Eldon,
whose advanced age and long tenure of the great seal gave
him no little influence in the House of Lords, had declared,
amidst the marked applauses of the Duke of Cumberland,
(the king's brother) and many other anti-reforming peers,
that they would do their duty; and every one perfectly
well knew what that expression meant in his mouth. In
Dublin, in Nottingham, in Kingsbridge, and many other
places, the anti-reformers were busily engaged in getting
up petitions, which, if not numerously, were 'respectably'
signed, and were sure to be thankfully and respectfully
welcomed by the majority of the assembly to which they
were addressed. At this momentous crisis, too, Lord
Ashley, an anti-reformer, came forward to contest the
representation of the county of Dorset with Mr. Ponsonby,
who was already in the field; and it was hoped by anti-
reformers that his personal popularity and family influence
would win him a triumph, which would give some colour to

the assertions they were industriously propagating, that the nation was cooling down in its zeal for reform, and that a reaction had begun. They were also making great use of the queen's name; while the reformers, on the other hand, were strongly insisting that Lord Howe, her chamberlain, and other officers of her household, who were members of the House of Peers, should be required either to support the bill or resign their offices.

At length the anxiously-expected 3rd of October arrived, and now the question, 'What will the Lords do?' must receive its answer. After the presentation and discussion of a large number of petitions, most of them in favour of the bill, but some of them in opposition to it, the order of the day for its second reading was read, and then, amidst deep silence, Earl Grey advanced to the table to address the House in support of it. It was a solemn moment—one of the most solemn that has ever occurred in the history of the British senate. The eyes of the whole nation—we may almost say of the whole world—were fixed on the Lords, and they felt it. And the premier was now standing before them to propose to an assembly—the majority of which he knew regarded him with a hostile respect—a measure which he had taken up in his youth, for which he had carried on what seemed a hopeless and almost quixotic struggle, through all the best years of his long public life, and which he was now in his old age enabled to bring forward as the first minister of the crown. There he stood, with his nobly-formed brow plainly betokening a meditative mind and a spotless soul, an eye sparkling with intelligence, and a patrician countenance and bearing which awed while it attracted, and indicated boldness and firmness associated with wisdom and prudence. There was a majesty in his manner that proclaimed the statesman. The solemnity of the moment was felt by all, but by none more than the earl himself. The recollections of the past and the responsibilities of the present rushed into his mind with overpowering force. He essayed to speak, but his agitation deprived him of utterance, and notwithstanding the sympathetic and encouraging cheers which proceeded from every part of the House, he was compelled to resume his seat. In a few moments he rose again, spoke in a very low tone, which grew louder as he proceeded, until each word became distinctly audible in every corner of the House. Less rhetorical than his great colleague Lord Brougham, he was not less eloquent, and the matter of his speech secured a continuance of that riveted attention which his demeanour, character, and subject had commanded before he commenced.

'In the course of a long political life, which has extended to half a century, I have had the honour of proposing to this and the other House of Parliament, amidst circumstances of much difficulty and danger, in seasons of great political convulsion and violence, many questions affecting the government of the political interests of this country, as well as the government of its domestic concerns. If at such times, speaking as I did in the presence of some of the greatest men that have ever graced this country, I experienced awe and trepidation, it was, as your lordships will readily believe, nothing to the emotions which affect me now, when I am about to propose to the consideration of your lordships a question involving the dearest interests of the nation—a question for the consequences of which I am more responsible than any man—a question which has been designated as subversive of the constitution, as revolutionary, as destructive of chartered rights and privileges, and as tending to produce general confusion throughout the empire, but which I solemnly and deliberately feel to contain changes that are necessary; to be a measure of peace and conciliation, and one on the acceptance or rejection of which I believe depends, on the one hand, tranquillity, prosperity, and concord,—on the other, the continuance of a state of political discontentment from which those feelings must arise which are naturally generated by such a condition of the public mind. Those members of the House who have observed the political conduct of so humble an individual as myself are aware that I have always been the advocate of reform. In 1786 I voted for reform. I supported Mr. Pitt in his motion for shortening the duration of parliaments. I gave my best assistance to the measure of reform introduced by Mr. Flood before the French revolution. On one or two occasions I originated motions on the subject. Although I have reverted to these facts in my previous political career, I do not stand here to advocate the measure of reform on the ground that I have never swerved from maintaining the necessity and expediency of its adoption; I am bound to entertain the conviction that in proposing a measure affecting the mighty interests of the state, the course I take is called for by justice and necessity, and essential to the safety of the country. Your lordships cannot have forgotten the agitation which prevailed throughout the country at the commencement of the last session—the general discontent that pervaded every part of the empire—society almost disorganised—the distress that reigned in the manufacturing districts—the influence of the numerous associations that grew out of that distress—the sufferings of the agricultural population—the nightly alarms, burnings, and popular disturbances, approaching almost to the very skirts of the metropolis—the general feeling of doubt and apprehension observable in every countenance. Noble lords will, no doubt, recollect these events; but I recollect, in addition, that there prevailed a general growing desire for the adoption of some measure of parliamentary reform. If the anxiety to urge forward that question had ever slept, it was only in appearance and partially, never really or completely. On the arrival of a season of difficulty the question was stirred anew,—a circumstance which of itself demonstrated the necessity of having it speedily settled. But granting that a measure of parliamentary reform is necessary, why have ministers gone to the extent of this measure, which, in the language of many, is revolutionary in spirit and subversive of the best principles of the British constitution? I hope to answer this question satisfactorily, and to prove to your lordships that there is nothing in the measure that is not founded on the principles of the British constitution,—nothing that is not perfectly consistent with the ancient practices of that constitution,—and nothing that might not be adopted with perfect safety to the rights and privileges of all orders of the state, and particularly to the rights and privileges of that order to which your lordships belong. Is it possible that the boroughs called nomination boroughs can longer be permitted to exist, when the people see the scenes which disgrace every election,—when they witness the most gross and scandalous corruption practised without disguise,—when the sale of seats in the House of Commons is a matter of equal notoriety with the open return of nominees of noble and wealthy persons to that House,—when the people see these things passing before their eyes as often as a general election takes place,—and when, turning from such sights, they read the lessons of their youth, and consult the writings of the expounders of the laws and constitution, where they find such practices stated to be at once illegal and inconsistent with the people's rights, and where they may discover that the privileges which they see a few individuals converting into a means of personal profit are privileges which have been conferred for the benefit of the nation? It is with these views that the government has considered that the boroughs which are called nomination boroughs ought to be abolished. In looking at these boroughs, we found that some of them were incapable of correction, for it is impossible to extend their constituency. Some of them consisted only of the sites of ancient boroughs, which, however, might perhaps in former times have been very fit places to return members to Parliament; in others, the constituency was insignificantly small, and from their local situation incapable of receiving any increase; so that, upon the whole, this gangrene of our representative system bade defiance to all remedies but that of excision.' After dwelling at great length on the provisions of the measure, replying to the objections which had been urged against it, and referring to the dangers which would arise from its rejection, he then proceeded:

'I especially beg the spiritual portion of your lordships to pause and reflect. The prelates of the empire have not a more firm friend than I. But if this bill should be thrown out by a narrow majority, and the scale should be turned by their votes, what would be their situation? "Let them set their houses in order."* I have said, and I am not the man to recall what I have said, that by this measure I am prepared to stand or fall. The question of my continuance in office for one hour will depend on the prospect of my

---

* This phrase, as we shall see by the sequel, gave great offence to the prelates. It must be admitted that they had some reason to complain, when we consider the whole of the passage from which it was quoted. ' Set thine house in order; for thou must die, and not live' (2 Kings xx. 1; Isaiah xxxviii. 1). I almost think, judging from Earl Grey's general character, that he used the expression inadvertently, without remembering the context. Certainly it was not his habit to employ such menaces.

being able to carry through that which I consider so important to the tranquillity, to the safety, and to the happiness of the country. I must repeat, that no danger which might be attendant on the rejection of this measure could be obviated by the introduction of one of less efficiency. At all events, if such a measure is introduced, it will not be by me. I am convinced that the people will not cease to urge their rights; and if your lordships should reject this bill, it is more than probable that you will hereafter have to consider a measure in which much greater concessions will be demanded. Most fervently do I pray that the Almighty Being will so guide and direct your lordships' counsels, that your ultimate decision may be for the advancement of his glory, the good of his church, the safety, welfare, and honour of the king and the people.'

Lord Wharncliffe, one of the most moderate of the opponents of the bill, and who candidly admitted the desirableness and necessity of a considerable reform in Parliament, followed, and, at the close of a long speech against the bill, moved that it should be rejected. At a subsequent period of the evening, finding that the terms of this proposition were unusual, and might be regarded as insulting to the House of Commons, he desired to substitute for it the customary formula, 'That the bill be read a second time this day six months.' Ministers resisted this change, wishing to retain the advantage which the motion as originally worded gave them in debate. However, after a long discussion, they yielded to the majority, and allowed the amendment to be couched in the usual terms.

Lord Melbourne—courteous, candid, sensible, and inoffensive—addressed the House on the second day of the debate. He said that he had opposed reform as much as any man. He had opposed the extension of the suffrage to the great towns of Manchester and Birmingham; but he had done so because he felt that if that measure were granted, it must lead to farther measures; and his whole speech showed that he supported the bill rather because he dreaded the consequences of a refusal of concession to the demands of the people than because he loved reform. In the course of his observations, he said that he could not concur in the censure which had been passed on the House of Commons for the time and consideration they had be-

stowed on the bill. It was perfectly impossible that they
could have done otherwise; and he did not think that any
time had been needlessly consumed, or that the delay had
been at all extravagant, considering the great importance
of the measure adopted by them.

In the course of the same sitting the Duke of Wellington
spoke strongly against the measure. On all occasions, but
especially on this, he was sure to be listened to with
attention; but this attention was a tribute paid rather to
his high character and his fame as a warrior than to his
capacity as a statesman or his merits as a speaker. The
commencement of his speeches was indeed usually effective, from the strong common-sense view which he took of
the question before the House; but, unhappily for himself
and his auditors, he never knew when to stop, and often
destroyed the favourable impression he had made in the
beginning of his address by continuing to speak after his
ideas were exhausted. His speeches were rendered still
more tedious by a defective elocution, caused by the loss of
several of his teeth, which often prevented many consecu-
tive sentences from being heard even by the most attentive
listener. He explained and defended his conduct with
reference to the question of reform; he stated his objections to the present measure; he gave it as his opinion,
that under the system it established the king would not be
able to carry on the government of this country, on the
principles on which governments had been conducted at
any former period; and declared his intention of voting
against the second reading of the bill.

Lord Brougham delivered his opinions on Friday, October 7th. As they have been published in the well-known
collection of his speeches, we do not think it necessary to
attempt to give an account here of one of the most able
and eloquent addresses ever delivered in either House of
Parliament. He concluded by imploring the House not to
reject the bill.

Lord Lyndhurst—inferior to Lord Brougham alone in
the power of his eloquence, and greatly his superior in tact
and mental agility—rose to reply. He expressed the feeling of all present when he characterised his great rival's
speech as an elegant and splendid display, never surpassed
on any former occasion even by his noble friend himself.

He dwelt at great length on what he denominated the revolutionary violence of the measure; and in reference to the argument that, inasmuch as they assented to the principle of the bill, they should read it a second time, he replied that they assented to its object, but they opposed its principle. After mentioning several objections he entertained to the measure, the noble lord thus proceeded:

'But all these objections vanish into insignificance when compared with the aggregate consideration I am now about to mention. The bill takes 157 members from the aristocratic part of the House of Commons. It gives back 65 in the shape of county members; but it gives also 50 members to the populous towns, to be elected by such a constituency as I have described. What would the representatives of such places be? We may judge by the persons who are at present the favourite candidates. The difference is not a difference of 50 members, but a difference of 100; for 50 are taken from the aristocratic part and given to the democratic part of the House. But then there are 35 more to be taken away; so that in fact the aristocratic part of the House will lose 135 members. The same consequences will result in Scotland, where the democratic part of the members will utterly overwhelm the aristocratic part. Then look at Ireland. Three-fourths of the representation of Ireland will be in the power of the Catholics. I must say, that I think the whole will form what the noble duke near me has described—namely, a fierce and democratic assembly.' He then proceeded to state what he conceived would be the consequence of this change. He believed that Earl Grey and his associates, after having opened the floodgates, would be carried away by the torrent—that a republic would be established—that the Protestant church in Ireland would be destroyed, and church property in both kingdoms confiscated.

'This,' he concluded, 'is the crisis of your lordships' fate: if you now abdicate the trust reposed in you, you will never be able to resume those trusts; your rights, your titles, and the liberties of the country will be trampled in the dust. The guardianship of the constitution has been intrusted to you; and if it should be despoiled while in your custody, the blame will rest with you, and with you only. But if, on the contrary, you preserve it unimpaired, you

will receive the thanks of all reasonable men of the present
generation, and your memory will live in the gratitude of
posterity, to whom, by your instrumentality, the invaluable
blessings of the British constitution will have been trans-
mitted uninjured and undiminished.'

Lord Tenterden, the chief-justice, gave utterance to
the prevailing wish and opinion of the legal profession
when he announced that it was his intention to vote for the
rejection of the bill. Dr. Howley, archbishop of Canterbury,
followed him. No prelate had ever more worthily filled
the throne of Lanfranc, Anselm, Becket, and Laud, and
none had ever more fully commanded the reverence of the
House of Lords. Briefly, hesitatingly, and with evident
deep feeling, he declared that he should have supported a
moderate reform, but that this bill he regarded as destructive. 'If,' he concluded, 'it should be your lordships'
pleasure to pass this bill, I shall rejoice if I find my apprehensions groundless; and if, on the contrary, your lordships
should deem it expedient to throw the bill out, and that
popular violence—which I do not anticipate—should result
from this proceeding I will cheerfully bear my share of the
general calamity, and I shall have the consolation, for the
few years or days I may have to live, of reflecting that I
have not been actuated by sinister motives, but that I
opposed the bill fairly and in perfect purity of heart,
believing it to be mischievous in its tendency and dangerous
to the fabric of the constitution.' It was evident, from
the assenting cheers of the bishops behind him, that the
venerable prelate uttered the prevailing sentiments of the
episcopal bench. These declarations of the heads of the
legal and clerical professions, though not unexpected, were
ominous of the fate of the bill. The Duke of Sussex, the
king's brother, declared that he should vote for the bill, and
his cousin, the Duke of Gloucester, briefly announced his
intention to vote against it.

The morning of the 8th of October was already far spent
when Lord Grey at length rose to reply. He retorted with
telling effect upon Lord Lyndhurst the charge of inconsistency, which that noble lord had insinuated against him;
and after some remarks in defence of the bill, he thus concluded:

'I have observed symptoms of an intention to attack

government with a view to overthrow it. All I can say is this, that to this measure, or to a measure of the same extent, I am pledged. A noble and learned lord has said that if I abandon office, it would be a culpable abandonment of the king. It is for me to consider what I will do. I certainly will not abandon the king as long as I can be of any use to him. I am bound to the king by obligations of gratitude, greater perhaps than any subject ever owed to a sovereign, for the kind manner in which he has extended to me his confidence and support, and for the indulgence with which he has accepted my offers and best endeavours to serve him. But I can only be a useful servant to the king whilst I am able to carry measures which are necessary to the security of the country, as well as to my own character. If I should once lose my character, the king had better have any man in the world for his servant rather than me; for as for abilities, I pretend not to them, nor to the other qualifications which long habits of office give. All that I can pretend to is, an honest zeal, a desire to do my duty in the best way I can, sensible of my deficiencies, but feeling that there is no personal sacrifices I am not bound to make for my king, whose friendship to me can never be obliterated from my heart, whatever may happen, to the last moment of my existence. Place was not sought by me. I can appeal to the history of my whole life to prove that I do not desire office. I found myself in a situation in which I thought that I could not shrink from serving my country and my king, and I accepted office very much against my inclination. I have lived a long life of exclusion from office. I have no official habits. I possess not the knowledge that official habits confer. I am fond of retirement; and in domestic life I live happy in the bosom of my family. Nothing but a strong sense of duty would have tempted me to embark on these

"stormy seas,
Bankrupt of life, but prodigal of ease."

I have quitted my retirement from a sense of duty to my country and my king, whom I shall continue to serve as long as his majesty may be pleased to require me; but if Parliament and the country withdraw their confidence from me, and I find that I can no longer be a useful servant to the king, I will resign office; and when in retirement, I shall at least be able to look back to having done my best to serve both king and country.'

These words extorted loud cheers of assent and approval not only from the supporters of the ministry, but from the Duke of Wellington and many of the Opposition peers; and at the conclusion of the speech, all sides expressed their sympathy by clapping of hands and stamping of feet —marks of approbation which, if not altogether unprecedented in the House of Lords, were very unusual.

After a few words of explanation from the Duke of Wellington and Lord Lyndhurst, the House divided, when there appeared:

For the amendment: Present	. . .	150
Proxies	. . .	49—109
Against . . . Present	. . .	128
Proxies	. . .	30—158
Majority against the second reading . . .		41

The House adjourned at twenty minutes past six o'clock in the morning.

Meanwhile the French were engaged in abolishing the hereditary peerage; an event which, though not much referred to, was no doubt a good deal in the thoughts of noble lords—producing different results, according to the various constitutions of their minds and the different ways in which it was regarded. By the great majority of the people it was hailed as an omen of what was coming in England.

CHAPTER IV.

THE REFORM BILL CARRIED.

Never perhaps had the whole English nation been in such a state of feverish and excited expectation as on that Saturday, the 8th day of October, 1831—on the dawn of which we left the peers walking out of their own House, after having thrown out the Reform Bill. The news spread through the country with the speed of lightning, producing wherever it came alarm, disappointment, or indignation. Every man felt as if he were walking on ground from which a volcano might burst forth. The people could do nothing, think of nothing, talk of nothing, but 'the bill.' The very women and children caught the contagion of the prevalent feeling, and were ardent reformers or violent anti-reformers. By the Tories the intelligence was welcomed with an exultation which was largely chastened with alarm. But the former feeling they were compelled to repress, for the reformers were not in a mood to tolerate its manifestation. By these latter the tidings were received with a deep feeling of exasperation, which only needed a leader and a distinct aim in order to produce great results. A stirring word thrown among the multitude at that moment might have produced a revolution. But no such word was spoken; indeed the leaders of the movement, while desiring that the popular enthusiasm should be sustained, as being necessary to the success of the bill, were also anxious that it should be curbed, and fully alive to the destruction that might result from its possible excesses. However, expressions of disappointed hope and fixed resolve were not wanting. In London and in many other towns the shops were closed, and the bells of the churches muffled. The shopkeepers of Spitalfields decided to keep a political fast-day, and to close their shops on the following Wednesday. A run for gold was commenced, and caused

no little alarm to the governors of the Bank. About 200
members of the House of Commons met at Willis's Rooms,
and unanimously agreed that resolutions should be submitted to the House of Commons, affirming that it was
expedient to declare their unaltered and undiminished
attachment to the great measure of reform, and their
determined purpose to support the king's ministers in the
present crisis; a resolution which, as we shall presently see,
was speedily carried out. The same evening, and within
twelve hours of the fatal division, the common council met,
and passed similar resolutions.

But while these efforts were being made to secure the
ultimate success of the bill, the popular indignation against
the authors of the nation's disappointment was being loudly
and strongly vented. The reforming press, at once expressing and stimulating the general feeling, threw off all the
restraints it had hitherto imposed on itself, in the hope of
soothing the anti-reforming lords into compliance with the
nation's desires. The abolition of the House of Peers was
frequently suggested. Still more violent was the language
employed by the orators who addressed the meetings which
were now again being held in every part of the metropolis
and of the United Kingdom. The whole force of the popular rage was directed against the majority of the House of
Lords. On Monday, October 10th, a great crowd assembled
along the line of road from Whitehall to Parliament-street.
The obnoxious peers and members were protected from
personal violence by a very strong party of the new police,
but they were received with roars of execration, which it
was said at the time would have drowned a peal of thunder.
The cheers which greeted the reforming peers and members
were equally loud. The bishops especially were objects of
popular detestation, and could not appear in the streets
without danger of personal violence. Many of the temporal
peers were assaulted on their way to or from the House.
The Duke of Newcastle, who was peculiarly obnoxious to
the reformers, was personally assailed, and his house was
attacked by an infuriated mob. The Marquis of Londonderry, riding in a cabriolet, was stopped, violently struck,
and would probably have been murdered, but for the presence of mind of the driver, who whipped the horse forward
into a gallop, and saved his master from the exasperated

populace. The anti-reforming peers—irritated by the treatment to which they had been exposed, and ascribing it in some measure to the language employed by Earl Grey and other ministerial speakers in the late debate—loudly complained of the alleged remissness of the government in not suppressing violence, which tended to intimidate the opponents of the bill, and to prevent them from voting according to their convictions. This impression produced a scene in the House of Lords on the evening of the 11th of October, almost rivalling in the violence of the language employed that which occurred on the eve of the dissolution. Of all the assailants of the church at this time, few surpassed Lord King in the frequency or bitterness of their invectives. If ever there was a good hater he was one, and the clergy, and especially the bishops, were the objects of his peculiar aversion. He took every opportunity of attacking them, and with no little ability and effect. At this period of their deep unpopularity his assaults were more bitter and persistent than ever. On the evening in question he presented a petition from a parish in Suffolk against an alleged unjust exaction of tithes; and in doing so made some very severe reflections on the conduct of the clergy. Lord Ellenborough called him to order, but he persisted in the same line of offensive remark.

The Earl of Suffield, who followed him, strongly censured the conduct of the bishops, observing that if they had, as usual, supported ministers instead of opposing them, they would have carried the bill. He was interrupted and called to order by Lord Carnarvon. Hereupon the lord chancellor interfered; and after giving his opinion on the question of order, added, 'Good God, my lords, the charge against the right reverend prelates of anything like self-interest in their conduct in this House is the very last imputation that can be made against them. It may be true that the bench of prelates have recently departed from their habitual course of supporting all administrations—it may be true that they have just opposed the government in a great national measure—it may be true that they have thought of tripping-up his majesty's government—'

Lord Ellenborough: 'I rise to order.'

Earl Grey: 'I very much regret that the topic has been introduced. To discuss the motives of the prelates is not consistent with order, and I think the noble earl has rather overstepped the order of the House.'

The Earl of Suffield: 'I regret that I should ever deviate from the order of debate. I will not question either the votes or the motives of the right reverend prelates; but surely I have a right to review their recent conduct as a matter of fact. I will say, then, as a fact, that the votes of the right reverend prelates have always been in favour of ministers; and now for the first time, when government stands in need of their votes in favour of a great national measure intended for the general benefit of the country, I find the bench of bishops have turned against the government. This I state as a fact, and I will state more—'

Lord Wynford: 'Order, order, order.'

The Bishop of London: 'I concur in the extreme inconvenience of introducing such topics of discussion; but I will not sit still and suffer to pass unnoticed the observations proceeding from the woolsack. I did not take any part in the late memorable debate, nor have I expressed any observations or uttered any opinions on the object of it; but when the noble lord on the woolsack went so far as to indulge in a vein of sarcasm on the bench of bishops— when he even insinuated, or rather asserted, that the bench as a body had been influenced by a desire to trip-up his majesty's government, I speak with perfect confidence that no such thought has ever entered their minds. So far as the interests of the church are concerned, not one of them has had any occasion to blame his majesty's present ministers. Whether the bench by their votes on a recent occasion have pursued a course of wisdom, is a different question; but I venture to assert that it has been a course of conviction and integrity.'

The Bishop of Llandaff said a few words.

The Bishop of Exeter, by far the ablest and the most courageous of all the prelates, and one of the most eloquent speakers in the House of Lords, next rose to vindicate his brethren from the attack that had been made on them. Usually his speeches were as remarkable for the calmness and courtesy of their manner and delivery as for the force and fulness of their matter; but on this occasion he spoke with a warmth very unusual to him. 'The bishops,' he exclaimed, 'have opposed this measure because, in their consciences, they cannot approve it; and they are ready to brave the censures of the mob, even when urged and instigated by those whose duty it is to restrain its ebullitions. I defy any noble lord to state a single instance in the history of this country in which any members of this House have been so vilified and insulted as the bishops have been within the last year, and that, too, by men of the highest station in his majesty's councils. I do not apologise for my warmth; for I should be ashamed of myself if I could be cool on such a subject. If the attack on the bench of bishops had been made in a moment of excitement, to that excitement I should have submitted; but upon the mere presentation of a petition, and that a petition of no consequence, a noble lord has abused the church as the great arch-disturber of all order, and another noble lord charged the bishops with being bound together in a conspiracy against the liberties of the country, and against "all that could constitute the welfare and happiness of the people."'

Earl Grey: 'What the right reverend prelate has uttered is the most unprovoked, the most intemperate, and the most unfounded insinuation that I have ever heard from any member of this House. The right reverend prelate said that every man who has spoken from this side of the House has spoken in a tone of sarcasm and reprobation of the recent conduct of the bishops. I ask if that observation is true, and if it could with truth be applied to the few words that have fallen from me?'

The Bishop of Exeter here attempted to explain, but was compelled to resume his seat by loud cries of 'Down, down.'

Earl Grey continued: 'I appeal to every noble lord whether there was anything in what I said at all like what the right reverend prelate attributed to me. Did I not reprobate the discussion altogether? Did I not state it as my opinion that the discussion was altogether inconsistent with the orders of the House? and did I not do all I could to stop it? On what ground, then, could the right reverend prelate make an attack so intemperate and so utterly without any pretext or foundation? I ask the right reverend prelate whether it has ever been my custom to say anything whatever offensive to the church, or anything that was not in support of it? The right reverend prelate said he had

heard, from a person holding the highest situation in the
government, frequent attempts to degrade, insult, and vilify
the church. Whether the right reverend prelate alluded
to me or to my noble friend on the woolsack, I know not,
but of this I am perfectly sure, that of neither could the
observation be made with any justice or truth. The right
reverend prelate was not content with this want of truth,
but he uttered it with an appearance of a spirit that but
little became the garment he wears. It was the grossest
injustice I ever heard. He said that those who were
charged with the care of the public peace, and were bound
to support the institutions of the country, had actually
been the instigators of a mob to insult the bench of bishops.
I cannot conceal the contempt and indignation with which
I heard the charge. I dare the right reverend prelate to
state, if he can, one single syllable of truth to support the
falsest and most calumnious accusation which I ever heard.
If any man could be capable of such conduct, no reprobation could be sufficiently severe against him. So far from
encouraging proceedings such as the right reverend prelate
alludes to, I am one of the very first who would exert the
full powers of the government to protect those whose votes
were hostile to me. I call on the right reverend prelate to
support what he has said by proofs.'

The Bishop of Exeter: 'As I am called upon to produce
proofs of what I asserted, irregular as it may be to refer to
the debates which have recently taken place, yet under the
peculiar circumstances of my case, I hope for the indulgence
of your lordships, in being allowed to refer to the proceedings in question. It must be within the recollection of
every noble lord who hears me, that in the first night of
the debate on the bill, the noble lord, without any one thing
to excite him from the bench of bishops, had thought himself justified in calling on the bench seriously to take to
mind what would be their position with the country, if
there was a narrow majority of lay lords against the bill,
and if it were discovered that the bishops had voted with
that narrow majority. To call upon any set of men—to
call upon one of the great states of the realm (as they are
called by the sages of the law and by the law itself)—to
call upon them by way of menace of popular indignation,
has the tendency, a tendency which the noble lord perhaps

little suspected, to excite the odium of the people. Has not that odium been excited, and have not the bench of bishops been exposed to its effects? The noble lord assumed the character of a prophet, and told the bishops "to set their houses in order." It is true that the noble lord did not conclude the sentence. He left that for us to do. But it was impossible not to know that he referred to words in which the prophet had threatened destruction. The noble lord in the same speech took special care to remind the bishops that certain important questions were in agitation, which might take the turn which would prove favourable or unfavourable according to the conduct of the bench on that night. What are those questions? If the noble lord meant that schemes of confiscation were in contemplation—that the bold among the multitude would be encouraged, and the multitude goaded on to more immediate execution—then indeed I could conceive that the conduct of the bishops on that night might have the effect of driving the multitude to such purposes. Have I said anything which the proofs I have produced have not fully substantiated?'

Earl Grey: 'I ask the right reverend prelate why he did not make the serious charges he has now brought forward when the words he imputes to me were fresh in the recollection of the House, and when he could have made those charges in a regular manner? For my part, I think that the right reverend prelate's proofs correspond very little with his assertions. The right reverend prelate charged his majesty's ministers with having purposely done all in their power to encourage tumult and excite the mob to acts of popular violence.'

The Bishop of Exeter: 'Most solemnly do I declare that I do not think I have used any such words. Upon my honour and conscience, I did not use those words.'

Earl Grey: 'The right reverend prelate in his anger was not likely to recollect what words he did use.'

The noble lord then went on to re-assert his charges against the bishop, and concluded by saying: 'The right reverend prelate has uttered a foul and calumnious aspersion, totally unfounded in truth, nor has he in the least benefited himself by the explanation he has entered into.'

The Duke of Wellington: 'The question before the House

is merely the reception of a petition. A noble lord has attacked the bench of bishops for having always servilely supported every government of arbitrary principles, whilst on the Reform Bill they deserted the government because its principles were liberal. I call upon the noble lord to state what he means by a government of arbitrary principles, and which administration he accused of having such principles. I have been at the head of administration for some time, and I choose to ask the noble lord on what his charge is founded. For the last ten months there has been but one division in this House upon which the bishops could give their votes against ministers; and if upon the Reform Bill the bishops have departed from their usual course of giving their support to the treasury benches, it is because the bill is such that they could not conscientiously support it. It is not fair to bring such charges against a body of men, on the ground of difference of opinion.'

The Duke of Newcastle and the Marquis of Londonderry stated that they had been attacked by a violent and riotous mob, and bitterly complained that they had not received the protection to which they were entitled.

Lord Melbourne assured them that the first desire of his majesty's government in general and of himself in particular was to afford every possible protection both to the persons and properties of all his majesty's subjects. He deeply lamented the excitement which prevailed in the metropolis at present, and sincerely lamented that any noble lord or other individual should have been exposed to acts of outrage and violence.

Some further conversation took place on the subject, in the course of which Lord Wharncliffe gave testimony to Lord Melbourne's zeal and activity as secretary of the home department. The conversation was interrupted by the entrance of a message from the House of Commons, bringing up the Consolidated Fund Bill, and the subject was dropped.

On the 12th of October an immense procession of delegates from nearly every parish of the metropolis marched to St. James's, to present an address to the king. It was computed that it contained 60,000 persons, almost all of them adult males. The leaders of the several bodies of delegates of which the procession was made up were introduced to the home secretary, who expressed his regret that he had not sooner been made acquainted with their wish to present addresses, as he had no doubt that, under the circumstances, his majesty would have waived the usual court etiquette, and received the heads of the delegations in person. As it was now too late to do this, he recommended them to give the addresses to the county members, Messrs. Byng and Hume, who would no doubt gladly present them. This suggestion was at once followed; and after an interval of about an hour, Mr. Hume re-appeared, and assured the parties who had intrusted the address to him, that he had presented it to his majesty, informing him that it had been passed at a meeting of nearly 40,000 persons, and that it prayed him to retain his present ministers, to use all constitutional means to promote the passing of the Reform Bill, and to remove from his court and household all those persons who were opposed to the measure. Mr. Hume added, that he had the happiness to say that his majesty had distinctly promised that the prayer of the petition should be complied with; that every effort should be exerted to insure the success of the Reform Bill; that all persons about his court who were opposed to the bill should be removed from the offices they held; and that he also emphatically stated that he had the highest confidence in his present ministers. After making this announcement, which was received with tremendous cheering, Mr. Hume exhorted the assemblage to disperse peaceably.

This advice was followed by most of those to whom it was addressed; but some of the vast crowd, who had either formed part of the procession, or who had congregated to witness it, were bent on mischief. The houses of the Duke of Wellington and the Marquis of Bristol were attacked, and the windows demolished. Several collisions took place between the police and the mob in various parts of the metropolis. The Duke of Cumberland was dragged from his horse on his way back from the House of Lords, and rescued with difficulty by the exertions of the police. Poor hot-headed Lord Londonderry was the object of another assault. He was on his way to the House of Lords, when he fell in with a mob of some 4,000 persons. A man in the crowd called out, 'There goes the Marquis of Londonderry.' He was instantly assailed with hisses and pebbles, whereupon he pulled out a pistol, but was prevailed on by a friend who accompanied him to abstain from discharging it, and to retire to the Horse Guards, where a large body of troops was drawn up; but before he reached them he was struck by a stone, which inflicted a severe wound on the right temple.

While these things were being done in the metropolis, the same spirit was manifested elsewhere. It is true that Sudbury, famous in the annals of corruption, rang its church bells and fired cannon to celebrate the rejection of the bill; but these demonstrations could not be made elsewhere with safety, if indeed at all. At Derby, when the intelligence arrived, it was received, as it was almost everywhere, with tokens of sorrow and disappointment. The church-bells were muffled, and continued throughout the night to send forth their mournful music. There was, however, at first no disturbance, and in all probability none would have occurred, if a few of the more foolish and violent anti-reformers had not thought proper to give three cheers in the market-place for the glorious majority of forty-one. This silly demonstration stung to madness some of the hotter reformers, and a serious tumult was the consequence. The houses of several of the principal anti-reformers were assailed and their windows smashed. The mob, excited by this first breach of the peace, attacked several other houses in the same manner, and did not always discriminate between reformers and anti-reformers.

They also besieged the borough gaol, which was successfully defended. A young man, of the name of Haden, was killed by a stone which struck him on the face, and several rioters were killed and wounded. The arrival of the military prevented farther mischief.

At Nottingham the violence of the mob was even greater than at Derby. The castle, which was the property of the unpopular Duke of Newcastle, was burnt to the ground. Colwick Castle, the seat of Mr. Musters, was also fired; but the flames were speedily extinguished. Mrs. Musters, whose maiden name was Chaworth, the first love of the celebrated Lord Byron, and the lady to whom his earlier poems were addressed, fled in terror from the burning mansion, and took refuge in a summer-house; but the fright produced an illness which terminated fatally a few months after. At Beeston a factory was burnt down; and the house of correction was attacked, but saved by the timely arrival of the 15th Hussars. At Loughborough there were serious disturbances. Belvoir Castle was attacked. On the whole, however, the disappointment, though severe, was borne with creditable patience, but this was in a great measure owing to the determination of ministers to retain office. The question of resignation had been very seriously considered. While they were deliberating upon it, they received a message from the king, now thoroughly alarmed at the state of the country, begging them to retain their places; it was also intimated to them that this was the wish of the majority of the peers. They therefore resolved to retain their offices, and this resolution was justly regarded as a pledge that the struggle would be renewed as soon as possible. They hastened to confirm this expectation, and to promise another measure of equal efficiency with that which had just been rejected. These declarations were imperatively called for. The danger was imminent, and ministers knew it, and did all that lay in their power to tranquillise the people, and to assure them that the bill was only delayed, not finally defeated.

Lord Brougham especially, on Wednesday, October 12th, in his place in the House of Lords, referring to the outrages which had been committed, condemned them in the strongest terms, declaring that the authors and abettors of such acts were the worst enemies of reform. 'The people,' he continued, ' who are zealously, anxiously, and devotedly desirous of the passing of that great measure should not permit themselves, on account of any temporary disappointment in that respect, to be betrayed into proceedings which could alone be expected from the bitterest foes of the success of that momentous measure which they have so much at heart—they should not allow any temporary defeat which their hopes and wishes may have experienced to drive them into a course of proceeding inconsistent with the public tranquillity and destructive of the peace of society. I call upon them, as their friend and as the friend of reform, not to give way to any such unfounded disappointment. I tell them that reform is only delayed for a short period. I tell them that the bill will pass,—that the bill must pass,—that a bill founded on exactly similar principles, and equally extensive and efficient with the bill which has been thrown out, shall in a very short period become part and parcel of the law of the land.'

This timely declaration did much to allay the irritation that prevailed, and to reconcile the people to a delay which they hoped would not be of long duration. Meanwhile the House of Commons lost no time in speaking out. In accordance with the determination of the meeting held on the Saturday on which the bill was rejected, on the Monday following Lord Ebrington moved and Mr. Dundas seconded the following resolution, which was carried the same evening by a majority of 131: 'That while this House laments the present state of a bill for introducing a reform into the Commons House of Parliament, in favour of which the opinion of the country stands unequivocally pronounced, and which has been matured by discussion the most anxious and the most laborious, it feels itself imperatively called on to re-assert its firm adherence to the principal leading provisions of that great measure, and to express its unabated confidence in the integrity, perseverance, and ability of the ministers, who, in introducing and conducting it, so well consulted the best interests of the country.'

The outrages which had been committed and the prevailing popular excitement were brought under the notice of the House of Commons on the evening of October 12th, in reference to a great meeting which had been held at Birmingham, and which was said to have been attended by 150,000 persons. At this meeting very violent language had been held in reference to the rejection of the bill by the House of Lords. One of the speakers exclaimed: 'When Hampden refused the payment of ship-money, his gallant conduct electrified all England, and pointed out the way by which the people, when unanimous and combined, might rid themselves of an odious and oppressive oligarchy. I declare before God, that if all constitutional modes of obtaining the success of the reform measure fail, I will be the first man to refuse the payment of taxes, except by a levy on my goods. I now call upon all who hear me and are prepared to join me in this step to hold up their hands.' These words were received by the vast multitude with indescribable enthusiasm; and when the speaker called on those present to hold up their hands in token of their determination to refuse the payment of taxes, a forest of hands was immediately raised, amidst the most tremendous cheering. He then added: 'I now call upon those who are not prepared to adopt this course to hold up their hands, and signify their dissent.' Not a single hand was lifted up, and the shouts and cheers were redoubled.

At the same meeting a vote of thanks was passed to Lord Althorp and Lord J. Russell, and forwarded to them by Mr. Thomas Attwood, a banker, of Birmingham, who, as president of the Birmingham Political Union, occupied the chair at this meeting. In acknowledging this compliment, Lord J. Russell used the following expression: 'It is impossible that the whisper of a faction should prevail over the voice of a nation.'

Sir H. Hardinge, amidst the loud assenting cheers of the Opposition, denounced this phrase as insulting to the House of Lords, and as improperly identifying the government with the political unions, and especially that of Birmingham, under whose auspices the meeting had been assembled.

Lord J. Russell, after stigmatising in the strongest terms the outrages that had been committed, and especially those which had been directed against the mansion of the Duke of Wellington, to whom the country was so much indebted for his past services, defended the expressions he had employed in his letter to Mr. Attwood, and explained that he did not mean to apply the phrase 'whisper of a faction' to the whole majority of the House of Peers, but only to a small self-interested portion of that majority.

Lord Althorp, referring to the charge of his having written a letter to the Birmingham Political Union, declared that he had written no letter whatever to the body known by that title. He admitted that he had addressed a letter to the chairman of a meeting at Birmingham, consisting of 150,000 persons, expressing his sense of a vote of thanks with which so large a portion of his fellow-countrymen had thought fit to honour his conduct; and he could not think that in doing so he had acted by any means in a manner unworthy of his station. In acknowledging to the chairman of the meeting the honour thus conferred on him, he had taken the opportunity to recommend that gentleman to use his influence for the prevention of acts of violence, or illegal and unconstitutional excesses.

Sir C. Wetherell vehemently condemned the letters of Lord Althorp and Lord J. Russell, and gave notice of a motion for an address to the king, praying his majesty to issue a special commission to try the offenders concerned in the outrage of burning down the Duke of Newcastle's castle in Nottinghamshire. The following evening Sir C. Wetherell was not in his place at the time when this motion should have come on. However, late in the evening he proposed it in the shape of an amendment to another motion. In supporting his proposition he indulged in his usual strain of vehement invective against his opponents, and especially against the members of the administration. In the course of the discussion which followed, the attorney-general stated that no person concerned in the firing of Nottingham Castle was yet in custody, and therefore there were no prisoners whom the proposed commission could try. Of course the proposal was negatived.

The public mind was now completely re-assured with respect to the retention of office by the ministry and the renewal of the attempt to carry the bill; but this fear was succeeded by an apprehension that concessions would be made to the Lords, and that much of the efficiency of the bill would be lost. The nation was also anxious to have the matter at once brought to an issue, and, in its impatience of delay, did not consider sufficiently the fatigues and anxieties to which both the government and the legislature had been exposed, and the absolute necessity that existed for a short respite from their labours. This impatience was increased by a circumstance which arose out of it. Earl Grey returning home at a quarter-past eleven o'clock at night, found Dr. Carpue and seventeen other reformers, who had been delegated from different parishes in the metropolis, and had come without any previous notice, to communicate to him the opinion of their friends, and to recommend that after a prorogation of seven days, the Reform Bill should be again brought forward and proceeded with until carried. Lord Grey, justly offended at their impertinent intrusion, rebuked them in his mild, lofty, aristocratic way, and sent them away deeply offended. In this mood they reported that

Parliament would be adjourned over Christmas; that Lord J. Russell's bill would not be revived; that no extensive creation of peers would take place; and that a bill would be brought in which would satisfy the Tories and the bishops, who were now willing to submit to what they called a moderate measure of reform, and which the delegates and reformers generally thought likely to prove much more remarkable for its moderation than for its efficiency. Reports of discussions in the ministry itself were also rife; it was said that the chancellor thought the bill much too violent, and that he headed a party in the cabinet who were labouring to bring the premier over to his views.

These reports were so widely disseminated, and produced so much discontent and alarm, that it was thought necessary to give them an authoritative contradiction. The ministry had already insisted on the dismissal of Lord Howe, the queen's chamberlain, and other officers of her majesty's household, who, in their own persons, or those of their near relatives or connections, had opposed the bill. Earl Grey, in a letter to Sir J. C. Hobhouse, and both he and Lord Brougham in the House of Lords, flatly contradicted the rumours that had been circulated. The latter, after declaring that there had not been any difference between Earl Grey and himself as to the minutest particulars of the bill, gave the following account of his own labours and those of his colleagues: 'I must avow my opinion, that for the session to commence after so brief an interval, and for the chancellor—I mean the chancellor in another house—to begin his labours again, and for my noble friend who has introduced the bill to renew his advocacy of the measure, I must pronounce my opinion that this would be physically impossible, after having given three months day and night to deliberation and discussion. None feels more than I do the impossibility of continuing such exertions. It was just twelve months last Friday since I began hard work in London, and during all that time I have enjoyed no respite or relaxation, with the exception of two days at Christmas and Easter, and even they were chiefly spent upon the road. During that period I have been occupied from six or seven in the morning until twelve and one at night; and if any man is so unreasonable as to say that I ought not to be allowed to enjoy a little repose, with that man I will not pause to reason. I will throw myself on the good sense and kind feeling of my countrymen, and I am confident that they will not bring in a verdict of guilty. Whatever advice may be offered as to the time of prorogation, the people of England may rest assured that it will be given on a solemn principle of public duty, and with a view to the carrying of that great measure, to which none can feel more devoted than myself and my colleagues. The public will see, when the measure is again before Parliament, the wisdom with which we have acted; and that the period that will intervene is no longer than is required, I will not say in justice, but in mercy.'

At length, on the 20th of October, the indispensable business of the session having been transacted, the king in person prorogued the Parliament to Tuesday, the 22nd day of November, with the usual formalities. The royal speech on this occasion contained the following passage: 'The anxiety which has been so generally manifested by my people for the accomplishment of a constitutional reform in the Commons House of Parliament will, I trust, be regulated by a due sense of the necessity of order and moderation in their proceedings.

'To the consideration of this important question the attention of Parliament must necessarily again be called at the opening of the ensuing session; and you may be assured of my unaltered desire to promote its settlement, by such improvements in the representation as may be found necessary for the securing to my people the full enjoyment of their rights, which, in combination with those of the other orders of the state, are essential to the support of our free constitution.'

Meanwhile the anti-reformers, who had been terrified at the first violences which followed the rejection of the Reform Bill, and thought that their oft-repeated predictions of revolution were about to receive an immediate fulfilment, finding that the crisis had passed without any very serious disturbances, and seeing that the people bore their disappointment with patience and calmness, began to take heart, and to assert that a reaction had commenced, and that the people were sick of the bill. They saw with delight, while reformers marked with silent regret, that

Lord Ashley, the anti-reforming candidate for the county of Dorset, had beaten his opponent, Mr. Ponsonby, a moderate reformer, by some thirty-six votes; that at Liverpool the moderate reformer, Lord Sandon, son of Lord Harrowby, one of the leading opponents of the bill, had triumphed over Mr. Thornley, the thorough-going reformer, by a majority of 849 at the end of the second day, when Mr. Thornley retired from the hopeless contest; that in Pembrokeshire, Mr. Greville, the reform candidate, had withdrawn from the contest with Sir J. Owen, an anti-reformer, at the end of the second day, finding himself in a minority of 108. On the other hand, it was some consolation to them to find the county of Cambridge returning the reform candidate, Mr. Townley, by a majority of 536 over his opponent, Captain Yorke.

But while the Tories were congratulating themselves on the elections they had gained, and triumphantly pointing to them as proofs of commencing reaction, they were very seriously disquieted by the proceedings of the political unions which, as already mentioned, had been established in Manchester, Liverpool, Birmingham, and other large towns, and were every day being formed in smaller boroughs, and agitated for reform more and more strongly. A union of this kind had recently been formed in the metropolis. These associations were receiving a sort of military organisation, and were acting together in concert for the promotion of reform. The *Times* and other ministerial journals applauded the movement, and urged reformers to establish similar bodies in every part of the kingdom. The proceedings of existing unions and the formation of new unions were carefully and triumphantly chronicled. The embodiment of a 'conservative guard,' to resist the 'rich opponents of reform and the ragged promoters of disturbances,' was strenuously advocated; and on the last day of October we find Sir F. Burdett occupying the chair at a great meeting of the inhabitant householders of the metropolis, convened for the purpose of forming a National Political Union, whose great object should be to obtain good government, and preserve social order through a full and efficient representation of the people in the Commons House of Parliament. These unions, all along a source of constant alarm to the anti-reformers, were now beginning to be regarded with no small uneasiness by many sincere reformers, who feared that they might prove unmanageable, and dictate to Parliament and the government changes far more violent and organic than any which had been hitherto proposed. The king himself had long been strongly impressed with this feeling, and continually urged his ministers to suppress these formidable associations, while it was still possible to do so. The ministers themselves began to participate in these disquietudes, and accordingly on the 2nd of November a proclamation was issued, in which they were denounced as unconstitutional and illegal.

This proclamation was not issued too soon. Before it appeared, an event had occurred which greatly augmented the prevailing alarm. The city of Bristol was the theatre of an outbreak which filled the kingdom with consternation. The office of recorder in this city was held by Sir C. Wetherell, and in virtue of that office he exercised within the county of Bristol (for Bristol was at that time a county as well as a city) all the functions of one of the judges of the realm, and was received, when he came down to hold the assizes, with honours similar to those which were usually paid to the judges. It was his duty to hold the usual gaol delivery at this time. Having been, as we have seen, the most active, persevering, and prominent of all the opponents of the bill, he was peculiarly obnoxious to its supporters outside, whose hostility was not disarmed by the experience of the wit and humour he displayed in resisting the measure, and which rendered him almost a favourite with the reformers inside the House. The Bristol mob was notoriously one of the fiercest * in England, and Sir C. Wetherell was at that moment of strongly excited political passions the most unpopular man in England. It was therefore anticipated that riotous demonstrations would be made on the occasion of his visit, and some of the citizens of Bristol tried to dissuade him from holding the gaol delivery, which might, from the state of the calendar, have been postponed without much inconvenience. The representations thus made were referred to the home secretary, Lord Melbourne, who did not think it necessary to interfere, but left Sir Charles to act according to his own judgment. Each probably thought that the event would

* See Macaulay's *History of England*, vol. II. p. 99.

prove favourable to his party. Sir C. Wetherell no doubt
hoped that all would pass off quietly, and that he should be
able to refer to his reception at Bristol as another proof of
the reaction which, by dint of continual assertion, he and his
friends had really begun to believe in; and Lord Melbourne
was probably not sorry that he should have an opportunity
of witnessing and showing to the country the full extent
of his unpopularity, not expecting that the demonstration
would proceed beyond hootings and execrations. Precautions, however, were taken which were thought sufficient to meet any emergency at all likely to arise, and to
preserve public order. The whole police force of the city
was mustered. The sailors of the port refused to be sworn
in as special constables for the protection of Sir Charles;
but a considerable number of citizens were enrolled, and a
handful of troops had been sent to the vicinity and placed
at the disposal of the magistrates, with the express understanding that they were not to be called in except in case
of necessity. Sir Charles made his public entry into the
city on the 29th of October. He appeared in a carriage
drawn by four grey horses, many hours earlier than the customary time, at Totterdown, and much nearer the Guildhall
than the place at which he was usually received. It was
hoped that by this means the opening of the commission
would have been quietly effected before the arrival of the
recorder was known. Sir Charles here quitted his own
carriage, and took his seat in that of the high sheriff,
amidst the yells, groans, and hisses of the mob, which had
already assembled, notwithstanding the precautions that
had been taken. The carriage was escorted by a large
number of special constables, and on each side of it was
a gentleman mounted on horseback. It was preceded and
followed by the usual cortege of mayor's and sheriff's
officers. As the procession advanced, stones began to be
thrown at the carriage, and the crowd became denser,
louder, and more violent. Females of the lowest class
were present in great numbers, and were observed to be
particularly violent in the expression of their feelings, and
in endeavouring to excite the men to make an attack on
the recorder. Some of the attendants were severely injured by the stones aimed at the carriage. At length the
Guildhall was reached; but the pressure of the crowd was

so great, that it was only after a severe struggle, which lasted some minutes, that Sir Charles was at length conducted into the building, and took his seat on the bench. The doors of the hall were then thrown open, and in a very short time the area set apart for the general public was crammed with spectators. The recorder was naturally agitated in consequence of the violent efforts he had been obliged to make to force an entrance; but in a few minutes he recovered his composure, looked round the court, and smiled and nodded to some of his acquaintances.

The opening of the commission was commenced in the usual manner, but the formal preliminaries were carried on amidst noise, confusion, and interruption, which rendered them quite inaudible. An imprudent attempt to put down the tumult made by Serjeant Ludlow, the town-clerk, served only to increase it. The court adjourned to the following Monday, October 31st. Sir Charles then quitted the bench amidst groans and yells, mingled with cheers for the king. A dense crowd filled the whole of the way leading from the Guildhall to the Mansion-house, and hooted and hissed him as before, except in front of the commercial rooms, where a compact body of his admirers had posted themselves, and greeted him as he passed with loud cheers. He reached the Mansion-house after considerable delay, but without injury. The constables who remained outside used their staves much too freely, and one of the crowd was killed by a blow on the head which he received. This increased the exasperation of the mob. But the constables kept them at bay, till unfortunately, at four o'clock, half the constabulary force were allowed to retire for the purpose of obtaining refreshments, with the understanding that they were to return at six o'clock, and release those who remained. The mob, encouraged by their departure, became more daring in their attacks, and began to gain the upper hand. The mayor, himself a reformer, now came forward, accompanied by some of the magistrates, and begged the people to retire quietly to their houses, and implored them not to impose on him the necessity of reading the Riot Act and calling in the military. While he was speaking, several large stones were thrown at him, one of which passed close to his head, and the person standing next to him was struck, and had his hat knocked off. As the crowd still continued to increase in number and violence, at five o'clock the Riot Act was read, whereupon the rioters made a rush on the constabulary, and completely routed them. Most of them were disarmed and severely beaten. One was compelled to throw his truncheon through the Mansion-house windows, others fled; and one of these last was chased into the flat dock, and with great difficulty saved from being drowned. A few took refuge in the Mansion-house, which was at once attacked by the triumphant mob. The windows and sashes of the building were shivered, the shutters beaten to pieces, the street-door broken open, and the rioters forced their way into two rooms on the ground-floor. During this attack Sir C. Wetherell escaped in disguise, clambering over the roofs of the adjoining houses, and quitting the city as quickly as possible in the disguise of a postillion. Unfortunately his departure, the knowledge of which might have put an end to the disturbances, was not publicly announced till the following noon. The mayor and the other occupants of the Mansion-house barricaded themselves as well as they could in that part of the building which the mob had not yet entered, but into which they were endeavouring to force their way. To effect this object, the rioters tore up the iron palisades in front of the house, and some young trees growing near, and converted them into weapons of offence and destruction. Walls were thrown down to furnish bricks, which were hurled through the upper windows, and straw and other combustibles were placed in the dining-room for the purpose of burning down the building. In a few minutes more the house and its inmates would probably have been burnt, had not the military made their appearance at this critical moment. The mob quickly evacuated the building, but did not desist from their attacks on the outside; and they were encouraged by the appearance of a large body of the worst characters of the neighbourhood, whom the tidings of the riot had brought into the city in great numbers. The mob received the troops with loud cheers. Such was the state of affairs when Major Mackworth, aide-de-camp of Lord Hill, the commander-in-chief of the forces, reached the Mansion-house. He found it filled with special and other constables, who had taken refuge in it, and who added to the prevailing confusion without being of any service. With the consent of the mayor, he formed them into four divisions, one of which he posted in the rear of the Mansion-house, another at the side, and the third in front. Colonel Brereton, who commanded the troops, instead of acting with the vigour and decision which the circumstances required, trotted his men up and down the square, shook hands with the rioters till his arm was tired, harangued, entreated, threatened, exhorted them to disperse, and even waved his cocked hat when they shouted for the king and reform. At length Serjeant Ludlow, astonished at his temporising conduct, plainly asked him whether he had received any orders which prevented him from obeying those he had received from the magistrates; and on being answered that his orders were to place himself under their directions, the serjeant at once distinctly required him to clear the streets. Colonel Brereton then commanded a charge, and the rioters were driven from the square and neighbouring streets in great confusion, but without any wounds being inflicted. Nevertheless many of the mob took refuge in narrow passages and on board ships lying in the harbour, from which they annoyed the cavalry with stones and other missiles. One rioter was shot by a soldier, at whom he had thrown a stone, and others received sabre wounds.

At an early hour of the morning of Sunday, October 30th, the people again began to assemble in the square, and by seven o'clock the mob already amounted to several hundreds, but they seemed to be drawn thither by curiosity, and manifested no disposition to renew the disturbances of the preceding day. Unfortunately the colonel ordered the soldiers to their quarters. Their departure was the signal for a fresh attack, during which the mayor and his companions escaped over the roofs of the houses, and made their way without molestation to the Guildhall.

The mob, now in undisputed possession of the Mansion-house, occupied themselves in destroying and flinging out into the square the furniture of the rooms which they had not been able to enter on the Saturday. Others descended into the cellars, which contained about three hundred bottles of wine, of which nearly a third part was carried off and drank, or wasted in the square. A disgusting scene followed. Persons of all ages and of both sexes were seen greedily swallowing the liquors, while scores lay on the ground in a state of drunken insensibility. Others, excited, but not stupefied, spread themselves over the town, adding to the confusion and consternation which everywhere prevailed. The troops were now brought back; but the people, flushed with victory, maddened with wine, and exasperated by the death of the man who had been shot the night before, received them with a shower of stones, bottles, and bricks. The rioters evacuated the upper part of the Mansion-house, but those in the cellars still continued their carouse. One of the aldermen now appeared, read the riot act, and endeavoured to persuade the mob to retire. He then desired Colonel Brereton to order the troops to fire. This the colonel, however, flatly refused to do, alleging that it would render the mob so infuriated that they might overcome the troops, and the city be given over to slaughter. He urged that it would be better policy to try to keep the rioters in good humour till the following morning, when reinforcements would probably arrive.

The mayor in vain summoned his fellow citizens to his assistance. Only a very small number of citizens answered his appeal by coming to the Guildhall, and the few who appeared said that they would not risk their lives unless supported by the military. At this juncture Colonel Brereton, in spite of the remonstrances of the magistrates, removed his troops. As they withdrew, they were followed by a large body of rioters, who continued their assaults on them, until, provoked beyond endurance, they faced about and fired repeated volleys on their assailants.

A vast mob had now assembled. One portion of it went to the Bridewell, another to the city gaol, which had been erected ten years before, at a cost of 100,000*l.*; others proceeded to the toll-houses at Princes-street bridge, at the Well, and at St. Philips; others, again, to the Gloucester county gaol. All these buildings were broken into and set on fire. The military, few, tired, and ill-supported, rode in vain from one conflagration to another.

The next object of attack was the bishop's palace. At first the number of rioters who attempted to break into it was so inconsiderable, that the few persons who were on the premises were able to hold them in check. The mayor, being informed that the palace was in danger, came to the spot accompanied by a handful of citizens, whom he was able to collect at the moment, and the military who were protecting the Mansion-house followed. The mob at once attacked it, forced an entrance, and set it on fire. The party at the palace, seeing that it was not at the moment seriously threatened, and finding that the Mansion-house was on fire, returned to the square. But they were now too late to be of any service there. Already the whole of the back of the building was in flames, and the front was occupied by a set of wretches engaged in firing the various rooms, who appeared at the windows, receiving the soldiers with loud shouts of triumphant derision. The fire spread with appalling rapidity; and many of these reckless creatures, unable to make their escape, were consumed by the flames they had assisted to kindle. In about twenty minutes the roof fell in, and brought down the whole front of the building with a tremendous crash.

The soldiers remained idly gazing at the destruction which they came too late to avert. But, while useless in the square, they might have been of great service had they remained at the bishop's palace. No sooner had they quitted it than a fresh body of assailants arrived, overpowered the servants who were left in charge of it, set it on fire, and in a short time reduced it to ashes. An attempt was also made to burn down the cathedral, but was frustrated by the efforts and persuasions of five respectable inhabitants, who, to their honour be it recorded, were all dissenters.

The Mansion-house being now destroyed, it was thought useless to keep the soldiers any longer in the square. They were therefore ordered to the Guildhall, where their commanding officer and the magistrates had been sitting: it had been attacked on the previous night, and it was feared that it would be the next object against which the efforts of the rioters would be directed. But a portion of the mob in the square, bent on farther mischief and finding no one to resist them, fired the house adjoining the Mansion-house, and by twelve o'clock at night the whole mass of buildings between the Mansion-house and Middle Avenue were in flames. Among these was the Custom-house, a very large building, which was so speedily fired in different parts, that many of the incendiaries were unable to escape, and perished in the burning building. All this mischief was effected by a small party, consisting chiefly of boys. They went about their work in a very systematic manner, giving the inmates of each house half an hour's notice before firing it. The leaders were armed with axes, and some of them carried pots of turpentine and brushes, with the help of which they produced the complete conflagration of a house in a few minutes. With their axes they cut holes in the floors of the burning houses, to allow the air to enter and fan the flames. The fire extended to the house in the adjoining streets, and, as many of the principal wine and spirit vaults were in this quarter, they burnt with great fury. Three men were reduced to cinders. Others flung themselves from the windows, and were severely injured by the fall; among these was a woman, who shortly after expired. Two leaped from the roof, and were killed on the spot; two boys, who had attempted to escape, were seen frying alive in the molten lead which rained from the roof to the pavement. Altogether the rioters had fired the Mansion-house, the bishop's palace, the Excise-office, the Custom-house, three prisons, four toll-houses, and forty-two private dwellings and warehouses.

But what were the respectable inhabitants doing while their city was in flames? Major Mackworth tells us that he went that evening to the council-house, and found some two hundred persons there, under the presidence of an alderman, engaged in a very stormy discussion. They were all crying out, 'We are willing to act, but we have no one to direct us.' The major, one would think, was just the man they wanted. He was an officer of experience, cool, clear-headed, and knew, as we have already seen, how to bring a handful of men to bear with effect on a mob. However, he found that they would not act to any good purpose, and retired disgusted with their folly and party spirit, but arranged to meet them in College-green at six o'clock on the following morning, when he promised to endeavour to organise them into a body capable of being of some service. As for the dragoons, harassed as they had been by repeated and useless marches, coming too late, or if coming in time, not ordered to act, they had been of little use, and were now thoroughly wearied. The mayor however, roused by the conflagration in the square to a sense of the necessity of acting vigorously, sent at twelve o'clock a letter to Colonel Brereton, authorising him to take whatever steps or give whatever orders he might think fit, to restore and preserve the public peace, as well with the troops he had at present under his command as with any others that might subsequently arrive. In consequence of this communication, the 3rd Dragoons, who had been withdrawn to their quarters, were brought back into the square.

On Monday morning Major Mackworth punctually presented himself at his place of rendezvous, but not a single citizen met him there. He therefore went in search of the dragoons, whom he found quietly patrolling the square with Colonel Brereton at their head. Two sides of the square were in flames, and the rioters, numbering about a thousand persons, were forcing their way into the corner house on the side of the square nearest to the docks. The major at once saw that if this house were once fired, the shipping, which was closely moored in the very heart of the city, would soon be in a blaze, and the greater part of Bristol would be destroyed. He therefore at once said to Colonel Brereton, 'We must instantly charge;' and without waiting for an answer, he gave the word 'Charge, and charge home.' Colonel Brereton then charged at the head of his men, and the rioters fled in all directions: many of them were cut down and ridden over; some were driven into the burning houses, from which they never returned; and the dragoons, after sabring all they could come at in the square, re-formed and charged down a neighbouring street, then returned to the square once more, and rode at the miserable mob in all directions.

Still they were but a handful of some twenty-five men, and the mob dispersed in one place reassembled in another. Major Mackworth therefore galloped to Keynsham, about six miles distant, whither the 14th Dragoons had been led, and brought them back to the city, from which they had been hooted the day before, but in which they were now welcomed as deliverers. On the road they were joined by a dozen of the Bedminster yeomanry, and entered the city, charging the rioters vigorously. One troop pursued the

Kingswood colliers, who had been very active in the work of destruction, two miles along the Gloucester road. The other executed charges in the city, cutting down all who resisted, and retook the gaol. And now troops and yeomanry came flocking in from all quarters. Major Mackworth, who had handed over the 14th to their commanding officer, Major Beckwith, organised the yeomanry, the pensioners, and the special constables; and the tranquillity of the city was restored. It should be mentioned, in justice to the Bristol rioters, that notwithstanding all the drunkenness and excited passions that prevailed, no act of personal violence could be laid to their charge.

The disposition which these disturbances manifested was by no means confined to Bristol. There was perhaps not a town in the empire in which accidental circumstances might not have produced similar disturbances. Nay, it was by no means improbable that the insurrection might have spread from Bristol to other places, and have become almost universal. Probably it was the consciousness of this fact that paralysed Colonel Brereton, and prevented the magistrates from giving their directions with that decision which would have insured obedience. Had they positively and peremptorily in writing required him to act, he probably would have acted, and the riots would have been suppressed; not indeed without bloodshed, but with far less loss of life than actually occurred. But they recommended rather than ordered, and tried to shift the responsibility of acting off their own shoulders on to those of the military commander. We need not be surprised at their hesitation, nor at the still greater and more culpable backwardness of Colonel Brereton. The political atmosphere was everywhere charged with electricity, and this all men felt. About the same time that this terrible destruction of life and property took place at Bristol, there were riots at Bath, riots at Worcester, riots at Coventry, riots at Warwick, and in other towns. The destruction of the bishop's palace at Bristol was by no means a solitary instance of the detestation in which the bishops and clergy, but especially the bishops, were held at this moment. The bishop of London was absent from the division on the second reading of the bill. His absence did not exempt him from the hatred with which his order was regarded. He had been announced to preach at St. Ann's

Westminster; but finding that on his appearance in the pulpit the congregation would leave the church, or perhaps even maltreat him, he did not fulfil his engagement. At a somewhat later period, Dr. Ryder, bishop of Lichfield, a man of the highest character, after preaching a charity sermon at St. Bride's church, was grossly insulted, and in danger of being killed by the infuriated populace, who surrounded the sacred building, and waited for the bishop's departure from it. The archbishop of Canterbury, the saintly and venerated Howley, coming to Canterbury to hold his primary visitation, was insulted, spat on, and with great difficulty, and by a very circuitous route, brought to the deanery, amidst the yells and execrations of a violent and angry mob. The bishop of Bath and Wells being expected to visit the latter city, a popular commotion was apprehended, and troops were sent for his protection. On the 5th of November the bishops in many of the towns, and especially the cathedral towns, were substituted for Guy Fawkes, and received the honours usually bestowed on that worthy. The bishops of Winchester and Exeter were hanged and burned in effigy close to their own palaces. Nor was this feeling confined to the persons of the clergy. It engendered a savage Vandalism towards those sacred buildings, which we, with all our mechanical advantages, vainly strive to rival. The author of this work, then a boy, well remembers the fierce shout of applause which rent the air at a large public meeting at Canterbury, when one of the speakers suggested that the noble cathedral of that city should be converted into a stable for the horses of the cavalry. Such were the disastrous consequences of identifying the church with a party in the state, and that too the party which was engaged in resisting progress passionately demanded by the mass of the people, and essential to the safety and well-being of the state.

The news from France served to increase the prevailing uneasiness and alarm. Before the country had recovered from the consternation produced by the Bristol riots, intelligence arrived that disturbances of a far more serious and alarming character had broken out in Lyons. The anti-reformers, half in terror, half in triumph, pointed to these outbreaks as evidences of what might be expected if the Reform Bill should pass. These events, too, had an unfavourable influence on many timid though sincere reformers, and particularly on the king, who daily became more and more alarmed. Still the great body of the nation were as fully resolved as ever not to rest until they had obtained a measure of reform as strong and as effective as that which the Lords had rejected. With this determination was associated a strong desire to humiliate the Upper House; in fact, this latter feeling had become almost if not quite as earnest as the wish for reform itself. Meanwhile trade and manufactures were everywhere suffering most seriously from the prevalent alarm and agitation, and the industrial stagnation greatly increased the popular discontent and the general impatience to have the bill re-introduced into Parliament as speedily as possible. It was rumoured that ministers did not intend to assemble Parliament before January; and the *Times* and the other reform journals expressing the wishes and opinions of the great majority of the people, vehemently deprecated this delay. At length, to the great satisfaction of all but the anti-reformers, it was authoritatively announced on the 21st of November that Parliament would reassemble on the 6th of December; on which day accordingly it met, and the session was opened by the king in person, with the usual formalities. The speech which his majesty delivered at the opening of the session contained the following passages:

'I feel it to be my duty, in the first place, to recommend to your most careful consideration the measure that will be proposed to you for the reform of the Commons House of Parliament. A speedy and satisfactory settlement of this question becomes daily of more pressing importance to the security of the state and the contentment and welfare of my people.

'The scenes of violence and outrage which have occurred in the city of Bristol and in some other places have caused me the deepest affliction. The authority of the laws must be vindicated by the punishment of offences which have produced so extensive a destruction of property and so melancholy a loss of life; but I think it right to direct your attention to the best means of improving the municipal police of the kingdom, for the more effectual protection of the public peace against similar commotions.'

On Monday December 12th Lord J. Russell brought forward the third Reform Bill. In asking leave to introduce the bill, he spoke in a tone which showed that the recent occurrences had caused him to regard with considerable alarm the consequences that might result from another disappointment of the people's wishes; and his speech was evidently designed to allay the excitement which prevailed out of doors, as well as to persuade his hearers that the danger which attended a prolonged resistance was greater and more imminent than any danger which could arise from concession. Of the new features introduced into the bill he gave the following statement: 'With regard to the principle of disfranchisement, we formerly took the census of 1821, and a certain line of population; but since that time the census of 1831 has been nearly completed. It is, however, liable to the objection of being made at a time when disfranchisement was connected with a small population, and persons might have been gathered together in certain of these small boroughs in order to make up the required number of 2,000. We have therefore preferred to take as a test the number of houses instead of the number of persons. And as we do not wish to place towns with several mean houses in a situation of greater advantage than towns with a smaller number of better houses, we have not taken the number of 10$l.$ houses only, but the number of all houses rated to the assessed taxes up to April last. Ministers have obtained much information from gentlemen whom we sent down to draw the limits of boroughs; and from this mass of information Lieutenant Drummond, who is at the head of the commission, has been instructed to make out a series of a hundred boroughs, beginning with the lowest, and taking the number of houses and the amount of their assessed taxes together. From this return Schedule A has been framed. It was necessary then to draw an arbitrary line somewhere as to the number of houses and amount of taxes below which a borough should be deemed too inconsiderable to enjoy the right of electing members. We have hence taken the number of fifty-six, which was found in the bill of last session, and the result is, that some boroughs which formerly escaped disfranchisement will now be placed in Schedule A, while others will be raised out of it and placed in Schedule B. The boroughs which will be placed in Schedule A in consequence of this change are, Aldborough (Yorkshire), Ashburton, Amersham, East Grinstead, Okehampton, and Saltash. There is another borough regarding which there are some doubts as to its limits. Supposing Ashburton * to be one of the fifty-six, then the boroughs that are to be raised out of Schedule A into Schedule B are Midhurst, Petersfield, Eye, Wareham, Woodstock, and Lostwithiel. Schedule B, which in the last bill contained forty-one boroughs, will be reduced to thirty. It was formerly proposed to diminish the House by twenty-three members; but it has now been thought desirable to conciliate those who objected to the diminution by leaving the present number of its members undiminished, more especially as this can be done without sacrificing any of the principles of the bill. It is proposed that of these twenty-three members, ten should be given to the most considerable towns in Schedule B; that one should be given to Chatham, so as to render that town independent of Rochester; and one to the county of Monmouth. Tavistock will be one of the towns removed from Schedule B. I have desired every information respecting that borough to be collected, and it will be laid before the House; and if any gentleman should still say that there has been unfair dealing with regard to it, I can only say that such an assertion will be false and unfounded. The remaining members will be given to the following large towns, to which the late bill gave one member each: Bolton, Brighton, Bradford, Blackburn, Macclesfield, Stockport, Stoke-upon-Trent, Halifax, Stroud, and Huddersfield. With regard to the 10*l.* qualification, ministers have never had the slightest intention to change it either in amount or value. The right was formerly limited to those who had not compounded with their landlords for the rates, and who had resided in the house for twelve months. Under the new bill all persons of full age and not legally disqualified, occupying a house, warehouse, or shop, separately or jointly, with land of the yearly value of 10*l.*, would be entitled to vote. The former bill continued the franchise to all existent resident freemen and apprentices, and others with incorporate rights. The present

* It was subsequently transferred to Schedule B.

bill will continue the franchise to all freemen possessing it by birth or servitude for ever, provided they reside within the city or borough, or within seven miles of the place of voting.'

Such were the principal changes announced by Lord J. Russell. Sir R. Peel, after expressing his readiness to postpone all discussion till the second reading, dexterously availed himself of the fact admitted by Lord J. Russell, that most of these changes had been suggested in the debates which had taken place in committee. 'I congratulate the House,' he said, 'on the great escape they have had from the bill of last session, and I must express my deep gratitude to those to whom we are indebted for that escape from a danger which I never fully appreciated till now. The advantages of those maligned delays and objections are now visible throughout every part of the bill. There is scarcely an amendment which has been offered from this side of the House that has not been adopted; and these amendments are now all urged by the noble lord as so many improvements in the plan. I am not surprised to find the noble lord so severe on the late bill, but I own I was not prepared for such a sacrifice to the *manes* of the last Parliament as the adoption of General Gascoyne's resolution. It is now declared to be the deliberate conviction of the king's government, that the objections we made to the former bill were well founded. I cannot therefore but rejoice at the delay which has taken place.' A long debate ensued, in which the Opposition announced that they still regarded it as a dangerous and revolutionary measure, and were determined to resist it to the last. Many reformers expressed their strong dissatisfaction at the changes made in the bill. Cobbett, on the other hand, who was by no means partial to the government, publicly stated that he considered that they had fully redeemed the pledge they had given in promising that it should be at least as efficient as that which the House of Lords had rejected, and declared that it was even a better measure. In spite of the protestations of the Opposition, the second reading was fixed for Friday December 16th.

On that day accordingly the question was brought forward by Lord Althorp. He contented himself by simply proposing it, adding that when it was disposed of, he should move that the House at its rising should adjourn till Tuesday the 17th of January 1832. All parties were now anxious to shorten a discussion, the prolongation of which would serve not to delay the progress of the bill, but to abridge the vacation. Lord Porchester, however, moved its rejection, in a speech in which he stigmatised this measure as more objectionable than its predecessors; and after two nights' debate the House divided on Sunday morning, when the numbers were as follows:

For the second reading 324
For the amendment 162
                                       ———
Majority 162

This majority of exactly two to one was greater by more than fifty votes than that which passed the preceding bill, and exceeded by twenty-six votes that by which its second reading was carried.

And now the country was more and more occupied with a consideration which for months past had been engaging its attention. The question now was no longer, 'What will the Lords do?' but 'What will be done with the Lords?' The extreme radical party clamoured loudly for the abolition of the hereditary branch of the legislature, but the great majority of reformers were continually urging ministers to resort to a large creation of peers; and much was to be said in favour of this expedient. During the last fifty years the enemies of reform had been almost without interruption in possession of power, and it was affirmed that they had filled the House of Lords with peers who were the ardent defenders of the abuses and corruptions which the bill aimed at removing. It was pointed out that, of the peers created before 1790, one hundred and eight voted in favour of the bill, and only four against it; while of the peers who owed their elevation to Mr. Pitt, fifty voted for the bill, and one hundred and fifty against it. The bishops too, who owed their elevation to the bench to anti-reform premiers, had almost unanimously opposed the bill. It was urged therefore that ministers owed it to themselves and to their party to create such a number of peers as would restore the equilibrium of the House in reference to the reform question. At first ministers did not lend a ready

our to these suggestions. The king was strenuously opposed
to such an exercise of his prerogative; Lord Grey was
almost equally averse to it; and most of the other members
of the cabinet, being either peers themselves or closely connected with the peerage, were very unwilling to take a step
which must destroy the independence of that branch of the
legislature. Still there appeared to be no other means of
carrying the bill; and strong as were the objections of the
ministers to create peers, they were justly still more apprehensive of the consequences which would result from the
frustration of what they themselves had denominated the
just demands of the people. The subject was frequently
discussed; at first with the idea that the creation of ten or
twenty peers might suffice. One by one the ministers
became convinced of the necessity of the measure. Lord
Brougham was the first convert, and, once convinced, he
advocated it with all the ardour and impetuosity that
belonged to his character. Earl Grey held out long, the
Canning section of the cabinet still longer; but finally all
were brought to the conclusion that the creation of a large
body of peers, though much to be deprecated and regretted,
was the only means of preventing far more terrible evils.
Still the repugnance of the king to this expedient remained
rather strengthened than diminished. He had, indeed, in
the first instance, cordially approved the bill, and had
supported ministers in their endeavours to carry it; but he
had candidly informed them that he would not consent to
swamp the House of Lords for that purpose. He had indeed, tardily and reluctantly agreed to create the small
number of peers which it was thought would suffice to
carry the second reading, but beyond this he would not go.
If therefore the bill should pass that stage, and the Lords
should materially alter the character of the bill—as, from
the avowed opinions of the majority, there was every reason
to expect that they would—the ministers would be obliged
either to violate the pledges they had given, by accepting
alterations which would, in their own and the popular
opinion, impair the efficiency of the measure, or abandon
their bill and retire from office. The question therefore
was for the present left in abeyance. The ministers could
only resolve to deal with the difficulty when it arose, and
work upon the prudence or the fears of the majority of the

peers, in the hope of averting the necessity for a creation which they themselves still continued to regard as a great though perhaps necessary evil.

Thus, amidst the anxieties of reformers on the one hand, and the dread of revolution on the other; amidst incendiary fires now again prevailing,* and Asiatic cholera spreading through the country; † amidst distress of trade and dread of coming bankruptcy; amidst the horror created by the crimes of Burke, Hare, and Williams,‡—the year 1831 went gloomily out; but the majority of the nation, now thoroughly exasperated by the obstinacy of the anti-reform peers, hailed with a grim consolation the abolition of the hereditary peerage in France, and hoped that this example would be speedily followed in England.

The new year opened with a series of trials arising out of the disturbances which followed the rejection of the Reform Bill by the House of Lords. Special commissions were sent down to Bristol and Nottingham to try the rioters of those neighbourhoods, great numbers of whom were convicted. Colonel Brereton and Captain Warrington were tried by court martial. The former committed suicide; the latter was sentenced to be cashiered, but by the recommendation of the court was allowed to sell out. Later in the year the mayor of Bristol was tried before the Court of King's Bench, but was honourably acquitted, the jury giving it as their opinion that, in a situation of great difficulty, and when deserted by those from whom he was entitled to expect aid and encouragement, he had conducted himself with great firmness and propriety. The parties chiefly to blame were the householders of Bristol, who neglected to come forward when summoned by the mayor to aid him in the preservation of the peace of the city. It is satisfactory to know that they were compelled to pay a rate of ten shillings in the pound on their rentals, to defray the cost of the damage, which would have been prevented had they done their duty. Four men, named Davis, Kayes,

* Numerous incendiary fires occurred in the neighbourhoods of Bedford, Cambridge, Canterbury, Devizes, and Sherbourne, in November and December; there were no fewer than eleven between the 23rd and 28th of the latter month.
† It did not appear in the metropolis until the beginning of February.
‡ These wretches committed murders for the purpose of selling the bodies of their victims to surgeons for dissection, and their teeth to dentists.

Gregory, and Clarke, were executed at Bristol; and three, named Beck, Hearson, and Armstrong, at Nottingham.

Parliament reassembled on the 17th of January, and on the 20th it was moved and agreed in spite of the opposition of Mr. Croker, that the House should go into committee on the bill. Then the old game of procrastination and delay was played over again by the Opposition. The first great battle was fought on the question whether the number of fifty-six should be retained in Schedule A. Defeated on this question, the Opposition contended in vain for an alteration of the number of boroughs contained in Schedule B, now reduced to thirty. A long discussion took place respecting the returning officers of the boroughs. Colonel Sibthorp endeavoured to save his county of Lincoln from division. Both these attempts were defeated. On the general questions of these divisions of counties, many of the usual supporters of the government opposed them, wishing that four members should be given to the undivided county, rather than two to each division; but, on the other hand, many of the Opposition supported the ministerial proposition, and, after a protracted debate, it was sustained by a majority of 215 to 89. But it would be tedious and useless to enumerate even the principal of the various and almost innumerable discussions that were raised. Suffice it to say that the Opposition repeated their old artifices and their stale arguments and declamations about democracy and revolution, and that by steady perseverance ministers at length succeeded in triumphing over all opposition; that the bill passed through committee on the 14th of March, was read a third time by a majority of 355 against 239, and finally passed the House of Commons on Friday March 23d. On the following Monday, Lord J. Russell, attended by a large number of members, once more carried it up to the House of Lords. There it was read a first time on the motion of Earl Grey, and it was agreed that the second reading should be moved on Thursday April 5th; but at the request of Lord Wharncliffe, subsequently postponed to the following Monday.

Lord Wharncliffe, in making this request, spoke on behalf of a small body of peers headed by himself and Lord Harrowby, which for the moment held the balance between the contending parties in the House of Lords, the members of which, under the names of 'waverers' or 'trimmers,' became for a short period the heroes of the day. When the Reform Bill was thrown out by the peers, Lord Wharncliffe led the Opposition, and proposed its rejection in a form which he found it necessary to alter, because it might be regarded as insulting to the House of Commons. Lord Harrowby also had spoken very strongly against the principle of the bill; and all the waverers either voted against the second reading, or were absent from the division. Their opposition to the bill had, however, been expressed in terms much less uncompromising than those employed by the Duke of Wellington and most of the Tory speakers, and approved by the majority of the peers. Lord Wharncliffe especially had admitted that a very large measure of reform must be conceded, and both he and Lord Harrowby voted against the second reading. They hoped, therefore, that when the bill was reintroduced, it might be modified in such a manner as to meet their views, and enable them to support the second reading; and they were the more desirous that this should be the case, because they dreaded above all things a large creation of peers in case the bill should be again rejected on the second reading. The king himself entertained very similar views, and hoped, by means of the waverers, to escape from the embarrassing situation in which he foresaw that he would be placed. Lord Grey, too, was no less anxious to avoid a large creation of peers. Negotiations were therefore carried on, commencing soon after the rejection of the bill, between the king and the waverers, through the medium of Sir Herbert Taylor, his majesty's secretary, with the full cognisance and approval of the premier. But Lord Grey and the government were deeply pledged to introduce a measure fully equal in efficiency to that which the House of Lords had rejected, and the very object of the waverers was to diminish that efficiency in the sense in which the term was understood both by the ministry and the nation. All therefore that the government could do, with every desire to meet and conciliate them, was to make such alterations in the bill as, without rendering it less acceptable to the nation or more palatable to them, might afford them an excuse for supporting the second reading when the bill came again before the House of Lords. And this is the true key to almost all the alterations which were made in the measure on its third introduction. Some of the features to which Lords Wharncliffe and Harrowby had particularly objected were withdrawn; but they were balanced by other concessions to the popular feeling, such as the enfranchisement of a greater number of large towns. This was all the waverers could gain by their long negotiations; and though they were very far from being satisfied, they resolved to vote for the second reading. Accordingly, when it was introduced, Lords Harrowby and Wharncliffe stated that they still strongly objected to it as it stood; but that they thought that some concession should be made to public opinion, and that they would vote for the second reading, and accept the principle of the measure, but would endeavour to improve its details in committee, and expunge those portions of it which they regarded as too democratic. At the same time, they intimated that if they should fail in this attempt, they would vote for the rejection of the bill on the third reading. The bishop of London was still more explicit. He not only promised to vote for the second reading, but declared that he would not support any amendment that would go to alter the bill so as to mutilate or destroy its essential principles, and by that means bring it into such a state that the Commons would refuse to agree to it. These frank declarations were met with equal frankness by Earl Grey. He said that the expressions of his noble friends, and especially those of the bishop of London, afforded him great satisfaction; that he was apprehensive that some alterations might be proposed to which he could not accede; but he promised that he would give due consideration to the proposals in the true spirit of conciliation. On the other hand, the Duke of Wellington announced that he could not follow the example of Lords Wharncliffe and Harrowby; the bill was not reform, but in many respects it was revolution; and Lord Grey himself had insisted that it was really, truly, and in principle, exactly the same measure as that to which they had refused to give a second reading. These declarations expressed the feelings and opinions of the great majority of those by whose votes the bill had been previously rejected.

On Monday, the 9th of April, the question of the second

reading was brought forward. Lords Harrowby and Wharncliffe justified at great length the course which they had already announced that they would take, and the Duke of Wellington, in accordance with his previous declaration, gave the bill the same uncompromising opposition as before.* In order to encourage the anti-reforming peers to vote against it, he contradicted the assertions which were so generally propagated, and so confidently made, that the king was in favour of the bill. 'It cannot be denied,' he said, 'that the Parliament was elected under circumstances of real excitement, which has ever since been kept up by the circulation of reports that the king wishes for a reform in Parliament such as the present bill proposes. Now, my lords, I do not believe a word of any such thing. My opinion is, my lords, that the king follows the advice of his servants; it is also my opinion that the part taken in the king's name on this subject will make it very difficult to do otherwise than reform Parliament. I am fully persuaded, my lords, that it is a mistake to suppose that the king has any interest in this bill; and I am satisfied, that if the real feeling of the king were made known to the country, the noble earl would not be able to pass the bill.'

This declaration, which it was felt that the duke would not have hazarded if he had not had the best authority for making it, plainly intimated that the king was not favourable to the bill as it stood, and would not be sorry to see it greatly modified. Besides, looking at the question with a view to the influence which the division would have on the greater or less amount of reform to be ultimately conceded, the duke thought—and perhaps rightly thought—that it would be better to refuse the second reading than to go into committee on it, even though the rejection should be followed by a large creation of peers. He probably reckoned on the known repugnance of the premier to a measure which would inflict a blow on the independence of his order, from the effects of which it

* Before the debate commenced, the Duke of Buckingham favoured the House with the outlines of a plan which he gave notice that he should propose, if the ministerial measure should be rejected on the question of a second reading. As, however, the event which the noble duke contemplated did not occur, and his plan went no farther, it is not necessary to give any account of it.

might never recover. The duke also, no doubt, wished to carry on the game of delay which was being played by his party, and by rendering necessary another recommencement of the contest, to weary the reformers into a compromise. His opinion was strenuously supported by Sir R. Peel. On the other hand, many of the lords, believing that the minister had obtained the king's consent to a creation of peers in case the bill should be rejected on its second reading, and feeling that the independence of their House, and their own individual importance, would be seriously affected by a large addition to their number made under such circumstances, were disposed either to absent themselves or vote with Lords Harrowby and Wharncliffe for the second reading. Earl Grey and his colleagues did their best to encourage these dispositions. The premier especially held out hopes of considerable concessions in committee. In his reply, at the conclusion of the debate, referring to a portion of the speech of Lord Lyndhurst, he said:

'The noble and learned lord says, that I will not consent to any alteration in the bill. To that objection I will make the same answer that I made in October,—that it does not depend on me, for that it depends on your lordships. When the bill goes into committee, I shall certainly feel it my duty to resist any alterations which I may think inconsistent with the main object which the bill proposes to carry into effect. But if it can be shown that any injustice has inadvertently crept into any of the schedules,—if it can be shown that any qualification *not so small as ten pounds* will be less open to fraud and abuse,—I will not resist the correction of such circumstances. It is, at the same time, perfectly true that I should strongly oppose any diminution of the number of fifty-six boroughs which it is proposed to disfranchise, and any increase of the *ten pounds* which it is proposed to fix as the minimum of qualification. *But the decision on these points will depend on the House, and not on me.* My opinions are as I have stated them to be, but it is in the power of the House to make such alterations as may, in their opinion, render the provisions of the bill more accordant with the principles of it.' At the conclusion of this address the House divided, when the numbers were:

Content	Present	. . .	128
	Proxies	. . .	56—184
Non-content	Present	. . .	126
	Proxies	. . .	49—175

Majority in favour of the second reading . 9*

Thus, by the assistance of the waverers, the second reading of the bill was carried, though by a majority so small † as plainly to show that the Opposition would have the game in their own hands. The House adjourned at the beginning of the following week for the Easter vacation, and did not resume its sittings until the 7th of May, when it resolved itself into a committee on the bill. Lord Grey on this occasion manifested the same conciliatory disposition as before, and moved the omission from the first clause of the bill of the words 'fifty-six,' thus leaving, for the present, undetermined the number of the boroughs to be disfranchised, and giving at least the appearance of freedom to the debates that were to follow.

The Opposition, however, were not satisfied with this concession. Lord Lyndhurst moved that the consideration of the disfranchising clauses should be postponed until the enfranchising clauses had first been considered; so that instead of making enfranchisement a consequence of disfranchisement, disfranchisement might follow enfranchisement. The noble lord, and those who supported him, made many protestations of their desire to give the bill a friendly and candid consideration, and of their willingness to disfranchise a large number of boroughs. Lord Wharncliffe, in particular, distinctly stated, that while he thought it to be his duty to vote with Lord Lyndhurst, he was determined to go the full length of disfranchising at least the number of boroughs contained in Schedule A. In fact, the proposal was put forward as being simply a question of the order in which the clauses of the bill were to be considered in committee; and it might seem to be a matter of little importance whether the order proposed by the ministry or that contended for by their opponents should be adopted; but the real question at issue was, whether the control of

* The number of the bill's supporters on this occasion, as compared with the last, had increased from 158 to 184; while the Opposition had diminished from 199 to 175.

† The majority of those present at the division was only two, and proxies could not be used in committee.

the committee was to be in the hands of the friends of reform, or of those who had all along been its open enemies, and who, if they were now prepared to allow the bill to pass in any shape, notoriously yielded because they durst no longer resist the plainly-declared will of the nation. Ministers therefore wisely resolved to take the first opportunity of bringing this question to an issue. Accordingly, after several of them had strongly contended that the proposal of Lord Lyndhurst was opposed to the principles of the bill, Earl Grey distinctly warned the House that he should regard its success as fatal to his measure; thus intimating to the Opposition lords, that if they voted for it, they must be responsible for the consequences of the rejection of the bill. In spite of this warning, Lord Lyndhurst's motion was carried by a majority of 35; there being 151 in favour of it, and 116 against it.

Earl Grey at once moved, that the House should resume, adding that he should also move, that the further consideration of the bill should be delayed till Thursday, the 10th. This notice was equivalent to an intimation that the ministry would either obtain the king's permission to create peers, or resign their places. The Opposition sincerely deprecated both these alternatives. They had resolved to make considerable concessions, and hoped to force the Government to meet them half-way. This, however, the administration would not and could not do. The Opposition therefore determined, as a last resource, to place their own plan of reform before the country, hoping to gain a considerable amount of adhesion to it; and Lord Ellenborough, who moved the amendment for the rejection of the bill on the second reading, gave a programme of the reform which he and his friends were prepared to support. 'I will merely say, that having, in conjunction with other peers, given the most serious consideration to the great principles of the bill; having well considered the claims possessed by the towns included in Schedules C and D;* having likewise considered the reasonableness, under existing circumstances, of carrying into effect the changes which these clauses, taken in conjunction with other parts of the bill, would create; having reflected on the proposal to give additional members to the counties; and having at

* The enfranchising schedules.

the same time very strong objections to Schedules B and E,* the result of the amendments to be proposed would have been to give enfranchisement to an extent such as would have made it necessary (unless an inconvenient increase of the members of the House were resorted to) to disfranchise the boroughs contained in Schedule A, which, with Weymouth, would cause a reduction of 113 members. Another proposal would have been to prevent persons from voting for counties in respect of property situated in boroughs, and to adopt a more clear and certain mode of ascertaining the genuineness or value of holdings; while both the 10l. qualification should be adopted, and the scot-and-lot right of voting retained.'

Such was the plan of reform which terror and the fear of worse had wrung from the anti-reform peers. It was put forward with the view of inducing the ministry to accept the offered concessions, or of appealing to the country if they declined them. So far as the administration was concerned, the hope of influencing them, if seriously entertained, was completely disappointed. Earl Grey, with cold politeness, rejected the overture thus made to him. He sarcastically congratulated the noble lord and the House on the progress he had at length made in the principles of reform, and especially on his expressed intention not to touch the 10l. qualification, and to preserve the scot-and-lot right of voting where it at present existed, thus rendering this 'democratic measure still more democratic.' The House accordingly resumed, and the farther consideration of the bill in committee was postponed to Thursday.

Nothing now remained for the ministry but to recommend such a creation of peers as would enable them to carry the bill through the House of Lords without important modifications. The king, as we have already intimated, entertained the most decided objections to this step. He had, with great reluctance, so far yielded as to consent to the creation of a few peers, if it should be found absolutely necessary to carry the bill; but he wished that every possible expedient should be tried to avoid this dire necessity. When, therefore, it came to be a question of

* The former containing the places to be deprived of one member, the latter those to have outlying districts annexed to them.

the order in which the clauses of the bill were to be taken,
the king was fully justified, according to the understanding
which existed between himself and his advisers, in refusing
to create peers. But besides this, a great change had come
over him in regard to the Reform Bill. There is every
reason to believe that he had in the first instance given it his
cordial approval; that he had frankly and honestly supported his ministers in their endeavours to carry it; and
had, at the same time, candidly stated to them the length
to which he was prepared to go with them, and the point
at which he was resolved to stop. But in following the
discussions on the measure, he had been gradually more
and more influenced by the predictions of revolution, which
were uttered by men who enjoyed a high reputation for
political sagacity, and by the parallel which was often
drawn between the commencement of his reign and that
of the unfortunate Louis XVI., which seemed to be borne
out by the increased agitation which pervaded the country,
and by the rapid wane of his popularity. He saw too, with
great dissatisfaction, the growing feeling which prevailed
against all hereditary authority. Thus the Reform Bill, if
it had not become absolutely odious to him, was certainly
viewed by him with much less complacency than before;
and this feeling extended to the ministry by which the
bill was introduced, and whom he naturally regarded as
the authors of the unpleasant—not to say dangerous—
dilemma in which he found himself placed. When therefore Lord Grey and his colleagues required him to choose
between a creation of peers large enough to enable them
to carry the bill unimpaired or their resignation, he accepted
the latter alternative, cordially thanking them at the same
time for the services they had rendered to himself and the
country during the period of their administration. In all
this there is nothing that is not perfectly intelligible,—
nothing to justify the charge of systematic dishonesty and
duplicity which has been brought against this monarch,
but which was certainly never believed by those whose
constant official intercourse with him afforded them many
excellent opportunities of forming a correct judgment of
his character, and whose penetration was unquestionably
equal to the task of fathoming a deeper mind than that of
William IV.

On the evening of May 9th, Earl Grey announced in the House of Lords the king's acceptance of the resignation of his ministry, and moved that the order for going into committee on the next day should be discharged, adding that he did not think it necessary to fix another day for the purpose. The Earl of Carnarvon, one of the most violent opponents of the measure, stigmatised in very strong terms the conduct of the ministers. 'My lords,' he exclaimed, 'the noble lords opposite may act as they think fit; we know the grounds, the slight grounds, which their defeat of Monday evening afforded them for one of the most atrocious propositions with which a subject ever dared to insult the ears of a sovereign. We have heard, what I naturally expected to hear, that his majesty, who was among the first to recommend reform, upon broad and constitutional principles, finding himself reduced to the alternative to which his ministers ventured to reduce him, has acted as became a sovereign of the house of Brunswick, and by so doing has established an additional title to the respect and affection of his subjects. But, my lords, it shall not go forth to the public that, because the noble lords opposite have determined to abandon this measure, this House is unwilling to enter into the discussion of its merits. I therefore move that your lordships proceed with the consideration of the Reform Bill in committee on Monday next.' Earl Grey replied to this attack with that severe dignity, which on such occasions no one could more effectually assume, and to which his lofty figure, his commanding attitude and aristocratic bearing gave peculiar force and effect. 'My lords,' he said, 'I am too much accustomed to the ill-timed, violent, personal, and unparliamentary language of the noble earl who has just sat down, to be much affected by the disorderly attack which he has made on my colleagues and myself. Nor is it for the defence of myself personally against the imputations which the noble earl has thought proper to cast on me, that I again rise to address your lordships. I trust, my lords, that in the estimation of your lordships and the public, my character is such that I may without presumption consider myself as sufficiently guarded from the danger of suffering by such imputations. The noble earl has been pleased to qualify the advice which I thought it my duty to tender to my sovereign as atrocious and insulting'; and there were other noble lords on that side of the House who appeared to agree with the noble lord in that opinion. All I can say is, that I deferred giving that advice until the very last moment; until the necessity of the case and my sense of public duty imposed upon me an obligation which appeared to me to be imperative. But I appeal to your lordships, whether, until that period shall arrive, I am called upon to notice the accusation.'

The motion of the Earl of Carnarvon was adopted, and the House separated.

In the House of Commons Lord Althorp made an announcement similar to that which had been made by Earl Grey in the House of Lords. Lord Ebrington immediately gave notice that, on the following day, he would move a humble address to his majesty on the present state of public affairs: he added, that he should also move that the House should be called over on the occasion.

In pursuance of this notice, Lord Ebrington, on May 10th, moved a resolution, imploring 'his majesty to call to his councils such persons only as will carry into effect, unimpaired, in all its essential provisions, that bill for the reform of the representation of the people which has recently passed this House.'

After a long discussion on the resolution, the House divided, when the numbers were:

For the motion	283
Against	203
Majority	80

If the state of the nation was alarming at the last rejection of the bill, it was much more so now. It soon became evident that the feeling in favour of the bill had become more intense and general. At no place was it more distinctly manifested than at Birmingham, which at this time exercised a more powerful influence on the destinies of the bill than the other great towns of the empire, not only on account of its central position and comparative proximity to the metropolis, but also as being the heart of a district densely peopled by a rugged and robust race, who were united almost to a man in determined support of reform.

On the very day on which Lord Lyndhurst's motion was carried, a meeting had been held, in anticipation of the rejection or mutilation of the measure by the House of Lords, at which 200,000 persons were said to have been present, and at which very violent language was used and very violent resolutions adopted. When therefore the news of the resignation of Earl Grey's ministry reached Birmingham, it produced a ferment. Everywhere it was resolved not to pay taxes, and not to purchase property which might be distrained for the payment of taxes. This determination was announced in notices placed in most of the windows in the town, and would unquestionably have been carried out, not in Birmingham only, but throughout the empire; and not only by the lower classes, but also by many of the upper and middle classes. Lord Milton desired the tax-gatherer to call again, intimating that he might find it necessary to refuse payment; and when afterwards asked in the House of Commons whether he had really used this language, he replied, 'Certainly.' It was a significant fact, that four Catholic priests, and a large number of Quakers, joined the Birmingham Union at the moment when it seemed almost ripe for rebellion.

On the 10th of May the common council of the city of London resolved that 'they who have advised his majesty to put a negative on the proposal of ministers to create peers have proved themselves enemies of the sovereign, and have put in imminent hazard the stability of the throne and the tranquillity and security of the country.' They also petitioned the House of Commons to refuse its supplies until reform should have been secured. The same prayer came from Manchester, Birmingham, Leeds, and in fact from almost every part of the kingdom. Everywhere the strongest determination was expressed, and the most violent proposals and the most outrageous language were welcomed with the loudest applauses. At a meeting of the inhabitant householders of Westminster, Mr. O'Connell elicited tremendous cheering by reminding his audience that Charles I. had been beheaded for listening to the advice of a foreign wife. The prayer of all the myriads of open meetings that were being held was, that the Grey ministry might be immediately reinstated, and the bill passed unmutilated. Of all the speeches made at this conjuncture, there is probably one only from which the reader will desire to have any extract, and that is the speech of the Rev. Sydney Smith. Every one is acquainted with his celebrated comparison of the House of Lords to Dame Partington, when the bill was rejected in 1831; and many no doubt will read with interest the following extract from his speech at Taunton at the crisis we have now reached, in which she is again referred to. 'One word before we part for an old and excellent friend of ours—I mean Dame Partington. It is impossible not to admire spirited conduct even in a bad cause, and I am sure Dame Partington has fought a much longer and better fight than I had any expectation she would fight. Many a mop has she worn out, and many a bucket has she broken, in her contest with the waves. I wish her spirit had been more wisely employed, for the waves must have their way at last; but I have no doubt I shall see her some time hence in dry clothes, pursuing her useful and honourable occupations, and retaining nothing but a good-humoured recollection of her stiff and spirited battle with the Atlantic.'

While these efforts were being taken to reinstate the Grey ministry, efforts were also made to embarrass their successors. One of these was a run on the banks. The streets of London were covered with placards on which were printed in huge letters—'Go for gold, and stop the Duke.' At the Manchester Savings Bank alone 620 persons had given notice for the withdrawal of deposits to the amount of 16,000*l*. Preparations were being made for a recourse to arms; and there can be no doubt that if the resistance to the popular will had been carried much farther than it was, a civil war would have broken out, or rather an immense and irresistible armed mob would have marched on London, and would have dictated their own terms to the king, the government, and the legislature. What these terms would have been, it is idle now to conjecture; they would certainly have gone far beyond the passing of the Reform Bill, and probably would have involved the overthrow of the monarchy, and a complete change in the form of government.

In the mean time the king consulted Lord Lyndhurst, who recommended that the Duke of Wellington should be sent for. The Duke, though his conduct on this occasion exposed him to much obloquy and aggravated his unpopularity, appears to have acted in a highly honourable manner. We may doubt his judgment in bringing on the crisis which he was summoned to deal with, but we cannot refuse our admiration to the self-abnegation and courage which he displayed. Entertaining the opinions he had all along avowed on the subject of reform, it was only natural that he should endeavour to defeat the measure which the government had brought forward, or, finding that impossible, that he should seek to render it as little objectionable in his eyes as he could venture to make it. But now that the crisis had occurred, his predominant desire was to save his sovereign from the humiliation of being compelled to solicit Earl Grey to return and of consenting to the creation of peers. The duke however felt that, after the strong declaration he had made against all reform, after the uncompromising opposition he had offered to the measure now before the House of Lords, he was not the man to carry it through, even in a modified form, or to accept office in an administration by which it was to be taken charge of. He could not but be aware of the danger to which he exposed himself, and of the imputations which his opponents would not be slow to heap on him. He therefore recommended that Sir R. Peel should be sent for and requested to form a government, promising at the same time that, whether in or out of office, he would give every support in his power to the new administration. But Sir R. Peel likewise felt that, after the uncompromising opposition he had offered to the bill, he could not accept an office from which he was certain to be ignominiously precipitated in less than a week after his entrance on it, unless he supported all the essential features of a measure he had so strongly denounced. The frightful responsibility which the state of the country imposed on an unpopular minister might well make a man of much stronger nerve than he possessed shrink from a position in which he would probably have to deal with a rebellion. Besides, the Catholic emancipation struggle was still fresh in his remembrance and in the recollection of all men; and if he were now to accept office and carry the Reform Bill, it would appear that the accusation that he had been actuated by a sordid love of the patronage and emoluments of office was really well-founded. Men, whose opinion is entitled to some weight, think that if he had accepted office at this juncture, he might have retained it. Looking at the state of the country at that moment, it appears to me that he must have been hurled from power almost before his ministry was formed, and perhaps the constitution would have fallen with him. But be that as it may, there can be no doubt that both on public and private grounds he exercised a very wise discretion in declining the offer. At the same time he promised, that if a ministry were formed from the political party to which he belonged, he would give it all the support he could; and there can be no doubt that this promise would have been honourably fulfilled.

Sir Robert Peel having declined to take office, there was no other man in the anti-reform ranks who possessed sufficient weight to form and lead an administration, except the Duke of Wellington. All the reasons that could be urged against Sir R. Peel's acceptance of office might with equal force be urged against the duke's accession to power, with the additional objection of the loss his ministry would suffer both in weight and in strength by Sir R. Peel's refusal to join it. But the duke's devotion to his sovereign prevailed over every other consideration, and seeing that no one else could be found competent to form such a ministry as the king desired, he accepted the thankless and perilous task. The king's eldest natural son had been created Earl of Munster by Earl Grey, at the solicitation of his father; but had since quarrelled with him, and been forbidden the court; he now returned, and was said to have taken an active interest in the formation of the new administration. But all these efforts were unsuccessful. The difficulties of the situation were insuperable. Even Sir R. Inglis and Mr. Davies Gilbert, two of the strongest Tories in the country, denounced the attempt to form an anti-reform ministry, which should pass the Reform Bill even in a modified shape. For a moment the duke thought of maintaining his position by the aid of military force, but he found that even the army could not be relied on; and having exhausted all his efforts and resources, he quailed at the first sighings of the storm he had raised, and wisely yielded before it burst forth. Mr. Baring, who throughout these transactions had acted as the mouthpiece of the proposed ministry in the House of Commons, announced, in his place in that House, amidst the loud cheers of the majority, that the commission given to the Duke of Wellington for the formation of a ministry was entirely at an end.

Nothing, then, was now left for the king but to yield to the almost unanimous wish of his people, and recall Earl Grey. It was evident that not only were the lower classes almost to a man in favour of the bill, but that even in the upper and middle classes the desire that it should be passed speedily and without any considerable change was rapidly spreading. Of this fact the character of the daily papers of the period affords a sufficient proof. These papers circulated almost exclusively among the classes we have just mentioned, and it appeared that out of thirteen, which was the whole number of them at the time, ten were on the side of reform, and that while, during the last ten days, more than 400,000 stamps had been issued to the papers favourable to reform, those issued to the anti-reform journals were under 40,000. The violence of language in which the former class of papers indulged at this period also furnishes an index to the feelings of their readers. A writer in the *Morning Chronicle* denominated the bishop of Exeter 'that obscene renegade Phillpotts.' Royalty itself was not spared. The amiable queen was stigmatised as 'a nasty German frow.' The king's natural children were thus referred to: 'The by-blows of a king ought not to be his bodyguard. Can anything be more indecent than the entry of a sovereign into his capital with one bastard riding before him, and another by the side of his carriage? The impudence and rapacity of the Fitz-Jordans is unexampled even in the annals of Versailles and Madrid. The demands made on the person of their poor drivelling begetter are incessant,' &c. &c. In fact, the king's popularity was now completely gone. He was no longer 'the patriot king' or 'the sailor king.' Dirt was thrown into his carriage as he came up to London; he was received in the metropolis with hisses, groans, execrations, and obscene outcries, and was with difficulty protected from personal violence by the exertions of the Guards who surrounded his carriage.

Earl Grey at once obeyed his sovereign's summons,

accompanied as usual by Lord Brougham. The king received them with evident ill-humour, and, contrary to his usual practice, kept them standing during the interview. But he at once consented to the creation of as many peers as the ministry might think necessary to enable them to carry the Reform Bill through the House of Lords, with the understanding that this power was not to be exercised until every means of avoiding the necessity for its employment had been tried; a condition which the two lords readily agreed to, as they and all their colleagues were extremely averse to the proposed step, and many of them would even have abandoned a great part of their bill, if they dared, rather than have recourse to it. This having been arranged, and it being understood that the ministers retained their offices, the king asked—'Is there anything more?' 'Sire,' said Lord Brougham, 'I have one farther request to make.' 'What!' replied the king, 'have I not yet conceded enough?' 'Yes,' replied the chancellor; 'I do not wish to ask any fresh concessions of your majesty, but simply to request you to put in writing the promise you have made us.'

The king was evidently irritated at a demand which seemed to imply a want of confidence in his promise, but he also felt that he could not resist. After a moment's hesitation, he took a small piece of paper, on which he wrote the following words, which he then handed to Lord Brougham:

'The King grants permission to Earl Grey and to his Chancellor Lord Brougham to create such a number of peers as will be sufficient to insure the passing of the Reform Bill—first calling peers' eldest sons.

'WILLIAM R.

'Windsor, May 17, 1832.'

The same evening, Sir Herbert Taylor, who was present at this interview, wrote the following circular note to the most active of the Opposition lords:

'My dear Lord,—I am honoured with his majesty's commands to acquaint your lordship that all difficulties to the arrangements in progress will be obviated by a declaration in the House of Peers to-night, from a sufficient number of peers, that in consequence of the present state of affairs they have come to the resolution of dropping their opposition to the Reform Bill, so that it may pass without delay, and as nearly as possible in its present shape.

'I have the honour to be, yours sincerely,

'HERBERT TAYLOR.'

On the evening on which this letter was written the Duke of Wellington, in his place in the House of Lords, gave a full explanation of the share he had taken in the transactions which had followed Earl Grey's resignation. He then withdrew from the House, and did not make his appearance in it again until the day following the passing of the Reform Bill. Lords Grey and Brougham, on the other hand, did not even yet declare positively that they would retain their offices. 'All I can state,' said the former, 'is that my continuance in office will depend on my conviction of my ability to carry into full effect the bill on your lordships' table unimpaired in principle and in all its essential details.' 'We shall not return to office,' said the chancellor, 'except upon the condition not only of our possessing the ability to carry the bill efficiently through the House, but also of being able to carry it through with every reasonable dispatch consistent with the due discussion of its various provisions.'

The fact is, that ministers were not at this moment aware of the proceeding of Sir Herbert Taylor, and they were most unwilling to use the power that the king had given them to the extent that would be required to carry the bill unimpaired, if the anti-reform peers persisted in their opposition to it. Therefore they were still in the greatest perplexity. They hesitated to use the power they had obtained. There were the people behind them, instant with loud voices demanding the bill. They had conjured up a spirit they could not lay and could not resist. They have been gravely censured for this, but most unjustly. The situation was most difficult; but the difficulty arose from the fault of those who had delayed reform so long that it was necessary to do in one bill and at one time what ought to have been done long before in twenty bills, spread over more than a century. That which—done in time— might have been effected quietly and without danger, was

now attended with imminent peril. The longer the delay
the greater the danger, and the more violent the required
change. The chief merit of the Grey ministry was, that
they dared to face the difficulties of the situation before
it was too late, and by proposing a strong measure of
reform prevented a revolution. The success of Sir Herbert
Taylor's communication to the peers removed every difficulty; and Earl Grey being asked, on the following evening, by the Earl of Harewood, whether it was settled that
ministers should continue in office, replied: 'In consequence
of my having received the king's request to that effect, and
in consequence of my now finding myself in a situation
which will enable me to carry through the bill unimpaired
in its efficiency, I and my colleagues continue in office.'
He accordingly moved that the bill should be proceeded
with on Monday.

Lord Harewood, after bitterly complaining that the independence of the House was destroyed, announced his
intention of withdrawing from farther opposition; and a
large number of peers followed the same course. A small
minority, disregarding the king's request, still offered a
pertinacious, and often factious opposition to its progress,
and, if they did not succeed in their endeavours, at least
had the satisfaction of venting their indignation in no
measured terms. Here is a specimen scene. In the course
of a discussion on the enfranchisement of Oldham, Lord
Kenyon exclaimed:

'The bill will be the destruction of the monarchy. By
forcing this measure on his reluctant sovereign, the noble
earl has placed the king in a situation in which he could
make no choice of a minister; and his advice to exercise
his prerogative in so unconstitutional a manner as to
destroy the independence of this House is abandoned and
atrocious—'

Earl Grey (interrupting, with great warmth and amidst
vehement cheering): 'Atrocious! my lords. I put it to your
lordships, is it consistent with the usages of this House,
or with ordinary propriety, that the noble lord should apply
such words to me? For my part I can only reject the
words with contempt and scorn.'

Lord Kenyon: 'I repeat, that I think such conduct most
abandoned and atrocious. Whether the noble lord be

pleased or not with my using the word *atrocious*, the privileges of the House have not been abrogated to such an extent that the noble earl can prevent me from saying that I shall always feel that it was the most atrocious act of the minister to give such advice to the king.'

Earl Grey: 'Anything more unparliamentary, disorderly, and atrocious than the applying of such words to me, I never heard in this House. It is for the House to act as may seem befitting its own dignity; but for me, all that remains to me is to throw back those words with the utmost scorn, contempt, and indignation.'

After some farther bickerings, the Duke of Cumberland interposed as a peacemaker, and the business of the committee proceeded. In six days the bill went through committee, and on the 4th of June it was read a third time and passed, 106 peers voting for it, and only 22 against it. Lords Wharncliffe and Harrowby, by whose assistance the second reading was carried, evidently thought that they had been duped by the ministry, and took the opportunity afforded them by the debate on the third reading of giving loud utterance to their disappointment and indignation.

On the 5th of June the amendments introduced into the bill by the House of Lords were submitted to the Lower House, and assented to. No objection was made to them from any quarter; nevertheless a long discussion took place, which had very little reference to the question before the House, but which presented one or two remarkable features. In the course of this debate Lord Milton avowed and justified his intention to resist the payment of taxes in case the Wellington Administration had been formed. Sir R. Peel also made the following remarks, to which subsequent events gave peculiar interest and significance: 'Whenever government come to deal with the corn laws, the precedent formed by the present occasion will be appealed to; and if they should be placed in similar circumstances of difficulty and excitement, the danger to the public tranquillity will be made a plea for overturning the independence of the House of Lords.' Little did he then dream, that when the dire consummation, which he thus lugubriously predicted, arrived he himself, by the aid of a reformed House of Commons, would constrain a reluctant House of Lords to sanction the entire abolition of the corn laws, and the subversion of the policy with which they were identified. It was also in the course of this debate that Lord J. Russell made the celebrated 'finality' declaration, which has so often been referred to as a proof that he and his colleagues were pledged to resist any attempt to carry further than they had done by their bill the reform of the House of Commons. His words were these: 'I think that, so far as ministers are concerned, this is a final measure. I declared, on the second reading of the bill, that if only a part of the measure were carried, it would lead to new agitations; that is now avoided by the state in which the bill has come from the other House.'

The measure thus at length adopted by the legislature swept away fifty-six nomination boroughs, returning 112 members, semi-disfranchised thirty more; making a sum-total of disfranchisement of 142 seats in the Lower House of Parliament. It gave the counties sixty-five additional representatives, and conferred the right of sending members to the House of Commons on Manchester, Leeds, Birmingham, and thirty-nine other large and flourishing towns previously unrepresented. On the other hand, it greatly impaired the direct influence of the working classes in the elections, by diminishing the number of the franchises in Preston and other towns, where, before the Reform Bill was carried, the suffrage was nearly universal. It must also be confessed that the mechanism of the measure was in many respects faulty. This was admitted by the late Lord Spencer—the Lord Althorp of our history—and has been pointed out by the late Sir J. Stephen, Mr. Chadwick, and other authorities. For this, however, the opponents of the bill were much more to blame than its framers and supporters. Their efforts were exerted not to amend, but to delay and defeat it. Not only did they bring forward themselves a multitude of motions with this view, but they also availed themselves of all the amendments proposed by the friends of reform to forward their obstructive designs. But the defects thus occasioned, though much to be regretted, are as dust in the balance when weighed against the solid gain obtained by the abolition of the crying abuses of the system which the bill swept away, as well as by the positive benefits of the system which it established. It conferred on some of the most powerful interests in the nation not perhaps all the influence in the framing of our laws to which their growing importance entitled them, but an influence sufficient to secure attention to their needs and requirements. The vast expansion of our trade, commerce, and manufactures, which has since taken place, could not have been effected if the landed interest had continued to possess that virtual monopoly of legislation which was taken from it by the Reform Bill.

Nothing now remained in order to give the bill the force of law but the formal assent of the king. It was earnestly hoped that he would have given it in person; and had he done so, he would probably have recovered a considerable portion of the popularity he had lost by his refusal to create peers. His ministers implored him to go down to the House of Lords; the reform journals urged him to attend, and promised a most enthusiastic reception, which unquestionably would have been given to him: for the people, now that their wishes were gratified, were quite prepared to forgive his past conduct. But the treatment he had received after Lord Grey's resignation, and the abuse with which he had been loaded by the reform press, had made a deep impression on his mind, and he peremptorily refused to give his assent in person. It was consequently given by commission, the commissioners being the lord chancellor, Earl Grey, the Marquis of Lansdowne, the Marquis of Wellesley, Lord Durham, and Lord Holland. The ministerial benches were crowded; those usually occupied by the Opposition were empty. One single prelate, Dr. Maltby, the now bishop of Chichester, represented the episcopal bench on the occasion. The speaker, followed by all the members present in the House, with the single exception of Sir R. H. Inglis, went up to the House of Lords, and announced on his return that the royal assent had been given to the bill. The announcement was received in silence, and the absence of the king gave rise to gloomy presentiments The bill had now become law, but its results yet remained to be seen. The agitation which the struggle had caused, and the passions it had roused, had by no means subsided; and the state of the public mind was such as to give rise to anxious forebodings, even in the hearts of the most sanguine supporters of the measure, as to the use which the nation would make of its victory. These fears we all know proved to be groundless. The dangers which menaced the state have passed away; the constitution has acquired new vigour; the tranquillity, contentment, security, and wealth of the nation have increased enormously; and many excellent measures have passed, to the great advantage of all classes, which an unreformed Parliament never would have entertained.

One of the most natural and obvious consequences of such a struggle as we have been describing was to give a more extensive circulation to existing newspapers, and to call fresh newspapers into existence. It had also the effect of producing a new description of political periodicals, containing many pungent political articles and personal attacks, but no news; so that being unstamped they were sold for a penny, while the price of newspapers was sixpence or sevenpence a number. These had only an ephemeral life; they appeared in great numbers during the reform excitement, and disappeared when it abated. Of these the most widely circulated and the most popular was the *Figaro*, which bore this motto on its title-page:

> 'True wit, that like a polish'd razor keen
> Wounds with a stroke that's hardly felt or seen.'

These papers were the precursors of *Punch*. But this year witnessed the commencement of a healthier and more durable class of cheap weekly periodicals, also sold at a penny; but from which both news and politics were altogether excluded, while a great deal of very valuable and interesting information was afforded by them. From their size, the character of their contents, and the engravings they contained, they were at that time regarded as miracles of cheapness. Of these we may specially mention the *Penny Magazine*, published by the Society for the Diffusion of Useful Knowledge, and circulating 200,000 copies; the *Saturday Magazine*, published by the Society for the Promotion of Christian Knowledge; and *Chambers's Edinburgh Journal*, each circulating 60,000 copies. This circulation was at that time regarded as almost marvellous; and the success of these periodicals constitutes an era in the history of our periodical literature, showing, as it did, that the people would willingly purchase, and even prefer, literature of a wholesome and improving character, if made interesting and sold at a price low enough to place it within their reach.

On the 21st of September in this year there passed away in peace one whose name is still a household word, whose works adorn almost every library, and are read with almost the same eager delight that they excited when they first appeared. We need hardly add, that we speak of Walter Scott. Clouds and darkness overshadowed his last years on earth, and the Reform Bill, so full of hope to some of his contemporaries, was to him big with disaster and despair. But he bore up under all with a cheerfulness that neither poverty, nor pain, nor illness, nor the apprehension of the evil to come, could quench. No man perhaps ever more completely transfused his own noble and generous character into his works, in which nearly all that is immortal of him still lives; and therefore it is needless to say more of him; but it would have been unpardonable in one who attempts to write the history of the year 1832 to allow the departure of so great and good a man to pass unremarked.

CHAPTER V.

THE FIRST REFORMED PARLIAMENT.

The struggle was at last over; but the emotions it had excited, like the ground-swell after the storm, still continued to agitate the public mind. The reformers, flushed with victory, made preparations for the coming contest with a vigour and enthusiasm which insured success. Many of them looked forward to the almost immediate introduction of universal suffrage, vote by ballot, annual parliaments; to the disestablishment of the church; and to various other great and organic changes, which they imagined would be the necessary and immediate consequence of the immense increase of popular power which had been effected by the great bill. Others among them, more moderate or more timid, gave their support to the government, which had announced that they intended the bill which they had succeeded in carrying to be a final measure, not indeed altogether precluding other important changes, but intended to determine the constitution of the House of Commons for the generation in which it was adopted. Many of them thought that reform had already gone too far in this direction, and would gladly have made the change less violent, if they had not been prevented from doing so by a sense of the impossibility of stemming the current of popular enthusiasm by which it was borne onwards. These, for the most part, gave their confidence and support to the Grey administration. On the other hand, the Tories, or, as they now began to be called, the Conservatives, were filled with alarm and almost overwhelmed with despair. Beaten and dispirited, they thought that the extreme measures which were at the moment so popular would speedily be adopted, and that reform would develop into anarchy and revolution. These fears caused them to put forth all the exertions of which they were capable, and the long interval which necessarily elapsed before the struggle between the two parties could be renewed at the hustings and the polling-booth enabled them in some degree to recover their drooping spirits. They had still a great superiority over their opponents in wealth and influence, and they hoped that by a large expenditure of money they might succeed, not indeed in obtaining a majority, for that was quite out of the question, but in returning a formidable phalanx to sit on the Opposition benches and obstruct and delay, as far as possible, the measures they dreaded. They knew that they could count on a large majority in the House of Lords, but that its action must in a great degree depend on the number of supporters they could muster in the House of Commons. If the majorities by which any measure which the Conservative party resisted was carried in the House of Commons were not very large, they knew that the Lords would be sure to reject the measure, or to so amend it as to render it in their opinion almost innocuous. The revision of the registers passed off quietly, and served to calm down still further the passions which the reform struggle had so powerfully excited. The revising barristers generally adopted the most liberal construction of the statute, and retained the names of all persons who were not distinctly shown to be disqualified for the votes they claimed. The revision, however, clearly showed, as indeed all parties had anticipated, that the vast majority of those on whom the Reform Bill had conferred the elective franchise were supporters of the government by which that measure had been introduced and carried through its different stages.

It was near the end of the year 1832 when the elections commenced, and they were not completed until after the beginning of the year 1833. The machinery of the bill fully answered the hopes and expectations of its authors. The revision had greatly facilitated the taking of the votes, as the only thing now to be ascertained was whether the persons tendering them had their names on the register. The plan of taking the votes at several separate polling-places, instead of at one central hustings, divided the mob, prevented disturbances or facilitated the repression of them. The diminution of the time over which the polling extended was a still greater improvement. In the place of fourteen days of turmoil, trouble, drunkenness, and riot, there were now only two days at the most; and though the state of towns during the elections was still far from being what

was desirable, comparative tranquillity prevailed. Of course
the ministerial party was the one which gained chiefly by
the dissolution. The Conservative party, whose ranks had
been so greatly thinned by two successive dissolutions,
suffered fresh losses by the present election. The rotten
boroughs, which had been their strongholds, were now disfranchised, and the new constituencies naturally showed
their gratitude to their political creators by generally returning representatives of the Whig party. Nevertheless
their losses were less disastrous than might have been anticipated, and they were able to boast that they had gained
some victories where defeat seemed to be inevitable. A
remnant, small indeed, but still larger than was hoped, of
the great party that carried General Gascoyne's amendment,
occupied the Opposition benches. Mr. Baring, one of the
most uncompromising opponents of the Reform Bill, was
returned for the county of Essex. Sir R. Vyvyan, whose
hostility to the measure had not been less marked, represented Bristol in the new Parliament. Lord Sandon was
elected by the still more important constituency of Liverpool. But these triumphs, dearly bought, were balanced
by very serious losses. Sir C. Wetherell, the ablest lawyer
and the most effective speaker of the high Tory party, was
rejected at Oxford. Sir E. Sugden, afterwards lord chancellor and Lord St. Leonards, lost his seat at Cambridge.
Mr. Croker had declared that he would never sit in a House
of Commons elected under the Reform Bill, and he kept his
word. On the other hand the radicals, who had expected
to gain most largely in this election, were disappointed in
their hopes. It is true that Cobbett, after having been
rejected at Manchester, found an asylum at Oldham; but
on the other hand, Hunt lost his election at Preston, where
the suffrage, which before the passing of the Reform Bill
was almost universal, had been considerably restricted by
that measure, which was far from going the lengths of the
ancient franchises, and which was consequently a measure
of disfranchisement in the places where they had prevailed.
In most of the boroughs, especially the larger ones, the
partisans of the ministers triumphed. Here and there a
large conservative proprietor was able to force himself or
his nominee on a borough in or near which his property
was situated. In the counties the influence of the nobility

and of the large landed proprietors secured for the conservatives a fair share of the representation. In Scotland, out of the fifty-three members, forty were ministerialists, ten conservatives, and three radicals. In Ireland, where O'Connell at this moment wielded an enormous power, a large proportion of his followers—men favourable to the repeal of the union and ready to lend their support to the most violent measures—were chosen. On the whole, the results of the election fully answered the expectations of the prudent and moderate supporters of the Reform Bill. Its effect was to increase considerably the large number of supporters of the ministry which the last House of Commons had contained, and to make that government one of the strongest administrations that had ever existed in England.

In the meantime the Asiatic cholera was spreading through the land, and exercising a sobering and saddening influence on the minds of all. Its ravages had not indeed proved as terrible as had been anticipated; still they caused no small alarm, especially as it was not yet known whether it would increase or decline in its severity. The winter had brought with it a very marked diminution of the pestilence; but what effect would spring and summer have on it? That question, often and anxiously asked, time alone could answer.

The first reformed Parliament was formally opened by commission on the 29th of January, 1833. Of course the first object that occupied the attention of the House of Commons was the choice of a speaker. The late speaker had intimated his intention of not again seeking reëlection, and in consequence a pension of 4,000*l.* a year had been settled on him, with a reversion to his son. It was observed however with displeasure by the conservative party, that he had not, according to the usual practice, been raised to the peerage. Some of the papers belonging to that party had remarked severely on this supposed violation of what was due to one who had so ably served the legislature and the country, and ascribed it to a disinclination on the part of the government to add to the already large phalanx of conservatives which was arrayed against them in the House of Lords. It gradually, however, became known that the government were actuated by a different and a more creditable motive. They thought that his long experience in the chair of the House would be peculiarly valuable in an assembly which contained so large a proportion of new members, and they therefore begged him to allow himself to be again put in nomination for the office he had already filled so long and with so much credit. He agreed to comply with a wish so flattering to him. This arrangement however was very far from being satisfactory to all the supporters of the ministry. The radicals especially contended that the chair of a reformed House of Commons should be filled by a reformer; and though the contest was quite hopeless, they determined to resist the nomination. Accordingly, when Mr. Manners Sutton was proposed by Lord Morpeth and seconded by Sir F. Burdett, Mr. Littleton, in spite of his own remonstrances and the strong support he gave to the claims of his rival, was proposed by Mr. Hume and seconded by Mr. O'Connell. The matter was pressed to a division, when 241 members gave their votes to Mr. Sutton, while only 31 supported his involuntary opponent.

After the usual swearing in of the members of the two Houses, on February 5th the king in person opened the session. His speech recommended to Parliament the careful consideration of the questions of the renewal of the charters of the Bank of England and of the East India Company; of the temporalities of the church, especially with regard to tithes, the collection of which had become very difficult, and caused very bitter disputes. The correction of the abuses of the church, and a more equitable distribution of her revenues, was also suggested, and a just commutation of tithes in Ireland strongly recommended. The king also requested the two Houses to confer on the government additional powers for the repression of disorders in Ireland, and expressed in energetic terms his determination to maintain the legislative union between the two countries, as being 'indissolubly connected with the peace, security, and welfare of his people.'

The address in reply to this speech passed the House of Lords with some criticism from the Duke of Wellington of the foreign policy of the government, especially in reference to Holland and Portugal, but without serious opposition. In the House of Commons, Mr. O'Connell assailed those parts of the king's speech that referred to Ireland with even more than his usual acrimony and violence. He denounced them as 'bloody, brutal, and unconstitutional;' he declared that the evils of Ireland arose not from agitation but from misgovernment, and that the attempt to put down agitation would not remove but increase them. Increase of crime always followed increase of force. Never had there been such a persecuting government as the present. They had persecuted the press, the people, and even the priests; but they had done nothing to restore tranquillity to the country. He complained bitterly of the administration of the law in Ireland, of the state of the magistracy, of the arbitrary rating of counties by grand jurors, and threw the blame of all these evils on the Whigs. He concluded these invectives by moving the following amendment to the address: 'That the House do now resolve itself into a committee of the whole House to consider of the address to his majesty.' Mr. Stanley, the Irish secretary, replied to the vehement harangue of the Irish agitator with little less vehemence. He taunted Mr. O'Connell on account of the caution he had displayed in avoiding the discussion of that measure which he had always been in the habit of representing as the only method of obtaining redress for the grievances of Ireland, namely, the repeal of the legislative union between the two countries. This panacea the government plainly told him, and, as Mr. Stanley believed, with the cordial support of the people, they would resist to the death. With that question Mr. O'Connell had not ventured to grapple, though he had told the people of Ireland that they should have a Parliament in College-green by next June.

In supporting the necessity of some stronger measures than the ordinary administration of the law, the Irish secretary drew a fearful but unexaggerated picture of the state of Ireland, affirming that the record of the crimes perpetrated in Ireland would almost surpass belief. He referred to some of the principal crimes that had been committed in Kilkenny and Queen's County during the last twelve months. In Kilkenny alone, during that period, there had been 32 murders and attempts at murder, 94 burnings of houses, 519 burglaries, 36 houghings of cattle, and 178 assaults, of such a nature as to be attended with danger of loss of life. In Queen's County, during

the same period, the number of murders was still greater—
namely, 60. Of burglaries and nightly attacks of houses
there had been 26, of malicious injuries to property 115,
and of serious assaults on individuals 200. This list,
formidable as it was, contained only the crimes of which
notice had been given to the police, which, in fact, constituted only a small portion of the offences really committed. So complete was the system of organisation
established by the midnight murderers and disturbers of
the public peace, that their victims dared not complain.
He had been willing to try the unaided powers of the law;
the experiment had been tried, and had failed. He maintained that Mr. O'Connell himself and his co-agitators had
instigated his ignorant fellow-countrymen to commit viola-
tions of the law. He denied the assertion that the government had systematically excluded the Catholics from the
magistracy, and mentioned the names of several Catholics
who had been raised by them to high legal positions. He
reminded the House, that if the sheriffs were, with a single
exception, Protestants, that was a circumstance over which
the government had no control, and for which it could not
be regarded as responsible. If they had exercised their
undoubted right of objecting to jurors in some cases, Mr.
O'Connell himself had carried the same right so far as to
call forth an indignant exclamation from Mr. Justice
Moore, a man of undoubted impartiality. The law was no
doubt sufficient, but the law could not be enforced; prosecutors, jurors, and witnesses, were all intimidated. The
majesty of the law must first be asserted, and then afterwards grievances might be redressed.

After Colonel Davis, Mr. Roebuck, Lord Althorp, and
Mr. Macaulay had successively addressed the House, Mr.
Sheil and other Irish members complained, and certainly
with some show of reason, that although Catholic emancipation had been granted by the legislature, the system
which was condemned still pressed heavily on their country.
They reminded the House, that there was not one Irishman
in the cabinet of Ireland; that the Irish secretary, when
examined before a committee of the House of Commons,
had declared that he knew nothing of Ireland. Admitting
the frightful nature of the disturbances that prevailed, they
declared that it was not a war of Catholic against Pro-

testant that lay at the root of these disturbances, but that it was misery and hunger that goaded the people to desperation. Mr. Hume complained that the speech gave no promise of the reductions and reforms which he alleged to be necessary. He demanded a thorough reform of the church, and supported, to a certain extent, the complaints of the repealers. Sir R. Peel, on the other hand, in a speech characterised by statesmanlike moderation, supported the address; and it was carried against Mr. O'Connell's amendment by 428 to 40, of whom 34 were Irish members; and against another amendment, moved by Cobbett, by 323 votes against 23.

After the adoption of some regulations, having for their object the expediting of the business of the House, Mr. Pease, the first member of the Society of Friends who had ever been elected to represent any constituency in the British Parliament, claimed to take his seat, as a knight of the shire for the county of Durham; and was allowed to do so on making his solemn affirmation instead of the usual oath.

It will be at once seen, from the account we have given of the king's speech, and of the debate on the address in reply to it, that the affairs of Ireland were likely to engross a large share of the attention of Parliament during the session of 1833, and that ministers felt that one of the most pressing works they had to accomplish was the pacification of Ireland. This had indeed become the most important question of the day. It influenced the course of legislation, the progress of civilisation, the fate of governments, and therefore cannot be omitted from any history of this country, however exclusively English its design may be.

Indeed, the state of Ireland at this period was a disgrace to the civilisation of the nineteenth century. The laws which had been passed for the protection of life and property had become a dead letter in many parts of it. Persons who hesitated to submit to the illegal dictates of Whitefeet, Blackfeet, and other emissaries of secret societies, were put to death in open day, in the presence of numerous spectators, with perfect impunity. The nearest relatives of the victims dared not institute proceedings against the murderers; jurors were afraid to attend the assizes, or were terrified into giving a verdict of acquittal in the face of the plainest evidence. Witnesses were compelled to quit their country in order to save their lives, if indeed they did save them. Even magistrates were deterred from doing their duty. The consequences of the impunity thus afforded to crime were such as might have been anticipated. There was a reign of terror throughout the greater part of Ireland, the like of which has scarcely ever existed in any other country. In the forcible and true language of a great writer, England, and Ireland too, were reaping 'at last in full measure the fruit of fifteen generations of wrong-doing.' The country was swiftly sinking into a state of barbarism, which only wanted cannibalism to be added to it in order to make it worse than that of the savages of New Zealand in the worst period of their history. We have already had something of its condition revealed to us in the debate on the address. A still more frightful statement of atrocities and horrors was submitted to the House of Lords by the first minister of the crown.

'Between the 1st of January and the end of December 1832 the number of homicides was 242; of robberies, 1,179; of burglaries, 401; of burnings, 568; of houghing cattle, 290; of serious assaults, 161; of riots, 203; of illegal reviews, 353; of illegal notices, 2,094; of illegal meetings, 427; of injuries to property, 796; of attacks on houses, 723; of firing with intent to kill, 328; of robbery of arms, 117; of administering unlawful oaths, 163; of resistance to legal process, 8; of turning-up land, 20; of resistance to tithes, 50; taking forcible possession, 2: making altogether a total of 9,002 crimes committed in one year, and all crimes connected with and growing out of the disturbed state of the country. I must unfortunately also state to your lordships that this system is in a state of progression, and is increasing rather than diminishing. I will not go farther into the details; but merely state a comparison between the three months ending with September, that is, July, August, and September,—and the three ending with December, that is, October, November, and December. The total number of crimes committed in the first three months was 1,279; the total number committed in the last three months was 1,646.'* It is evident that the government would have

* Hansard, 1833, vol. i. p. 731.

greatly failed in the discharge of the duty they owed to their sovereign and their country, if they had failed to deal with such a state of things with a decided and vigorous hand. It was clear that remedial measures which, from the nature of the case, must be slow and gradual in their operation, would not meet the emergency, and that whatever specific ministers might have for the chronic diseases of the body politic in Ireland, they must meet the state of things which existed in that country with severe and coercive measures, which would be prompt in their operation, and would enable the government to discharge with effect the first and most essential of its functions, the protection of life and property; and it was a fortunate circumstance both for England and Ireland that there was at this moment at the head of affairs a government strong enough to carry measures of coercion, and enlightened enough to see that such measures by themselves would not meet the extremity of the case, but that they must be attended or promptly followed by remedial measures, and measures of justice.

A bill was accordingly brought into the Upper House by Earl Grey, founded on the statement of which we have already quoted the most important portions. This bill proposed to give the lord lieutenant power to proclaim disturbed districts, to substitute courts-martial for the ordinary courts of justice under certain limitations and restrictions, the chief of which was that such courts should not try offences to which the penalty of death was attached without special authorisation from the lord lieutenant, and that even then they should not have the power of inflicting any sentence more severe than transportation. It was also ordered by the bill that the court-martial should be assisted by a king's counsel or serjeant-at-law, who should act as judge-advocate. All persons absent from their houses between sunset and sunrise were punishable by these courts. Powers were also given to enter houses for the purpose of searching for arms and ammunition; and persons who did not produce them when inquired for were to be punished. The distribution of seditious papers was also made a punishable offence. And lastly, the Habeas Corpus Act was to be virtually suspended within the limits of the proclaimed districts; but it was enacted by the bill that all persons apprehended should either be brought to trial within the space of three calendar months, or discharged from confinement.

In the House of Lords this bill encountered no serious opposition, and passed through all its stages without a single division. Some amendments suggested in a friendly spirit by the Duke of Wellington were readily admitted by the government, and adopted by the committee. An objection made by Lord Teynham to that provision of the bill which gave the lord lieutenant the power of proclaiming disturbed districts was put by him into the form of a motion, but was afterwards withdrawn.

Very different was the reception that the measure met with in the House of Commons. There it was viewed with great dislike not only by the followers of O'Connell, but by the radical party, and by many of those who generally supported the government. The bill came down from the House of Lords on the 22nd of February, but the first reading of it was postponed to the 27th. No sooner was this delay gained than Mr. O'Connell gave notice that he should move for a call of the House, and renew that motion as often as he perceived any diminution of its effect, as long as the bill was before the House. We will not go into the details of the struggle. The majority that supported the government rendered all opposition ineffectual and carried the bill through its different stages, admitting only such alterations as government consented to allow, with the exception of one clause, in which the majority indulged and displayed their hostility to the church in spite of the remonstrances of the government, and which declared that no district should be proclaimed only on account of the resistance which was offered in it to the payment of tithes. The clause which gave jurisdiction to courts-martial was hotly but unavailingly opposed, though many warm friends of the government supported the objections to it both by speech and vote.

On the 29th of March the bill was read a third time by a majority of 345 to 80, and passed the House of Commons. On its return to the Upper House, great dissatisfaction was expressed at some of the changes which the Commons had made in it, and more especially to that which enacted that resistance to the payment of tithe should not be regarded as a sufficient reason for proclaiming a disturbed district.

It was urged that this provision would be regarded by the Irish as an encouragement held out by Parliament to that resistance to the collection of tithe which was being offered in almost every part of Ireland. Earl Grey and Lord Brougham admitted that the proviso was a very objectionable one, and regretted that it had been introduced into the bill; but they both argued that in point of fact it would prove absolutely innocuous, and declared that under the bill the same protection would be given to the collection of tithe that was afforded to the collection of every other kind of property. The Earl of Harrowby, in order to take away from the clause the invidious character which the amendment had imported into it, proposed to add a farther proviso to the effect that no district should be proclaimed on account of the non-payment of rent or taxes. The House of Lords, however, rejected, by a majority of 85 to 45, an amendment which might have caused farther delay in bringing the measure into operation.

No sooner was the act passed than it was put in force in the county of Kilkenny, with very satisfactory results. A list of offences committed during the month of March which preceded the passing of the measure, and the month of May that followed its introduction, showed that even in that short interval it had effected a great diminution in the number of crimes that had been committed; for while the total number of offences perpetrated in the former of these two months was 472, the whole number committed in the latter was only 162. And this result was obtained without holding a single court-martial, and without applying any of those provisions of the act which had been most strongly opposed in the House of Commons. The volunteers, a body of men who had hitherto contributed largely to disturb the tranquillity of the county, were dissolved by proclamation, and disbanded without attempting resistance. The working of the Coercion Bill was greatly aided by another bill which was also carried through Parliament, and which empowered the Court of King's Bench to change the venue to an adjoining county, or even to Dublin, in cases where there was reason to expect that intimidation would be practised against prosecutors, jurors, or witnesses in the county itself. The carrying of this measure was followed by the transfer of Mr. Stanley from the Irish secretaryship to the Colonial

Office, and by the nomination of Sir J. C. Hobhouse to the office he vacated. This was an arrangement which satisfied all parties. Mr. Stanley was no doubt glad to escape from a post in which he was constantly at warfare with Mr. O'Connell and his followers; and they were glad to be rid of a minister whose unbending determination to make no concessions to them, and whose vigorous and scornful replies, rendered him both formidable and odious to them. They saw that nothing could be gained as long as he was the minister for Ireland; they hoped that his successor would prove more flexible and less unfavourable to their views.

We have already intimated that the ministers of the crown had determined that the coercive measures which they felt themselves compelled to carry should be accompanied, or speedily followed, by measures calculated to remedy the evils of which the Irish people justly complained, and to redress those grievances which were the chief causes of the disturbances that rendered coercion indispensable. The grievance of which the discontented party in Ireland complained most loudly, was the hardship of being obliged to pay tithes and cess for the support of a church in which they did not believe, and which they regarded as a badge of subjection. They averred that they desired its removal, and would be satisfied with nothing short of the entire extinction of tithes and all other taxes levied on them for the support of the Protestant establishment. Ministers were far from being prepared to concede these demands. They believed that the existence of a Protestant established church in Ireland was a necessary check on the aggressive spirit which, rightly or wrongly, they imputed to the Catholic church. So far from desiring to disestablish that church, they were anxious, both from political principle and sincere religious conviction, to strengthen it by removing its abuses, and to mitigate the hostility with which it was regarded by the bulk of the Irish population, by diminishing to some extent the burdens of which they complained, and which their religious opinions rendered trebly grievous to them. With this view they desired to sacrifice a portion of the tithe and commute the rest, and to farther facilitate its collection by transferring the payment of it from the tenant to the landlord. The funds were to be placed in the hands of a body of commissioners, to be called ecclesiastical commissioners, by whom they were to be applied in accordance with the provisions of the measure. The bill enacted that the bishops' lands, which were of great extent and for the most part leased at very low rents, should be sold; and the proceeds of the sales should be vested in the commissioners, who were to pay over to the bishops the same amounts as they received before the passing of the measure, and to apply the surplus to the purposes directed by the bill. In the next place, it was proposed that the number of bishops in Ireland should be reduced from twenty-two to twelve, and the number of archbishops from four to two. The future bishops were to be paid stipends, which, though ample and perhaps even excessive, would, on the whole, be considerably lower than those of the present holders of the sees. Lastly, the bill proposed to lay on the holders of benefices a graduated tax, in lieu of the first-fruits, to which they had been subject hitherto. It was intended in the first instance, that this tax should be levied on the clergy who were already in possession of the benefices; but it was subsequently determined that this provision should only apply to their successors. The bill, as at first introduced, contained a still bolder innovation. It provided that a portion of the funds obtained by the improved management of the bishops' lands, should be appropriated to non-ecclesiastical purposes. In support of this proposal it was urged, that though it was admitted that the church might rightfully claim all property which she at present possessed, Parliament might with no less reason assert her right to the disposal of the additional funds raised through powers conferred by her, to such purposes as she might deem useful and fitting. Ministers proposed to leave to the church all she now possessed, but not to endow her with funds the existence of which were due to the action of the legislature. This clause of the bill was highly acceptable to the repealers and to the English radicals, because it was regarded by them as a precedent for the secularisation of ecclesiastical property, which they hoped would at some future and no very distant time be applied not only to the Irish but also to the English establishment. But for this very reason the proposed appropriation was regarded with great abhorrence, not only by the conservatives but also by a large section of the ministerial party, which was attached to the church,

and strongly opposed to any measure which they thought
calculated to injure or weaken it, and especially to any
concession which seemed to them likely to substitute a new
Catholic ascendancy for the old domination of Protestantism.

In the cabinet itself there was a strong opposition to it.
The premier disliked it, the Earl of Ripon was even more
averse to it. Mr. Stanley, a devoted son of the church,
who supported the proposed reform of the Irish church
with a view to strengthen and enrich, not to impoverish
and despoil her—to increase the number of her members,
not to make a precedent which might hereafter be used to
cripple her,—was vehemently opposed to it. With him
Sir James Graham, the first lord of the Admiralty, also
sympathised; and even those ministers who favoured the
retention of this feature of the bill, for the most part regarded it as a sad necessity—as a sacrifice that must be
made in order to restore peace and tranquillity to Ireland.
The whole cabinet too was well aware that the clause
would certainly be rejected by the Lords, and they wished
to avoid a renewal of the state of things which had occurred
in 1831 and 1832, during the reform struggle. These considerations led the government to take the initiative in
moving the omission of this very important provision of
the Irish Church Bill. They were not, however, allowed
to make so great a change without violent protests and
strong remonstrances from the party that regarded this
clause as the most valuable portion of the government
measure. O'Connell himself exclaimed that it was the
basest act which a national assembly could sanction. But
the government majority enabled them to defy all the
efforts of the opponents of the measure.

Notwithstanding this concession on the part of the
ministry, a very formidable resistance to the bill was
anticipated in the upper House, where the great majority
was avowedly hostile to most of its provisions. Lord Eldon,
who led the opposing party, had taken the opportunity of
the presentation of a petition against the measure early
in April, to declare that he would oppose it to the end of
his life and to the utmost of his power; for he thought it
adverse to every established principle of government, and
full of spoliation. But the experience of last year had
taught many of the noble lords a lesson of caution, and

had made them unwilling to drive the government to extremities. At one time a collision did indeed seem inevitable. An amendment was proposed by the Archbishop of Canterbury respecting the appropriation of the revenues of suspended benefices. The great authority which his personal character and official position gave him obtained a majority of two in favour of it. The ministers suspended the progress of the bill in order to deliberate on the course they should adopt under the circumstances. It was a question with the cabinet whether they should give in their resignations, which would no doubt have produced a crisis similar to that which had occurred when they adopted that course in 1832, and which might have been attended by very serious results. After some consideration, however, they determined to go on with the measure, which was carried through its remaining stages without any very material alterations.

Another question which imperiously called for settlement was the question of Irish tithe. Hitherto it had been collected at the point of the bayonet, and it was rapidly becoming uncollectable even in that way. Almost every attempt to enforce the payment of the obnoxious impost was followed by an affray. Sometimes policemen were killed—sometimes the peasants. The clergy who attempted to enforce their rights, the men who obeyed the law and paid what was due, were assassinated, or lived in continual dread of assassination. Under these circumstances, the collection of tithes through the greater part of Ireland had become impossible. Many of the clergy, who were dependent on them for the support of their families, were reduced to the greatest distress, and in some instances brought almost to the verge of starvation. In 1831 and 1832, government had striven to put an end to a state of things so intolerable. They had advanced a million as a loan to the clergy. They had attempted to transfer the collection of tithes to the government, and to commute the tithe into a land-tax. But all these expedients were unsuccessful. The opposition to the tithe was still so great, that, though payment of some portion was obtained with great difficulty, the expenses of the collection exceeded in amount the sum actually levied. It seemed as though, if England would persist in maintaining a Protestant establishment in Ireland, she would be compelled to sustain it at her own cost. Little was really done this year. The pressure of other business and the difficulty of dealing with this matter led the government to postpone the question till it could be more maturely considered in all its bearings, determining to grapple with the difficulties that beset it in the next session.

The time had now arrived when ministers would at length be compelled to show how far they were prepared to satisfy the highly raised expectations of the people with regard to retrenchment and economy. Hitherto their shortcomings in this respect had been condoned on the ground of the formidable opposition with which they had to contend, and of the manner in which their time and attention had been engrossed by the Reform Bill. But now that these obstacles were removed, now that a reformed House of Commons was sitting, the overwhelming majority of whose members were deeply pledged to those reductions which the Whig party when out of office had strenuously advocated, such excuses as these could no longer be made for the government. It was not indeed possible that expectations such as those that had been raised should be altogether satisfied. Something however was done to meet them. It was announced that the present administration had abolished 1387 places, the total amount of the salaries attached to which was 231,406*l.*; but from this amount a sum of 38,000*l.* had to be deducted for retiring allowances, thus leaving a net saving of about 192,000*l.* In the diplomatic service a saving of 91,735*l.* had been effected; but of this amount 34,000*l.* was due to the regulations which had been introduced into that service by Lord Aberdeen during the Wellington administration, and of which therefore the present ministry could not claim the credit. In the revenue department a saving of 28,000*l.* had been secured by bringing 500 persons from the retired list into active service.

The income of the year ending April 5th, 1833, was 46,835,000*l.*, the expenditure 45,366,000*l.*; leaving an excess of income over expenditure of 1,487,000*l.* The minister proposed to take advantage of this surplus to abolish the duty on tiles, to reduce the duties on marine insurances, advertisements, houses, windows in shops, cotton and soap.

These reductions, it was calculated, would leave a surplus of 516,000*l*. There was nothing very brilliant in these financial operations—nothing to distinguish the budget of the Whig ministry very strikingly from those which had been introduced by some preceding administrations, or meet the expectations which were entertained throughout the country of what was to be effected by a reform ministry and a reformed Parliament. Diligent, assiduous, economical Mr. Hume was deeply disappointed. He complained that the reductions were quite insufficient, and urged that they should at least be pushed to the full extent of the surplus. Sir R. Peel, on the other hand, was of opinion that the chancellor of the exchequer went too far, and argued that by leaving so small a surplus he endangered the public credit, and ran the risk of involving the country in an expenditure which would very far exceed the amount of the reductions which he proposed to make. And not only was the budget unsatisfactory to the parties whom these two financiers represented, but their dissatisfaction was shared by many supporters of ministers in the House and still more in the country, where it had been expected that reform would produce, as one of its first fruits, an abolition of all pensions and sinecures, and an immense reduction of taxation. Nor was the discontent that was thus generally felt altogether groundless. The long exclusion of the Whig party from office had necessarily prevented them from acquiring that administrative experience which nothing but a long tenure of office could give; and their various subordinates, most of whom had been appointed by Tory ministers and belonged to the Tory party, were little able and still less disposed to suggest great and bold financial operations, such as might have induced the country to look indulgently on what they regarded as an over leniency on the part of ministers in dealing with pensions which were not the recompense of any service, sinecures, and other abuses. The expectations which had been raised during the reform struggle were such as no government whatever could have fulfilled; but more might have been done in this way than actually was done. The consideration of the details of the budget was deferred to a later period of the session.

A motion, however, was brought forward on the 26th of

April, which very nearly proved fatal to Lord Althorp's plan. Sir W. Ingilby proposed that the duty on malt should be reduced from 1*l*. 0*s*. 6*d*. to 10*s*. per quarter. In favour of this proposition he urged, that if adopted, it would not only have the effect of alleviating the agricultural distress, about which so much had been said in king's speeches and elsewhere, that it would not only benefit the landlord and the farmer, but that it would also be of great advantage to the public generally, by supplying them with cheap beer; and all this with very slight loss to the revenue, because the largely increased consumption which was sure to follow the reduction of the duty would in all probability keep the revenue nearly at the amount at which it stood before the taking off of the duty; in fact, it was asserted that the reduction of the price would double the consumption, so that there would be no loss of revenue at all. Others, again, thought that the motion did not go far enough, and advocated the getting rid of the expensive machinery for collecting this tax by abolishing it entirely. Various plans were also suggested in the course of the debate by the members of the agricultural party, by which any loss caused by this great reduction of duty might be compensated.

To these arguments in favour of the reduction Lord Althorp replied, that the success of the motion would involve a loss to the revenue of 2,500,000*l*., and he had no security that any great and immediate increase in the consumption would ensue, so as to diminish to any considerable extent this large defalcation, and he could not see any means by which a substitute for the tax could be provided, that would not be more unsatisfactory than the tax itself. It would be impossible that the service of the country could be provided for, or the interest of the debt paid, if the House should consent to sacrifice so large an amount of the taxation of the country, unless the House would consent to a property-tax, or devise some other tax as a substitute for that on malt. However, notwithstanding this strong declaration of the chancellor of the exchequer, Sir W. Ingilby's motion was carried by a majority of 162 to 152.

Ministers appeared at the time to accept this defeat with a good grace. Lord Althorp got up and said, 'The decision of the House has certainly placed his Majesty's government in a situation of considerable embarrassment. Of course, however, after the decision the House has come to, notwithstanding that the majority is not very large, I should be ashamed to make the least opposition or objection to carrying the resolution into effect.' It was therefore supposed that the government would reconstruct their budget, and find some substitute for the taxation which it had been resolved to repeal; and such in all probability was really their intention at the time. Farther consideration seems, however, to have satisfied them that it would be impossible, or at any rate very unadvisable, to attempt to carry out the resolution in which they had appeared to acquiesce. It was resolved to get rid of it by a side wind. Accordingly on the 29th of April Lord Althorp gave notice of an amendment on a motion of Sir J. Key, for the repeal of the house and window taxes, converting it into a motion for the reimposition of the duty which Sir W. Ingilby's motion had taken off. The supporters of that motion loudly complained of this as a violation of the assurance which had been given to the House by Lord Althorp when the motion was carried; and certainly the expressions which the chancellor of the exchequer was reported to have used seemed to warrant the interpretation which Sir W. Ingilby and his friends put on them. They appealed to the House, not to submit to the dictation of Lord Althorp, and not to undo a resolution which a few days before they had so deliberately adopted. Ministers, however, had no course open to them but to press their proposal, and this time they had taken good care that it should not be rejected. It was carried by 285 votes to 131. So that Sir W. Ingilby's proposition, which had before been passed by a majority of ten, was now set aside by a majority of 162. Notwithstanding the largeness of this majority, Sir W. still persisted, and moved for leave to bring in a bill founded on his original resolution; but the motion was lost by 258 votes to 162.

Various attempts were made to get rid of the house and window taxes, which were very unpopular in the metropolis and the great towns of the empire. They were all defeated by the steady determination of the chancellor of the exchequer to oppose a change which would utterly derange his budget, or compel him to resort to a tax on property; neither of which alternatives he was prepared to adopt.

With equal firmness government resisted all the efforts made by Mr. Hume and the rest of the radical party, to obtain the abolition of pensions and sinecures, and a large reduction of our land and sea forces.

The conduct of ministers in regard to these measures greatly disappointed the expectations of their supporters through the country, and produced a very marked diminution of the popularity which they had enjoyed from the time of the introduction of the Reform Bill. Sir J. C. Hobhouse at the time of his election for the city of Westminster had expressed himself strongly in favour of the abolition of the house and window duties. But convinced of the impossibility of finding a substitute for these imposts in the present year, he had voted against the motion for their abolition. Having done so, he determined to resign his seat, to explain to his constituents the reasons which had led him to give this vote, and to ask them to re-elect him. This honest and manly course did not, however, profit him. He was opposed by Colonel Evans, who belonged to the radical party; the electors refused to listen to the explanations he offered to them; and his opponent was returned by a large majority. About the same time a strong agitation was set on foot for the repeal of the assessed taxes. Crowded and enthusiastic meetings were holden in all parts of the metropolis. The Birmingham Political Union, which had so ardently supported the government at every emergency during the struggle for reform, now declared against them. Resolutions were passed by that body denouncing them as having betrayed the confidence of the people, and praying his majesty to dismiss them, as having 'proved themselves utterly unable or unwilling to extricate the country from the difficulties with which it is surrounded.' A public meeting was appointed to be holden on an open space of ground near the Coldbathfields prison, 'for the purpose of adopting preparatory measures for holding a national convention, as the only means of obtaining and securing the rights of the people;' in other words, for the purpose of overturning the government, and substituting another for it. A proclamation from the home office prohibited the holding of this meeting as illegal and dangerous to the public peace. However, in spite of the proclamation, the meeting assembled at the appointed time. The new police, a force at that time recently established, and very unpopular with the working classes, accustomed only to the mild inefficiency of the old constabulary, were ordered to disperse the meeting, and attempted to do so. They were accused of having acted with unnecessary violence. One of them was stabbed by a dagger and killed, another was severely wounded. The coroner's jury that sat on the body of the murdered policeman returned a verdict of justifiable homicide, which was quashed by the Court of King's Bench, as being utterly unwarranted by the evidence. Nevertheless, such was the spirit of the time, that when the murderer was tried, he was acquitted, in spite of the instructions of the judge and in the face of the clearest proofs of his guilt.

We have already seen that it was announced in the king's speech that the question of the renewal of the charters of the Bank of England and of the East India Company would be brought under the consideration of Parliament in the course of this session. It was perhaps a fortunate circumstance that these two charters expired in the very first year that a reformed House of Commons sat at Westminster. This renewal afforded the government an opportunity not only of reviewing its relations with the Bank and the system on which this institution was conducted, but of revising the whole banking system of the country. After due and careful negotiations with the governors of the Bank, they determined to propose to Parliament a renewal of its charter on the following conditions:

1. That its promissory notes were to be made a legal tender for sums of 5*l*. and upwards.

2. That one fourth part of the debt of 14,000,000*l*. at present due by the public to the Bank should be repaid during the present session of Parliament.

3. That the allowances hitherto made to the Bank for the management of the national debt and other public business should be continued, subject to a deduction of 120,000*l*. a year.

4. That the laws restricting the interest of money to 5*l*. per cent., which were commonly called the 'usury laws,' should be repealed so far as concerned bills not having more than three months to run before they became due.

5. That royal charters should be granted for the establishment of joint-stock banks within a certain distance of London, it being, however, understood that government was at liberty to withhold such charter, if it should in any case deem it advisable to reject the application for it.

6. That all banks should enter into a composition in lieu of stamp duties at present chargeable, at the rate of 7s. for every 100l. issued in notes.

7. That a bill should be introduced into Parliament to regulate country banks, the provisions of which should be such as to encourage joint-stock banking companies in the country to issue the notes of the Bank of England.

This plan, embodied in eight resolutions, was moved on the 1st of June. An effort was made, chiefly by those who wished to abolish the charter altogether, to postpone the consideration of the question till the next session, but was defeated by a large majority. That part of the plan which provided for the establishment of joint-stock banks having been dropped for the present by the government, on account of the great opposition that was likely to be made to it, the other resolutions were carried, and a bill founded on them passed both houses with some changes, the most important of which was that which provided for the quarterly publication of the Bank accounts, so as to enable the public to be acquainted with its exact position at the end of each quarter. This was an innovation of the highest value and importance. It enabled not only the government, but financiers and economists of all classes, both in and out of Parliament, to watch the monetary operations of the country, and thus pave the way for that remodelling of the constitution of the Bank which we shall have occasion to narrate hereafter.

Never perhaps in the history of the world had any government or any legislature been called on to deal with so important a question as that which was involved in the renewal of the East India Company's charter. They were to decide on the future administration of an empire which, including the territory directly or indirectly under the rule of the company, extended over a million and a half of square miles, contained not very far from two hundred millions of inhabitants, and had a seaboard of more than four thousand miles in length, from the mouth

of the Indus to the mouth of the Ganges. The House was
called upon to decide how this vast and rich country was
to be governed and traded with for the next twenty years.
It was a fortunate circumstance that the Reform Bill had
passed, and a reformed Parliament been elected, before the
question of the renewal of the company's charter was
decided; for otherwise the directors of this great company,
and other persons interested in the maintenance of the
monopolies and abuses connected with it, would in all
probability have returned to Parliament, by means of
rotten boroughs, a party of adherents sufficiently large to
have effectually prevented the government and the House
of Commons from dealing with this great question in the
manner in which the interests of England and India alike
demanded that it should be dealt with. A bare examination of the leading changes which were effected will be
sufficient to show how much they were influenced by the
existence of a liberal government and a reformed Parliament. The company enjoyed, under certain restrictions
which had been imposed upon it by previous charters, a
monopoly of the Chinese and Indian trade. At the renewal
of its charter in 1813, it had been required to publish its
commercial accounts separately from its territorial accounts.
This was a most important regulation, for it showed beyond
all doubt that the Indian and Chinese trades could be
carried on better by private merchants than by the monopolist company. It was therefore stripped entirely of its
commercial attributes, and became henceforth a corporation
for ruling British India, under the control of the British
government. Besides this great and beneficial change, the
restrictions on the entrance of Europeans into the country
under the company's authority were swept away. Offices
under the government were thrown open to natives and
foreigners; distinctions based on differences of race, colour,
and religion were abolished. Henceforward India was to
be governed for the Indians, and not for the English only.
As for the results of these great changes, we shall have
occasion to point them out at a future stage of our history.
The measure was received with great favour. It was
strenuously opposed in the upper House by Lord Ellenborough, and in the lower House by Mr. Silk Buckingham,
a gentleman who had been returned for Sheffield, but who,

notwithstanding a commanding presence and a fluent eloquence, enjoyed no influence in the House, and on this occasion found himself without a supporter. This complaisant acceptance of the government measure was due as much to the ignorance or indifference of honourable members with regard to Indian questions as to the intrinsic merits of the bill. But this apathy shows what might have been effected in defence of the abuses of the company by a small and well-organised band of monopolists in the House of Commons. It shows too how far England had moved away from that system by means of which corruption at home sheltered far worse corruption abroad, and under which, in the energetic language of Burke, the 'lawbreakers of India became the lawmakers of England.'

But greatly as these measures redounded to the credit of the Grey ministry, that which they brought forward and carried through for the abolition of slavery in the West Indies did them still higher honour, and shed a lustre on the session in which and the Parliament by which it was triumphantly carried. But the credit belongs above all to the English people, and especially to the English working classes, whose strong feeling on this point made itself felt in a reformed Parliament as it had never been felt before. At almost every election, conspicuous among the banners of the liberal candidates was one which bore the figure of a negro in chains, with this legend underneath, 'Am I not a man and a brother?' And now the time was come when the sincerity of those who had professed themselves on the hustings the friends of the negro, and on this ground had received much enthusiastic support, was to be tested. The honour, however, of taking the initiative in the matter, and of compelling the attention of the legislature to it, belongs not to the government, but to a private member. Mr. Buxton, a dissenter from the established church, a man of strong but unostentatious piety, much respected by all parties, brought this subject before the House, and by the steady earnestness with which he urged it in season and out of season, compelled the government to look the matter in the face, and to deliberate on the propriety of bringing forward a measure for the emancipation of the slaves in our West Indian colonies. Let us do justice to their conduct on this occasion, for it redounds greatly to their honour. There can be no doubt that it would have been an easy matter for them to have deferred the consideration of this difficult and embarrassing question at least to another session. There were many other measures which seemed to be logical and necessary corollaries of the great bill which demanded attention, and which the English people were clamorously pressing on their attention. Nevertheless the government determined without delay to bring in, and if possible carry through, a bill for the abolition of slavery in those parts of the British dominions in which it still continued to exist. To this resolution they were urged by numerous anti-slavery meetings, at which the pledges that had been given were strongly insisted on, and the crime of the continued toleration of slavery vehemently denounced. Accordingly on the 14th of May Mr. Stanley, who, as has already been mentioned, had recently exchanged the office of Irish secretary for that of colonial secretary, explained to a committee of the whole House the measure which the cabinet had determined to submit to the legislature. He proposed, in the name of the government, that slavery should at once cease, but that, in order to prepare the uneducated slave for the entire freedom that it was intended he should ultimately enjoy, and to guard against the excesses into which it was feared he would indulge, if allowed to pass without any interval from slavery to complete liberty, it was proposed that there should be a transition state of apprenticeship, which would gradually prepare him to become a free workman. Accordingly the colonial secretary moved the following resolutions, which embodied his plan:

'1. That it is the opinion of the committee, that immediate and effectual measures be taken for the entire abolition of slavery throughout the colonies, under such provisions for regulating the condition of the negroes as may combine their welfare with the interests of the proprietors.

'2. That it is expedient, that all children born after the passing of any act, or who shall be under the age of six years at the time of passing any act of Parliament for this purpose, be declared free; subject, nevertheless, to such temporary restrictions as may be deemed necessary for their support and maintenance.

'3. That all persons now slaves be entitled to be registered as apprenticed labourers, and to acquire thereby all the rights and privileges of freemen, subject to the restriction of labouring under conditions, and, for a time to be fixed by Parliament, for their present owners.

'4. That to provide against the risk of loss which proprietors in his majesty's colonial possessions might sustain by the abolition of slavery, his majesty be enabled to advance, by way of loan, to be raised from time to time, a sum, not exceeding in the whole 15,000,000*l*., to be repaid in such manner and at such a rate of interest as shall be prescribed by Parliament.

'5. That his majesty be enabled to defray any such expense as he may incur in establishing an efficient stipendiary magistracy in the colonies, and in aiding the local legislatures in providing for the religious and moral education of the negro population to be emancipated.'

The consideration of these resolutions was deferred to the 30th of May.

The first of these resolutions was adopted without any division, but not without much debate, the chief topic of which was the importance of conciliating the West India planters, and inducing them to accept the measure cordially.

The second resolution was also adopted, in spite of a motion, made by Mr. Hume, for the appointment of a committee to inquire into the probable efficiency of free labour, in order that the House might proceed on full and trustworthy information.

But it was on the third resolution, which embodied the system of apprenticeship, that the chief battle was fought; and the opposition to it was led by the most earnest friends of emancipation, headed by Mr. Buxton himself. He began by insisting that this part of the ministerial plan was founded on a fallacy, inasmuch as it was framed on a supposition, which he contended to be erroneous, that the emancipated slaves would not be induced to work by wages. He brought forward a variety of facts, intended to prove that when left to themselves they not only readily worked for wages, but that their labour was much more valuable when they were stimulated to it by the hope of a pecuniary recompense than when they were goaded on to it by compulsion and the fear of punishment. He believed that this part of the ministerial scheme would prove altogether unworkable, and therefore moved the rejection of the resolution which embodied it.

The plan was also condemned by Mr. Halcomb, who moved, as an amendment to the resolution, 'That it is expedient that all persons now slaves, and their children hereafter to be born, be declared free; subject nevertheless to such restrictions as may be deemed necessary for their support and maintenance, and for the future cultivation of the soil.'

Lord Howick also, who had resigned the office of secretary of the colonies on account of the objection he entertained to this part of the ministerial scheme, declared that it would be neither more nor less than an entire subversion of the existing relations of society in the colonies, and the organisation of a system that had never been tried in any age or country. It had not yet been shown in what manner the proposed system of apprenticeship would improve the character of the negroes, so as to render them more fit for the enjoyment of perfect liberty at the expiration of twelve years. His opinion was, that the negroes would be in a worse condition at the termination of the experiment than they were at its commencement.

The other side was taken by the members of government and their supporters, conspicuous among whom was the brilliant Macaulay, the influence of whose genius was vastly increased by the fact that he was the son of Zachary Macaulay, one of the foremost of the noble band of pioneers who, with Wilberforce and Clarkson, had fought the battle of emancipation at a time when the cause was unpopular, and victory far off. They earnestly contended that the step from slavery to apprenticeship was a great forward stride. The duration of the apprenticeship was a matter of comparatively little consequence, provided only that it was interposed as an interval of transition between slavery and perfect liberty. By insisting on this, they recognised the rights of property, conferred freedom from corporal punishment, secured respect for the domestic ties of the negro in his closest and tenderest relations, and a not inconsiderable share of the produce of his labour. The advocates of immediate and complete emancipation had been unable to show that the same amount could be produced in the West Indies by a system of free labour as was actually produced under the present order of things by a system of compulsion.

These arguments so far influenced Mr. Buxton, that he consented to withdraw his amendment, on receiving an assurance that this resolution left open the question of the duration of the apprenticeship; but he proposed to substitute in the place of it another amendment, by inserting words which would have the effect of securing that the labour should be for wages. This amendment he also consented to withdraw; but Mr. O'Connell, his seconder, pressed it to a division, and it was rejected by 324 votes to 40.

To the next resolution, which proposed a loan of 15,000,000*l*. to the planters, as a compensation to them for the loss of their slaves, a strong opposition was offered by the West India interest, as it was termed—the party in Parliament which espoused the cause of the planters; and ministers, fearing a defeat, consented to convert the proposed loan of 15,000,000*l*. into an absolute gift of the enormous amount of 20,000,000*l*.

The remaining resolution passed without any division; and the resolutions having been carried up to the House of Lords, were there adopted without alteration.

A bill based on these resolutions was then brought in, and went quietly through its various stages, with the single important change of a reduction of the term of predial apprenticeship from twelve years to seven, and that of non-predial apprenticeship from seven to five years.

Thus passed this glorious measure, which reflected the greatest honour on the men who for many years had struggled for it, on the government which proposed it, on the Parliament which in a single session adopted it, and on the nation in general, whose generous instincts responded to the appeals made to it, and purchased the liberty of the slave at so enormous a price. There is not perhaps to be found in the whole history of the world a more striking instance of national virtue, than that of a great people, uninfluenced by any meaner motive, compassionating the condition of a subject race in a far distant part of the world, freely and unrepiningly consecrating the enormous sum of twenty millions of money to purchase its freedom; and that too at a moment when they were earnestly pressing on their rulers the duty of retrenchment, and were suffering severely in almost every part of the kingdom.

The result of the passing of this measure, so far at least as the negroes were concerned, was most satisfactory. In the island of Antigua the planters resolved not to take advantage of the apprenticeship clause, but to manumit their slaves immediately and entirely. And it was found that, as the friends of the negro had predicted, the passage from slavery to free labour was effected without difficulty or disturbance. The success of the experiment in Antigua, and experience of the inconveniences of working the apprenticeship system, induced other islands to follow the example thus set to them; and in a short time, slavery, and all the precautionary modifications which were intended to be interposed between it and freedom, had almost entirely disappeared from the British dominions. Nothing could better illustrate the value of the Reform Bill than the fact that one of the very first uses which the people made of the power which that measure conferred on them, was to perform an act of national virtue unparalleled in the history of the world; and nothing tends more to illustrate the great truths of the close connection between every description of progress, and to show how speedily any great political advance that may be made by the people, is sure to be followed by corresponding moral, intellectual, and religious improvement.

While the interests of the negro were thus nobly championed, and his wrongs generously yet prudently redressed, those of the white labourer were not altogether forgotten. The hours of labour in the factories were not regulated by any law, and were excessively long. Not only men, but even women and children, were compelled to toil for twelve hours a day, and sometimes even for longer periods. The consequence was, that the inhabitants of the manufacturing districts of Lancashire and Yorkshire, who had been some of the finest in the kingdom, were becoming a dwarfed, stunted, and deformed race. Recruiting sergeants complained that, though towns and villages had grown up in every direction, they could not find as many men fit to be admitted into the ranks of the army as they could before amongst the sparse population which dwelt amidst the moors, which were now becoming covered with houses,

factories, shops, churches, chapels, schools, and mechanics'
institutes. A strong agitation was carried on for the
shortening of the duration of the hours of labour in
factories. It was strenuously opposed by most of the
employers of labour, under the idea that it was an
improper interference with their operations on the part
of government, and that it would injure, if not destroy,
their business. Political economists, too, victoriously
demonstrated the mischief and impropriety of what the
factory operatives and their friends in and out of Parliament were asking for. But the agitation went forward
nevertheless, and gained ground. Mr. Sadler, the member
for Leeds, had in the year 1832 introduced into Parliament
a measure which embodied the views of those who took the
lead in the agitation. But the House of Commons at that
time was too earnestly occupied with the reform struggle
to be able to pay much attention to his representations;
and the majority of that assembly were prejudiced against
Mr. Sadler, who was known to be a decided anti-reformer;
so the measure, for that session, was thrust aside, and
referred to a committee upstairs. In the election which
took place after the passing of the Reform Bill, Mr. Sadler
was rejected at Leeds, and was not in this Parliament. But
the question fell into good hands—those of Lord Ashley,
better known to this generation as the Earl of Shaftesbury.
When the bill had been read a second time, Lord Althorp
opposed its farther progress, and moved that it should be
referred to a select committee. But the strong government found itself too weak to withstand the feeling that
prevailed in favour of immediate legislation on this great
question. It was decided, by a majority of 164 to 141, that
Lord Ashley's bill should be submitted to a committee of
the whole House.

In another instance the government was more successful.
The bill, as brought in by Lord Ashley, provided that persons under eighteen years of age should not be allowed to
work more than ten hours a day. The government succeeded in substituting a provision limiting the labour of
persons under fourteen years of age to eight hours a day.
Thereupon Lord Ashley gave up the bill into the hands of
Lord Althorp, by whom it was carried through. It enacted
that persons under eighteen years of age should not be

required to work more than sixty-nine hours in the week and provided for the appointment of inspectors of factories whose duty it would be to see that the provisions of the bill were duly carried out. This was a most valuable feature in the measure, as the reports made in accordance with it supplied the legislature with the information which enabled it at a subsequent period to deal with the factory question in a more vigorous and satisfactory manner. We must not omit to mention that the act also contained provision for the education of the children who were not to be employed more than eight hours a day, and thus paved the way for the introduction of that half-time system which has since been inaugurated with such happy results. Parliament dealt with the question now for the first time, cautiously and imperfectly; but it dealt with it quite as strongly as the information it then possessed warranted it in doing. It has been often and truly said, that men cannot be made virtuous or religious by act of Parliament; but it is equally true that acts of Parliament may remove the impediments which prevent men from carrying into effect the dictates of virtue and religion. This we think the Reform Bill pre-eminently did; and we cannot regard it as a mere accident, but as a natural sequence of cause and effect, that the very first session that followed the passing of the Reform Bill witnessed the abolition of slavery, and the first step in the shortening of the hours of labour in factories. That these two measures were equal in importance we do not pretend to affirm; but we point to them as being both fruits of the same spirit of Christian benevolence, which certainly never before had a freer course, or had exhibited the power of religion and morality on so grand a scale.

But while engaged with these acts of humanity and benevolence, Parliament was not allowed to forget the humbler duty of endeavouring to carry forward those improvements in the constitution of which the great measure of last session was expected by the people to be only the commencement. It was soon found that the Reform Bill in removing one evil had aggravated another. It had put a stop to the sale of boroughs; it had not by any means put an end to the sale of votes. On the contrary, it soon appeared that the increase of the number of voters had been followed by an increase of bribery, corruption, and intimidation. Perhaps never before or since had these malpractices been carried to a greater extent than they were during the general election that had recently taken place. Certainly they had never before been so effectually dragged to light. The conservatives, especially strong in the amount of their wealth and property, and frantic with the dread of impending revolution, endeavoured to stem the torrent of democracy, which, as they imagined, was about to sweep away all that was holy and venerable and morally beautiful in the land. With this view they exerted all the influence which their wealth and position gave them in order to return men representing their opinions to the new Parliament. The other party had less ability and less need to resort to such means; nevertheless they, too, had recourse to them when they found that they could not succeed without them. The House of Commons, at the very commencement of the session, was besieged with petitions complaining of improper practices which had been employed at elections, and calling on the House to endeavour to put a stop to them for the future. It was shown that at Liverpool, at Warwick, at Stafford, at Londonderry, and at many other places, bribery, corruption, and intimidation had been carried to quite scandalous lengths, and it was felt that this was a reproach to the reformed Parliament which ought to be wiped away.

The remedy for these evils which most naturally suggested itself was the ballot; and before the introduction of the Reform Bill it had been strongly pressed on the government by the radical party. As we have already seen, some disappointment was expressed by the members of that party when it was found that the Reform Bill did not contain any provision for the introduction into it of their favourite remedy for corruption; and Lord J. Russell, in his opening speech, explained that the government had not thought it expedient to embody a ballot clause in the bill, on the obvious ground that it was desirable that the two questions should be kept distinct, and that each should stand on its own merits. The radical party had acquiesced in the propriety of this separation of the two questions, and had joined cordially in the national chorus which demanded the bill, the whole bill, and *nothing but* the bill. But they had done so with the expectation that the ministers would take up the question of secret voting as a preventive of bribery and other corrupt practices, and, that the passing of the Reform Bill would soon be followed by the passing of a ballot bill. Finding, however, that government did not intend to introduce a measure on this subject, Mr. Grote, one of the members of the city of London, and the author of a well-known History of Greece, brought in a bill for the substitution of secret for open voting in all parliamentary elections. Lord Althorp, who had formerly voted for the ballot, opposed Mr. Grote's motion, on the ground that the Reform Bill had rendered it unnecessary, and that the malpractices complained of were not sufficiently numerous to render such a change desirable. Sir R. Peel insisted that the ballot would make the House of Commons more democratic, and in his opinion it was too democratic already; besides, he urged that they should wait and see how the Reform Bill worked before they introduced farther organic changes. As for the arguments in favour of the change, this generation has been so familiarised with them in repeated annual debates on the subject, that it is not necessary to introduce them here; but it may at least interest the reader to know, that on the first introduction of the question in the first session of the reformed Parliament, the proposal was rejected by 211 votes, against 106 in favour of Mr. Grote's motion. This result was, no doubt, due to the opposition of the government, and also to an honest desire on the part of many sincere reformers to give the Reform Bill a full and fair trial before taking any farther steps in advance.

Another change, which a large and influential portion of the party that supported ministers hoped to see speedily adopted, was a shortening of the duration of parliaments, for the purpose of giving constituents a more complete control over their representatives. This measure, like the ballot, for some time formed the subject of annual motions, though it has not been pressed with the same persistency. Mr. Tennyson, the representative of the metropolitan borough of Lambeth, a man of high character, easy elocution, and great knowledge of parliamentary laws and customs, brought it forward on this occasion and in some following sessions. The advocates of this change were greatly divided among themselves in their opinions on the subject. The more extreme members of the radical party desired annual parliaments; others were in favour of triennial; and others again of quadrennial or quinquennial parliaments. To unite as far as possible all who desired a shortening of the duration of parliaments, Mr. Tennyson on the 24th of July moved for leave to bring in a bill to revive the Triennial Act; a proposal which had the double recommendation of being a middle term between the different opinions of his supporters, and of being a return to a practice which had already existed, and which had been set aside in a not very regular manner, on grounds of temporary expediency. The conservative party left ministers to fight their own battles against a large section of their own supporters. They would no doubt not have been sorry to see ministers defeated on this question, knowing that the measure was not likely to be carried through the lower House, and that, even if carried, it was sure to be rejected by the House of Lords. The government objected to Mr. Tennyson's motion on various grounds. It was brought forward at too late a period in the session; it would prevent the great experiment of reform from having a fair trial; it was not as much needed now as it had been before the House of Commons was reformed; it was calculated to impair the power of the crown, which required to be maintained and supported; it rendered members too dependent on the caprices of their constituents, and government too much exposed to the influence of the temporary and fluctuating passions of the people, as distinguished from their settled and fixed opinions. For these reasons they resisted Mr. Tennyson's motion, which was accordingly rejected, though the majority against it was only 49.

Thus the Reform Bill escaped for the present those large and important modifications which most of its opponents had feared would speedily follow its adoption, and which many of its supporters deemed to be absolutely necessary to the completion of their triumph. It was clear that this Parliament was determined that it should be left untouched in all its main features, and should have a full trial. They were not, however, unwilling to make such improvements in its minor details as the experience of its working at the last election had suggested, and which were recommended by its authors as evident improvements of their measure. Thus the following resolution was adopted:

'That in all cases where a select committee appointed to try the merits of an election for any county, city, or borough report to this House that they have altered the poll, by adding or striking out the names of any voter on such poll, Mr. Speaker shall issue his directions thereupon to the clerk or other officer, as the case may be, with whom the register of such county, city, or borough is deposited, to alter and amend such register, by striking out the names of such voters as have been struck off the poll, and by adding such names as have been added to the poll by such select committee.' Some other alterations proposed to be made in the Reform Bill, but which were opposed by the government, were rejected.

We must not here omit to mention, as indicating the spirit of this Parliament, that a bill for relieving the Jews from their civil disabilities was introduced by Mr. Grant, and passed through the House of Commons, but was rejected by the Lords.

The session was prolonged to the 29th of August, when it was brought to a close by the king in person. His speech announced the appointment of two commissions; one for digesting into one body the enactments of the criminal law, the other for investigating the state of municipal corporations throughout the United Kingdom. It also announced the complete success of the measure which had been enacted for the control and punishment of the disturbers of the public peace in Ireland. The powers which that measure conferred had only been exerted to a very limited extent, and it was hoped that they would soon cease to be necessary.

This terminated a session which, if it did not altogether remove the apprehensions of the anti-reformers, at all events completely disappointed the predictions of speedy ruin and revolution in which they had indulged, and in the truth of which they had sincerely believed. If the reformed Parliament had not accomplished all that the more sanguine reformers hoped for, it had adopted many great and important measures. It was accused indeed of violence and vulgarity; but, judged by what it did and what it ob-

stained from doing, it certainly deserves a very different
character. Never had any Parliament effected greater
things or displayed more prudence and moderation. Ireland tranquillised; West-Indian slavery abolished; the
charters of the Bank and of the East India Company
renewed and greatly improved; a factory bill passed; the
Reform Bill retained in its integrity, and farther organic
changes in the same direction for the present declined;
bribery and corruption discouraged; some important law
reforms carried; the first step taken towards the establishment of a national system of education by an educational
grant of 20,000*l.*;—such are the chief features that distinguish the first session of the first reformed Parliament.
They entitle it to our gratitude and respect; and they
show that in a country where institutions rest on such
solid foundations as those of England, progress however
rapid, and innovation however bold, is not attended with
any danger to their stability. The government had now
passed the zenith of its popularity. In the nature of things,
the enthusiasm which had been felt for it during the reform
struggle could not be sustained. It must be followed by
lassitude, disappointment, and reaction. The expectations
that had been raised could not be fulfilled, and their frustration was sure to be attended with discontent and mur-
murings. Reasonable men acquiesced in the propriety of
not hurrying on too fast after so great a change, and were
content to wait patiently for a few years for the other
changes they thought to be still desirable. But the great
mass is not reasonable. They had expected more from the
Reform Bill than any measure whatever could have produced, and blamed the ministry for not working miracles
and performing impossibilities. The exemplary patience
and diligence of this Parliament was not the least of its
merits. The session of 1831, with all its long duration,
obstructive delays, and endless speeches against time, gave
918 hours to its work, which was far more than had been
given to it by any previous Parliament; but in the session
of 1833 no fewer than 1270 hours were devoted by the
House of Commons to its legislative duties.

We must not omit to record the death of William Wilberforce. He lived long enough to hear that the bill for the
abolition of slavery in the British colonies, the measure to

DEATH OF MR. WILBERFORCE.

which he had devoted the greater part of his life, had been read a second time in the House of Commons, and that its success might now be regarded as morally certain. He died three days after that event, and consequently before the abolition bill had become law. Of all the advocates of the measure, he was the most eloquent, the most persevering, and the most distinguished; and this is much to say when we remember that such men as Clarkson, Zachary Macaulay, Brougham, and Buxton were associated with him. He had been the intimate friend and associate of Pitt, Fox, Dean Milner, and all the foremost men of his time; and there can be no doubt, that if he had given himself to politics, he would have attained to the highest offices of the State. But he relinquished these prospects in order to devote himself to the cause of humanity and religion;—to the discharge of those duties which according to his views Christianity required from men who occupied the position and enjoyed the opportunities of doing good which God's providence had assigned to him; and so he employed an extraordinary eloquence, set off by a voice of marvellous power and sweetness, to advocate and defend the cause of the oppressed, the suffering, and the helpless, and that too at a time when such championship involved the loss of popularity and influence. In the year 1780, being then only twenty-one years of age, he was elected member for his native town. In 1784 he was chosen for Yorkshire. He continued to represent that great county in six successive Parliaments, till 1812. He then became member for the small borough of Bramber, which he represented in three Parliaments; and finally retired from the House of Commons in the year 1825, having sat in that assembly for forty-five years. During the whole of that time he exerted all the influence which his position and brilliant talents gave him to plead with greater effect in favour of those measures of justice and humanity to the advocacy of which he had determined to devote his life. He was indeed of the straitest sect of our religion; but he softened the moroseness of his creed by the geniality and cheerfulness of his disposition. He died on the 26th of July, in the 74th year of his age. He had expressed a wish that his funeral might be as private as possible. But the general respect and affection with which he was regarded caused this wish to be overruled, and he

was buried in Westminster Abbey, close to the tombs of
Pitt, Fox, and Canning. Around his open grave stood
the royal dukes of Sussex and Gloucester, the venerable
Archbishop Howley, the Duke of Wellington, Lord Chancellor Brougham, who for many years had been associated
with him in his advocacy of the cause of negro emancipation, the Marquis of Westminster, and a large number of
members of Parliament, as well as many of those who had
sustained with him the burden and heat of that glorious
struggle for human freedom in which he had for so many
years been the foremost fighter. Such a tribute of respect
to one who had cast from him the ordinary objects of
ambition, that he might devote himself to the pursuits of
beneficence, was a glorious testimony to the worth of the
services he had rendered, and of the man by whom they
had been performed. But one that was still more glorious,
and which would have been far more in accordance with his
own feelings and wishes, was the final adoption of the bill
for the abolition of slavery in the only part of the British
dominions in which it yet existed, in the manner in which
he would have wished it to be adopted. He lived not indeed
to see this fondest wish of his heart actually accomplished,
but he did live to see the triumph secured, and to know the
full extent of it.

We must interrupt here our political narrative, to take
notice of some events which were occurring in the scientific
and the religious world. The first that strikes our attention
when we so pause—the first, at least, in order of time—
is the commencement of the British Association for the
Advancement of Science, in the year 1831. The idea which
this society embodied was not of English growth; it
originated in Germany, where an association of somewhat
similar character, long and strenuously recommended by
the learned Professor Oken, held its first meeting in the
city of Leipsic in the year 1822. This first meeting was
not a very brilliant success so far as numbers went; it was
attended by only about twenty citizens of Leipsic itself, and
twelve strangers. But this was perhaps a fortunate circumstance; for a large concourse probably would have excited
the jealousy of the German governments of that day, and
have caused the speedy suppression of the association. But
what government could be alarmed by an association that

only mustered thirty-two members? In 1823 the association met at Halle, in 1824 at Wurzburg, in 1825 at Frankfort, in 1826 at Dresden, in 1827 at Munich. By this time it had established a reputation; and so it was recognised and welcomed by Louis Maximilian, King of Bavaria, who treated the congress with marked honour, appointing Oken, its founder, to the professorship of physiology in the university of Munich. This royal patronage gave a great impulse to the career of the association; and when the congress of 1828 was held at Berlin, the illustrious Humboldt was appointed president of the year. The King of Prussia, the heir-apparent, the other princes of the blood royal, the foreign ambassadors, and a large number of the Prussian nobility, were present at an entertainment to which the president invited the savants who attended this scientific congress. Yet the number of members was only 464. Of course the constitution and proceedings of this German association became known in England, and seemed to present an opportunity of carrying out thoughts and ideas which were occupying the minds of some of our most eminent scientific men. Sir Humphry Davy, Sir John Herschel, Mr. Babbage, and Sir David Brewster were loudly complaining that science was on the decline, and were appealing to the government and to the public to arrest its downward course. Sir David Brewster in particular asserted that 'the sciences and the arts of England are in a wretched state of depression, and that their decline is mainly owing to the ignorance and supineness of the government; to the injudicious organisation of our scientific boards and institutions; to the indirect persecution of scientific and literary men by their exclusion from all the honours of the state; and to the unjust and oppressive tribute which the patent law exacts from inventors.' The remedy which he proposed for the state of things thus described was one evidently suggested by the proceedings of the German association, of whose history we have just given a brief outline. 'An association,' said he, 'of our nobility, clergy, gentry, and philosophers, can alone draw the attention of the sovereign and the nation to this blot upon its fame.'

Accordingly, in the year 1830, only two months after, Sir David proposed that a great scientific reunion should be held at York. That ancient city was chosen because it seemed to be the most central and convenient point for the assemblage of the men of science of the three kingdoms, and because it could boast an active philosophical society, whose rooms would be available for the meetings of the association, and whose members would undertake the labour of making the necessary arrangements. The first meeting was at York on the 29th of September, 1831, and its members were carrying on their calm and abstract discussions just at the time when the newspapers and the mass of the English people were passionately asking, in reference to the great bill, What will the Lords do? The number of members of the association who came together at this its first meeting, was under two hundred. Perhaps the smallness of the number was in some degree owing to the excitement and anxiety which still prevailed with regard to the fate of the Reform Bill. But small as it was, whether we regard the interest and importance of the object which brought them together, or whether we look at the attendance at subsequent meetings of the association, it was large when compared with the number present at the first meeting of the German association. However, this smallness in the number of those who attended the York congress was to some extent compensated by the scientific eminence of many of those who took part in its proceedings; among whom we may enumerate Dalton, Brisbane, Greenhough, Lloyd, Pritchard, Howard, Pearson, Murchison, Smith, Robinson, Harcourt, and Scoresby.

In 1832 the association held its second meeting at Oxford, on the 18th of June; and though Parliament at this time was still sitting, though the excitement which attended the reform struggle had not yet subsided, about seven hundred members attended. In the year 1833 the third meeting, held at Cambridge on the 18th of June, and consequently during the parliamentary session, was attended by upwards of nine hundred members. And we will so far anticipate the course of time as to add, that the meeting of 1834, held at Edinburgh on the 8th of September, was attended by twelve hundred and sixty-eight members. So rapid and so steady was the progress made by the association during these first years of its existence.

If it should be asked, what were the objects of this congress, the answer is, to give a new impetus to the pursuit of science, to convert scientific decline into scientific progress. The means by which it was proposed to effect this object were thus indicated by Mr. Harcourt: 'To point out the lines of direction in which the researches of science should move; to indicate the particulars that most immediately demand investigation; to state problems to be solved, and data to be fixed, and to assign to every class of mind a definite task.' There were besides two other objects which the originators of the association put forward; but as these were soon laid aside, we need do no more than specify them here. They were to amend the laws relating to patents, and to agitate for a government provision to encourage and reward scientific research.

There can be no doubt that there was much quackery in connection with the meetings of the association; a great deal of self-advertising; that fluent and presumptuous mediocrity often thrust aside modest genius and patient research; but after all deductions on these accounts—and very large ones should be made for them—there still remains a great residuum of good resulting from these meetings. They made science popular; they inspired men, and especially young men, with the ambition of distinguishing themselves in the walks of science, as they had before had the ambition of distinguishing themselves in the walks of politics, literature, and war; they collected the results of the investigations made in different parts of the kingdom, and substituted in many instances organised and concerted inquiries for investigations that were vague, desultory, unsystematic, and isolated. Like everything else human, the association has its good and its bad side, and has been made the subject of glowing encomium or of cutting ridicule, according to the disposition of its critics or the standpoint from which they regarded it.

In later years it has, as we all know, attained to large and important dimensions, and undertaken many useful scientific inquiries, which have been attended by a very large increase of human knowledge. It has not only made known new facts, but it has also proclaimed new ideas; a point which many older societies calling themselves 'philosophical' have very much neglected.

While this important movement was going forward in the scientific world, the ecclesiastical world was being still more deeply stirred. We have already seen how unpopular the clergy had become, owing to the part they had taken in the reform struggle. This feeling of hostility found vent in a loud outcry for church reform, which was taken up partly by friends of the church, who hoped by the reformation of its abuses to recover for it some portion of its former popularity; but still more by avowed or secret enemies, who regarded the reform of the church as a first step towards its destruction. Innumerable pamphlets issued from the press during the years 1831, 1832, 1833, of which we need only notice a few that attracted considerable attention, either by their own merits or the station and character of their authors. In the beginning of February, 1831, appeared the *Church Reformer's Magazine*, edited by William Eagle, Esq., barrister-at-law. In the course of the same month there appeared a letter from R. M. Beverley, Esq., addressed to the archbishop of York, and proposing a complete separation of church and state with a confiscation of church property: this pamphlet, distinguished by the violence of its language, obtained a circulation far beyond its merits. Strongly contrasting with it in all respects was the letter of Dr. Burton, Professor of Divinity in the University of Oxford, who sought simply to restrain pluralities, and provide by the taxation of livings of the value of more than 200*l.* per annum a fund for the augmentation of poorer benefices. On the 22nd of August, 1832, Lord Henley, an Irish peer, published an elaborate pamphlet on the subject of church reform, in which he proposed the abolition of all sinecures, pluralities, non-residence; of all titles not scriptural, such as deans, prebendaries, rectors, vicars, &c.; and to have only two classes of clergy, bishops and ministers; the bishops to be removed from the House of Lords, convocation to be restored, and the authority of the episcopate to be greatly diminished. He also proposed to make the services of the church more congregational, and to 'take away all such reliques of Popery as chanting, and all anthems, solos, duets, voluntaries, &c.' In January, 1833, Dr. Arnold, the celebrated head master of Rugby, published his 'principles of church reform' in a pamphlet replete with counsels of wisdom, but at the same time displaying a strange ignorance of the state of public feeling on this subject. His scheme was an attempt at the comprehension of all Christians within the pale of a great national church. He proposed to retain episcopacy, and to leave the bishops in undisturbed possession of their seats in the House of Lords. All ministers of religion to be episcopally ordained, all services to be performed in the parish church, where the liturgy of the church was to be celebrated in the morning, and services with extempore prayers and adapted to the views of dissenters at other parts of the day. Of course the utmost latitude of belief would be allowed to exist in the church reformed according to these notions. Dr. Arnold thought that by this means the church might be made to comprehend all dissenters except a few Quakers and Roman Catholics; and that when this was done all conscientious objection to the payment of tithes, church-rates, &c., would be removed. These proposals, which might perhaps have found favour in an ecclesiastical millennium, were scouted both by churchmen and dissenters at a time when the spirit of religious party raged with a violence and bitterness rarely if ever equalled. This bold avowal of what were then called, in opprobrium, the principles of religious liberalism, caused great alarm both in high and low church circles, and had no small share in the production of an ecclesiastical phenomenon which gave an altogether new form to the struggle between the new and old ideas, brought about an altogether new division of parties in the church, and was the commencement of a great religious movement, of which the end is not yet. I allude to the appearance of the Tracts for the Times, or as they were more commonly called, from the place of their publication, the Oxford Tracts. The history of their origin is very important, as illustrative of the solidarity which exists between every kind of progress, whether political, social, intellectual, moral, or religious. It is a significant fact, that the tracts began to appear within less than a year after the passing of the Reform Bill, and within a few short months from the suppression of two archbishoprics and eight bishoprics in Ireland. Nor was this an accidental coincidence. Any one who reads the memorials of Richard Hurrel Froude, the *Apologia* of J. H. Newman, or the other literature of tractarianism, cannot avoid seeing how closely the publication of the tracts was connected with the political events which occurred within the two or three years that preceded their appearance. But in order that we may fully comprehend the connection that existed between the two classes of events, we must briefly consider the changes which had gradually taken place in the relations between the English church and the state.

The men who in the reign of Anne and of the two first Georges met every attempt to extend the principles of religious liberty with the cry of 'The church is in danger' meant exactly what they said. The idea of a church existing in separation from the state, or without the assistance of tithes and endowments, or even with a considerable curtailment of these aids, did not enter into the calculations either of those who raised the cry or their opponents. The two distinct ideas of a confiscation of the revenues of the church and the cessation of her existence were confounded in men's minds. We do not mean to say that if their attention had been drawn to the subject, they would not have recognised the distinction; but attention was not drawn to it, and so the distinct ideas which in our time are represented by the three words, disestablishment, disendowment, and destruction, were in their minds confounded. Hence they regarded every advantage gained by dissenters and Roman Catholics as a step towards the destruction of the church. But they viewed with more especial alarm every proposal for their admission into the legislature, one of whose chief functions they considered to be the representation of the lay element of the church, as convocation, though in abeyance, was the representation of its clerical element. And this feeling maintained its ground through all subsequent struggles. It animated the resistance to the repeal of the test and corporation acts, and the proposal for Catholic emancipation. Hence, too, the clergy and the warm supporters of the church were never weary of extolling the church as by *law established*, and insisting on that legal establishment as constituting its chief claim to the respect and attention of the people. But the long suspension and final repeal of the test and corporation acts, the adoption of Catholic emancipation, the admission of Quakers, and the proposed admission of Jews into the House of Commons, the hostility against the church, which had been engendered by the events that preceded and attended the reform struggle, spread alarm and terror through the ranks of the zealous churchmen, and made them anxiously ask, what would become of them and their church if the support of the law should be withdrawn from it, and what course they should take if the church should come to be by law *dis*established. Nor was the composition of the first reformed House of Commons at all calculated to reassure their minds or to allay their fears. There could be no doubt that the great majority of that assembly was perfectly prepared to welcome and to carry any measure against the church that might have been brought forward by the government, and that in the temper in which men's minds then were, the nation would have received such a proposal with an enthusiasm little if at all inferior to that which had been excited by the introduction of the Reform Bill. It is true that the government, so far from being disposed to make any attack on the temporalities of the church, was composed of men the majority of whom were anxious to preserve to it all the possessions and privileges it then enjoyed, and even to increase its influence by such just and moderate reforms as were demanded by public opinion, and calculated to disarm most of the hostility with which it was popularly regarded. But these favourable dispositions of the government were unknown to the generality of the clergy, who looked upon them as enemies, and imagined an intention to injure where there really was a sincere desire to befriend. On the other hand ministers were irritated by the suspicions and the opposition of the clergy, and some of them showed their sense of it by language and acts on which the panic-stricken churchmen put the worst construction, and from which they drew the direst omens for the future. It was feared, too, that the men now in power would soon be displaced by men who openly avowed that they were prepared to go all lengths against the church. Its downfall had been predicted by the anti-reformers as an event sure to follow the passing of the Reform Bill, and it was thought that the prediction was about to be accomplished, both by those who desired and those who dreaded its fulfilment.

The English church was at this time divided into the high church and low church, or, as they then preferred to be styled, the orthodox and evangelical parties. The former was vastly superior in numbers among the clergy, the latter in zeal and acceptance with the people. The former could claim almost all the bishops and men holding the higher preferments in the church, and most of the country churches; the latter had churches in most of the large towns, which were generally crowded with congregations drawn from other parishes as well as their own. The former were scrupulous observers of the rubrics and canons of the church; the latter were often careless even to slovenliness in their performance of the service, the only part of which they seemed to regard as important was the extemporaneous sermon, often an hour or an hour and a half long. But they most delighted in prayer-meetings, at which they could cast off altogether the fetters which the law of the church imposed, and preface the long extemporaneous sermon by a long extemporaneous prayer. Both these parties vied with each other in their hostility to the Roman Catholic church, and in the violence with which they resisted the Catholic Emancipation Bill. But the orthodox party based their opposition on civil and political grounds. They declaimed against the obedience which the papists gave to an extra-national head, as being inconsistent with their allegiance to the crown; against the celibacy of the clergy; against the evils and dangers of the confessional; the persecuting spirit of Romanism; the denial of the cup to the laity, and the hatred with which the Romish church was supposed to regard the civil and religious liberties of the nation. The evangelicals, on the other hand, denounced the Pope as the Antichrist of the Thessalonians, the scarlet whore of the Book of Revelations; the church of Rome was to them the mother of abominations; they loudly declared that any alliance with her was a compact with idolatry, and would bring down on the nation that entered into it the just judgments of God. They were incessant in their attacks on her, and their exposures of her alleged abuses. Such was the state of parties in the church at the moment when the reform struggle took place, which by itself, and the consequences it drew after it, impressed a new direction on men's minds, and gave birth to the party of whose views the Tracts for the Times were the exponents.

From the time of the Reformation, if not even before it, all great church movements have had their source in the University of Oxford; but none perhaps so visibly and exclusively as the tractarian movement, as it was speedily called. It was commenced by a small knot of young men, most of them under thirty years of age. The two most energetic and original minds among them were Richard Hurrel Froude and John Henry Newman. Froude died at the early age of thirty-three of a pulmonary complaint, but lived long enough to witness the commencement of the tracts, and to rejoice in their unexpected success. Newman was the prime mover and real leader of the movement, and one who, not only by his writings, but by his sermons, his conversation, and above all by the influence of his pure motives and lofty intelligence, nurtured and carried it forward. With them soon came to be associated two kindred spirits, less energetic indeed, but not less firm or less earnest—Dr. Pusey, the learned young Regius professor of Hebrew, and Keble, the sweet singer of the Church of England, whose *Christian Year* will live as long as that church endures. With these were associated other men of less mark and note, of whom William Palmer and Arthur Perceval were the chief. They were connected with the higher authorities of the church and a large body of the most influential of the clergy by Hugh Rose, chaplain to the archbishop of Canterbury, and regarded as the first theological and German scholar of his day. Purer, holier, and more unselfish men than those who composed this little band never lived. Amidst all the violent attacks of which they have been the subjects, none has ever questioned the purity of their motives or the excellence of their characters. They were all, without exception, men of the highest principle and of the most spotless lives. They were also, without any exception, thoroughly loyal to the church of which they were the brightest ornaments. And it was on account of the strong faith in her that they were led to make the exertions they did to defend and strengthen her. They saw that she was in danger from without, but still more from within. They saw that the advocates of what they called 'religious liberalism' were gaining ground in her, and were, as they thought, still more to be dreaded than the open enemy that assailed her from without. Against both of these foes they came forward to defend her with a generous and unselfish devotion. It is true indeed that the position which they took up was suggested by the impending attacks on the temporalities of the church, and more especially by the proposal to appropriate to secular purposes a portion of the revenues of the Irish establishment; but they thought more about the increase of her usefulness than the preservation of her revenues, and they wanted not only to defend but to transform her. They looked at the history of Christianity in its earliest days, and as they read, they asked themselves, Why is the church, once so full of vigorous life and power, so weak and powerless now? And the answer they gave to that question was, 'She is weak because she is cowardly; because she is afraid to proclaim the principles on which her power is based, and the consequence is, that her power has departed from her. The true remedy for her present weakness, the true salvation in her present dangers, the true means of resisting the assaults that are being made on her, is courageously to proclaim her divine mission, to make men see and know that she is no "act of parliament church," no mere creature of the Reformation, but that she is a free and apostolic branch of that Catholic church for which we pray in our liturgy, and which we uphold in our creeds.'

Such were the general objects of the young men who commenced this movement. The particular doctrines by which they hoped to effect their aims are very clearly exhibited in the following passages from the first tract, bearing the date of September 9th, 1833.

'I am but one of yourselves, a presbyter; and therefore I conceal my name, lest I should take too much on myself by speaking in my own person. Yet speak I must; for the times are very evil, yet no one speaks against them.

'Is not this so? Do not we "look on one another," yet perform nothing? Do we not all confess the peril into which the church has come, yet sit still, each in his own retirement, as if mountains and seas cut off brother from brother? Therefore suffer me, while I try to draw you forth from those pleasant retreats which it has been our blessedness hitherto to enjoy, to contemplate the position and prospects of our holy mother in a practical way; so that one and all may unlearn that idle habit which has grown upon us of owning the state of things to be bad, yet doing nothing to remedy it.

'Now then let me come at once to the subject which leads me to address you. Should the government of the country so far forget their God as to cut off the church, to deprive it of its temporal honours and substance, *on what* will you rest the claims to respect and attention which you make upon your flocks? Hitherto you have been upheld by your birth, your education, your wealth, your connection; should these secular advantages cease, on what must Christ's ministers depend? Is not this a serious practical question? We know how miserable is the state of religious bodies not supported by the state. Look at the dissenters on all sides of you, and you will see at once that their ministers, depending simply upon the people, become the *creatures* of the people. Are you content that this should be your case? Alas, can a greater evil befall Christians than for their teachers to be guided by them, instead of guiding? How can we "hold fast the form of sound words," and "keep that which is committed to our trust," if our influence is to depend simply on our popularity? Is it not our very office to *oppose* the world? Can we then allow ourselves to court it? to preach smooth things and prophesy deceits? to make the way of life easy to the rich and indolent, and to bribe the humbler classes by excitements and strong intoxicating doctrines? Surely it must not be so; and the question recurs, on what are we to rest our authority when the state deserts us?'

The answer that this writer of the tract gives to his own question is as follows:

'There are some who rest their divine mission on their own unsupported assertion; others who rest it upon their popularity; others on their success; and others who rest it upon their temporal distinctions. This last case has been perhaps too much our own; I fear we have neglected the true ground on which our authority is built—our APOSTOLICAL DESCENT. We have been born not of blood, nor of the will of the flesh, nor of the will of men, but of God. The Lord Jesus Christ gave His Spirit to His Apostles; they in turn laid their hands on those who should succeed them; and those again on others; and so the sacred gift has been handed down to our present bishops, who have appointed us as their assistants, and, in some sense, representatives.'

The author of this tract further affirms, that every one

of the clergy is bound to believe this—does in fact believe it, though the belief may not be sufficiently impressed on his mind; and in proof of his assertion he quotes the words which the form for the ordination of priests appointed by the church puts into the mouth of the bishop:

'Receive the Holy Ghost, for the office and work of a priest in the church of God, now committed to thee by the imposition of our hands. Whose sins thou dost forgive, they are forgiven; and whose sins thou dost retain, they are retained. And be thou a faithful dispenser of the word of God and of His Sacraments, &c., &c.'

These passages present very distinctly the scope and objects of the tracts, and the motives which led their authors to undertake them. They wanted to show that the church was a body distinct from the state; and capable of existing without its patronage and support. They did not indeed aim at obtaining disestablishment, for they thought that there were advantages in the union of the church with the state; but they did not regard a separation from the state, and even a partial or entire confiscation of her revenues, with the panic alarm with which the old high churchmen and evangelicals looked forward to such an event. Among themselves they spoke more freely and hopefully of such an occurrence than they thought it safe to do in public and among their followers. The saying of a northern divine, in intimate and frequent communication with the leaders of the body at Oxford, was frequently quoted— 'Give us our own, and let us go.' They hoped to see her under the divinely ordained government of bishops, priests, and deacons, not merely preaching the gospel and administering the sacraments, but taking a high and independent stand, and exercising a profound influence on the religion and morality of the nation. They hoped to see her, by example and precept, encouraging virtue and denouncing vice, the leader of the education of the people and of all good works in the land, proclaiming truth and denouncing heresy; being once again, in fact, what the Christian church was in the first ages of her existence.

Such was their dream. It was the dream of noble and generous minds; but it was by no means a new idea. It was an idea which manifested itself very early in the history of Christianity; it was the idea with which the Roman church started, and which she has never entirely lost sight of; it was an idea which many of our reformers had entertained; it was an idea which Laud and those who acted with him had tried to realize; it was an idea which was kept up by some of his school after the Restoration; it was the idea on which the non-jurors were thrown back when they, with some of their bishops, withdrew from the church; it was an idea which continued to haunt the minds of the clergy, and now and then to make its appearance in their discourses, up to the end of the reign of William III.; but from that period it had fallen into almost complete oblivion. It was indeed familiar to the clergy, not only of the orthodox, but of the evangelical schools, who were acquainted with the writings of the old divines of their church; but it was a sort of esoteric doctrine about which they were discreetly silent, or at which they just timidly hinted in their discourses. Mr. Newman himself tells us that after he had been some years at Oxford he was 'taught the doctrine of apostolical succession' by a friend as he walked with him once in the college gardens; and he remembers to have heard it with impatience. However, though this teaching seems to have made at first a slight, if not an unfavourable impression on his mind, he afterwards proved to be an apt scholar. Dr. Blomfield, the bishop of London, a man who subsequently showed considerable sympathy with the tractarians, greatly offended them at first by contemptuously remarking, that apostolical succession was a notion that had gone out with the non-jurors.

But gone out or not, it was now to be brought back again; and not only brought back, but avowed, proclaimed, and insisted on with a boldness and distinctness that had never been displayed in its proclamation at any former period. Passages were diligently culled from the early fathers and from theological writers of all ages, in which the doctrine had been more or less expressly asserted, and these were formed into catenas, which made a considerable impression on the readers of the tracts; lists of bishops were also given from the earliest times to the present day, intended to show that the asserted succession from the time of the apostles was at least an actual and ascertained fact.

The sudden apparition of such views, thus nakedly, boldly, I may almost say offensively, put forward and pressed to their logical results with an unsparing hardihood, produced an effect which their authors in their most sanguine moods could hardly have anticipated. By a very large number of the younger clergy and by many students of both universities these views were embraced with all the generous ardour that belonged to their age. Among the elder clergy there were not a few who accepted opinions for which their previous studies had prepared them. The primate was not unfavourable to them. The bishop of London, as we have already had occasion to mention, sympathised with them to a certain extent, though he had offended them by his sneer at their favourite doctrine of apostolical succession. Their own diocesan, the bishop of Oxford, was very well disposed towards them. Other bishops and church dignitaries were at first inclined to countenance and support them, under the belief that they were strengthening the church against the life-and-death struggle that was evidently awaiting her; though not a little alarmed at the audacious and almost reckless disregard of public opinion which they displayed. Their doctrines seemed to combine the charm of novelty with the authority of antiquity. They had fallen into such complete neglect and oblivion, and yet they found so much support in the language and formularies of the church, and particularly in her ordination services, that they came on men as a resurrection of old and forgotten truth peculiarly adapted to the wants and circumstances of the times. The consequence was, that they were received with great favour by a large number of churchmen both of the orthodox and evangelical parties, to whom they seemed to furnish a new and powerful weapon of defence against the encroachments of Popery on the one hand, and of religious liberalism on the other. A large portion of the evangelical party, however, whose favourite doctrines they indirectly assailed, regarded them with growing suspicion and dislike. A small section of churchmen, headed by Arnold, Whately, and Hampden, the precursors of what we now call the broad church party, were still more strongly opposed to them. But these were then few and far between — ecclesiastical Ishmaelites, whose hand was against every man, and every man's hand against them. Outside the church there was but one opinion with regard to them, and that was a feeling of strong and earnest disapproval. The success of the tracts was much greater, and the outcry against them far louder and fiercer, than their authors had expected. But the support and the opposition they met with both tended to embolden them to speak out their opinions still more plainly and resolutely. The tracts which at the commencement had, as their name denoted, been small and simple, by degrees, as they proceeded, became large and learned theological treatises. Changes too came over the views of some of their writers. Doctrines which probably would have shocked them at first were put forward with a recklessness which success had increased. Alarm was excited; remonstrances stronger and stronger were addressed to them; but these belong to a later period.

It now only remains that we should endeavour to appreciate the very remarkable ecclesiastical phenomenon that we have been endeavouring to explain. What shall we say of it? That some truth and some rightness must have been at the bottom of this movement is to my mind proved by the fact of its rapid spread and long continuance. No idea lives and is widely diffused except in virtue of some truth that is in it. Falsehood, pure and unadulterated falsehood, cannot live—must speedily die. And if I should be challenged to show what germ of truth there was in this movement, my reply would be: If there was nothing else in it, there was at least this—that a church, that is to say a body that exists in a nation claiming to promote the practice of virtue by the proclamation of truth, must produce as authority for doing so some better credentials, must appeal to some higher proof of its mission, than acts of Parliament or establishment by law.

On the 4th of February, 1834, the king opened the second session of the reformed Parliament. In the speech which he delivered on this occasion he referred to the unsettled state of affairs in Spain, Portugal, Belgium, and Holland; he congratulated the Parliament on the manner in which the act passed during the last session for the abolition of slavery had been received in the colonies, and on the progress that had already been made in carrying out the intentions of the legislature. His Majesty also referred to the report of the commissions appointed to inquire into the state of the municipal corporations, into the administration and effects of the poor-laws, and into the ecclesiastical revenues and patronage in England and Wales. He announced the intended introduction of a measure for the final settlement of the tithe question in Ireland, and the determination of the government to maintain the legislative union between the two countries.

The speech, and the address in reply to it, were criticised in the upper House by the Duke of Wellington, and defended by Earl Grey; but no amendment was proposed, and no division took place. In the lower House, amendments moved by Messrs. Hume and O'Connell were rejected. In the course of the discussion on the address, Sir R. Peel sarcastically remarked, that, experienced as he was in speech-making, he could not but admire the great skill with which the framers of the king's speech had avoided saying anything at all.

On the 13th of February Mr. O'Connell brought a double accusation against Baron Smith, one of the Irish judges. In the first place he alleged that he scarcely ever appeared in his court till half-past twelve o'clock; that he commonly came in, wrote a letter, and then departed without taking any part in the proceedings of the court; that when sitting as a judge at the assizes, he had tried fourteen prisoners between six in the evening and six on the following morning; that the jury were asleep, the prisoners worn out, the witnesses were either not to be found or had been drinking, and were not in a condition to give correct evidence. Several other accusations of the same nature were brought against the learned baron. In the second place Mr. O'Connell accused him of introducing into the charge which he delivered to the grand jury political attacks of a very violent, undignified, and irritating character, and this too on occasions which afforded nothing to call for or excuse the introduction of political topics; as, for instance, when the cases to be heard were for such offences as cow-stealing and pig-stealing. He concluded by moving that these accusations should be referred to a select committee.

Mr. O'Connell certainly seemed to have made out a

primâ facie case for inquiry. It might indeed reasonably be doubted whether the kind of investigation which he proposed was the most proper under all the circumstances of the case, but that the charges were such as deserved investigation could hardly be disputed. Accordingly the motion for a select committee was supported by many members of the government; but was strongly opposed by Sir J. Graham. Nevertheless the motion was carried by a large majority. But a few days afterwards Sir E. Knatchbull moved that it should be rescinded, and the House agreed to his motion; thus rendering itself obnoxious to an imputation of fickleness and undue haste, which the conservative minority both in and out of doors were not slow to fasten on, and did not allow to be soon forgotten.

We must not altogether pass by a motion made by Mr. O'Connell for the repeal of the legislative union between England and Ireland; nor that 'for the appointment of a select committee to inquire and report on the means by which the dissolution of the parliament of Ireland was effected; on the effects of that measure in Ireland, and upon the labourers in industry and the operatives in manufactures in England; and on the probable consequences of continuing the legislative union between the two countries.' The former motion was not pressed; and the latter was so certain to be rejected, that it was generally believed that it was brought forward with no other motive than that of stimulating the flagging zeal of Mr. O'Connell's supporters in Ireland, and keeping up the amount of the tribute raised there for him, and perhaps too for the purpose of preventing the question from coming into the hands of some meaner agitator, who might thus transfer to himself a large portion of the popularity which Mr. O'Connell now enjoyed. These considerations prevented his proposals from receiving any serious consideration. The great Irish agitator did indeed give notice of both of these motions on the first day of the session; but he only brought forward the second, which was met on the part of ministers by a call of the House, and an amendment, proposed by Mr. Spring Rice, declaratory of the importance of maintaining the legislative union between Great Britain and Ireland, to be followed up by an address to the crown embodying this declaration. This amendment was carried by a majority of 523 to 38; and the address founded on it was carried up to the House of Peers, where it was unanimously adopted, and presented to the king, from whom it received such a reply as the government might be expected to advise.

Very different from these hollow and unreal attempts to obtain the repeal of the union was the motion made by Mr. Ward for the reduction of the revenues of the Irish church, which deserved and at once obtained the earnest serious attention of the House and the country, and was supported by a great force of public opinion not in Ireland only, but in England and Scotland also. It was becoming every day more and more evident, that the position of the church in Ireland was one of the main causes, if not altogether the chief cause, of the discontents that prevailed there, and that nothing short of a radical change in this respect would give peace to Ireland, or enable the English government to dispense with those coercive enactments which the disturbed state of that country rendered necessary. Circumstances too were forcing on the consideration of the tithe question. All the expedients to which the government had resorted had proved unsuccessful. It had expended 26,000*l.* in collecting 12,000*l.*, and there seemed to be no likelihood that it would be more successful in future. An arrangement had been made between the government and the clergy, but would soon come to an end; and it was not likely that, after such experience of its working, it would be renewed. To add to the embarrassment of the position, the members of the government were at variance among themselves as to the course which should be adopted. They were all agreed in the determination to uphold the established church in Ireland. It was evident, by diminishing the incomes of the bishops and some of the dignitaries of the church, by redistributing its funds, and by suppressing parishes which contained few or no Protestant parishioners, a considerable surplus could be obtained, which some of them thought might be applied either to the payment of the Roman Catholic priesthood, or to the erection and maintenance of schools, while other members of the cabinet would not listen for a moment to any proposal to devote any portion whatever of the revenues of the

Irish church to other than Protestant and ecclesiastical purposes. On the other hand, there was a strong party, both in the House of Commons and in the country, which was anxious to seize this opportunity of asserting the principle that Parliament had a right to devote a portion of the funds of the Irish church to purposes not strictly ecclesiastical, hoping that if they could once get this principle distinctly recognised by the legislature, it would be easy to obtain farther applications of it, not only to the Irish, but also to the English church. Accordingly great interest was excited by the motion which Mr. Ward, member for St. Albans, brought forward, and which asserted the justice and necessity of immediately depriving the Irish church of a portion of her temporalities; and as the principle involved in his resolution has caused the rise and fall of many administrations, it demands our serious attention, although it presented itself to the House of Commons in the guise of a purely Irish question.

In bringing forward his proposal, Mr. Ward showed that the collection of tithe was the real cause of the disturbance and discontent that prevailed in Ireland. He also pointed out that the resistance offered to the payment of tithe had become well-nigh universal; that it extended to Protestants as well as Catholics, and existed in all parts of the country: he therefore argued that nothing but some change in the appropriation of the tithe could appease the discontent that universally prevailed, or produce even a momentary calm. The chief cause of the hatred with which this impost was regarded was, that while the great majority of those who paid it were Catholics, the purposes to which it was applied were exclusively Protestant; and this grievance could not be remedied by any change in the manner of collecting the impost. The present arrangement would expire on the first of November, and then the clergy must either return to the old system, or once more become a burden on the resources of this country. Military force and civil process had both been tried, and tried in vain. Between 1825 and 1832 the army maintained in Ireland had varied from 19,000 to 23,000, being as nearly as possible the same amount of force as was required for our Indian empire, and within one-third of the force that was required to occupy all our colonies in the other three quarters of the world. This army had cost the country during the last year upwards of a million of money, besides the annually increasing expense of a police force, amounting to nearly 300,000*l.* During the five preceding years 17,981 tithe cases had been heard annually in ecclesiastical courts, and at quarter sessions before the assistant barristers. Large sums had been granted to schools and institutions which had Protestant proselytism for their object; but the religion of the people of Ireland seemed to be rendered dearer to them by every attempt made to shake its hold on their affections, and by the flagrant abuses of the established church itself, of which none was more striking than the disproportion that existed between its wealth and the number of its members.

Mr. Ward brought forward returns to show that only about 600,000 persons, or not one-fourteenth of the population of Ireland, adhered to the communion of the established church there; and he endeavoured to prove that the revenues belonging to the church amounted, not, as the chancellor of the exchequer had calculated, to 600,000*l.*, but to a million, Lord Althorp having omitted in his estimate to reckon the value of the glebe lands, which Mr. Ward put down at 400,000*l.* or upward. Another abuse of the Irish church which Mr. Ward denounced was the unequal division of its revenues, and the enormous sums that were paid to rectors or vicars who had little or nothing to do. There were 176 benefices the value of which varied from 800*l.* to 2,800*l.* per annum, 407 from 400*l.* to 800*l.*, and 386 from 400*l.* to 200*l.* Again, non-residence prevailed to an extent that was not surprising, considering how little the clergy had to do. It appeared that in 1814 there were 664 residents and 543 non-residents; in 1817, 665 residents and 544 non-residents; in 1819, 758 residents and 531 non-residents. Some of the resident clergy did duty for the most trifling remuneration, in some cases as low as 18*l.* a year, but the average was 70*l.* a year. And Mr. Ward forcibly asked: 'What sort of a feeling is it calculated to create in Ireland when they see the actual work of that wealthy church done for a comparatively small sum?' He did not however mean to abolish this establishment altogether, but to do away with the glaring disparity that existed between the scales of duties and compensations. He would not give 800*l*. or 1,000*l*. to the rector of a parish containing only ten or twelve Protestants, and even then forming, as in many cases they did, merely the family of the rector or vicar, brought into the parish for that very purpose. In cases where only the remnant of a Protestant flock existed provision might be made for a curate, without going to the expense of a rector. After explaining what he thought should be done, and asserting at some length the right of Parliament to dispose of church property, he concluded by moving the following resolution:

'Resolved, that the Protestant episcopal establishment in Ireland exceeds the spiritual wants of the Protestant population, and that it being the right of the state to regulate the distribution of church property in such a manner as Parliament may determine, it is the opinion of this House that the temporal possessions of the church of Ireland as now established ought to be reduced.'

The facts and arguments contained in Mr. Ward's speech pointed at a result far beyond that of the resolution which he moved. He showed that the maintenance of the Irish church, in one way and another, cost the English government a sum far exceeding the amount of the revenues that belonged to that church, excessive as they were, and that consequently it would be far cheaper and every way better to pay the Irish bishops and clergy out of the English taxes than to continue the system which then existed. And yet so slowly does common sense and justice make its way, even under a reformed Parliament, that some thirty-five years elapsed before Mr. Ward's resolution could get itself carried into effect; and it would probably have remained a dead letter for a longer period, had not a great statesman at length made up his mind to deal boldly and finally with the question raised in the first reformed Parliament in this year 1834.

The motion was seconded by Mr. Grote, at the conclusion of whose speech Lord Althorp rose and requested the House to adjourn, in consequence of circumstances which had come to his knowledge since he entered it. He could not at present state the nature of those circumstances, but he trusted that the House would believe that he would not make such a proposition without being convinced of its propriety. The motion announced in such ominous terms showed that a ministerial crisis had arisen, and was at once agreed to.

Lord Ebrington, who, as the reader will perhaps remember, had in similar emergencies come forward to assist the ministry, at once got up an address to Earl Grey, which was signed by a large number of supporters of the administration in the lower House, and in which they entreated his lordship to retain his place at the head of the ministry, expressing their unaltered confidence in him. The premier, in his reply, declared that he intended to make every personal sacrifice that was required of him in support of the principles of the administration; but he complained of the embarrassment and mischief that were produced by the reckless desire of innovation. In proceeding in a course of salutary improvement he found it indispensable that the government should be allowed to go on with deliberation and caution, and above all that they should not be urged by a constant and active pressure from without to adopt measures the necessity for which had not been fully proved, and which were not regulated by a careful attention to the settled institutions of the country both in church and state.

When the House of Commons reassembled, it had transpired that the members of the cabinet who were opposed to an appropriation of the funds of the Irish church to other than ecclesiastical purposes had withdrawn from the ministry. They were, the Duke of Richmond postmaster-general, the Earl of Ripon privy seal, Mr. Stanley colonial secretary, and Sir James Graham first lord of the Admiralty. It was at first thought that the loss of these members of the cabinet, and especially of Mr. Stanley and Sir J. Graham, would break-up the administration; but it was determined to proceed; and the vacancies caused by these withdrawals were filled by the Marquis of Conyngham, who became postmaster-general, the Earl of Carlisle privy-seal, Lord Auckland first lord of the Admiralty, and Mr. Spring Rice colonial secretary. The re-election of the last-mentioned gentleman at Cambridge was opposed by Sir E. Sugden, but was carried by a majority of twenty-five votes.

But though the men who most decidedly objected to Mr. Ward's motion had now quitted the ministry, those who still remained were not prepared to assent to it. In the first place the king was strongly opposed to it; and as he shortly afterwards took an opportunity of expressing his disapproval of it in a very extraordinary manner, it is more than probable that he had already announced to Earl Grey the feeling with which he regarded it, and his desire that it should in some way or other be got rid of. No doubt, if the matter had been pressed by his advisers, he would have been forced to give way, as he had been forced to consent to a creation of peers to enable the government to carry the Reform Bill through the House of Lords, and as he had before been compelled to yield on the question of the dissolution of the Parliament in 1831; but he would probably not have conceded the principle of appropriation without a break-up of the ministry, and perhaps another dissolution. Add to this, that though Earl Grey and several other members of the cabinet were not prepared, like Mr. Stanley and the seceding ministers, to deny that Parliament would be warranted in appropriating any portion whatever of the revenues of the Irish church to other than Protestant and ecclesiastical purposes, they were nevertheless very unwilling to commit themselves to the course indicated by Mr. Ward. They regarded the maintenance of the Protestant church of Ireland as demanded by strong considerations of policy as well as of religion. Jealousy of the church of Rome, the upholding of Protestantism, and the importance of establishments, had been cardinal points in the creed of the Whig party in every period of its history. Ministers felt strongly the injustice of the then existing state of things in Ireland, and they saw clearly that, for the sake of the preservation of the church and the removal of the discontent prevailing in that country, it would be politic to devote a portion of the surplus funds of the establishment to the joint education of Catholics and Protestants, or even to the payment of the Catholic clergy. But the time for the latter of these measures, which they thought the most advisable of the two, had not yet come. The English people were too strongly opposed to such a proposal to admit of its being made with safety. The government therefore determined to stave off the difficulty. Commissioners were hastily selected, and a commission hurriedly issued addressed to any two or more of them, directing them to visit every parish in Ireland, and 'to ascertain on the spot, by the best evidence they could procure there or elsewhere, the number of members of, or persons in communion with, the united church of England and Ireland in each benefice or parish, distinguishing in the case of such benefices as comprise more than one parish the number belonging to each parish separately and to the union collectively; and also to state the distances of the parishes in each union from each other respectively; to state the number and rank of the ministers belonging to or officiating within each benefice, whether rector, vicar, or curate, and whether resident or non-resident, and whether there is a church or glebe-house thereon:' in a word, the commissioners were not only to inquire into the temporalities of the Irish church, but also into the relative proportions of the number of churchmen, Roman Catholics, and dissenters in Ireland. The issue of a commission of this kind had been recommended some time since by the lord-lieutenant of Ireland, and the cabinet now adopted the recommendation as a means of extricating themselves from the difficulties in which they found themselves placed. Lord Althorp, after announcing the decision to which the government had come, begged Mr. Ward to be satisfied with the concession they had made to his views, and to withdraw his motion until it could be ascertained whether any, and if so what, surplus was likely to be disposable for the purposes he had indicated. Mr. Ward however declined compliance, on the ground that everything portended a speedy change of ministry, in which case the commission might prove wholly ineffectual. Under these circumstances the government resorted to the usual means of getting rid of an inconvenient discussion—the previous question was moved, and, after some debate, carried by a majority of 120; a majority which however would have been much greater if a large number of the conservative party, who were much more strongly opposed to the success of Mr. Ward's resolution than the members of the government, had not gone away before the division took place.

The haste with which the commission was expedited showed that it was caught at by the government as an expedient for extricating them from a difficult and embarrassing position; at the same time, it could not be denied that it was very desirable that the way should be prepared for legislation on the question by such accurate information as a commission would obtain. Evidently it could serve no good purpose to affirm an abstract principle before the government and the Parliament were in possession of the materials which should enable them to embody it in wise and effective legislation. Even after the information was obtained the question would still be surrounded with difficulties, because the revenues which one man might deem excessive might appear to another to be barely sufficient. Amidst the variety and contradiction of the statements that were made on the subject of the revenues of the Irish church, it seemed necessary that their approximate amount at least should be ascertained before any further steps were taken in the matter.

Nor was this the only Irish-church question that occupied the attention and endangered the stability of the ministry. Tithe bill after tithe bill had been passed, and all had failed most signally. The arrangement made under the last tithe bill would terminate on the 1st of November in this year, and for the sake of the peace and tranquillity of Ireland, as well as to keep the clergy from starving, it was necessary that ministers should again take up the question. A new tithe bill was introduced, the object of which was to convert the tithe, first into a rent-charge payable by the landlord, and ultimately into land; and it was proposed that the clergy should accept something short of the amount to which they were entitled by law collected without difficulty, in the place of a larger sum which could only be obtained, if obtained at all, at the cost of riot and bloodshed. We will not weary the patience of the reader by attempting to follow out all the vicissitudes which this unfortunate measure underwent, or to give any idea of the floods of parliamentary eloquence and ineloquence that were poured forth on it. We shall content ourselves with saying, that the bill, though introduced by Mr. Littleton, the Irish secretary, on the 20th of February, did not pass the House of Commons till the 5th of August. In the long interval between these two dates, it was altered to meet the objections of the Irish party, modified to meet practical objections that were urged against it from both sides of the House, considerably changed in consequence of the resignation of Mr. Stanley and his party, and assailed by him with a vehemence of vituperation seldom equalled in the House of Commons. In a speech applauded to the echo by the Tories, but which gave bitter offence to his former political associates, the honourable gentleman stigmatised the bill, as it now stood, as a system of plunder, and that too not a system of plunder characterised by the straightforward course which bold offenders followed, but marked with all that timidity, that want of dexterity, which led to the failure of the unpractised shoplifter. In another part of the same speech he compared his late colleagues to thimble-riggers at a country fair, whose art consisted in dexterously conveying or shifting the pea from one thimble to another, while the party who guessed under what thimble the pea was deposited, in the end found that the result of his speculations was the loss of his money. So the Irish secretary had suggested, the church pocket, the state packet, the perpetuity fund—first the landlord, then the tenant—so that it was impossible to guess under which thimble the treasure lay; and the end would be, that in taking up the thimbles, it would be found that the property had disappeared. Again, in speaking of one part of the plan, he stigmatised it as 'petty larceny, for it had not the redeeming quality of bold and open robbery.' In justice to Mr. Stanley it should be added that he is said to have afterwards expressed to Earl Grey his deep regret at having been led, in the heat of discussion, on a question on which he felt very strongly, to speak so disrespectfully of his former colleagues. But this attack, proceeding as it did from the prospective heir of the earldom of Derby, was very damaging to the government, and was industriously echoed and reëchoed by their opponents.

The coercion bill of the last session had worked so well, had produced so great a diminution of the number of predial and political outrages, that there could be no doubt whatever as to the policy and necessity of renewing it. But the government had to consider anxiously in what shape it should be renewed. No necessity had arisen for employing the court-martial clauses, and therefore it was thought useless to reënact them. There was a division of opinion in the cabinet on the question of the continuance of the clauses which conferred on the lord-lieutenant the power of preventing the holding of public meetings intended to promote political agitation. The majority, strongly influenced by Earl Grey, were of opinion that the powers should be continued. A minority, however, thought that it would be expedient to conciliate the Irish party by leaving them out of the renewed act; but in deference to the judgment of the head of the government and of the majority of their colleagues, they waived their objections, and agreed to support the clause in the House of Commons. Amongst those who belonged to this section of the cabinet was Lord Althorp, on whom, as leader of the House of Commons, the duty of defending the bill and conducting it through the lower House devolved. Lord Wellesley, the lord-lieutenant of Ireland, a man of very inferior capacity, appears to have displayed great indecision in reference to the public-meeting clauses of the bill. On the 18th of April he recommended their renewal; in June he wrote to Earl Grey proposing that they should be abandoned, not for the sake of Ireland, but because he had been informed that it would facilitate the passage of the bill through the lower House, and might lead the Commons to grant the other powers which the bill conferred for a longer period. But being asked to give his opinion only with a view to the government of Ireland, on the 7th of July he concurred in the view taken by Earl Grey and the majority of the cabinet. Meanwhile Mr. Littleton, who, as Irish secretary, had suggested the abandonment of the public-meeting clauses, expecting that the representation which he had urged the lord-lieutenant to make would lead to such a settlement of the question as he desired, after consulting Lord Althorp, who advised caution, but said he saw no great harm in his taking the step, communicated to O'Connell what he then supposed to be the intention of the government with regard to the public-meeting clauses. O'Connell, whose tribute was diminished, and whose personal prestige was greatly damaged by the operation of these clauses, had determined to offer a violent and factious opposition to the measure that contained them. He had accordingly made preparations for resistance with his usual vigour and ability. He had summoned his followers to his assistance; he had determined on having a call of the House. A vacancy having occurred in the representation of Wexford, a ministerial candidate was in the field. O'Connell put forward a repealer. He prepared an address to the reformers of England and Ireland, in which he appealed to them from the present ministry, and denounced the government, but more especially Lord Grey in the most violent terms. 'Brother reformers,' he wrote, 'from the insulting injustice of the present weak and wicked administration I appeal, not without hope, to your sense of right and justice. Is it just that Ireland should be insulted and trampled on, merely because the insanity of the wretched old man who is at the head of the ministry develops itself in childish hatred and maniac contempt of the people of Ireland? I observed this trait of madness in the character of Lord Grey's mind so long ago as the year 1825. I published my opinion on this subject at that period; and experience has confirmed the judgment I formed and promulgated respecting him nine years ago. In fact, there appear to be but two leading ideas in his mind. The first regards the procuring for his family and relations the greatest possible quantity of the public spoil; I believe no minister ever had the one-twentieth, perhaps not the one-fiftieth part of the number of relations receiving public pay as Lord Grey has, nor so few deserving such payment. He and his family are indeed a cruel infliction on these countries. The second, but subordinate, sentiment in Lord Grey's mind is hostility to Ireland, evinced by every act and deed of his administration. Ireland never was so unsatisfactorily, so badly governed as since the present ministry came into power. They have done everything to insult and degrade all parties and all classes in that country; they have done nothing which could serve or satisfy any portion of the people except the few who, like the Plunkets, have been gorged with the public plunder. The ministry have not one single friend, nor even one nominal friend, in Ireland—nay more, those whom they have enriched out of the public treasury hate and despise them in public, and avow their hatred and contempt in the circles of private life. Never was Ireland so badly, so unsatisfactorily governed. But, will you believe it, brother reformers, Lord Grey is not content with the oppression of last year; he actually threatens to renew the coercion bill again! Come forward, then, I respectfully implore, and teach the insane dotard who is at the head of the administration, that Englishmen and Scotchmen are alive to the wants and sufferings and the privileges of the people of Ireland.'

Matters were in this state when, as we have seen, Mr. Littleton, with the privity of the leader of the House of Commons, but without consultation with the first minister of the crown or his other colleagues, sent for O'Connell and informed him in strict confidence, that the clauses which conferred on the lord-lieutenant the power of preventing public meetings would not be renewed. After he had given this assurance, he found to his dismay that the cabinet had decided that those clauses should be retained. He lost no time in acquainting O'Connell with the disappointment of his expectations. O'Connell naturally indignant, and supposing that he had been designedly duped, at once called on him to resign his office, and brought the matter before the House.

Mr. Littleton admitted that he had been guilty of gross indiscretion, but complained of the breach of confidence on Mr. O'Connell's part. O'Connell defended himself from this charge. He said 'I never would have divulged the communication made to me, if I had not found that it had been used to gain an advantage over me by trickery. It was not I who sought the Irish secretary; I was sought by him. I had nothing to ask from him; he sent for me. He had no right to send for me to go to his office; I did not want him. If he wanted me he knew where I lived. The election for Wexford was coming on. One of the candidates was a Whig: I thought it my duty to put up a repealer. In these circumstances the interview took place. I admit the conversation was confidential, but that confidence was limited. That secrecy would never have been broken by me, if I had not been tricked and deceived by the Irish secretary. . . . I told him he might reckon on the fullest assistance from myself and that of the party to which I belonged for such a purpose. I was going out of the room, when he addressed to me this observation—that if the coercion bill should be brought into that House, it would not be brought in by him. Such was the conversation between him and me. In consequence of that conversation I wrote over to the county of Wexford; and the candidate whom I had started there on the repeal interest declined the contest. Another gentleman started on the same interest. He wrote over to me, requesting that I would send one of my family to canvass the county

with him. I acted upon the right honourable gentleman's
distinct declaration, and I declined interfering; and what
was the consequence? The Whig candidate on the first
day had a majority of 114 over his opponent. But what
has since taken place affords a positive proof, that if I had
interfered, and if some one connected with me had gone
through the county the majority would have been decidedly
on the other side. That election is still going on; and up
to the post-hour on Monday last, the majority of the Whig
candidate had been beaten down to 18.* Was not that a
proof that I should have carried that election, if I had not
been kept neutral by the delusion—by the deception—
practised upon me?'

Mr. Littleton denied, and no doubt with perfect truth,
that he had intended to deceive Mr. O'Connell. In fact,
he had deluded himself and had communicated his delusion
to a very dangerous opponent; but when he discovered the
mistake, he did his best to correct its effects. The moment
the decision was taken by the cabinet, Mr. O'Connell was
informed of it; first by a common friend, and then, as
already related, by Mr. Littleton himself. Mr. O'Connell,
however, insisted that a very important fact had been
omitted in Mr. Littleton's statement. 'When he made the
communication to me,' said the member for Dublin, 'I told
him that I wished the report of 1832, on the disturbances
in Ireland, to be printed. He said emphatically, "There is
no occasion for it to be printed; you will be satisfied of
that by the announcement made by Earl Grey in the House
of Lords to-night." I said in reply, there is only one course
for you to take—to resign: for after the manner in which
you have acted, you will be otherwise guilty of a deception
on me. His reply was, "Say nothing of that to-day."'

The following dialogue ensued:

Mr. Littleton: 'I declare, on my honour as a gentleman,
that I said no such thing.'

Mr. O'Connell: 'On my honour as a gentleman, you did.'

Mr. Littleton: 'I declare solemnly before the House, and
upon my honour as a gentleman, that I never did.'

Mr. O'Connell: 'Do you mean to deny that you spoke of
resignation?'

Mr. Littleton: 'I never said any such thing. I deny

* Eventually the repeal candidate was returned.

solemnly, on the honour of a gentleman, that I made any
statement of the kind.'

Mr. O'Connell: 'Then why did I not make my motion
for the printing of the report?' I want to know that.'

Mr. Littleton: 'I cannot answer for that; I do not know
anything about it. It is true that you declared your intention of moving for the printing of the report, and said
something about the bill. I did not in reply say a word
about resigning. To the best of my knowledge, my reply
was as nearly as possible in these words: "I trust that,
whatever your feelings and opinions on the subject may be,
you will not divulge them to-night; but that you will wait
until to-morrow, when you can ascertain the particular
nature of the bill in Lord Grey's speech."'

Mr. O'Connell: 'That was not what you said, nor anything like it.'

Two days after, Mr. Littleton tendered his resignation;
but it was refused, his colleagues declaring that they valued
his services much too highly to dispense with them on such
grounds. The coercion bill went through the House of
Lords unaltered. In the House of Commons the revelations
so maladroitly made by the Irish secretary placed the
government in a very critical position. How could Lord
Althorp, as leader, press on the House clauses to which it
was now known that he was opposed? He therefore
tendered his resignation, and persisted in it, in spite of the
efforts made by the premier to induce him to change his
determination. Thereupon Earl Grey, already anxious to
be relieved from a position which had become painful to
him, and only prevented from carrying out his intention
of retiring by the importunities of his colleagues, determined to resign; and on July 9th he spoke for the last time
in the House of Lords as premier. Never perhaps did any
man occupy a higher position in the eyes of his peers and
in those of his countrymen than Earl Grey filled at that
moment. His life-long championship of the cause of reform,
and the manner in which he had carried the Reform Bill
through the legislature, had won for him the affectionate
veneration of his own party, and the respect of his opponents. The firmness he had displayed in reference to
Ireland, and especially his recent conduct on the coercion
question, had to a great extent atoned in their eyes for his

advocacy of those changes which they had so strenuously but unsuccessfully resisted. All acknowledged his sterling worth, his earnest patriotism, his great abilities, his long and valuable services to the state. When the order of the day was read, he rose to give his last explanations; but his feelings overcame him, and he was unable to proceed. The Duke of Wellington generously and skilfully relieved his embarrassment by presenting petitions. When this was done, Earl Grey rose again, and spoke as follows:

'I really feel ashamed of the sort of weakness I have shown upon this occasion. I have recently been honoured with an interview with his majesty, and the personal kindness I experienced has quite overpowered me. I have, however, a duty to perform, and whatever be my present incapacity, I will to the utmost of my ability discharge it; and in rising to propose that you should agree to the report that has just been brought up, I have to state that I no longer do so as a minister of the crown, but as an individual member of the legislature strongly impressed with the necessity of passing the act in order to invest the government of Ireland, into whatever hands it may fall, with a power which I believe to be necessary to the maintenance of law and order in that country.' After relating the events which had brought about his resignation, he thus proceeded: 'I have for some time felt the increasing difficulties of the situation in which I was placed become so painful and so much above the remaining strength and energy that I possess, that I have long wished to retire from office. Both my late and present colleagues well know that I expressed this wish most anxiously at the close of the last session of Parliament. I gave up that determination in consequence of the strong and united representations of my colleagues, who urged that my retirement would occasion the immediate dissolution of the government, and might place his majesty in a painful situation. Since the commencement of this session, some of the most powerful members of the government have separated from it. This was most painful to me, on personal as well as public grounds; and feeling how inadequate I was to discharge the duties of my office, I felt anxious then to retire. That resolution was so decidedly taken, that I thought nothing could have diverted me from it. I was induced, on the representations of my remaining colleagues, to depart from it; as also in consequence of an application of a great number of the members of the House of Commons, and from my anxious desire to carry through those measures that were in progress, and which were essential to the true interests of the country. I also felt how unjust it would be to his majesty to resign at such a period of the session. . . . Then arose this new circumstance, which has deprived me of the assistance of the chancellor of the exchequer, the leading member of government in the Commons, on whom my whole confidence rested, whom I considered as the right arm of my government, and without whom I felt that it was impossible that government could go on. Former breaches had weakened it. This new breach has placed us in a situation in which I cannot, to any useful purpose, continue in the situation which I hold. Receiving my noble friend's resignation, I felt that there was no alternative left but to tender at the same time my own. These resignations have been accepted by his majesty; and I now discharge the duties of my office only till such time as his majesty can supply my place.'

It was generally expected that the retirement of Earl Grey would draw after it the dissolution of the ministry of which he was the head. It was true that Lord Brougham had announced that he himself and several of his colleagues felt it a duty that they owed to their king and country in the present crisis of affairs to retain their offices; on the other hand, Lord Althorp in the House of Commons announced that the administration was at an end. He was indeed even more impatient to retire than the aged premier. 'Nature,' he used to exclaim, 'intended me to be a grazier; but men will insist on making me a statesman.' However, the withdrawal of Earl Grey, by removing the great difficulty in which the government was placed, facilitated the continuance in office of his colleagues. He alone in the cabinet seems to have held a very decided opinion with regard to the clauses to which Mr. O'Connell had so strongly objected, and which had been the subject of the communication made to him by Mr. Littleton. It is true, the retention of those clauses had been supported by a majority of his colleagues; but that support was given rather out of deference to Earl

Grey's opinion than from any belief on their part in the necessity that existed for them. Lord Althorp, therefore, by the advice of Earl Grey, reluctantly consented to remain in office, and the other members of the government came to the same resolution. Lord Melbourne became first lord of the treasury and head of the cabinet, a few official changes took place, and the coercion bill, shorn of the public-meeting clauses, went forward with the assent of those who had hitherto so vehemently opposed it.

The appointment of Lord Melbourne to the chief place in the administration took most men by surprise. In ability and reputation he was far below his predecessor. He had never been a conspicuous politician. As a follower of Mr. Canning he had abetted that statesman in his resistance of the very moderate instalment of reform which the Whigs at that time submitted to the House of Commons. He had indeed given a doubtful and hesitating support to the Reform Bill; which he accepted as a necessary concession to the public opinion of the country, rather than as a measure desirable in itself. To say that he was inferior as a speaker to Lord Grey is not to say enough. He was totally devoid of eloquence, and generally spoke with a hesitation and embarrassment which were painful to his hearers, and which only partially disappeared when he was animated by debate or excited by contradiction. What he said was plain and sensible, but had hardly sufficient merit to balance the defects of his delivery. He was a man of fashion, but had displayed in office a degree of ability and diligence of which his previous career and his known character had given no promise. The fears of his friends and the hopes of his opponents were disappointed by his able administration of the Home Office in a very difficult and delicate crisis of affairs. Still, he had not shown himself more than a tolerably good home secretary, and most men were astonished to find that one so little known as a politician should be placed at the head of the government at this trying moment. The only explanation, as far as we know, that could be given of this appointment was that his strong good sense, firmness of purpose, suavity of manner, and thorough goodness of heart recommended him to the king, to his colleagues, and to both parties, and enabled him to manage them better than many men of greater ability and more unbending character could have done.

The number by which the coercion bill passed through its last stage in the House of Commons sufficiently showed how thoroughly the members of that assembly were wearied of the discussion of Irish questions. Only 60 voted in favour of the bill, while those who voted against it were 25. In the upper House the Duke of Wellington moved an amendment which had for its object to reinstate the public-meeting clauses in the position they had originally occupied in the bill; but he did so merely to give himself an opportunity of criticising the conduct of the ministry in reference to these clauses; and his motion led to a debate, but was not pressed to a division. There can be no doubt that the changes which had been made in the measures of the government, and the manner in which they had truckled to O'Connell, had seriously weakened them, and paved the way for the speedy return to power of a party which the Reform Bill appeared to have annihilated, but which now began again to be full of hope. The popularity and prestige of the ministry was still farther damaged by their conduct with regard to the Irish tithe bill, into which they allowed O'Connell to introduce a very important change, compelling the landlords to take the tithe at once, instead of holding out to them the strong inducement of a discount of 40 per cent. if they did so. Mr. O'Connell's proposal was recommended by many considerations of expediency. It would give immediate relief to the tenant; it would prevent the discontent that would arise if one tenant paid a pound while another with an exactly similar holding only paid twelve shillings; but the chief attraction of his plan was that it would enable the House, wearied out by the protraction of the session, to get rid of the bill in two more sittings; for it was known that if this provision were adopted, O'Connell would at once withdraw from his opposition to the measure. This last inducement was irresistible. Ministers were obliged to yield, against their own judgment, to the impatience of their supporters, but the concession made to a man who had been so distinctly denounced in the king's speech very seriously damaged them; while the great radical party, much stronger in the country than in the House, bitterly complained that the measures which they expected to see follow the Reform Bill, and which they regarded as essential supplements of that measure, were thrust aside to make way for long Irish debates.

Several church questions of great importance were brought forward this session, though with no other noteworthy result than that of freely ventilating them. A motion made on the 13th of March, 'to relieve the archbishops and bishops of the established church from their legislative and judicial duties in the House of Peers,' was supported by 58 votes to 125. The question of the admission of dissenters to the universities gained greater attention. The way for the introduction of this measure had been prepared by the presentation of several petitions, most notable among which was one from resident members of the University of Cambridge, signed by two heads of houses, nine professors, amongst whom were Airy, Sedgwick, Musgrave (afterwards archbishop of York), eleven tutors of colleges, and forty-one other members of the senate. This petition was presented in the House of Lords by Earl Grey, and in the House of Commons by Mr. Spring Rice, both of whom announced that the government was prepared to support a measure for giving effect to the prayer of the petitioners. It was stated, in the course of the discussion which followed the presentation of these petitions, that the statutes excluding dissenters from taking degrees had been forced on the universities by King James I., much against the will of many who held high academical offices at the period when they were imposed. It was therefore suggested, that what had been enacted by royal authority might be repealed by royal authority. Accordingly, on the 17th of April Colonel Williams moved an address to the king, 'requesting his majesty to signify his pleasure to the universities of Oxford and Cambridge respectively, that these bodies no longer act under the edict or letters of James I, 1616, by which he would have all who take any degree in the schools to subscribe to the three articles of the thirty-sixth canon, with the exception of those proceeding to degrees in divinity; nor to require the declaration, namely, "that I am *bonâ fide* a member of the church of England," nor any other subscription of like effect or import.' As, however, it seemed doubtful whether the crown possessed the power which had been exercised in this instance, and as an address to the crown must be made on the assumption that it had that authority, it was thought better to proceed by a bill, which was accordingly introduced into the lower House by Mr. Wood, one of the members for South Lancashire. The measure was supported by the government, and somewhat coldly and hesitatingly by Mr. Stanley, now out of office and taking a very independent course. On the other hand, it was strenuously resisted by all the members for the universities, by Sir Robert Peel, and the conservative party generally. To counterbalance the effect of the petition which had made so strong an impression in favour of the bill, a more numerously signed petition of resident members of the University of Cambridge deprecating the proposed innovation was presented. The bill passed the House of Commons, notwithstanding all opposition, by 164 votes to 75. The conclusion of this debate took place in the midst of laughter, shouting, coughing, cock-crowing, and most disreputable uproar; the speaker strenuously, but vainly striving to maintain order. The bill was rejected in the upper House; there being 85 votes in favour of it, and 187 against it.

Another ecclesiastical question submitted to the decision of the House of Commons was that of church rates. This impost had for some time past been a subject of growing discontent not only to dissenters, but also to many churchmen. Hitherto the opposition to it had taken the shape of an objection to the amount or the disposal of the rate rather than to the rate itself. The various items of expense were scanned with a very jealous eye, the meetings for the purpose of levying the rate were held in the churches, and the sacred edifices were often profaned by scenes of a very painful character; violent and acrimonious contests arose when, as was often the case, a poll was demanded. But now the dissenters began to think of getting rid of the impost entirely; and when every other privilege and advantage which the church claimed was being called in question, it was not likely that this would escape notice. It was felt that the question of tithes stood on a very different footing from that of church rates; the former being devoted to the support of the clergy, the latter to that of the fabrics in which they ministered, and of the services there performed; the former being in the nature of a rent charge, and partaking of the sacredness which attached to landed property, while the latter was a tax which, it was argued, the legislature had as much right to abolish as any other tax. The dissenters complained that it was a payment applied to the support of services which they conscientiously disapproved, while they contributed to support their own places of worship. To these reasons in favour of the abolition of the church rate it was replied, that if it were admitted, for the sake of argument, that the rate was a tax, it could not be denied that it had been longer in existence than any other tax whatever; that the ratepayer bought his property with the full knowledge that it was subject to the impost, and had paid for it accordingly, therefore it did not belong to him, but to the church; and it was not right that he should be allowed to retain it. To the plea of conscience it was answered, first, that conscience could not urge a man to keep in his own pocket money that belonged to the church; and next, that if such a plea should be admitted, it would be fatal to all taxation, because some portion of the public funds are applied to purposes which the tax-payer disapproves. Thus Quakers might plead a conscientious objection to war, dissenters to expenditure on the church, Protestants to Maynooth grants. These arguments, however, failed to convince the opponents of the rates, and the agitation against them was carried on with greater violence than ever. To put an end to the church-rate contests which annually raged in all parts of the kingdom, producing an immense amount of contention and ill-will, Mr. Divett, member for Exeter, and a churchman, moved, on the 8th of March, 'that it is just and expedient that effectual measures should be taken for the abolition of the compulsory payment of church rates in England and Wales.' Lord Althorp announced that he intended to deal with the question not by resolution, but by a plan embodied in a substantive motion; and at his request Mr. Divett withdrew his resolution, and on the 21st of April Lord Althorp moved, 'That after a fixed time church rates should cease and determine, and that in lieu thereof a sum not exceeding 250,000*l.* should be granted from the land tax, to be applied to the expenses of the fabrics of the churches and chapels in such a manner as Parliament should direct.' In bringing forward this resolution, Lord Althorp said, 'It is not intended that the annual grant should be spent in aid of all the purposes to which church rates are now applied; but that it should be paid into the hands of the church commissioners, which are at present a temporary, but whom it would be found necessary to make a permanent body, to be applied as the repairs of the fabric should require. It will be found from the returns that the sum hitherto applied is not quite 250,000*l.* But then it should be recollected that in many instances the church rates have been mortgaged. These mortgages will form the first lien on this 250,000*l.*; but I do not think it will require much to satisfy these claims, and I have no doubt that the funds I propose to cover the expenses will prove amply sufficient. As the law now exists, the rector or lay improprietor is bound to repair the chancel. It is my intention to relieve them from this charge, and in lieu of it to impose on them the charge of finding the necessaries for divine service. Thus the grant will provide for the maintenance of the fabric of the church, of the chancel, and for the expenses of the churchyard. The persons who hold the pews will be bound to keep them in repair. In my plan there is no provision for organs or bells, or other things that might be considered as church luxuries. If these things are thought necessary, they must be supplied by voluntary contributions. According to the system which I propose, it will be necessary to have some fresh check on the expenditure. The vestry is a very inefficient check. The first check under my plan will be the limited amount of the sum at the disposal of the commissioners, which they cannot exceed. In addition to this, when the churchwardens and the clergyman think that repairs are necessary, they will in the first place have to call in the surveyor of the county, to examine and declare whether these repairs are in fact demanded by the state of the fabric or no. The result of the whole is, that although 250,000*l.* is to be taken from the land tax, and church rates are to be done away with altogether, the people of England would be relieved from a very heavy tax.'

The fate of this carefully meditated and nicely-balanced

project was such as might have been anticipated. It was expected and intended by its authors to please everybody. It pleased nobody. The object of the dissenters was not to transfer the maintenance of the churches from the rates to the land tax, nor was it to obtain a better system of checks on the expenditure of the money. What they wanted was, to be released from all contribution, direct or indirect, towards the support of the churches. The transfer of that support to the general taxation of the country would deprive them of the control over the expenditure which they now possessed, as well as of the means of agitation which the present state of things afforded them. The stories of the seizure of the poor man's bed or his Bible, which circulated through the kingdom with immense effect, would no longer be available; and the rate would be perpetuated in another form. But if the dissenters were hostile to the proposed measure, the clergy and the zealous churchmen generally were not less opposed to it. Had they been wise, they would readily have paid the price which the chancellor of the exchequer demanded of them, in order to get rid of an agitation which did greater damage to the church than the whole value of the rate could compensate. Instead, however, of closing with the offer, and giving the ministry that support which policy dictated, the champions of the church found fault with the smallness of the proposed grant, and objected to any part of the expense of carrying on the service being thrown on the congregations. Some of those who held this language were undoubtedly actuated by a sincere zeal for the church; but many of them were chiefly anxious to embarrass the ministry, and would have gratefully and warmly received the same measure, if their own party had been in office and brought it forward. However, the government carried the resolution by a majority of 256 to 140, and probably might have passed a bill founded on it; but the unfavourable reception it encountered from those whom it was intended to conciliate so disgusted the government, that they determined not to carry the matter any farther.

To the other abortive attempts at ecclesiastical legislation made during this session, are to be added a tithe commutation bill and a dissenters' marriage bill introduced by Lord J. Russell. His plan was, to have the banns asked in church as before, but to require the clergyman, on payment of a fee of half-a-crown, to give the parties a certificate of the asking, which certificate would be a sufficient authority to a dissenting minister to celebrate the marriage in any dissenting place of worship licensed for the purpose by the justices of the peace, on the application of twenty resident householders. The dissenters were too conscious of their own power, and too much elated by their previous successes, to accept this boon when they hoped soon to be able to dictate their own terms. They therefore rejected a concession which a short time before they would have accepted with gratitude; and the government again yielded to an opposition which they might have overcome.

After reading this long list of legislative failures, to which we shall yet have to make some additions, the reader may be impatient to ask—were they counterbalanced by any legislative successes? To this question it may be answered, that if Parliament had done no other work during this session, it might still have pointed with pride to the fact of its having passed the new poor-law. We have already referred to the agricultural distress that prevailed; to the miserable condition to which the agricultural labourer was reduced; to the riotings, machine-breakings, and rick-burnings to which their misery had instigated them. It was now becoming daily more evident, that the root of all this misery and crime lay in the maladministration of the poor-laws. The evil was an old one, but it was now rapidly approaching a climax. A sort of fatality seems to have attended all our legislation on this subject. Every measure that had been adopted had only served to introduce new mischiefs and to aggravate those it was intended to cure. The statute of Elizabeth, designed to make the indolent industrious, and to check vagrancy and mendicity, and quite capable, under proper administration, of effecting these objects, had in its actual working covered the land with able-bodied paupers and sturdy mendicants. The laws against bastardy had fostered unchastity. The 3 & 4 William and Mary, and the 9 George I., which had been passed to put a stop to the extravagant dispensation of poor rates, produced increased extravagance, and frustrated every attempt at a more economical administration. The various laws of settlement, originally devised to protect parishes from large immigrations of paupers, had enabled wealthy parishes to thrust the maintenance of their superabundant labour on small and poor parishes. Thus, after three centuries of bungling and inefficient legislation on the subject, the work had to be begun again, and Lord Grey's government boldly grappled with the gigantic difficulty. Wisely determining to base their legislation, not on assertions and theories, but on a careful preliminary inquiry carried on by competent investigators, they issued a commission, which was composed of Dr. Blomfield, bishop of London, Dr. Sumner, bishop of Chester, and afterwards archbishop of Canterbury, Mr. Sturges Bourne, Mr. Nassau Senior, and three others. They were especially directed to inquire into those exceptional cases in which a careful administration of the law had produced good results, as well as into those in which a careless and wasteful administration had brought forth its natural fruits. The inquiry was chiefly carried on by assistant commissioners, of whom Mr. Edwin Chadwick was the most active, and the one whose recommendations were chiefly followed. Their inquiries revealed a multitude of abuses and stupidities in the administration of the poor-laws far beyond what was previously known or suspected. Jobbery reigned supreme almost everywhere. Tradesmen exacted exorbitant prices from the parish, and bribed the parish officers to wink at their extortions. In many instances the rates were used to influence and corrupt the electors of parliamentary boroughs. The attempts which in some cases were made by the overseers to prevent imposition were generally overruled by the magistrates. The scale of relief given acted as an inducement to improvident marriages. In many instances it was found that the able-bodied paupers received higher allowances than the infirm and disabled. In the workhouse the pauper was overfed with beef and mutton, while the man who earned his food by the sweat of his brow could scarcely obtain bread; and the pauper often received in relief a larger amount than the industrious and independent labourer was paid in wages. When relief was once obtained, it was regarded as a kind of vested interest, to be continued through life. Often pauper parents begat pauper children; and so on to the third and fourth generation. Relief was given in the most careless manner, and with gross partiality.

In Buckinghamshire it was allowed to all who chose to ask for it. The recipients were often known to be thieves or prostitutes. In many instances the allowance was extorted by violence and threats. Since the commencement of the machine-breakings and rick-burnings, the amount had greatly increased, the allowance often being, in fact, a bribe given to the rioters in the hope of propitiating them. In some cases at least, it was shown to be the cause of the outrages committed. Relief was insolently demanded for children whose fathers were receiving high wages, or wasting their earnings in drunkenness and disorderly living. In Sussex labourers refused to work; preferring to live on the parish allowance.

Such an administration of the poor laws was producing the harvest of ruin, degradation, and crime, that might naturally be expected from it, and in great abundance. Whole parishes had been pauperised, parochial relief having been substituted in them for wages. Farmers discharged their labourers, that they might receive them again partly paid by the parish; and manufacturers in Durham adopted the same plan, thus throwing the burden of paying the wages of their workpeople on the shopkeepers and other ratepayers. This system was demoralising all classes of labourers; destroying veracity, industry, frugality, and all the domestic virtues, and fostering vice, profligacy, and drunkenness. It led men to dissipate their earnings, that they might entitle themselves to become recipients of parochial relief. Much of the money given in relief was carried at once to the beer or gin shop, and spent there. Early and improvident marriages were contracted. Men went from the church to the overseer's office to ask for a loaf of bread or a bed to sleep on. Under the baneful influence of this system, the rates were steadily increasing, labourers were becoming paupers, farmers were reduced to the condition of labourers, capitals were being eaten up; and it was evident that, unless some stop was put to it, the end must be universal pauperism, degradation, and starvation. The existing law afforded no means of checking the progress of the mischief. The efforts of the parish officers were counteracted by the magistrates, even in places where the relief was administered with the greatest care it was often found impossible to control the demand for it; and in some a

' decrease in the population was attended by an increasing expenditure in parish allowances.

It must not be supposed that the labouring classes of England were thus sinking deeper and deeper without resistance. No, the great mass of them were still earnestly struggling to maintain their honest independence. To most of them the name of pauper, in spite of the advantages it carried with it, was a brand of shame and degradation. The independent labourer was still distinguished from the pauper, if not by higher remuneration, at least by greater sobriety and self-respect, by more decency in his clothing, more civility in his manners, by the greater cleanliness of his wife, his children, and his house. The man who worked early and returned from his work late for a pittance which the operation of the poor-laws was continually diminishing, could still proudly exclaim, 'Thank God, I am not a pauper; thank God, neither I nor any of my family ever received parish relief.' But poverty and misery compelled many to relinquish this boast, and drew them into the whirlpool of pauperism.

It was, of course, the duty of the commissioners not only to discover the evils of the system, but also to recommend a remedy for them. Some high authorities on the subject, among whom we may mention the names of Lord Brougham, Mr. Senior, and Miss Martineau, had been strongly of opinion that the only effectual remedy for the state of things which the poor-laws and their maladministration had produced was to be found in their entire abolition. This opinion, however, after due consideration, was rejected by the commissioners, who represented that it was desirable that provision should still be made for the relief of the infirm, aged, and those who, though willing to work, could not obtain employment; but that such alterations should be made in the law as would put a stop to the existing abuses and maladministration.

The changes which they resolved to recommend were first suggested by Mr. Chadwick; and we cannot better describe them than by borrowing the recommendations which he made to the commissioners.

'1. That the existing system of poor-laws in England is destructive to the industry, forethought, and honesty of the labourers, to the wealth and morality of the employers of labour and of the owners of property, and to the mutual good-will and happiness of all. That it collects and chains down the labourers in masses without any reference to the demand for their labour; that while it increases their numbers, it impairs the means by which the fund for their subsistence is to be reproduced, and impairs the motives for using those means which it suffers to exist; and that every year and every day these evils are becoming more overwhelming in magnitude and less susceptible of cure.

'2. That of those evils, that which consists merely in the amount of the rates,—an evil great when considered by itself, but trifling when compared with the moral effects which I am deploring,—might be much diminished by the combination of workhouses, and by substituting a rigid administration and contract management for the existing scenes of neglect, extravagance, jobbing, and fraud.

'3. That by an alteration, or even—according to the suggestion of many witnesses—an abolition of the law of settlements, a great part, or, according to the latter suggestion, the whole of the enormous sums now spent in litigation and removals might be saved, the labourers might be distributed according to the demand for labour, the immigration from Ireland of labourers of inferior habits be checked, and the oppression and cruelty to which the unmarried, and those who have acquired any property, are now subjected, might, according to the extent of the alteration, be diminished, or utterly put an end to.

'4. That if no relief were allowed to be given to the able-bodied or to their families, except in return for adequate labour, or in a well-regulated workhouse, the worst of the existing sources of evil—the allowance system—would immediately disappear; a broad line would be drawn between the independent labourers and the paupers; the number of paupers would be immediately diminished, in consequence of the reluctance to accept relief on such terms, and would be still farther diminished in consequence of the increased fund for the payment of wages occasioned by the diminution of rates; and would ultimately, instead of forming a constantly increasing proportion of our whole population, become a small well-defined part of it, capable of being provided for at an expense less than one-half of the present poor rates.

'5. That the proposed changes would tend powerfully to promote providence and forethought, not only in the daily concerns of life, but in the most important of all points—marriage.

'And lastly, That it is essential to every one of these improvements that the administration of the poor-laws should be intrusted, as to their general superintendence, to one central authority, with extensive powers; and as to their details, to paid officers, acting under the consciousness of constant superintendence and strict responsibility.'

Such were the views and recommendations on which the new poor-law bill was based. Mr. Chadwick's ideas were as nearly carried out in this measure as their novelty and boldness would admit, with the addition of bastardy clauses, intended to check the unlimited increase of pauper population, which the old poor-law had so fatally encouraged. The best thing the Parliament could do with it evidently was to examine it as carefully, and pass it through as speedily as possible, without much change in its details. This accordingly was what Parliament did. Great complaints were made of one part of the bill, which, while stopping all out-door relief, provided that the goods and furniture of the person admitted into a workhouse should be sold, and that not only in cases where the pauperism was likely to be permanent, but where there was reason to hope that it would probably only be transient, as when it was caused by depression of trade, or other accidental circumstances; and it was indignantly asked, When a man is thus situated, will you make him sell his loom, or his tools, or his bed; so that when he comes out of the workhouse again he will be destitute, helpless, and without the means of carrying on his trade, or providing the most necessary articles for his family? But the answer given to this question was, that though no doubt there were instances in which an honest and industrious workman might, without any fault of his own, be reduced to such poverty, yet men were generally brought to this condition by improvident marriages, reckless expenditure, or neglect to make provision against a rainy day; and that therefore it was necessary, in justice to the honest and hard-working ratepayer, that the property of the rate-receiver should be made available to the last penny before he was allowed to become a burden on the community; and that thus the working classes should be practically taught the bitter but salutary lesson of self-help—the lesson of reliance on their own industry, frugality, temperance, and providence, rather than on the public purse.

Another part of the scheme which caused great dissatisfaction, and gave rise to loud complaints, was that which required the separation of wives from their husbands, and children from their parents, while they were in the workhouse. Endless was the sentimental declamation that was poured forth on this subject by those who constituted themselves the defenders of the pauper. But nothing could be more reasonable than that the man who was obtaining his daily bread, not by the sweat of his own brow, but by the labour of others—who consumed without producing—should, at least during the period of his voluntary dependence, be prevented from loading his supporters with fresh burdens, and produce a generation of paupers, to press with additional weight on the overburdened industry of the country. Besides, decency, propriety, and economy, all rendered these arrangements necessary; and had Mr. Chadwick's ideas been fully carried out, the classification would have been much more perfect. His motto was, 'Aggregation in order to segregation;' in other words, large unions, in order that every distinct class of paupers might come under a separate and appropriate management. But whatever might be the hardships of the separations to which we have alluded, the pauper could at any time put an end to them, by ceasing to be a pauper and withdrawing from the workhouse, which he was always at liberty to do, by giving twenty-four hours' notice. The provision, however, to which so much objection was made, applied only to the able-bodied labourer, and not to the infirm and aged.

The transfer of the control hitherto exercised by magistrates to elected guardians acting under the authority of a central body, was naturally opposed; as was also the removal of that great fetter on the freedom of labour—the law of settlement. But the chief resistance was to what were called the bastardy clauses, which threw the support of an illegitimate child on the mother instead of on the putative father. Those clauses were, with the consent of the ministry, so far modified as to allow the father to be made subject to a claim from the guardians of the poor for expenses incurred in the delivery of the child, together with such weekly sum as the support of the child would cost the mother, provided that her testimony was supported by other evidence. A clause of the bill, rendering the child's parents and grandparents liable to support an illegitimate child, was withdrawn; but it afforded Mr. Cobbett an opportunity, of which he availed himself, of venting his spleen against the king's family and pensioners in general, by moving that the same principle should be applied to paupers on the pension-list; a proposition which was supported by the votes of sixteen members in addition to that of its proposer. Clauses were added excluding the members of the commission to be appointed to carry out the provisions of the bill from having seats in the House of Commons, and limiting its operation to five years; so that at the expiration of that period Parliament might have an opportunity of revising its work, in the light of the experience gained during the interval. An attempt, made by Sir J. Whalley, to throw out the measure on the second reading, was defeated by 319 votes against 20; and it passed its last stage by a majority of 187 to 52.

When it reached the House of Lords the second reading was proposed in a speech of great ability by the lord chancellor, in which the various provisions of the bill and their advantages were lucidly exhibited. Lord Winford indeed opposed the motion; but the Duke of Wellington not only gave the measure his powerful assistance, but generously declared that it was *the best bill ever devised;* and as some of his party had complained of the lateness of the period of the session at which it was introduced into that House, he said that there was plenty of time during the present session to carry it regularly through all its stages. He warmly recommended that part of the bill, which provided for a central board to control and give uniformity to the administration of the poor-law throughout the country. At the same time, he referred to one or two provisions of the bill, which he hoped might be amended. Notwithstanding this hearty approval of the measure by the leader of the Opposition in the upper House, it was strongly resisted by a small section of the peers; but the second reading was carried by a majority of 76 to 13.

As we have already seen, the bastardy clauses of the bill had been altered in the Commons to meet in some degree the objections that had been made to them. This concession, however, was far from satisfying the party that opposed their enactment; a strong agitation had been raised against them out of doors, and the *Times* newspaper, which had all along shown itself hostile to the measure, exerted the whole power it possessed over public opinion against this feature of it. The bitterness of its opposition had been much increased by an accidental circumstance. The lord chancellor, while sitting in his court, wrote a note to Lord Althorp, suggesting that they should set the *Times* at defiance, and expressing in no measured terms his opinion of one of its editors. This note he afterwards tore up without sending it. The pieces were carefully picked out of the waste-paper basket, pasted together, sent to the editor of the *Times*, and printed in his newspaper; whereupon Lord Brougham, being unable to discover the culprit, dismissed all the officers of the court. In the House of Lords the opposition to the bastardy clauses was led by the bishop of Exeter, who, as we have already seen, was one of the ablest debaters in the House, and a man who exercised a greater influence in the country than all the rest of his episcopal brethren. He eloquently dwelt on the wrong done to the woman by throwing on her the whole burden of supporting the child, and he adduced many facts tending to show that female incontinency might be checked without resorting to such injustice. He was ably answered by a brother prelate, the bishop of London, who was one of the most active of the commissioners, and well acquainted with the reasons which had led to the adoption of these clauses. Lord Radnor stated that his experience as a magistrate had taught him that the law of bastardy as then administered produced a mass of perjury that it was truly frightful to contemplate. Lord Brougham stated that the object of this part of the bill was not to make women chaste and men continent, but that if it had been constructed with that view, it could not have been more effectual. The law as it then stood was contrary to common sense, and fostered a crime only second to murder—the detestable crime of wilful and corrupt perjury. The division was a close one, the bishop of Exeter's amendment being supported by 34 votes to 38. But when he renewed his attempt in another shape, the numbers on both sides were higher, 71 supporting the view of the bishop, and 82 voting with the government. Some changes of no great importance were made in the bill by the peers, which were all agreed to by the Commons, with the single exception of a provision relating to the admission of dissenting ministers into the workhouses: and thus this great and beneficial measure became the law of the land. Mr. Chadwick, the real author of the measure, was appointed secretary to the commissioners, and ably and diligently superintended its application. The bill did not receive the royal assent till the 14th of August, but no time was lost in bringing it into operation. This consequently took place at a period of the year when there is employment for all in the agricultural districts; and thus this great change was much less felt than it would have been if made at a different season. The hopes of its authors were more than fulfilled, and the predictions of its opponents signally falsified. The introduction of the new act was speedily followed by diminished rates, higher wages, employment for all who sought it, a cessation of riots, rick-burnings, and machine-breakings, a great improvement in the habits and character of the working classes, and a marked and surprising diminution of the number of illegitimate births. The Bashaws, as the commissioners were called by their more intemperate opponents, used the great discretionary powers confided to them with prudence and moderation. The persons elected for guardians of the poor were for the most part persons of high respectability, and discharged the duties imposed on them by the act with zeal and fidelity. An abundant harvest helped to mitigate the hardships inseparable from so great and sudden an alteration. There was indeed a small remnant of inveterately demoralised paupers who would rather eat the bread of idleness than obtain their food by the labour of their own hands and the sweat of their own brow. These raised a loud outcry against the *bastilles*, as the new workhouses were termed by the opponents of the act, and they received encouragement from some who should have known better. But they gradually and slowly fell into the ranks of industrious labourers, or were obliged to submit to the terms which the law properly imposed upon them as a condition of receiving the public money. Never perhaps was so great a transformation wrought in the habits of the working classes so effectually or with so little disturbance.

The truth of these assertions will be best exhibited by pointing out a few of the results actually achieved by it; and this we will do, though of course in doing it we must anticipate a little. In the four unions of Milton, Blean, Bridge, and River, containing altogether a population of 41,409, there were 954 able-bodied paupers at the time of the formation of the unions; but in June 1836 there were only five. All the rest were employed within the unions, with the exception of about two dozen, all of bad character, who had either gone to seek work elsewhere or joined the British legion in Spain. In the county of Sussex, which before the passing of the act had been one of the most deeply pauperised in the kingdom, there were at the time of the formation of the unions 6,160 able-bodied paupers. In less than two years after the introduction of the new poor-law that number was reduced to 124. In 1836 the act was in operation in twenty-two counties, and the average reduction in the rates in those counties was $43\frac{1}{2}$ per cent. It had been predicted by the commissioners of inquiry, that the application of the principles they recommended would restore and improve industry, create and confirm habits of frugality, increase the demand for labour and the wages of the labourer, diminish discontent, and improve the moral and social condition of the working classes. In less than two years after the passing of the act these predictions had been fulfilled.

The subject of 'agricultural distress' was still kept before the legislature. The new poor-law was the measure of all others best calculated to relieve it; but the country gentlemen were anxious to get some other and more speedy remedy for it. Hence the Marquis of Chandos, who had become the leader and spokesman of the agricultural party, moved, 'that in the remission of taxes due regard be paid to the necessity of relieving agricultural distress.' Mr. Cobbett too proposed the repeal of the malt tax; a measure of relief which the farmers were continually hoping to obtain. Mr. Hume introduced a motion for the repeal of the corn-laws, the time for the serious and dispassionate consideration of which had not yet arrived. He was, however, supported in a very able speech by Mr. Poulett Thompson, who then filled the office of vice-president of the Board of Trade, and who on this question separated himself from his colleagues. These motions, however, for the present produced no practical result, and the agricultural interest gained little or nothing by them.

At the unusually early period of the 14th of February, Lord Althorp made a preparatory statement of the general features of his intended financial operations in a committee of ways and means, which was, on the whole, very satisfactory, and showed that the pledges of economy and retrenchment which the Whig party had given to the country had not been forgotten or neglected by the Whig ministry. In the course of the three years during which they had held office, they had reduced taxes to the amount of 3,335,000*l.*; and yet on the 5th of January 1834 they found themselves able to deal with a surplus of 513,000*l*. By changing the duty on tea to an *ad valorem* duty, and by certain operations in the tea market, the control of which had at the last renewal of the East India Company's charter been transferred from the company to the government, the chancellor of the exchequer hoped to have at his disposal a surplus revenue of 2,600,000*l*. From this a deduction of 800,000*l*. must be made to meet the interest of the 20,000,000*l*. which Parliament had granted last year to the West India proprietors. But there would still remain a clear disposable surplus of 1,800,000*l*.

Admitting that there were other taxes which, in his opinion, it was more desirable to remove, Lord Althorp announced that it was his intention to repeal the tax on houses, on account of its great unpopularity. He expected to be able to propose the repeal of some other taxes, but he was not able to specify them at that time; but he called on those who were in favour of the repeal of the house tax to give him their support in his resistance of other reductions of taxation, which would render that repeal difficult, if not impossible. The measure would relieve the country of burdens to the amount of 1,200,000*l*. It was true that it would not remove the agricultural distress that was so much complained of; but it was hoped that the new poor-law and tithe-commutation bills, which government introduced in the course of this session, would greatly alleviate the distress that prevailed throughout the agricultural districts.

Though this statement was made at the very beginning of the session, the budget itself, which it anticipated in its chief features, was not brought forward till the 25th of July. In introducing it, the chancellor of the exchequer informed the House that the receipts for the year ending July 5, 1834, amounted to 46,914,586*l.*; while the expenditure for the same period had been 44,737,556*l.*; leaving a surplus of income over expenditure of 2,177,030*l.* On the strength of this surplus, he proposed to make the following reductions:

House tax	£1,200,000
Customs	200,000
Starch	75,000
Stone bottles and sweets	6,000
Almanacs	25,000
Small assessed taxes	75,000
Total	£1,581,000

A farther deduction however would be made from the surplus, in consequence of reductions that it was proposed to make in the Irish excise duties, for the purpose of checking the practice of illicit distillation. Lord Althorp admitted that the surplus was small; but looking to the history of recent times, and regarding the buoyancy and elasticity of our present resources, he entertained the fullest confidence that no danger whatever would arise from relying on so small an estimated excess of revenue.

Another financial operation carried out in the course of this year was the conversion of the 4 per cent. annuities granted in 1826 into 3½ per cent. annuities redeemable on the 5th of January, 1840. This was effected by the help of the savings'-bank funds. The number of those who declined to accept the terms proposed by the government was much larger than had been anticipated, and they had to be paid off in full. However, the proposed reduction was carried into effect without difficulty on the 10th October in this year.

Some other attempts at legislation made during this session, though abortive, demand a passing notice. The bill for the removal of the civil disabilities of the Jews, rejected during the last session by the Peers, was again carried in the lower House, and once more rejected by the

Lords. A motion for altering the law which compelled members of the House of Commons accepting office under the crown to present themselves for re-election, deserved and obtained considerable attention. The present administration had been seriously embarrassed through the rejection of the attorney-general by his constituents when he went before them again, in consequence of his acceptance of office. Lord Althorp, while admitting the difficult position in which the law sometimes placed the government, and particularly the embarrassment which the rejection of the attorney-general had caused them, opposed the motion, which was accordingly rejected. On the 15th of May, Mr. Tennyson asked for leave to bring in a bill to shorten the duration of Parliament. In the debate which arose on this motion, annual, biennial, triennial, quadrennial, and quinquennial parliaments, all found their advocates: and one member—Mr. James—suggested the retirement of a third part of the House annually. But all these opinions united were not numerous enough to obtain a consideration of Mr. Tennyson's bill, or overcome the natural reluctance of the majority to appear more frequently than heretofore on the hustings. The same fortune attended a motion made by Colonel Evans, to modify or repeal those clauses of the Reform Act which made the payment of rates and taxes by a certain day necessary to the exercise of the parliamentary franchise. The proposed change was resisted by the government, and the motion lost. A bill for the prevention of bribery, introduced by Lord J. Russell, went through both Houses; but the Peers, acting on the recommendations of a select committee, to which it had been referred, introduced amendments so extensive as utterly to change the character of the measure. As these amendments, according to the forms of the House, could not be considered without making the bill pass again through committee, and as there was no prospect of bringing the two Houses to an agreement with respect to them, Lord J. Russell withdrew the measure. A bill for the disfranchisement of the freemen of Warwick who had been guilty of gross corruption, and for the extension of the right of voting for the representative of that borough to the inhabitants of the surrounding districts, was carried through the Commons, but rejected, after some discussion, by the Peers, on the motion of the lord chancellor. A similar fate befell bills of a like character relating to Hertford, Stafford, Liverpool, and Carrickfergus; in all of which bribes seem to have been very extensively dispensed among the freemen; a class of voters who were most open to corrupt influences, and the preservation of whose franchises under the Reform Bill the liberal party had reluctantly conceded, and had frequent reason to regret. The House of Commons, which had carefully investigated the charges brought against the voters of these boroughs, and had come to conclusions in reference to them which were diametrically opposed to those at which the Lords had arrived, showed their disapproval of the decision of the upper House by resolving that the writs of three of the inculpated boroughs—Hertford, Warwick, and Carrickfergus—should be withholden until the 20th of February next.

This session was damaging to the ministers. The vigour and firmness they had displayed in the debates on the Reform Bill had raised expectations which had not, and perhaps could not, be realized. A general feeling prevailed, and was very strongly expressed by many of the leading journals which had hitherto warmly supported them, that in many respects, and especially in their manner of dealing with Irish questions, they had displayed a great want of capacity. The opposition they offered to the measures which a large number of their supporters deemed necessary complements to the Reform Bill, and their steady discouragement of all proposals for the enlargement of the suffrage, the introduction of the ballot, the shortening of the duration of Parliaments, caused great discontent. It was true that the new poor-law which they had carried through was a most valuable measure, and one which might well be pleaded as a set-off against more serious errors and deficiencies than those of which they were accused. But it was not one of those measures that call forth the enthusiastic admiration of a people; and the benefits it conferred on all classes of the community, and especially in the agricultural districts, had scarcely begun to be felt, while the hardships and sufferings inseparable from the first introduction of so great a change in the habits and condition of the working-class were at their height. The government was too reforming for the Tories, who besides could neither forget nor forgive their intro duction of the Reform Bill, or their manner of carrying it through. It was too conservative for many of its own supporters, who blamed its deference to the House of Lords; were disappointed to find that the Reform Bill had not been followed up by the measures which had been held out to them as certain to result from it; and saw with great dissatisfaction the government steadily adhering to a policy of finality. The immense popularity they had enjoyed at the time of their accession to office and during the whole duration of the reform struggle, had given way to a feeling, not so much of hostility, as of indifference almost approaching contempt. The losses which the cabinet had sustained by the secession of many of its members had increased this indifference. The king and the conservatives greatly mistook the mind of the country when they imagined that it was undergoing a conservative reaction. Ever since William had been compelled to take back his Whig ministers after calling in the Duke of Wellington, he had considered that one of his most important prerogatives had been invaded, and felt deeply and personally humiliated in consequence; and had ever since been impatient to seize the first favourable opportunity of getting rid of the advisers that had been forced on him by the will of the nation.

This resolution was no doubt greatly strengthened by the strong disapproval with which he regarded the proposed appropriation of the revenues of the Irish church; and their coquettings with O'Connell. He had already displayed these feelings in an altogether unprecedented manner. On the 28th of May, the day observed as the anniversary of his birthday, the very day after the introduction of Mr. Ward's motion and the resignation of Lord Stanley and his friends, just when Earl Grey was prevented from resigning by Lord Ebrington's address—at this critical moment, the Irish prelates, with the Irish primate at their head, presented an address to the king at the birthday levee, signed by seventeen Irish prelates and some 1400 of the Irish clergy, in which they expressed their attachment to the doctrine and liturgy of the church to which they belonged, promised to assist in reforming real abuses, but deprecated undefined changes in the doctrine and discipline of the church, which persons widely differing among themselves were understood to have in contemplation. Instead of giving to this address, according to the usual practice, a written answer prepared in concert with his advisers, the king, after conversing with the prelates who had presented the address, made this reply in tones of great earnestness, and the tears running down his cheeks: 'I now remember you have a right to require of me to be resolute in defence of the church. I have been, by the circumstances of my life and by conviction, led to support toleration to the utmost extent of which it is justly capable; but toleration must not be suffered to go into licentiousness; it has its bounds, which it is my duty and which I am resolved to maintain. I am, from the deepest conviction, attached to the pure Protestant faith which this church, of which I am the temporal head, is the human means of diffusing and preserving in this land. I cannot forget what was the course of events that placed my family on the throne which I now fill. These events were consummated in a revolution which was rendered necessary, and was effected, not, as has sometimes been most erroneously stated, merely for the sake of the temporal liberties of the people, but for the preservation of their religion. It was for the defence of the religion of the country that the settlement of the crown was made which has placed me in the situation which I now fill; and that religion, and the church of England and Ireland, the prelates of which are now before me, it is my fixed purpose, resolution, and determination to maintain. The present bishops, I am quite satisfied (and I am rejoiced to hear from them and from all the same of the clergy in general under their government), have never been excelled at any period in the history of our church by any of their predecessors in learning, piety, or zeal in the discharge of their high duties. If there are any of the inferior arrangements in the discipline of the church—which, however, I greatly doubt—that require amendment, I have no distrust of the readiness and ability of the prelates now before me to correct such things; and to you, I trust, they will be left to correct, with your authority unimpaired and unshackled. I trust it will not be supposed that I am speaking to you a speech that I have got by heart; no, I am declaring to you my real and genuine sentiments. I have almost completed my sixty-ninth year, and though blessed by God with a very rare measure of health, not having known what sickness is for some years, yet I do not blind myself to the plain and evident truth, that increase of years must tell largely upon me when sickness shall come. I cannot therefore expect that I shall be very long in this world. It is under this impression that I tell you, that while I know that the law of the land considers it impossible that I should do wrong—that while I know that there is no earthly power that can call me to account—this only makes me the more deeply sensible of the responsibility under which I stand to that Almighty Being before whom we must all one day appear. When that day shall come, you will know whether I am sincere in the declaration which I now make of firm attachment to the church and resolution to maintain it. I have spoken more strongly than usual, because of unhappy circumstances that have forced themselves on the observation of all. The threats of those who are enemies of the church make it the more necessary for those who feel their duty to that church to speak out. The words which you hear from me are indeed spoken by my mouth, but flow from my heart.'

This speech was of course received with transports of joy by the prelates to whom it was addressed, and by the members of the united churches, to whom it was diligently distributed. By the king's ministers it must have been regarded with far different feelings. What private remonstrances they offered to their master we cannot tell; but they must have felt that it was an open declaration of hostility against the policy to which they had committed themselves, and an appeal to the country against it. After this, if before, they could not cherish any illusion with regard to the intentions of their royal master. They must have felt that he would dismiss them as soon as he thought that he could do it without subjecting himself again to the humiliation of being obliged to ask them to take office again. The death of Earl Spencer, which raised Lord Althorp, his oldest son, to the upper House, afforded William, as he thought, the opportunity he desired. When therefore, on the 14th of November, Lord Melbourne submitted to him the changes he proposed to make in the ministry in consequence of the vacancy of the chancellorship of the exchequer, his majesty told him that he was of opinion that the business of the country could not be carried on by such a ministry as it was now proposed to constitute, and that he had made up his mind to call in the Duke of Wellington. The Duke advised that the task of forming a new administration should be confided to Sir R. Peel, who had gone to Rome, intending to pass the winter there. He was at once sent for, but as some time must elapse before he could return, the Duke himself filled provisionally the offices of first lord of the treasury and secretary of state. Lord Lyndhurst received the great seal on the 21st of November. On the 9th of December Sir Robert arrived in London, and at once accepted the task imposed on him. He soon succeeded in forming a ministry, and as it was evidently impossible for his government to stand its ground in the face of so large a majority as was arrayed against it in the House of Commons, he determined to appeal to the country; and on the 30th of December a proclamation was issued, announcing the dissolution of Parliament. Sir Robert also published a manifesto to the nation under the form of an address to his constituents at Tamworth, in which he announced the policy he intended to pursue, and asked for a fair trial on behalf of himself and his ministerial colleagues. In this carefully prepared document, he thus indicated the spirit in which he was resolved to act: 'Our object will be, the maintenance of peace, the scrupulous and honourable fulfilment, without reference to their original policy, of all engagements with foreign powers, the support of public credit, the enforcement of strict economy, and the just and impartial consideration of what is due to all interests—agricultural, manufacturing, and commercial.'

Before the dismissal of the Melbourne ministry, the two chambers in which the legislature assembled had been destroyed. The evening of the 16th of October was just closing in when flames burst from several parts of the edifice, and spread so rapidly that some persons who were inside had great difficulty in escaping. In a very short time the two Houses, with almost all the offices and buildings that belonged to them, were wrapped in one tremendous conflagration, which lighted up all London. Presently every street leading towards the burning mass was thronged as it had never been thronged before. Dense crowds occupied the various open spaces from which the progress of the flames could be watched. A deep red glare overspread the river, the Abbey, the hall of William Rufus, and the neighbouring houses, presenting a striking contrast to the white moonlight which illuminated the stones of old Westminster-bridge, and threw its beams on the dark mass of human beings that covered the pavement, the roadway, and even the parapets. Unfortunately, the tide at this moment happened to be unusually low, and this rendered the supply of water so scanty, that at first only a few fire-engines, and these not very advantageously placed, could be brought to bear on the burning pile. It appeared to the spectators that no human efforts could save Westminster-hall, and even the Abbey itself was thought to be in imminent danger. The flames, crackling and rustling with prodigious noise, compared by those who heard it to very loud firing of musketry, speedily destroyed the two Houses of Parliament, the interior of the tower containing the library of the House of Commons, which fell a little after midnight with a tremendous crash, and most of the residences and offices connected with the chief buildings. The tide had now risen, and an ample supply of water was obtained from the river; the floating fire-engine was brought up, and played on the still burning ruins with prodigious effect. An eye-witness wrote: 'More vigorous exertion and more active zeal were never witnessed;' but most of the exertion was misdirected, and a good deal of the zeal uselessly expended, for want of due organization and a directing head. Each insurance company sent up its own fire-engines, which were worked under the uncontrolled management of their own officers. By three o'clock the flames had sunk down, having devoured nearly all the combustible matter within their reach. Westminster-hall was saved, and so too was the speaker's residence, but almost all the rest was destroyed. The myriads who had crowded the streets and covered the bridges had gradually gone to their homes, and none were now left to watch the final extinction of the flames but the soldiers, the police, and the firemen.

Among the first to hasten to the scene of destruction were Lord Melbourne, Lord Althorp, Lord Duncannon, the home secretary, and Sir J. C. Hobhouse, the ministers then in town. The home secretary mounted on to the roof of the House of Commons to direct the efforts of the firemen there, and bravely refused to descend from his dangerous post till all others had quitted it. In two minutes after his departure, the roof on which he had been standing fell in. Next morning, when the citizens came from their houses, they found Westminster-hall erect amidst a mass of blackened and unsightly ruins. Thus at last disappeared a building which Guy Fawkes had vainly attempted to destroy with gunpowder, and which Mr. Hume, equally in vain, had been long labouring to remove by more regular and constitutional means.

It was at first supposed that this destruction was the work of incendiaries, and it was asserted very confidently that persons had been seen running to and fro, and setting fire to the buildings in several parts. But it was soon ascertained that the fire was the result of nothing more criminal than very gross carelessness. A workman of the name of Cross had been employed to burn the old wooden tallies formerly used in the court of Exchequer. He had been directed to burn them slowly and carefully; but being impatient to finish his work, in which he was engaged for more than ten hours, he disregarded this injunction, and threw great numbers on at a time. The consequence was, that the flues became intensely heated, and being in contact with a good deal of old dry timber, set it on fire; and this was the reason why the fire, which had no doubt been long smouldering, burst out in several places almost simultaneously.

This catastrophe was not much to be regretted. The buildings which had been destroyed were quite unsuitable for the accommodation of the legislature of the United Kingdom, and the necessity of erecting new Houses of Parliament had long been felt and acknowledged; but it is probable that if this accident had not occurred, the old premises would have been occupied and extended from time to time for a much longer period. Fortunately, a large portion of the records, and that the most valuable, was saved. As Parliament had to be farther prorogued only a week after the fire occurred, the library was fitted up as a temporary House of Lords, and a contiguous committee-room served as a place of assembly for the few members who represented the House of Commons. The king offered to give up Buckingham Palace, now nearly ready for his own reception, to the legislature; but it was ultimately determined that some of the old buildings should be refitted until a more permanent arrangement could be made.

The 25th day of July in this year witnessed the death of the great philosopher-poet S. T. Coleridge; a man in whom gigantic industry and lofty virtues alternated with ignoble indolence and deplorable vices. Born at St. Mary's Ottery, educated first at Christ's Hospital and afterwards at Cambridge, where, however, he did not complete his academical career, he found in 1792 a congenial spirit in Robert Southey: and the two, fired with the enthusiastic hopes of universal human regeneration, which the dawn of the French Revolution inspired, dreamed all kinds of Utopias, and tried hard to realize their dreams. But the horrible sequel of the French Revolution quenched the bright anticipations which its dawn had excited. Through life he was a dreamer and a thinker, not a doer. He married; tried to found in America what he called a Pantinocracy, or retreat for the universal regeneration of the human race; but other dreams and the tide of events floated him to Lisbon. On his return to England he became a preacher of Unitarian Christianity, and a writer of plays and pamphlets. In 1798 he spent two years travelling in Germany, in company with Wordsworth, and thus acquired that taste for German literature by which tinge all his later writings are tinctured. On his return to England in 1800, he took up his abode at Keswick, where his two friends Southey and Wordsworth also resided. Here he exchanged his strong anti-trinitarian opinions for equally strong trinitarian opinions, and during the rest of his life was the vehement and intolerant denouncer of every form of unitarianism. He became a most zealous and affectionate son of the church of England, and sympathised with the anti-reformers as far as it was possible that a man of his lofty intelligence could do. His works are replete with profound thought and the loftiest eloquence; and nothing but poverty and indolence prevented him from producing a system of philosophy which would in all human probability have been of inestimable value. Perhaps few men ever lived who have more powerfully influenced understandings of the highest order. We believe that Dr. Arnold, Keble, Pusey, T. Carlyle, Gladstone, the two Newmans, the two Froudes, Colenso, and the writers both of the *Tracts for the Times* and *Essays and Reviews*, were all largely, though perhaps unconsciously, indebted to the seeds of thought which were directly or indirectly sown in their minds by his writings or conversation.

CHAPTER VI.

CORPORATION REFORM.

When Sir Robert Peel accepted office, he probably entertained no very sanguine hope of being able to sustain himself in it for any length of time. He knew how large a majority his opponents had in the House of Commons, and though he might hope to diminish that majority by an appeal to the country, he could hardly expect to change it into a minority. Had he been consulted before the dismissal of the late ministry, he would probably have given his advice against the step. But now that it had been taken, he determined to do all he could to deserve victory, if he could not achieve it. With the view of strengthening his government, he made overtures to Mr. (now Lord) Stanley and Sir J. Graham. They declined to join his administration, but promised that, as independent members of the House of Commons, they would give it a fair trial. The policy announced in his Tamworth address made, on the whole, a favourable impression. There was a general feeling of confidence in Sir R. Peel, not only as an able administrator, but as one who would not offer an obstinate resistance to the public opinion of the country, when once it was clearly declared. On the other hand, it was felt that he was not the man to attempt those bold and organic changes which reformers hoped to obtain from the Whigs, but which they knew would not be conceded, except at the last extremity, by the Tories. The long and obstinate opposition that Sir Robert had offered to the great measure of reform was remembered to his disadvantage, and it was felt that the man who had so strongly resisted it was not the man who ought to be intrusted with the care of carrying out the policy which that great measure had inaugurated. It was true that a large number of reformers had been grievously disappointed by the resistance which the Whigs had opposed to wishes and expectations which had no small share in placing and keeping them in office. But it was known that they were preparing a measure of municipal-reform, and it was expected that they would accept and carry out the policy indicated in Mr. Ward's motion for the appropriation of the surplus revenues of the Irish establishment. There was therefore a somewhat cold but yet very decided preference of them in the country; and it remained to be seen how far the influence of the government, which in many places was still considerable, the lavish expenditure of money, and the power which was still wielded by the Tory party, would enable the new administration to counterbalance this preference. The Whigs while they thought themselves secure in office had treated the radical party almost with disdain, but they now courted it, and let it be understood that they would give it greater influence if they should succeed in regaining office. The commencement of the elections was ominous for the new administration. The City of London, which had previously returned three reformers now sent four. All the metropolitan boroughs elected radicals. On the other hand, Bristol, Leeds, York, Newcastle, Exeter, Hull, Warrington, and Halifax, each sent to the House of Commons a supporter of the new ministry, to replace a supporter of their opponents. At Liverpool and Leeds the conservatives headed the poll. In the counties they gained largely. In Hampshire Lord Palmerston lost his election. In Berkshire, Buckinghamshire, Cambridgeshire, Denbighshire, Derbyshire, South Devonshire, South Essex, West Gloucestershire, South Hampshire, South Lancashire, South Leicestershire, Lincolnshire, East Norfolk, South Northamptonshire, North Shropshire, East Suffolk, West Suffolk, East Surrey, West Surrey, South Warwickshire—and to this long list was added in the course of the year Devonshire, Inverness-shire, and Staffordshire—the Tories gained seats which had before been filled by liberals; thus showing how strong a reaction had taken place among the agriculturists, and how rapidly and completely, thanks to Lord Chandos, the great territorial proprietors were recovering the influence they had formerly enjoyed. The ministerial party could boast that they had a majority of English members. In Scotland the relative strength of the two parties was little altered by the dissolution. In Ireland, where unscrupulous corruption on the one side wrestled with lawless intimidation on the other, the following, or, as it was then called, the *tail*, of O'Connell was somewhat diminished. On the whole, it was evident, as all thoughtful men had foreseen, that though the appeal to the country had greatly swelled the Tory ranks, it still left to their opponents a decided majority, in the face of which it would be impossible for the new administration long to retain office. Sir Robert Peel was, however, none the less determined to strain every nerve and put forth every effort in order to place himself in a favourable position before the new House of Commons and the country. He laboured in the preparation of a number of measures which he intended at least to propose before being driven from office. He appointed an ecclesiastical commission, composed of the two archbishops, the bishops of London, Lincoln, and Gloucester, and some of the chief members of the government, to consider the condition of the church in England and Wales, and to prepare a plan of church reform. He hoped that the measures which he was engaged in framing would contrast so favourably with those which had been brought forward by his predecessors, that they would strengthen the feeling in his favour that prevailed in the country, and if they did not enable him to retain office now, would at least pave the way for his future return to it.

The first business of the new House was, of course, the appointment of a speaker. We have already seen how strongly the late ministers had in the previous Parliament supported the election of Sir C. M. Sutton to that office. They now resolved to oppose his re-election, partly for the purpose of inflicting a defeat on the ministry, and partly because they believed that Sir C. M. Sutton had gone out of his way to assist in the formation of the conservative ministry, by taking part in some meetings of the privy council summoned by them. Mr. Abercromby, one of the members for the city of Edinburgh, and an office-holder in the late administration, was requested to allow himself to be put forward in opposition to the late speaker. He at first refused; but ultimately yielded to the earnest solicitations of Lord J. Russell. The interest excited was immense. Never before had so large a number of members been present. The division was closer than had been anticipated, Mr. Abercromby winning by only ten votes; the number being 316 in his favour, against 306 for the late speaker. It was remarked, however, that Sir C. M. Sutton had a majority of 23 English votes. Of the Scotch members, it was found that 31 supported their own countryman, while 18 voted for his opponent. Thus on the English and Scotch votes together Sir C. M. Sutton had a clear majority. But the Irish votes decided the triumph of the Whig candidate, and this was the first parliamentary indication given of the fact that the late ministers had come to an understanding with Mr. O'Connell, and had secured his co-operation.

The address in answer to the king's speech afforded the leaders of the Opposition an opportunity of inflicting a second defeat on the ministerial party. In the upper House there was much debate, but no division. In the lower House an amendment, strongly censuring the dissolution, was carried by 307 voices to 302. An attempt to alter this decision on the bringing up of the report of the address was abandoned by the ministry as hopeless. Here, again, the supporters of the government consoled themselves by remarking that a majority of 32 English members voted with them, and that the Opposition carried their point only through the support given them by O'Connell and his tail. O'Connell's adhesion to the Whigs was still more signally marked by an announcement he made, that he intended for the present to withdraw from the agitation of the repeal question, in the hope that the reform of the Irish corporations would put an end to the power of the Orange faction, and would give to Ireland all she could hope to obtain by means of a domestic legislature.

Rumours were very rife that the government contemplated another appeal to the country, and the dread of such a step prevented many Opposition members from voting against them. Lord J. Russell, therefore, as leader of the Opposition, endeavoured to draw from Sir R. Peel a declaration of his intentions on this point. But his efforts were baffled by the wary tact of the premier. 'With respect,' he said, 'to the question with which I was threatened by the noble lord on a former day, but from which I think that he has himself now receded, the question as to the dissolution of Parliament, I cannot help thinking it possible that in the interval he has referred to a question put in the month of April, 1831, to Lord Grey. There were then rumours very prevalent as to the dissolution of Parliament, and not without good cause. But the question to which I refer was put on the 21st of April, and on the 22d Parliament was dissolved. On the 21st of April, 1831, Lord Wharncliffe said: "I wish to ask his majesty's ministers whether there is any truth in the statement that they have advised his majesty to dissolve Parliament, and that it has been resolved to adopt that course." Lord Grey, in reply, said: "I believe the noble earl's question will be admitted to be one of a very unusual nature, and can hardly bring myself to believe, that when he put it, he expected an answer. But whatever his expectations may have been, I have only to say, I must decline answering his question." I am sure, that if the noble lord would on any subject submit to a rebuke from any one he would not object to one coming from Earl Grey. But I will be more explicit with him than Lord Grey was with Lord Wharncliffe. He has asked me whether or not I have countenanced rumours which he says are prevalent, respecting a dissolution of Parliament. I tell him in reply, that by no act or expression of mine, directly or indirectly, have I sanctioned or countenanced such rumours. I will tell him with equal fairness, that I have never discussed with anybody the case hypothetically in which a dissolution might be considered necessary. I must, at the same time say, that it would be unbecoming in me, as a minister of the crown, to consent to place any prerogative of the crown in abeyance, or to pledge myself how I should advise the crown as to the course it should pursue.' By this dexterous handling of the matter Sir R. Peel kept the Opposition in doubt as to his real intentions, and left the Damocles' sword of another dissolution still hanging over their heads. Mr. Hume thought to bring matters to a crisis by moving that the supplies be limited first to six, and then to three months; but by the advice of his friends he abandoned both these projects, and, after several days of irresolution, he ended by moving that the navy estimates should be referred to a committee with a view to the reduction of their amount; but this motion was rejected by 146 to 60.

The next contest in which the government was engaged was with some of its own supporters. On the 10th of March the following resolution was moved by the Marquis of Chandos: 'That it is important that the present duties on malt should altogether cease and determine.' Sir R. Peel, who had aided the Whig ministers in resisting the repeal of a portion of this tax in 1834, now strenuously withstood the attempts that were made to repeal it entirely, and was assisted by the late ministers, who were induced, not only by the recollection of his conduct, but by the prospect of having themselves to frame the budget, to use their utmost efforts to defeat the motion. Thus as, by the aid of Sir R. Peel, Lord J. Russell had been enabled to maintain the tax against his followers, so now, by the aid of Lord J. Russell, Sir Robert maintained it against his, and especially the country members, many of whom had pledged themselves on the hustings to vote for the repeal of this unpopular tax. After a long debate, in which Sir R. Peel surpassed himself, the motion for the repeal was rejected by a majority of 138; 192 having voted for it, and 350 against it.

Another event happened at this time, which shook the tottering administration, and nearly brought it down. It was announced that the Marquis of Londonderry, who had on two occasions so nearly fallen a sacrifice to the rage of the London mob, had been appointed to the important post of ambassador at St. Petersburg. He had many claims to this appointment. He had served on the staff of the Duke of Wellington, and had filled the office of adjutant-general, much to his grace's satisfaction, from 1809 to 1813. In 1813 he was employed as assistant minister at Berlin; and in 1814 he had been sent as ambassador to Vienna; and when recalled at his own desire, from that mission, he had received from Mr. Canning a letter in which his services were warmly acknowledged and the loss of them regretted. He had published a History of the Peninsular War, of which he had furnished the facts, while a reverend friend had attended to the grammar and the composition. But the experience he had enjoyed had not made him wise. He was very unmeasured in his language. He had attacked the authors of the Reform Bill with a violence and rashness that damaged the cause he espoused much more than that which he assailed. All this, however, would not probably have prevented the appointment from taking effect, if he had not obtained for himself a most unenviable reputation by coming forward on all occasions as the defender of the most arbitrary and despotic acts of the absolute monarchs of the Continent, and still more by having denounced the unhappy Poles as a nation of rebels. At that moment there was throughout England a strong and general sympathy with the sufferings of Poland, and it seemed intolerable that a man should be chosen to represent England at the Russian court who would so entirely misrepresent the sentiments of the nation. On the other hand, the dangers he had run in the Tory cause, the manner in which he had employed the influence derived from his large estates and princely revenues in promoting the return of supporters of the present ministry, the liberality with which he had contributed to the funds with which the battle of conservatism was fought at the last election, gave him a strong claim on his party. It is very unlikely that a statesman so wary and calculating as Sir Robert Peel would willingly have consented to place him in a position in which he might have done great and irreparable mischief. He probably yielded to the influence of the Duke of Wellington. If he expected that the appointment would pass unchallenged, he was speedily undeceived. Mr. Sheil took the matter up by moving ' An address to his majesty for a copy of any appointment, made within the last four months, of an ambassador from the court of London to St. Petersburg, and of the salary and emoluments attached to such embassy.' As the appointment had not been formally carried, the motion was set aside; but the opinion of the House was significantly manifested in the discussion which took place on it. Even Lord Stanley, who up to this time, had warmly supported the government, abandoned and censured them on this question. Lord Londonderry withdrew his claim to the office; and thus the difficulty was got over, not however without some damage to the administration. This untoward circumstance did not prevent Sir R. Peel from bringing forward the measures he had prepared with so much diligence. As these came to nothing, or at best furnished a few hints to his successors in office, we will review them very briefly.

On the 17th of March Sir Robert brought forward his dissenters' marriage bill. He proposed that marriages should be celebrated in the usual manner for those who desired to be married according to the rites of the church. Others were to appear before a magistrate of the hundred in which they resided, at least seven days before their intended marriage, and must make oath that they were of the age of twenty-one, or, if not of age, that they had obtained the consent of their parents and guardians, and that they were not aware of any lawful impediment to the validity of the marriage. A copy of this contract was then to be forwarded to the clergyman of the parish, and to be entered by him in the parish register, for which service he was to receive a fee of five shillings. After this the parties would be at liberty to superadd any religious ceremony they thought proper. This plan did not altogether meet the views of the dissenters; but it found more favour with them than the Whig bill of the preceding year. A tithe bill exhibiting the legislative dexterity, the diligence, and statesmanship of the premier, had to be dropped, and was afterwards brought forward in a somewhat changed form by Sir Robert's Whig successors.

The ecclesiastical commissioners, urged forward by the active premier, reported on the 19th of March. But, as their recommendations were carried out under Sir Robert's successors, we shall have occasion to speak of them hereafter.

On the 12th of March two bills were brought in by the attorney-general, also based on the report of a commission, for the better maintenance of church discipline, and for the reform of the ecclesiastical courts. By these measures it was proposed to bring into one the whole of the ecclesiastical courts, amounting to about 400, that existed in the country.

The case of Colonel Tremenhere would be undeserving even of this passing reference, if it had not furnished the occasion of another party struggle and ministerial defeat. The colonel had excluded some slopsellers of Chatham from the barracks in that town. He was accused in a petition to the House of Commons of being actuated by a desire to punish them for having voted against the government candidate at the recent election; and in support of this charge some words which he was alleged to have used were cited.

The colonel denied the words imputed to him, and alleged that the slopsellers had been excluded to prevent the men from some ships which were paid off from being defrauded by them. In support of this assertion it was stated that the order, which was issued in January while the ships were being paid off, was rescinded on the 14th February. Mr. Hodges, member for East Kent, moved on the 24th of March that the matter should be referred to a select committee, and, notwithstanding the explanations that had been given, and in spite of the opposition of the government, his motion was carried by a majority of 31. The committee never reported, and the matter was dropped. On the 26th of the same month Mr. Tooke moved an address to his majesty, beseeching him 'to grant his royal charter of incorporation to the University of London as approved in the year 1831 by the law officers of the crown.' Memorials against the proposed charter had been sent from the two Universities, and from the Colleges of Surgeons and Physicians, and the motion was opposed by the government, but carried against it by 246 votes to 136.

Notwithstanding these repeated defeats, Sir R. Peel distinctly announced that it was his intention to retain office until a vote should be passed by the House of Commons, which distinctly implied that an administration possessed of more public confidence and greater ability to discharge its public duties could be formed. He challenged Lord J. Russell to bring forward a direct vote of want of confidence; a challenge which his lordship declined, declaring that he would wait for the measures of reform which the government had promised to bring forward.

It was by no means an easy matter for the Opposition to agree on any point on which they could combine against their astute opponent, and inflict on him such a defeat as would compel him to retire. The bills which he brought forward were, to a great extent, reproductions of measures which the Whigs had introduced, with certain manifest improvements suggested by the discussion which the measures had undergone in the previous session. Gentlemen who had voted in favour of these bills before could hardly vote against them now. Such was, to a great extent, the case with regard to the Irish tithe-commutation bill which Sir R. Peel introduced, and which the leaders of the Opposition reproached him with having borrowed almost entirely from

them. They therefore resolved to join issue with the
government on the question of the appropriation of the
surplus revenues of the Irish church to non-ecclesiastical
purposes; a question which, as we have already seen, they
had previously staved off by the appointment of a commission, but which they now brought forward as a means
of driving Sir R. Peel from his post. Accordingly Lord
J. Russell, as leader of the Opposition, on the 30th of
March moved the following resolution:

'That this House resolve itself into a committee of the
whole House, in order to consider the present state of the
church establishment in Ireland, with the view of applying
any surplus of the revenues not required for the spiritual
care of its members to the general education of all classes
of the people, without distinction of religious persuasion.'

The debate that ensued was so interesting and important,
whether we regard the question discussed in it, the consequences which depended on the decision of the House, or
the characters of many of those who took a conspicuous
part in it, that we are persuaded we shall be complying
with the wishes of our readers by giving a condensed
account of what was said by the principal speakers.

In moving his resolution, Lord J. Russell expatiated on
the advantages of religious establishments, but argued that
an established church could only deserve the character of a
useful institution when it fulfilled the objects for which it
was established; and to show what those objects were, he
quoted the following passage from the writings of Paley:

'The authority of a church establishment is founded on
its utility; and whenever, upon this principle, we deliberate
concerning the form, propriety, or comparative excellence
of different establishments, the single view under which we
ought to consider them is that of a scheme of instruction;
the single end we ought to propose by them is the preservation and communication of religious knowledge. Every
other idea and every other end which have been mixed up
with this, as the making the church the instrument and
ally of the state, converting it into the means of strengthening or diffusing influence, or regarding it as a support of
regal in opposition to popular forms of government, have
served only to debase the institution, and to introduce into
it numerous corruptions and abuses.

'This (said Lord John) being what an established church

ought to be, the question is, whether these great objects have been advanced by the way in which the church revenues have been appropriated in Ireland, and whether it has furthered the religious instruction which that church ought to be the means of bestowing. In the earlier part of the last century the revenues of the Irish Church did not exceed 160,000*l.* per annum; they now amount to no less than 791,721*l.*, in round numbers 800,000*l.* While this enormous increase has taken place, has there been a corresponding increase in the number of conversions to the Protestant faith, or has the activity, zeal, and success of the clergy been such as to warrant the continuance of this revenue? In too many instances the conduct of the clergy has been the reverse of what it ought to have been. Not very long ago it was considered an advantage to a clergyman to have few Protestants in his parish, because he thus had a fair excuse for neglecting his duty. Even up to a late period many of the established clergy considered themselves rather as members of a great political body than as set apart for the purpose of communicating religious instruction. What has been the consequence? In the county of Kilkenny in 1731 there were 1055 Protestants; in 1834 there were only 945. In Armagh at the same period the Protestants were to the Catholics as three to one; now they are only as one to three. In the county of Kerry the proportion of Catholics to Protestants is much greater. I believe the whole Protestant population of Ireland does not exceed 750,000, and of these, 400,000 are within the ecclesiastical province of Armagh. In nine dioceses the proportions are as follows:

Diocese.	Members of Established Church.	Roman Catholics.	Presbyterians.	Other Protestant Dissenters.	Total.
Ardfert	7,529	297,131	..	27	304,687
Down	30,583	61,465	101,627	3,557	197,232
Dromore	35,687	58,516	59,385	831	154,409
Kildare	13,980	122,577	9	384	136,950
Kilfenora	233	34,606	4	..	34,815
Killaloe	19,140	359,585	16	326	379,076
Leighlin	20,404	170,083	198	281	190,966
Lismore	8,002	207,658	164	382	216,236
Meath	25,626	377,430	671	199	403,920
Waterford	5,301	43,371	110	443	49,225
	160,492	1,732,452	162,184	6,439	2,067,558

It is clear from this, that while in some parts of Ireland the members of the established church are sufficiently numerous to require a considerable number of beneficed clergymen, in other parts they form so small a proportion that it could not be either necessary or right to maintain as large an establishment as in other parts of the country. Nothing can set this in a clearer light than the following example, taken from the diocese of Ferns:

Parishes.	Value.		Established Church.	Roman Catholic.
Taghmon	£446	Glebe .. £50	133	2,920
Ballyoormick	94		10	501
Ballynitty	82		21	390
Dunleer	153	Glebe .. 6	159	1,460
Drumcar	63		120	1,528
Monachebone	107		9	737
Moyleary	173	Glebe .. 20	13	1,148
Capp.g	120		1	530
Ruthdrumaim	82	Glebe .. 20	7	662
Carrickbogget	57		..	332
Port	142	Glebe .. 5	5	800
Ullard	280	Glebe .. 45	50	2.213
Glaig	440		63	4,999
Ossory	62		4	107
Dairoon	69		7	313

Numerous instances of the same kind may be adduced, all showing that of the 800,000l. which form the revenue of the Irish church, a large portion is given to a very small portion of the people, while all the rest derive from it no benefit whatever. It is true that within the last twenty years greater attention has been paid to the spiritual wants of the members of the church. In this respect I believe that the church of Ireland now stands high. But it is not enough to build churches and glebe-houses in order to convert men from one persuasion to another. The occurrences of late years have very much diminished the probability of such conversions. In defiance of all history and experience, it was thought fit some years ago to call public meetings, in order to make Protestants out of Catholics by controversy and dispute. The Catholic clergy, being thus provoked, advised actual resistance to payment to the clergy of the opposing church. I am far from deeming that resistance justifiable, and far less the encouragement that was given to it; but it did take place, and its very existence presented an additional obstacle to the gaining over of any great class of the Irish to the church of England. That resistance has prevailed for several years; it has become so inveterate, that all the exertions of the clergy and of the government to enforce the collection of tithe has become unavailing. Thus the establishment has not merely failed to diffuse spiritual and religious doctrine among the great mass of the populace; it has produced a system which continually brings the clergy into collision with the people—which has led to scenes of civil strife and bloodshed—has brought about a state of things utterly irreconcilable with the true ends of all church establishments—and has now made it plain, that those great and paramount objects will never be aided by limiting the spiritual instruction of the people of Ireland as it hitherto has been, and by applying the revenues of the Irish church to maintaining the doctrines of the establishment, and to no other purposes whatever.

'This being the case, there must be reform; and that reform should consist in adapting the establishment to the wants of those who belong to it, and making no unnecessary additions. If the House adopts this principle, it cannot do otherwise than greatly reduce the ecclesiastical establishment of Ireland. Whatever may remain after that reduction, ought to be applied to some object by which the moral and religious instruction of the people of Ireland might be advanced. The use to which I propose to apply the surplus is general education, according to the system adopted by the national board in Ireland, and according to which individuals of all persuasions can receive religious and moral instruction, and be brought up in harmony together. No measure would tend so much to produce peace in Ireland. From the earliest times it has been the wish of Parliament to improve that country by education. This was the object of the statute that introduced diocesan schools. Afterwards it was considered desirable to have a system of education which would not interfere with any man's religious faith. Since the establishment of the national board of education in Dublin, which was introduced by Lord Stanley, a better kind of education has been enjoyed, and moral and religious instruction has been conveyed generally to the people, without interfering with the opinion or shocking the feelings of any sects. If, then, I can show that public advantage requires that some portion of the revenues of the establishment should be applied to religious education and charity, how can my opponents maintain that they hold church property more sacred than I do? To say that it should be partly distributed and partly kept sacred, partly interfered with for public objects and partly considered as private property, does seem to me to couple in one proposition the utmost absurdity with the utmost inefficiency. It is said, that the land which pays the tithe belongs to the Protestants in the proportion of fifteen to one. I could understand that argument, if an established church existed only for the rich; but as it is intended for all classes of society, and especially for the benefit, instruction, and consolation of the poor, it is not enough to tell me that those who originally contributed to the revenue were Protestants, for I am bound to look on its effects on the whole of Ireland. Besides, whoever they may be on whom the charge of maintaining that church ultimately falls, it is notorious that it is now levied on Catholics, who derive no benefit from the establishment.

'I am charged with inconsistency in reference to this question, because last year I objected to pass such a motion as this without inquiry. But it must be remembered that Sir R. Peel, without waiting for the report of the commissioners, has declared that he would in no case consent to the application of church property to any but ecclesiastical purposes. He has declared that the commission may go on, but that he shall care for its reports only so far as they may enable him to make a better distribution of church property among its members. If that is the case, it is quite necessary that the House should come to some distinct resolution on the subject, and that it should not be going on night after night, and week after week, without knowing whether the ministers of the crown do or do not enjoy the confidence of the House of Commons on this great and important question.'

The debate was continued on the evenings of the 31st of March and the 1st and 2nd of April. After Sir E. Knatchbull and Mr. Ward, the mover of the original appropriation clause, had addressed the House, Sir J. Graham said: 'Why is it that some members are so anxious to get at the small sum which may arise out of the proposed appropriations of the revenues of the Irish church, and which will not, I believe, amount to more than 100,000*l.* per annum? I believe it is the wish of many of those who support the present resolution to take these revenues, not because the state is poor, but because the church is rich; not that the state may gain, but that the church may lose them. I believe in my conscience, that if the appropriation is once allowed, in a very short time the Protestant religion will cease to be the established religion in Ireland, and ultimately in England too. It was to avoid this very danger that the Irish legislature had stipulated, in the treaty of the Union, for the safety of the Irish church. They made it an essential and fundamental article of the Union, that the united church of England and Ireland should for ever be maintained. Such being the case, shall the Commons of England now, even before many of the parties to that compact have passed away, ungenerously withdraw from it that main and moving consideration which induced an independent legislature to enter into it?

'Is this a course likely to add to the peace of Ireland? No; if peace is the object of this measure, its success is indeed hopeless. Peace has indeed been the promise which Ireland has made for important changes and concessions, but that promise has always been broken. Expectations and assurances of tranquillity were held out to induce Britain to give way; while the real design, and the design now openly declared, was to proceed step by step till the Protestant Church is annihilated. Mr. Sheil, in his examination before the select committee of the House of Commons in 1824-25, said: "I am convinced that it will not be in the power of any—no matter how great his influence might be, no matter how perverse his ambition might be—to draw large convocations of men together in Ireland; nothing but the sense of individual injury produces these great and systematic gatherings, through the medium of which so much passion and so much inflammatory matter is conveyed through the country. . . . I am perfectly convinced that, neither upon tithes, nor the union, nor any other question, could the people of Ireland be powerfully and permanently united." Dr. Doyle declared, before the same committee: "I conceive that the removal of the disqualifications under which Roman Catholics labour would lessen considerably those feelings of opposition which they may at present entertain with regard to the establishment, chiefly for this reason,—that whilst we labour under the disabilities which now weigh on us, we find that the clergy of the establishment, being very numerous and very opulent, employ their influence and opulence in various ways to oppose the progress of our claims; and I do think that, if these claims were once adjusted, and the concessions that we desire granted, the country would settle down into a habit of quiet, and that we should no longer feel the jealousy against the clergy that we now feel, because that jealousy which we do feel arises chiefly from the unrelaxed efforts which they have almost universally made to oppose our claims. We should view them, then, if these claims were granted, as brethren labouring in the same vineyard with ourselves." Every one of these hopes has been falsified, every one of these promises has been forgotten, and in their place has come triumphant exultation over the approaching downfall of the Protestant church. What better witness can there be to the designs of the Catholics than Mr. O'Connell, of whom Lord J. Russell is now the accredited agent? No farther back than October, 1834, Mr. O'Connell spoke out in a published letter addressed to Mr. Crawford, and discussing the proceedings regarding tithes in the last session of Parliament. He there said: "It is quite true that I demanded for the present but a partial reduction—it was three-fifths—of the tithes. Why did I ask for no more? Why did I not demand the abolition of the entire? Because I had no chance in the first instance of getting the entire abolished. And you perceive that I was refused the extent that I asked, being three-fifths, and only got from the House of Commons two-fifths. I had therefore not the least prospect or probability of destroying the entire; and because I am one of those who are and have been always ready to accept any instalment, however small, of the debt of justice due to the people—the real national debt—I have been and am ready to accept any instalment of that debt, determined to go on and look for the remainder as soon as the first instalment shall be completely realised. It is totally untrue that I acquiesced in the perpetual continuance of the remaining three-fifths of the tithes." Nor did he leave them in the dark as to the appropriation of church property; for in another letter, in September, 1834, he says: "My plan is, to apply that fund to the various counties of Ireland, to relieve the occupiers of land from grand-jury cess. ... My plan is, to defray all the expenses of dispensaries, infirmaries, hospitals and asylums, and to multiply the number of those institutions, until they become quite sufficient for the wants of the sick."* That is to say, that church property is to be granted to the landlords of Ireland to enable them to do that which, without confiscation, they are bound to do by the law of humanity, if not by the law of the land—namely, to provide for the relief of their poorer brethren.

'I press on all those who lay claim to the name of sincere and genuine Whigs, to oppose this mischievous and disastrous resolution. Whig principles consist not in death's-heads and crossbones denunciations of those who venture to exercise their religious principles according to their consciences, nor in prayers for mercy limited to them in heaven, but not to extend to them on this side of the grave. Whig principles consist not more in the love of civil liberty than in jealousy of the Catholic religion as an engine of political power, when it arrogates to itself a right to ascendancy, and claims to put other religions under its feet; above all, I consider genuine Whig principles to consist in a warm attachment to the Protestant religion as by law established. I have on this question a strong religious feeling. It is a vital question, on which no farther compromise can be made. I have carried compromise on it as far as principle will allow; but farther I cannot go. The property which was set apart by our ancestors to maintain and propagate the Protestant religion is sacred, and ought to be applied to sacred uses. They who minister at the altar ought to live of the altar. That principle is high as heaven, and you cannot reach it; strong as the Almighty, and you cannot overturn it; fixed as the Eternal, and you cannot unfix it. It is binding on you as a legislature of Christian men acting on Christian principles, and no consideration on earth will induce me to compromise or destroy it.'

* The reader will be interested in observing how clearly Mr. Gladstone's plan was foreshadowed in these quotations.

Omitting the speeches of Lord Howick, Mr. Sheil, and several others of lesser note, we come to that of Mr. Gladstone. The following speech, containing the early impressions of a celebrated statesman on a question on which he afterwards thought and acted so differently, will on that account be read with interest.

Mr. W. E. *Gladstone*: 'The noble lord and those who have spoken on the same side of the question have proceeded on totally unproved assumptions—they have gone on the gratuitous and unsustained supposition, that there exists a surplus revenue over and above what is necessary for the due maintenance of the church in Ireland. I think church property as sacred as private property; but I should say, that the former was sacred in persons, and the latter to purposes. At the time of the reformation, the legislature, composed of the representatives of the country, having changed the established religion, changed to the same extent the appropriation of church property. If Protestants should ever again be in a minority in this House, I, for one, avow my conviction that a return to the ancient appropriation would be the fair and legitimate consequence; but until that is the case, I shall raise my humble voice as a Protestant against the principle involved in the motion before the House. The great grievance complained of in Ireland is, that the Protestant establishment there is paid for by the Roman Catholic inhabitants. Now is such in reality the case? Are tithes paid for that purpose? or are not tithes rather a part of the surplus profit of the land, which goes not to the cultivator of the land, but to its owner? Tithe is paid by the landlord, and the grievance complained of exists rather in theory than in reality. But if there are evils arising out of this question of tithes, is not the present government prepared to redress them? Has not the government a tithe bill before the House, the object of which is to place the payment of tithes where it ought to be, on the landlords? The principal argument of Lord J. Russell is, that the Irish church property is not duly applied, and does not answer the purposes for which it was originally intended. Well, admitting that, and granting also that there were general abuses and neglects in the administration of the church of Ireland, he might fairly ask, had not the same general vice prevailed also,

and to like extent, in its political government? The
present motion opens a boundless road; it will lead to
measure after measure, to expedient after expedient, till we
come to the recognition of the Roman Catholic religion as
the national one. In principle you propose to give up the
Protestant establishment; if so, why not abandon the political government of Ireland, and concede the repeal of the
legislative union? I come next to the question of a surplus
church revenue in Ireland. When the supposition of the
existence of a surplus causes a convulsion in this House
and throughout the country, the noble lord ought to have
waited till he could prove by official documents the existence of such a surplus. The number of benefices in Ireland
is 1450; and, according to the returns, the average income
of each is 275*l.* Is that too much? The noble lord who
brought forward this motion calculated the number of
persons belonging to the established church in Ireland at
750,000. I believe that they amount to upwards of a
million, or at least to a million ("Oh! Oh! from the
Opposition). If I am wrong in my calculation, the fault
rests with the noble lord, who has brought the subject
under discussion before we have received full information
on it. Allowing that there are a million of Protestants in
Ireland, each of its 1450 rectors would have a flock of 700
souls in a country where the population is scattered over a
wide extent. Is that number too small to occupy the attention of a clergyman? If the people of Ireland were all
Protestants, the present establishment in that country
would be totally and ludicrously disproportionate to their
wants. I submit that there is no surplus, as far as the
House of Commons can be aware, of the available revenues
of the church of Ireland. Mr. Senior, a gentleman intimately connected with some of those who are most favourable to the Irish church commission, has declared in a
pamphlet on this very important subject, that there is
reason to believe that the report of the commissioners will
show that there is a considerable Protestant population in
most parts of Ireland, and that if the church is to be
suppressed only in those districts where it is now needless,
the proportion of parishes in which it is got rid of will not
be large. The proposition, therefore, to which the House
is invited to assent is alike impracticable and unjustifiable:

impracticable, because the moral means of maintaining the state of things it proposes to create will be lost; unjustifiable, because there is no principle on which the Protestant church can be permanently upheld, but that it is the church that teaches the *truth.* The system we are now called on to agree to involves the existence of church establishments. I hope I shall never live to see the day when such a system shall be adopted in this country; for the consequences of it to public men will be lamentable beyond all description. If those individuals who are called on to fill the high functions of administering public affairs should be compelled to exclude from their consideration the elements of true religion, and to view various strange and conflicting doctrines in the same light, instead of administering those noble functions, they will become helots and slaves.'

Lord Stanley: 'When the House is called on to adopt the present proposition as the only means of pacifying Ireland, it behoves them to remember what has been the result of the concessions already made, and to consider how far this additional concession is likely to produce unanimity and cordiality. Mr. Littleton has candidly admitted that he cares little for the resolution; that he looks to the great and vital disease, which, according to him, can only be removed by cutting out the affected part. Is the House prepared to admit the principle involved in that argument, and to expose themselves to all the successive assaults which they will have to sustain from the well-marshalled phalanx which I see arrayed on the opposite benches? I congratulate the member for Dublin (O'Connell) on the position he now occupies as compared with that which he filled last year. O, how proud is the triumph enjoyed by one of the parties at the opposite side of the House, and how bitter the submission of the other! In my opinion it matters little whether the amount of the annual revenue of the Irish church is 400,000*l.* or 800,000*l.*; though I firmly believe that on inquiry it will be found not to exceed 400,000*l.* The whole sum available for the parochial clergy would not, I am assured, if fairly divided amongst them, exceed an average of 200*l.* per annum to each. And yet, with no prospect of a higher revenue to the members of the clerical body in Ireland, the House of Commons is gravely called on to appropriate the amount that may be left.

'We have been frequently told in the course of this debate, that if we would agree to this resolution, the war would close, peace and quietness would spread themselves through the land; that abstract resolution of the House of Commons would at once, and at a single stroke as it were, allay for ever the heart-burnings and animosities, the civil broils and contentions which afflict Ireland from one end to the other. Do not assertions of that nature exceed the credibility of any rational being? Notwithstanding the resolution, the same people will suffer distraint—blood and violence will be continued—the small farmers and proprietors now banded in resistance to tithes will continue in the same condition. In a word, does the resolution touch a single atom of the pressing and substantial grievance?

'An argument in favour of this resolution has been drawn from the example of Scotland, and from the Catholic religion being established in Canada, both of which instances merely prove that the faith of treaties is to be preserved, while the present motion says that it ought to be violated. In Canada we found a district of the country Catholic, when we took possession of it by right of conquest, and we entered into solemn treaties, by virtue of which we were bound to recognise within the particular limits the religion of the majority of the inhabitants as the religion of the state. There we could not introduce a Protestant episcopal church consistently with the obligations of our treaty; but in all the rest of Canada, where we were free to act, we have introduced the Protestant religion, and made a fund in every district for the support of Protestant ministers. In Scotland prelacy was found uncongenial, not merely to the numerical majority of the population, but to the majority of those possessing property in the country, and gifted with intelligence. Presbyterianism was the religion of their choice, and by the act of union they were established in the full right and exercise of it. But in Ireland the religion of the state was by the solemn obligation of treaties to be Protestant. We are bound by virtue of the faith of treaties to maintain the Roman Catholic religion in Canada, the Presbyterian in Scotland, and the Episcopal in Ireland.'

Mr. O'Connell: 'I shall content myself with laying down the broad principle, that the emoluments of a church ought not to be raised from a people who do not belong to it. Ireland does not ask for a Catholic establishment. The Irish desire political equality in every respect, except that they would not accept a shilling for their church. I am told that I am disposed to repeal the legislative union, and how do you reconcile me to it? By showing that you are unwilling to do justice to Ireland. My opinion is well known, but I am ready to give it up. The union never has had fair play. I am told that the House is disposed to do justice to Ireland; let them not tell me so, but show it. Let them beware of disappointing the just expectations of the people of Ireland, and thus instigating them to appeal to the wild justice of revenge. All that the Catholics require is justice—equal and even-handed justice. What they want to know is, whether there is a prospect of happier days; whether a new era has sprung up; and whether a dawn of comfort and prosperity has beamed on Ireland. This resolution would be an earnest and a pledge of better times; its rejection would be a proclamation to Ireland that the legislature despises in regard to it all principles of justice.'

Sir R. Peel: 'If the House is clearly of opinion that the public interest requires the abandonment of a national compact, the violation of a long prescription, and the abrogation of the laws affecting property, I am not disposed to deny the abstract absolute right of the legislature to do all these things; but I maintain that before doing so, it must be convinced by arguments approaching to demonstration of the absolute necessity of the case. Three measures have expressly confirmed the property of the church. The Act of Union differed from any ordinary law in this: that it was a national compact, and contained the conditions on which alone the Protestant Parliament of Ireland resigned itself and its church to us, inserting as part of the compact, of equal force with the compact itself, that "the continuance and preservation of the established church in Ireland shall be deemed and taken to be an essential and fundamental part of the union." The Emancipation Act of 1829 likewise partook of the nature of a compact. If it is irrevocable as regards the privileges it conferred on the Catholics it is equally so, unless some great and urgent necessity should arise to compel a change, with respect to the assurances that it gave to Protestants. They were led to believe that, no privilege which it conferred on the Catholics would be exercised to disturb or weaken the Protestant religion or government; that the removal of the civil disabilities would give new security to the church of Ireland; but they little thought that, within five years from the passing of that act, the power which it conferred would be exercised to subvert the church establishment, as far as regarded the property of the church. Two years ago we passed the Temporalities Act, by which ten bishoprics were abolished and measures were adopted, in my opinion wisely, to cut off a certain number of superfluous livings, and to apply their revenues to the improvement of small livings. Some of those who devised that act contended that, according to one of its clauses, part of the fund obtained might be applied to secular purposes; but the subsequent abandonment of that clause and the whole tenor of the act showed that the principle of reserving ecclesiastical property for strictly ecclesiastical purposes was rigidly adhered to. Two years only have elapsed since the date of that act, and now, notwithstanding the Act of Union—notwithstanding the removal of the civil disabilities of the Catholics—notwithstanding the reform of the Irish church and the extinction of ten bishoprics—we are told that this resolution must be adopted as the indication of a new system, and as the commencement of a new era.

'The mover of this resolution says that the whole annual revenue of the Irish church is 791,000*l.* I assert as positively that it has not 450,000*l.* Now, I ask the House of Commons whether it is just or wise to come to a decision with regard to the disposal of a surplus when so great a difference of opinion prevails as to the sum itself. You have a right to insist on the noble lord's producing a practical plan; that is the only way to prevent the exciting of extravagant hopes and subsequent disappointment. The noble lord's proposition will not give satisfaction to any party—not to the people of this country, not to the Protestants of Ireland, not to the Roman Catholics.

'It has been argued that the Irish church has failed to effect the ends for which it was established—that there are not more than 1,000,000 Protestants to 7,000,000 Catholics, and that Protestantism is not on the increase. I maintain that hitherto causes have been in operation to impede the growth of Protestantism: civil disabilities, which enlisted men's pride on the side of Catholicism; abuses in the church; superfluous wealth, which created a prejudice against the Irish church. Those causes, which formerly prevented the spread of Protestantism, have been removed; what right, then, have we to legislate on the assumption of a supposed surplus?

'The best proof that the resolution points at no determinate or practical course is its own vagueness, and the consequent diversity of principles among those whom it has been framed to enfold; some professing at least that they must still maintain the church; others that the church is an atrocity; others that it is a nuisance because all establishments are bad; others that the Catholic clergy should be maintained by the state as well as the Protestant. Yet you call this a final settlement of the question. This resolution may have the advantage of enabling you to act together to-night, but you act on different principles and with different views. You are all aware that this is no final settlement; that it is only an instalment of that whole amount which is held in contemplation; that it is only an indication of the course you intend to pursue. Because you yourselves have taken a position that is untenable, you wish me to take it in common with you. But I will not consent to appropriate this property, which is ecclesiastical and connected with the Protestant establishment, to other purposes than those of the establishment. I will not assent to your resolution for the sake of Ireland, because I know that it will excite in that unhappy and susceptible country false hopes—hopes which you cannot realize, and yet hopes that you will shrink from disappointing. I tell you beforehand I will not act on your resolution. I shall oppose the motion for going into committee; in committee I shall oppose the resolution; and lastly, I shall oppose with all my strength the communication of that resolution to his majesty. I will do so because it wears all the appearance of a purpose to pass by the House of Lords. Why have not the movers of this resolution brought in a bill? Are they uncertain of their plan? Are they ashamed of presenting in the ordinary course the result of their calm, solemn, and mature deliberation? Do you consider it right to ask for a resolution of this nature under the unfair and dishonest pretence of making a communication to the crown, which might have been done in a modest manner without any parade or the excitement of the least commotion? If you think it right that a bill should be brought in on the subject, I will afford every facility. You may succeed in forcing your resolution on us. It may enable you to embarrass the future progress of the administration. But I tell you, notwithstanding your vaunted majorities here, you do not control public opinion. We may be weak here, but this I tell you, that there is a public opinion altogether independent of majorities, and which is not controlled by votes, but which must always hereafter be an essential element in every executive government. I never was more confident of anything than that the people will not sanction a motion to embarrass the government. They would sanction you in attempting a vote of want of confidence; that would be a usual course of proceeding. Why have you not the manliness to propose it? Why do you not say at once that you want to turn out the government by the introduction of this measure? Why, then, do you not displace us, and then carry on the measure triumphantly? I feel that I cannot undertake to enforce your resolution. I shall adhere to the principles of my own measure. I feel that such is the necessity for the settlement of the tithe question, that it will admit of no further delay. I shall press it forward; and if your determination to throw unusual impediments in the way of the government be plainly indicated, if you determine to obstruct it in principle and detail, I shall then see that it is not possible for me, consistently with my sense of duty, to remain in the situation that I have at present the honour to hold.'

A short reply from Lord J. Russell concluded the debate. On a division the votes were:

For the resolution 322
Against 289
  Majority in favour of the resolution 33

This division took place at three o'clock on the morning of the 3d of April, at the close of a debate which had lasted for three nights. Sir R. Peel proposed that the resolution should be considered in committee on the Monday following;

but the victorious majority would not tolerate even this slight delay, and the debate was renewed the same evening. We will not weary the reader with a description of the parliamentary fencing by means of which the ministers tried to keep their offices, and the leaders of the Opposition to force them to resign; it is enough to say that, after a long series of resolutions and discussions, the majority succeeded in fastening on the government the task of carrying into effect the resolution they had so strenuously opposed, and thus compelled Sir Robert to execute the threat of resignation with which he had concluded his speech on the original motion. On the 8th of April he announced to the House of Commons that he and his colleagues, by a unanimous determination, had resigned their offices. The manner in which this announcement was made was manly and dignified, and commanded the respect and sympathy of the House. Lord J. Russell generously declared that the retiring minister had acted entirely in the spirit of the constitution. The resignation of the administration was announced in the upper House by the Duke of Wellington.

Such was the result of this attempt to force a conservative ministry on the country. The results were, the needless turmoil and expense of a hotly-contested election; a vast expenditure of money; a great loss of time wasted in party strife which should have been devoted to public business; and an increase of the conservative opposition, a proportionate weakening of the Melbourne administration, compelling it to seek strength and stability in a closer alliance with O'Connell and his followers. And now the question arises, Who was really responsible for these mischievous results? On the principle that the king can do no wrong, the blame of them must be thrown first on the Duke of Wellington, who consented to fill Lord Melbourne's place provisionally, and next on Sir R. Peel, who accepted it definitely, and accepted with it the responsibility of Lord Melbourne's dismissal, as he himself honourably and frankly acknowledged. But history must not be arrested in its decisions by constitutional fictions. It judges sovereigns as well as their ministers, and in this instance it must condemn William IV. as having made an unwarrantable use of his prerogative, in order to place in power the party that he personally preferred. Had Lord Melbourne stated that he was unable to carry on the government, the king might, without any impropriety, have accepted his resignation. But Lord Melbourne did nothing of the kind. He had a large majority in the House of Commons, and he was quite prepared to go on when the king so unexpectedly dismissed him and his colleagues. This act was consummated before any adviser that the king might have recourse to in accordance with the forms of the constitution could have been consulted. It was an act done by the king on his own judgment, or on the advice of persons to whom he ought not to have listened in such a matter. It was only after the ministry had been actually dismissed that the Duke of Wellington was sent for. He ought to have recommended the king, under the circumstances of the case, to recall Lord Melbourne; and by not doing so he took on himself, probably without reflection, the responsibility of the dismissal. But this was an advice that he can hardly be blamed for not having given. His strong Tory principles, his hatred of the Reform Bill, by no means diminished by his experience of its actual working, prevented him from perceiving the nature and consequences of the step the king had taken. And even if he had disapproved that step, his chivalrous nature would have led him at all hazards to spare the king the humiliation of asking his discarded ministers to return to the posts from which they had been so summarily ejected. The conduct of the king and the duke together placed Sir R. Peel in an inextricably false position. We can hardly doubt, that if he had been consulted beforehand, his sound judgment and practical experience would have led him to recommend the king to wait for more certain proofs of the asserted reaction than he yet possessed. But when he returned from Rome, the time for giving such advice was past. The action of the king and the duke left him no option. After the government had been kept open for him so long, and in so unprecedented a manner, he could hardly have refused to accept it. All that remained for him to do was, to make an appeal to the people, in the desperate hope, that by the exertions and influence of the Tory party, he might obtain a majority in the new Parliament. That such a hope was not altogether quixotic the result of the elections proved. But the displacement of the ministry, and the dissolution of Parliament which that step drew after it, were grievous blunders; and though the Duke of Wellington and Sir R. Peel must share between them the constitutional responsibility, the verdict of posterity will attach the real blame to William IV. As for Sir R. Peel, he deserved the praise which his honourable rival in the House of Commons so warmly gave him, not only on account of the great diligence and ability he displayed in framing and conducting the measures he introduced, but for the very upright and honourable manner in which he acted under the extremely difficult and undesired circumstances in which he was placed.

On receiving the resignation of the ministry, the king sent for Earl Grey, and by his advice again entrusted to Lord Melbourne the formation of a cabinet; thus at last being compelled to undergo the mortification from which the duke and Sir Robert had striven to save him. The new ministry was, with one very important exception, nearly a reproduction of the one that had been a few months before so unceremoniously dismissed.*

* The following were the persons who composed it:—

THE CABINET.

First Lord of the Treasury	Lord Melbourne.
President of the Council	Lord Lansdowne.
First Lord of the Admiralty	Lord Auckland.
Chancellor of the Duchy of Lancaster	Lord Holland.
Woods, Works, and Privy Seal	Lord Duncannon.
Home Secretary	Lord J. Russell.
Foreign Secretary	Lord Palmerston.
Colonial Secretary	Mr. Chas. Grant (created Baron Glenelg).
India Board	Sir J. C. Hobhouse.
Secretary at War	Lord Howick.
Board of Trade	Mr. Poulett Thomson.
Chancellor of the Exchequer	Mr. Spring Rice.

NOT IN THE CABINET.

Joint-secretaries of the Treasury	Mr. Francis Baring.
	Mr. E. J. Stanley.
Attorney-general	Sir J. Campbell.
Solicitor-general	Mr. Rolfe.
Judge-advocate-general	Mr. Arthur Ferguson.
Postmaster-general	Earl of Minto.
Paymaster-general and Treasurer of the Navy	Sir H. Parnell.
Clerk of the Ordnance	Colonel Leith Hay.
Attorney-general for Ireland	Mr. Perrin.
Solicitor-general for Ireland	Mr. O'Loughlin.
Lord-advocate of Scotland	Mr. J. A. Murray.

Parliament having been adjourned, as usual in such cases, to allow the ministerial arrangements to be completed, reassembled on the 18th of April. In the upper House Lord Melbourne announced that he was once more at the head of a ministry, which he had succeeded in forming, not without great difficulties, some of which had been of a peculiarly severe and mortifying nature. He underwent a long cross-examination from Lord Alvanley, and the Duke of Buckingham, respecting the nature of his relations with Mr. O'Connell. Lord Brougham advised the premier not to answer. Lord Melbourne, however, disregarded this counsel, and gave a manful and straightforward reply to the questions which the two peers had put to him.

'The noble lord has asked,' he said, 'how far I coincide in opinion with Mr. O'Connell. Why, not at all. He has also asked me whether I entertain the same opinions which I held on a former occasion, which I apprehend refers to the time when the coercion act was under consideration. I certainly do entertain the same opinions, and I persevere in them. The noble lord then demanded of me whether I have taken any means to secure the assistance of Mr. O'Connell; and if so, on what terms. I do not know whether I shall have the assistance of Mr. O'Connell or not; but I can state most distinctly that I have taken no steps to secure it. As to tithes, I do not hesitate to say that I consider myself pledged to act on the resolution of the other House.'

Both Houses adjourned till the 12th of May, to allow

Solicitor-general for Scotland	Mr. Cunningham.
Lords of the Treasury	Lord Seymour. Mr. Ord. Mr. R. Stewart.
Irish Secretary	Lord Morpeth.
Vice-president of the Board of Trade and Master of the Mint	Mr. Labouchere.
Under-secretary of the Home Department.	Mr. Fox Maule.
Under-secretary of the Colonies	Sir G. Grey.
Secretary of the Admiralty	Mr. C. Wood.
Secretaries of the Board of Control	Mr. R. Gordon. Mr. V. Smith.

Lord Brougham did not appear in the list of the new ministry, and the great seal was put in commission, the commissioners being the master of the rolls, the vice chancellor, and Mr. Justice Bosanquet.

time for the re-election of the new ministers, and for other arrangements, which the change of administration had rendered necessary. The seats vacated were not in every case filled to the satisfaction of the new government. Lord J. Russell was defeated in South Devonshire by a conservative opponent, and was obliged to take refuge in the small borough of Stroud, where a vacancy was made for him, by the appointment of Colonel Fox to the secretaryship of the ordnance. Mr. Littleton, who had been made Lord Hatherton, and Mr. C. Grant, who had become Lord Glenelg, were succeeded in the seats they vacated by conservatives. Lord Palmerston was provided with a seat for Tiverton, which Mr. Kennedy, the sitting member, resigned to make room for him. Lord Morpeth's seat for Yorkshire was strongly contested; but he triumphed over his conservative opponent by a great majority.

The new ministry, considering the impossibility of carrying through many measures at the period of the session which had now been reached, determined to content themselves with endeavouring to pass a bill for the reform of the municipal corporations. In the middle ages the members of the corporations had been elected by the freemen of each town. But the Tudor sovereigns had infringed on this ancient liberty; and under the Stuarts the charters had been remodelled in such a manner as to take away, if not the appearance, at all events the reality of popular election, and to transfer to the crown the power of appointing the municipalities. The charters granted by William III. and his successors, were in the same form. Under such charters abuses of every kind had grown up, and municipal corruption was associated with parliamentary corruption, and was carried to even a greater height. When therefore Earl Grey's ministry had dealt so successfully with parliamentary reform, it was naturally expected that they would carry through an equally effective measure of corporation reform. The Whigs had accordingly accepted the obligation thus imposed on them. In 1833 they appointed a commission to inquire into the state of the municipal corporations in England. Their report had now been made, and the time had come for the fulfilment of the expectations of the English people on this subject. The ministry hoped that by dealing with this question in a vigorous and comprehensive manner, their party might recover much of that popularity which it had enjoyed during the great struggle for parliamentary reform. The commissioners appointed to carry out the inquiry do not seem to have been very happily chosen; at least it was clamorously alleged, that, with the exception of Sir F. Palgrave, who dissented from and protested against the report made by his colleagues, they were persons utterly unknown; and they certainly did not afterwards emerge from the obscurity with which they were reproached at the time that they were appointed to carry out this very important and delicate investigation. It was also complained, that their report added very little to the information on the subject already possessed by Parliament and the country. It was notorious that the various officers of the municipal corporations were elected by persons who had very little interest in the expenditure of the corporation funds; who were very accessible to all kinds of corrupt influences; and that the gross abuses existed which might be expected to arise and flourish under such circumstances. It was therefore argued that a bill might have been prepared without the formality of this previous investigation; and it certainly must be admitted, that the measure brought forward by the government was not so much based on the particular facts which the commissioners had elicited in the course of their inquiries as on general considerations; and that it applied everywhere the one remedy of popular control to all the various abuses which a practically irresponsible municipal government had caused to exist and flourish everywhere. But we will allow Lord J. Russell, who introduced the measure into the House of Commons on the 5th of June, to state briefly the reasons which had induced the government to prepare the measure, the evils which it sought to remove, and the remedies that it was proposed to apply to them.

'The number of persons under the government of municipal corporations to be touched by this bill is about two millions. A great number of these corporations govern populous towns; but there are others in which the municipal body is so small, that they are, in fact, not corporations in the ordinary sense of the word. I will speak in the first instance of places which are considerable boroughs, where the municipal corporation does not properly represent the property, the intelligence, or the population of the town. In Bedford the corporate body * is only one-seventeenth of the population and one-fourth of the property of the place. In Oxford there are 1,400 electors; but a great many of these are not rated inhabitants, and generally there has been so much treating, and so many corrupt practices at elections, that seldom more than 500 can be said to be free from them. In Norwich there are 2,231 resident freemen; but of these 1,123 are not rated at all, and out of the 1,123, 315 are paupers; and it is stated that out of 25,541*l.* raised by rates, no less than 18,224*l.* is on the property of persons who do not in any way belong to the corporntion. At Lincoln three-fourths of the corporate body are not rated, and nearly four-fifths of the population are excluded from it. At Ipswich there are 2,000 ratepayers; but only 187 of them belong to the corporation. At Cambridge the population is about 20,000, and there are 1,434 ten-pound houses; but there are only 118 freemen. The property produces in rates 25,499*l.*, of which not more than 2,111*l.* is paid by freemen. It should be the object of these corporations to represent the property, to share the general feelings, and to take care of the interests of the town over which they are placed. There are two modes of excluding this wholesome sympathy between the governors and the governed: the one, the more obvious and common mode, is where the corporation is an entirely select body, where there is no appearance of popular election, and where the government is carried on in total defiance of the general body of the inhabitants; the other, and in my opinion still more glaring abuse, is that which connects a few persons carrying on the government for their own benefit with a portion of the lower class of the people belonging to the town, whose votes they buy, and whose habits they demoralise.

'The consequences of these vicious modes are, that the grossest and most notorious abuses have prevailed. In the distribution of charitable funds, two-thirds, three-fourths,

---

* It is to be observed, that in this and many other places Lord J. Russell uses the term corporate body or corporation to include the whole number of persons by whom the governing body was elected, who were usually the freemen.

and sometimes a larger proportion have been delivered to
the Blue party, or to any other colour that is the favourite
symbol of the local government. The charitable estates,
instead of being employed for the general benefit of the
town, have been consumed for the partial benefit of a few
individuals, and not unfrequently in the feastings and
entertainments in which the mayor and other corporators have been in the habit of indulging. In some not
very large boroughs the expenses have amounted to 500*l.*
or 600*l.* a year, and the enjoyment has been confined to
the freemen on one side as some inducement to stand by
that side, and not to desert the corporation in any political
emergency. These facts are so fully established in the
reports of the commissioners, that I do not propose to enter
into them; yet I think I may venture to state one or two
instances which are particularly striking proofs of the way
in which, in some of the smaller places, corporate funds
have fallen into the hands of persons who have assumed
the duties of corporators, but have totally neglected them.
One of these is Aldborough, where the corporators have
been continually changed. They used to ask a regular sum:
the price of "an honest burgess" (such are the terms of
the charter) was 35*l.*; and one of the most "respectable
honest, and discreet burgesses" (still following the terms
of the charter) asked for, and was rewarded with, influence
to obtain a chancellor's living for a clergyman worth 100*l.*
a year. Whenever the patron of the borough was changed,
all considered themselves bound in honour to resign. The
members of the council are the Marquis of Hertford, two
members of his family, his solicitor, the superintendent of
his estates there, his steward, the Right Hon. John Wilson
Croker, a captain in the army or navy, and the chamberlain
of the corporation. The details respecting Oxford are
nearly similar. The Marquis of Hertford is one of the
honest men of Oxford, and the others consist of four or five
members of his family, his present steward, his former
steward, the superintendent of his estates, and the Right
Hon. John Wilson Croker. I mention these cases because
the main facts apply to a hundred other boroughs that I
could name which formerly returned members to Parliament. It has been proved by the investigations of the
commissioners, that, in large towns and in small, the

municipal corporations have not employed the powers with which they have been invested that their boroughs might be "well and quietly governed"—to use the words of some of the charters—but for the sole object of establishing an influence for the election of members of this House.

'I now proceed to the methods I propose to adopt for establishing really good government in corporate towns. We intend to include 183 boroughs in the bill I shall conclude by moving for leave to bring in, containing, as I have already stated, a population of about two millions. In the first enacting clause we declare that all powers in their charters and all practices under them inconsistent with the provisions of the bill are null and void, and shall totally cease and have no operation. And we propose that there shall be one uniform government applicable to all of them; one uniform franchise for the purpose of election, and a like description of officers, except in some of the larger places, in which there will be a recorder or some other such magistrate.

'I come now to the franchise. We think that it ought to belong to the permanently settled and fixed inhabitants of the town alone, and we propose, as a test of this, that they shall be persons who shall have been rated to the relief of the poor for three years, and who shall have regularly paid their rates for that term. There will be provisions introduced for taking care that the having received relief or the not having paid rates for a short time shall not exclude persons who have previously acquired the right of voting for a longer period than their inability to pay up their rates. We propose, then, that the right of voting shall be in the occupiers of houses, warehouses, and shops paying rates, using similar words to those of the Reform Bill. We propose likewise that they should reside within seven miles of the place.

'We propose that there should be only one body whom those persons are to elect for the government of the town, consisting of the mayor and common council, varying from fifteen in the smallest places, the inhabitants of which are about 2,000, to ninety in the largest towns. Twenty of the largest, which have more than 25,000 inhabitants, we propose should be divided into wards and a certain number of council-men be chosen for each ward; but with regard to the rest of the towns it is proposed that the whole of the common council should be elected together.

'We propose to preserve all pecuniary rights, exemption from toll, rights of common, and all personal rights of that kind, to those who now enjoy them during their lives; but that in future no person shall be admitted into these corporations, nor be burgesses of them, except by being permanent inhabitants, paying rates within the borough. We propose to abolish likewise the rights acquired by serving apprenticeship to certain trades, all exclusive rights of trading, with due regard to the pecuniary interests of persons now living.

'With regard to the election of the common council, we propose that its members should be elected for three years, but that one-third of them should go out every year. We propose that the mayor shall be elected annually by the council, and shall be during his mayoralty a justice of the peace for the borough and likewise for the county. We propose to give the council the power of appointing a town-clerk and treasurer, giving compensation where it can fairly be demanded.

'The most important part of this Municipal Corporation Bill relates to the management of the funds, the management of which certainly does not show at the present moment any great wisdom or economy on the part of the corporations with which we deal; for while the gross income of these corporations amounts to 307,000*l.*, the expenditure amounts to 377,000*l.*; besides which there is a debt of two millions owing to these bodies. When we come to look into particular cases, we find that some corporations have been incurring debts year by year up to within two years ago, while they were actually dividing among themselves the proceeds of the loans they raised. It is proposed therefore that the council shall have the power of appointing a committe in order to manage their financial affairs, and that their accounts shall be regularly audited and brought before the public.

'We propose that the common councils shall become trustees of charity funds which have been scandalously mismanaged, with power to appoint a committee for their management, composed of not less than fifteen persons, to be chosen not from the council, but from the general body of the burgesses.

'With regard to the administration of justice and police within the towns, we propose that the whole work and business of watching the town shall be placed completely under the control of the council. Then, with respect to another part of this measure, which refers to what I consider a part of the police of the town, and a part which has often led to very great abuses—I mean the power of granting alehouse licenses—it is proposed that this power shall not be mixed up or confounded with the duty of administering justice, but that it should be left to the council or a committee of the council. I think that the council elected by the rate-payers, as now proposed—although no doubt many of the members may have a desire to favour their friends or promote their own private views as a body—will always act under popular control, and be less likely to abuse the power of granting licenses than magistrates, in whose case the robe of justice is sometimes employed to cover a great enormity of abuses.'

The rest of the speech was devoted to the explanation of the provisions of the bill relating to the appointment of the unpaid magistracy, the arrangement of quarter sessions, the appointment of recorders and stipendiary magistrates.

Sir Robert Peel followed—not to oppose the introduction of the bill, for he candidly admitted the necessity that existed for legislation on the subject, but to criticise the speech of Lord J. Russell, and to express his own opinions on the subject of municipal reform. After making some introductory observations on the importance of the question and on the report of the commissioners, he thus proceeded:

'The noble lord said he would not refer to instances of particular corporations; but scarcely had the words escaped his lips when he referred to eight or ten corporations, with the circumstances of four-fifths of which he became acquainted by having access to documents which have not yet been laid before the House. We have no report upon Norwich, Oxford, Cambridge, Orford, Aldborough, or Ipswich; and yet these are the cases on which he has mainly founded his argument. There is a double ground of complaint against the noble lord. He first takes an unfair advantage of quoting from documents to which he alone has had access, thus precluding all answer or explanation which a reference to those documents might possibly afford; and secondly, he selects the case of corporations in which a particular class of political opinions predominate, thus warranting the inference that the party in the state holding those opinions had been specially, if not exclusively, the encouragers of corporate abuses.'

After referring to the corporations of Derby and Portsmouth, in order to show that the abuses complained of prevailed in boroughs under Whig as well in those under Tory influence, he thus continued:

'The better course is to look to the future; and I strongly advise all members of corporations readily and willingly to concur in an amendment of the existing system, but upon this express condition that the reform is to be a sincere *bonâ fide* reform, and not a mere pretext for transferring power from one party in the state to another; that the subject aimed at shall be a good system of municipal government, taking security, as far as security on such a subject can be taken, that the really intelligent and respectable portion of the community of each town be called to the administration of municipal affairs, and guarding against the future application of the charitable or corporate funds to any other but charitable and public purposes.'

Mr. Ewart mentioned that a sound system of municipal reform, corresponding in every respect with that now brought forward, but giving the privilege of voting by ballot to every householder, had been introduced in Prussia in 1808.

Mr. O'Connell said: 'There is an essential defect in the title of the bill—a deficiency of one word, which greatly diminishes the value of the measure. It is entitled "A Bill for the better regulation of Municipal Corporations in England and Wales." The word I wish to see annexed to it is "Ireland." In other respects, I do not think it possible to produce a measure more entitled than the present to universal approbation.

It was afterwards stated by the chancellor of the exchequer that his majesty's government intended to bring forward a measure of corporation reform for Ireland, as extensive in its provisions as that introduced by his noble friend.

On the 15th, the bill was read a second time without a division, and was in committee from the 22nd of June to the 20th of July—a period which, when we consider the boldness and importance of the measure, and the power possessed by those whose interests it invaded, cannot be regarded as unnecessarily long, and shows that it was not met in the factious spirit that had characterised the discussion of the Reform Bill. This arose partly from the experience the conservative party had acquired of the utter uselessness of such wanton waste of the time of the legislature, partly from the change which had taken place in the composition of the House of Commons, by the elimination of so many of those who had employed every artifice of delay to protract the debates on the Reform Bill; but it was also due to the candour and good sense of Sir R. Peel, who by his example and influence discouraged all needless opposition to a measure which he saw was demanded by public opinion and by the state of the municipal corporations.

The point on which the conservative party in and out of doors made its chief stand was embodied in the following clause: 'That after the passing of this act, no person shall be elected, admitted, or enrolled a citizen, freeman, liveryman, or burgess of any borough, or by any name member of any body corporate, in respect of any right or title, other than by occupancy and payment of rates within such borough, according to the meaning and provisions of this act.'

To this Sir W. Follett moved an amendment, reserving the rights which this clause took away from the freemen.

In order to understand this motion and the struggle to which it gave rise, it is necessary that the reader should be furnished with some general idea of the nature of the privileges which the amendment of Sir W. Follett was intended to preserve. The freedom of a borough, carrying with it the parliamentary and municipal franchise, might be acquired by birth, apprenticeship, redemption, *i.e.* purchase, marriage, or by the gratuitous gift of the corporation in each borough. The presentation of the freedom was a compliment often paid to successful military or naval commanders, or other persons of distinction to whom the corporators of the borough desired to testify their admiration and respect. In some boroughs the freemen enjoyed valuable rights of pasturage or a share in commons adjacent to the town, and of the proceeds of their sale if they should be sold; in others, they possessed the right of selling their wares and merchandise toll-free in any fair or market in the kingdom; in others, again, they participated in the monopoly of trading in the town which was possessed by the general body of its freemen.

In ancient times the freemen, as their name sufficiently intimates, constituted a sort of privileged caste in each borough; they were the élite of its inhabitants, and the fitting electors of the corporate body by which the town was governed. But this had long since ceased to be the case. In almost every borough, the governing class, taking advantage of the power they possessed of admitting whom they chose into the number of the freemen, had selected their own partisans, in order to strengthen and perpetuate their authority; and thus the freemen, had gradually come to be, as a class, though no doubt, with many honourable exceptions, thoroughly corrupt and degraded, and by long habit had been led to expect a fixed and often very valuable consideration for every exercise of their parliamentary or municipal franchises. The majority of them were bound to the Tories both by interest and gratitude; for the Tories generally paid them most liberally for their votes, and had preserved to them the parliamentary franchise when the Whigs had attempted to take it from them.

It was pointed out by Sir W. Follett that the clause, as it stood, would prevent persons, who otherwise would have become freemen, from enjoying that privilege; and would thus shut them out, from obtaining not only the municipal but also the parliamentary franchise, which Earl Grey's government had somewhat reluctantly allowed the freemen to retain: a concession they had great reason to regret, because these freemen proved to be, as had been anticipated and foretold, the most corrupt and purchaseable portion of the constituencies. But the same reason that led the government to desire the gradual extinction of this class of voters led the conservatives to contend vehemently for its retention, and to complain loudly that ministers were attempting in a covert and underhand way to introduce a most important change in the Reform Bill, to the finality of which they had so strongly pledged themselves. It was warmly contended, that if these persons were to be deprived of the privilege they had inherited, and which the Reform Bill had continued to them, it should at least be done by a special act of Parliament, and not be slipped in as an indirect consequence of municipal reform. On the other hand, it was argued by the government and their supporters that these freemen would be open to every species of corruption; that they were not necessarily residents or rate-payers; that they might come from gaol for the purpose of giving a vote; and if for these reasons they were debarred from exercising the municipal franchise, how could they be allowed to retain the parliamentary franchise? Sir W. Follett's amendment, as well as another intended to preserve the franchises and other privileges of those who either by birth or apprenticeship had acquired inchoate rights, was rejected. Thus, so far as the power of the House of Commons extended, the franchises of these freemen, with all the corruptions, monopolies, and other abuses with which they were connected, were doomed to final extinction. We must not here omit to notice one most valuable though indirect effect of this bill. By putting an end to the rights of apprenticeship and exclusive trading, it struck off one fetter on industry, as the poor-law, in dealing with settlements, had struck off another. Both of them, by preventing men from trading or working where they would, interfered most mischievously with the freedom of labour.

The bill provided no qualification for common councillors beyond that of their being rate-payers in the borough for which they were elected. It was proposed by Sir R. Peel on the 30th of June, that in case of the larger boroughs, which were in Schedule A of the bill, they should be required to possess a personal property of the value of 1000*l.*, or that they should be rated on a rental of not less than 40*l.* a year; and that in the case of the smaller boroughs, which were in Schedule B, they should possess a property of 500*l.* or a rated rental of 20*l.* a year. It was urged that this would be a practical carrying out of the intentions of the old charters, which directed that 'fit, discreet, and respectable' persons should be appointed to corporate offices. Sir Robert in support of his proposal referred to the fact that a clause similar to that which he proposed, had been inserted in the acts of Parliament which had been obtained for the government and regulation of Manchester, Birmingham, Wolverhampton, Bilston, Bolton, Oldham, Stoke-on-Trent—all of which towns were regarded as representatives of popular opinion. This proposal was also rejected. A like fate befell an attempt made by Lord Stanley to render the periods of election less frequent, by providing that one-third of the council should go out of office every two years instead of every year. Mr. Grote was unsuccessful in an attempt he made to introduce the ballot into municipal elections. Proposals for rendering town clerks irremovable, and for preventing municipal corporations from granting leases, were also rejected. The bill therefore, unchanged in all its leading features, went up to the Lords, where a decided majority was strongly hostile to it; afraid indeed to reject it; unwilling to come into collision with the Commons; they determined to alter it as much as they thought they could safely venture to do. Lord Melbourne showed in the speech in which he introduced the bill to the notice of the upper House how well aware he was of the feelings with which it was regarded by the majority of that assembly. His tone was deprecatory, and far different from that which Earl Grey had employed in introducing the Reform Bill. But this was due not so much to the difference in the characters of the two men as to the differences of their position. Lord Melbourne felt that his administration was not strong enough in the House of Commons and the country to warrant him in holding the language which Earl Grey had used. On the other hand, the House, warned by the result of the conflict on parliamentary reform and by the dangers they had then run, were very anxious to avoid a similar crisis. Accordingly most of the amendments which had been rejected by the Commons were substantially adopted in the House of Lords by large majorities. Their lordships began by deciding that they would hear counsel against the statements contained in the report of the commissioners; and the government, unable to resist the will of the majority, were happy to compromise the matter by agreeing that all the corporations who had petitioned for a hearing should be

represented by two barristers. In accordance with the
terms of this understanding, Sir C. Wetherell and Mr.
Knight were heard at the bar of the House. The bill as
amended by the Lords was brought down again to the
House of Commons, where a compromise was proposed by
Lord J. Russell, and accepted by the upper House with
some little modification. It was ultimately agreed that
one-fourth of the councillors should be aldermen holding
office for six years, half of their number being reëlected
every three years. A qualification was admitted, though
not precisely that which the Lords had adopted. A
difficulty which had been raised respecting the ecclesiastical patronage of corporations was got over by determining that the livings in their gift should be sold. The
clause conferring on town councils the power of licensing
public-houses was abandoned. It was not until the 7th
of September that the two Houses at length came to an
agreement, and this great measure, second only in importance to the Reform Bill, of which it was the natural sequel,
became the law of the land.

As the ministers had obtained office by means of the
resolution they had carried incorporating the principle of
appropriation with the Irish tithe-bill of their predecessors,
they were of course compelled to carry forward that measure
with the amendments they had introduced into it. Accordingly, on the 26th of June, Lord Morpeth, as secretary for
Ireland, brought in a bill which was to a great extent a
reproduction of the measure of the displaced government,
with an appropriation clause annexed to it. The provisions
of the bill relating to the collection of tithe were approved
by both parties, and the question of appropriation had been
decided, so far as the House of Commons was concerned, by
the victory which displaced the Peel administration. Lord
Morpeth endeavoured to prove that there would be a considerable surplus available for the purposes that the government contemplated. He proposed to suspend the appointment to every benefice in Ireland where the number of
Protestants did not exceed fifty. If there was no church,
glebe-house, or churchmen, the cure of souls was to be
given to a neighbouring curate, who should receive an
annual payment of 5*l*. In other parishes, the ecclesiastical
commissioners were empowered, with the consent of the

lord-lieutenant and others, to provide curates, under certain regulations, to take charge of them, with power to build churches where required. In the case of benefices of the value of more than 300l. a year, the lord-lieutenant was authorised to make such deductions from their value as he might think proper, provided that the income of the living was not reduced to an amount below 300l. a year. But in the twenty-six dioceses of Ireland, the number of parishes without a single member of the established church was 151; of parishes containing fewer than ten Protestants, 194; between ten and twenty, 198; between twenty and thirty, 133; between thirty and forty, 107; between forty and fifty, 77. Thus the total number of parishes that would come under the operation of the bill would be 860; and it was calculated that from them would be obtained a fund, to be called 'the reserved fund,' amounting to 58,076l., which would be employed, first, to pay the stipends of the neighbouring ministers or salaried curates to be appointed under the provisions of the bill; in the next place, to meet all the charges that might arise in the suspended parishes, to the erection of places of worship; and lastly, to the religious and moral instruction of all classes of the people without distinction of religious persuasion.

Sir R. Peel proposed to separate that part of the bill which related to tithe from that which related to the appropriation of the surplus, making them into two separate and distinct bills. This proposal was supported by Lord Stanley and Sir J. Graham. They endeavoured to prove that if all the requirements of the Irish church were met,—if a sufficient number of clergymen were to be maintained, and sufficient stipends provided for them,—if churches were to be built where needed, and the existing churches kept in proper repair, all the available funds of the Irish church would be employed, and instead of a surplus there would be a deficiency. On the ministerial side these conclusions were tacitly admitted or only faintly denied; but it was argued that the great grievance of Ireland—a grievance which, for the sake of the Irish church herself, it was desirable to abate—was, that revenues intended for the religious instruction of the Irish people should be monopolised by 800,000 Protestants, for purposes in which the 7,000,000 Catholics of Ireland not only took no interest, but strongly disapproved. They therefore contended that the two questions of the collection and the appropriation of Irish tithe were intimately connected, and ought not to be separated. These reasons were no doubt just and weighty; but the real consideration that weighed with both sides, and made each most anxious to carry its point, was, that both were well aware, that if the proposed separation of the two questions were carried, the Tithe Bill would be quietly passed in the upper House, and the Appropriation Bill rejected. On a division Sir R. Peel's motion was lost: the numbers were:

For the motion	282
Against	319
Majority for the government	37

This majority was not large enough to warrant the expectation that ministers would be able to carry the measure through the House of Lords, where an overwhelming majority was avowedly hostile to the principle of appropriation. The conservatives offered no farther opposition to its progress, knowing well how it would be dealt with in the upper House. The Lords made some important alterations in the provisions relating to the collection of tithes, and rejected the appropriation clauses. In vain did Lord Melbourne warn them, that if they persisted in dealing with the bill in this way, it would be abandoned by the government, and that the consequence of that abandonment would be, not only that the clergy, unable to collect their tithes, would be reduced to beggary, but also that the government would be compelled by law to take proceedings against them in the Exchequer Court of Ireland to recover from them 650,000l., which had been advanced to them from the public funds. Undeterred by these warnings, the conservative majority persisted in the course they had decided to adopt, and the bill was withdrawn. The government did not execute the threat they had held out in order to induce the Lords to accept the appropriation clause. A bill was brought in, and carried through both Houses without opposition, to release them from the necessity of prosecuting the Irish clergy.

There was yet another circumstance which contributed even more than the tithe question to keep up and increase the irritation and discontent that prevailed in Ireland—the existence and the conduct of the Orange lodges, by which the principle of 'Protestant ascendancy,' that is, the insolent domination of a small minority over the Catholic majority, was maintained. These Orange lodges exercised at this time so mischievous an influence over the destinies, not of Ireland only, but of England also; they so complicated the problems that English legislators were striving to solve; that a short sketch of their history seems to be called for here. The first Irish Orange lodge was founded in a village called Loughhall on the 21st of September 1795, and it gradually took the place of another Protestant confederacy, the members of which were called 'Break-of-day men.' The original object of both these associations had been to drive the Catholics out of the northern counties of Ireland by wrecking and destroying their houses. 'To hell or to Connaught with you!' was the device of these Protestant societies, by which 7,000 Catholics were stated to have been driven out of Armagh. At first the Orangemen all belonged to the lower orders; but they were soon joined by persons of position and education, and as early as the year 1798 a corrected report of the rules and regulations of the society was submitted to the grand lodge of Ireland, of which Thomas Verner, Esq., was the grand-master, and J. E. Beresford, Esq., the grand-secretary. The condition to which the conduct of the Orangemen had at this time brought the country was very forcibly stated in an address delivered by Lord Gosford, then governor of Armagh, to the leading magistrates of the county, whom he had convened for the purpose of submitting to them a plan intended to check the excesses by which the county was at that time disgraced.

'It is no secret that a persecution, accompanied with all the circumstances of ferocious cruelty which have in all ages distinguished that dreadful calamity, is now raging in this country. Neither age nor acknowledged innocence as to the late disturbances is sufficient to excite mercy, much less afford protection. The only crime which the wretched objects of this merciless persecution are charged with, is a crime of easy proof: it is simply *a profession of the Roman Catholic faith.* A lawless banditti have constituted themselves judges of this species of delinquency, and the sentence they pronounce is equally concise and terrible: it is nothing less than a confiscation of all property and immediate banishment. It would be extremely painful, and surely unnecessary, to detail the horrors that attended the execution of so wide and tremendous a proscription, which certainly exceeds, in the comparative number of those it consigns to ruin and misery, every example that ancient or modern history can afford. For where have we read—in what history of human cruelty have we read—of *more than half the inhabitants of a populous country deprived at one blow of the means as well as the fruits of their industry, and driven, in the midst of an inclement winter, to seek shelter for themselves and their helpless families where chance may guide them?* This is no exaggerated picture of the horrid scenes now acting in this country; yet surely it is sufficient to awaken sentiments of indignation and compassion in the coldest heart. *These horrors are now acting, and acting with impunity.*'

The resolutions moved by his lordship at the close of the address from which this extract is taken were adopted and signed by all the leading magistrates in a country where Orangeism was now rapidly spreading.

Lodges were nevertheless established in all parts of Ireland, and were joined by many magistrates. Their members were numbered by thousands, and even hundreds of thousands; nor were they confined to Ireland. Lodges containing great numbers of members were formed in all the principal towns in England; and some idea of the multitudes that were enrolled in them may be gathered from the fact that there were at one time upwards of 50,000 in London alone. They were also industriously extended to the colonies and dependencies of the British empire. In Canada, where, as we have already seen, circumstances not unlike those of Ireland existed, there were no fewer than 12,000 Orangemen. New lodges were even formed at Malta and on the shores of the Mediterranean. As they rose in respectability and increased in numbers, noblemen, members of parliament, and other persons of position and consequence sought and obtained admittance into them. The Duke of Cumberland, the king's brother, was the grand master of all the Orange lodges, with an absolute veto on their proceedings, and with the power of issuing orders, which every Orangeman was bound to obey. He attended the meetings of the grand lodge in great state. Lord Kenyon was the deputy grand master.

Nothing apparently could be more unobjectionable than the rules of this vast association. They breathed a spirit of moderation and toleration that was quite edifying. The members of the association were required to swear to 'defend the king and his heirs *so long as they support the Protestant ascendancy.*' The objects of the association are stated to be 'exclusively Protestant, but at the same time most tolerant in spirit.' An Orangeman's qualifications are 'faith, piety, courtesy, and compassion.' He must be sober, 'honest, wise, and prudent.' He must love rational society, 'and hate swearing.' Such was the ideal Orangeman, as portrayed by the founders of the institution. But the actual living Orangeman was a widely different creature. The usual place of meeting was the public-house, where political prayers were offered up, and various religious ceremonies gone through, in a manner that the habits, education, and feelings of the majority of the members of these societies will enable the reader to imagine. Every attempt made by English statesmen to apply to Ireland the most elementary principles of civil and religious liberty was encountered by these societies with bitter hostility, and fresh insults on their Catholic compatriots. The battle of the Boyne and the effigy of William III. were flaunted in the faces of the Roman Catholics, now beginning to feel their strength, and less disposed to brook these Orange insults. Of course there were hotheaded fools on both sides, and the faults and follies of the Orangemen were emulated, and perhaps even surpassed, by the Ribbonmen and other secret associations of Catholics. But the latter had been brought into existence by the provocations of the former; and though they greatly damaged the cause they were intended to serve, and helped by their crimes to keep alive the bitter feeling that existed on the other side, yet the mischief they did was not on the same great national scale as that inflicted by the Orange lodges. They were very serious to individuals; but they did not materially retard the pacification of Ireland, and were sure to disappear when its condition was sensibly ameliorated. We can easily guess with what feelings this Orange party would be regarded at this time by O'Connell's followers in Ireland, as well as by the radicals—nay, by the whole liberal party—in England; nor were the feelings of Sir R. Peel and the wiser portion of the conservative party more favourable to them. They could not but feel how much the Orangemen had done by their stupid bigotry to disappoint the hopes they had entertained of the beneficial results of Catholic emancipation. They could not, however, venture to manifest the contempt and dislike they felt for men who formed the bulk of their supporters in Ireland, and were therefore obliged to wink at, and even to palliate, the bigotry of these mischievous marplots. Such were the feelings with which the Orange societies were regarded by all sensible men, when it was discovered that there were a great number of them in the army; that the warrants constituting them were signed by the Duke of Cumberland, and this in direct contravention of general orders issued in the years 1822 and 1829, expressly forbidding the establishment or continuance of such associations in the army, and declaring them to be subversive of military discipline. The subject was brought under the notice of the House of Commons by Mr. Hume, who proposed that the House should send an address to the king, condemning the Orange lodges, and directing the especial attention of his majesty to their introduction into the army, under warrants signed by the Duke of Cumberland. Out of doors the matter assumed a still more serious aspect. The Duke was a Tory of the Tories, and the most unpopular man in the kingdom. The most absurd reports were founded on the facts that had been brought to light. It was alleged that there was a conspiracy on the part of the Orangemen to set aside the Princess Victoria, the next heir to the throne, in favour of the Duke of Cumberland; and though all well-informed persons saw that these suspicions were destitute of foundation, they were nevertheless extensively believed by the very ignorant; and they caused the matter to be discussed with a degree of interest and excitement which would not otherwise have been bestowed on it. On behalf of his royal highness, it was explained that the warrants had been signed by him in blank, and had subsequently been filled up in the manner already mentioned quite against his wish and intention. Lord J. Russell, while taking exception to many parts of the address, and particularly to the mention in it of the name of a member of the royal family, nevertheless expressed his surprise that the Duke of Cumberland had not withdrawn from a society in which his confidence had been so flagrantly abused. A committee had been appointed to investigate the matter; and in prosecuting their inquiries, they had been led to ask for a book belonging to a Colonel Fairman, an officer of these societies, which he steadily refused to produce, alleging that it contained references to private matters. His conduct being reported to the House, it was ordered that he should be committed to Newgate; but he managed to keep out of the way of the sergeant-at-arms till the end of the session; and an application to search his house for the book was refused, on the ground that there was no precedent for such a proceeding, except in the case of the South-Sea directors, where the circumstances were very different and the necessity for it much greater; besides which, it was ascertained that such a search was contrary to the practice of the law courts.

Some improvements were effected in the machinery of the Reform Bill during this session. The duration of polls was reduced from two days to one, which the experience of the working of the measure had shown to be amply sufficient; but the returning officer was empowered to adjourn the poll in case of a riot. It was also enacted that such a number of polling places should be provided as would reduce the number polling at each to 300 or less, and under certain specified circumstances to 100 or less.

A committee was appointed, in spite of the strong opposition of Lord J. Russell, to consider the best mode of setting apart a portion of the strangers' gallery for the accommodation of ladies who might wish to be present at the debates of the House; but when the report of the committee was brought up, it was rejected by a majority of three. Mr. Grote again proposed his ballot scheme, little thinking probably at the time for how many years it would be repeated, and how long a time would elapse before it was at last adopted.

On the 25th of May, the Marquis of Chandos, 'the farmer's friend,' and chosen champion of the agricultural interest, came forward to advocate the cause of the clients whose interests he had espoused with no ordinary self-devotion. He had declined office in the Peel administration, because it was offered on conditions which would render necessary a temporary cessation of his advocacy of their claims; and he now came forward to make another attempt to represent their grievances and to ask for redress. He proposed an address to the throne, referring to the frequent acknowledgments of agricultural distress which had been made in different king's speeches at the opening of several successive sessions, and asking for 'the immediate removal of some portion of the burdens to which the land is subject through the pressure of general and local taxation.' In making this motion, he dwelt on the heaviness of the county rates, on the cost of maintaining prisoners in gaols, of the expense of building and repairing of bridges, and mending roads by statute labour; he also complained of the exaction of a tax on carts having springs and cushions, from which carts destitute of those luxuries were exempted. The motion was met by the home secretary with a hostile amendment, which was supported by Sir R. Peel, on the ground that the adoption of the resolution would have the effect of raising expectations amongst the agriculturists which the government would be compelled to disappoint. The loss of this motion did not prevent Mr. Cayley, a representative of the north riding of Yorkshire, from bringing forward another remedy for the agricultural distress so much complained of. He proposed an alteration of the currency; a favourite motion of a section of the House. This scheme also was opposed by the leaders on both sides, and rejected.

The debate on the motion of Lord Chandos proved fatal to that extraordinary man William Cobbett. Though seventy-three years of age, and suffering from an affection of the throat, which rendered him inaudible except to those members who were seated close to him, he could not be induced by any persuasions to refrain from addressing the House in favour of the motion of the Marquis of Blandford for the repeal of the malt tax—a question in which he had for many years taken a warm and active interest. He again sat up late to take part in the voting on the supplies, and was completely prostrated in consequence. Nevertheless, he once more sat up to a late hour to give his vote in favour of the motion of the Marquis of Chandos on agricultural distress. He left London early the next morning, and went down to his farm at Ash near Farnham. Here his illness assumed a still more serious character, and he expired on the 18th of June. His life affords a striking instance of the manner in which the greatest disadvantages may be overcome by indomitable perseverance. With scarcely any school education, and with very little assistance of any kind, he succeeded, by his own resolute diligence and the most rigid economy of time, amidst a variety of other avocations, in making himself one of the first writers of pure racy English that has ever lived; in obtaining a competence by his own exertions; in becoming the leader of a powerful party, which owed its very existence to his eloquence and ability; and in obtaining for himself at length a place and an influence in the legislature of his country.

The budget of this year was not brought forward until the 14th of August. It showed an income a little below that of the preceding year, and an expenditure considerably greater, in consequence of the sum payable this year to the West India planters under the slave emancipation act, which might under certain circumstances amount to nearly a million, though it probably would not exceed 600,000l. or 700,000l. In the former case there would be a deficiency, in the latter a small surplus. But the uncertainty which existed on this point prevented the chancellor of the exchequer from doing more than making some small changes in the incidence of taxation on spirits, flint glass, and a few other articles.

The session of 1836 was opened by the king in person on the 14th of February. The Duke of Wellington in the upper House, and Sir R. Peel in the lower, took exception to a clause of the speech which recommended the two Houses to apply to the defects and evils that existed in the municipal corporations of Ireland 'a remedy founded on the same principles as those of the acts which have already passed for England and Scotland.' These words were objected to on the ground that they pledged Parliament beforehand to particular principles of measures not yet in existence. But the real motive of the objection was, that a corporation reform bill for Ireland, based on the same principles as those of England and Scotland, would inevitably transfer the government of the towns from the hands of the Protestants into the hands of the Catholics; a result which must follow the adoption of any measure of corporation reform that allowed a free election of the members of the corporations by the inhabitants of the towns whose municipal affairs they were to manage. In the House of Lord, the duke, followed as he was by a large majority, was master of the situation, and his amendment, faintly deprecated by the government, was adopted. In the House of Commons a similar amendment was rejected.

The affairs of Ireland still continued to force themselves on the legislature, and to occupy a large share of its attention. This arose from two causes: first, the still unsettled state of that country, which no government could disregard; and secondly, the position occupied by the Irish Catholic party, which, though not very numerous, was sufficiently large to hold the balance between the Government and the Opposition, and to give the majority to the one or the other, as it suited the purpose of its leader. O'Connell used the enormous power which this state of things placed in his hands very skilfully. He gave a steady support to the government; but he took good care to make them feel that the continuance of that support depended on their adoption of such a policy towards Ireland as he advocated, and would be instantly withdrawn, or even converted into bitter hostility, if they should swerve from it. It was no doubt for the purpose of conciliating him and the party he led that the paragraph relating to the principles of the Irish municipal corporations bill had been inserted in the king's speech.

No sooner did the business of the session commence than Mr. Hume, seconded by Sir W. Molesworth, led a fresh assault on the Orange societies. They insisted strongly on the dangerous nature of associations, the members of which were bound together by a solemn religious engagement, equivalent to an oath—the proceedings of which were wrapped in profound secrecy—which contained 300,000 members, all bound to yield the most implicit obedience to any order that might be given by their grand master the Duke of Cumberland, who was, as we have already seen, absurdly supposed to be aspiring to the English throne. To the resolution condemnatory of these societies moved by Mr. Hume, an amendment, also condemning them, but in more qualified terms, was proposed by Lord J. Russell, in the form of a resolution for an address to be presented to the king, requesting his majesty to discountenance the Orange societies and *all* political societies 'excluding persons of a different religious faith, using signs and symbols, and acting by affiliated branches.' Lord Stanley and Sir R. Peel advocated the omission of the words in the resolution which mentioned the Orange societies, admitting, at the same time—what they were far too enlightened not to see, and too candid not to confess— that those societies had proved very baneful to Ireland. Lord J. Russell, however, refused to admit the suggested change in his resolution, which was carried without a division. The king's reply was of course an echo of the address. Both were forwarded by the home secretary to the Duke of Cumberland, who answered that he had already recommended the dissolution of the Orange societies throughout Ireland. It was effected in some places with strong demonstrations of loyalty and submission, in others with murmurs and reluctance.

The next Irish question that occupied the attention of the legislature was a Corporation Reform Bill, framed in accordance with the pledge given in the king's speech. The Opposition exclaimed loudly against the measure, contending that it would intensify those evils of party ascendancy with which Ireland was already afflicted, by transferring to the Catholics the predominance which had hitherto been enjoyed by the Protestants. The conservatives proposed to obviate this danger, and to secure that the new corporations should contain some Protestant ingredients, by enacting that almost all the officers of the existing corporations, from the mayors and aldermen down to the butter and cheese tasters, should hold their respective offices till removed from them by death or in other ways, which they promised to specify in new clauses of the bill. It was farther proposed by them, that in some large towns the corporations should be allowed to continue to exist, while in others they were to be altogether suppressed, leaving certain members who were to take charge of charitable trusts. In those towns whose corporations they proposed to suppress, they suggested that the functions belonging to those bodies should be exercised by commissioners to be appointed by the lord-lieutenant.

These proposals are sufficient to show that the cry of

'justice for Ireland' was neither unreasonable nor unfounded; for had they been adopted, they would have placed Ireland on a very different footing from England and Scotland in respect to her municipal affairs, and yet on a footing vastly superior to that on which she had hitherto stood. The government wisely and rightly set its face against these suggestions, and the bill went through the lower House unaltered in its leading features. But when it got into the House of Lords, the majority of that assembly did what the minority of the lower House had vainly wished to do. Never perhaps was any measure so extensively changed in its passage through that House. Out of 140 clauses which the bill contained, 106 were virtually or actually thrown out of it, while eighteen fresh clauses were introduced. That the government should accept a measure thus mutilated, after the pledge they had given, was out of the question. When it came back into the lower House, Lord J. Russell moved that Dublin, Belfast, Cork, Galway, Kilkenny, Limerick, Waterford, Clonmel, Drogheda, Londonderry, Sligo, and Carrickfergus should have corporations selected in the manner provided by the bill; that twenty-two other boroughs should not have corporations, but elect commissioners to whom the corporate property and the right of appointing the various municipal officers should belong; that other boroughs, still less considerable than these, should be allowed to choose commissioners or not, as they might think fit; that the appointment of magistrates should be transferred from corporations to the crown. This compromise, proposed by the government and adopted by a large majority of the Commons, was rejected by the Lords, and the bill was consequently dropped.

The same fate awaited the Irish tithe bill, reproduced this session in a somewhat modified form. It was once more very fully discussed in the House of Commons, the conservatives again ineffectually attempting to get rid of the appropriation clauses; the House of Lords, on the other hand, getting rid of them by large majorities; whereupon Lord J. Russell raised a question of privilege, maintaining that some of the amendments introduced by the peers were invasions of the constitutional principle, in virtue of which the Commons claimed the exclusive right of dealing with all clauses granting money to the crown. He also condemned these amendments on their own merits, and moved that they should be taken into consideration that day three months—in other words, that the bill should be abandoned. After some discussion this motion was carried by a majority of 29.

In England the question of tithe commutation was not clogged with any such difficulties as the introduction of the appropriation clauses had imported into the Irish measure. It was alike the interest of the Government and the Opposition, of the tithe-payer and the tithe receiver, that it should be speedily and finally settled. In consequence of this general agreement no difficulty was to be apprehended in either House of Parliament. Ministers therefore adopted, with some modifications, the plan that Sir R. Peel had introduced during his brief term of office. The bill passed through both Houses with little alteration. Only one amendment made by the Lords was objected to when the bill came back to the Commons, and the Lords did not insist on it. Thus a great scandal, a great grievance, a great clog on the operations of the agriculturist, a great source of unpopularity to the clergy, and a great social evil, was at length quietly taken out of the way.

Another great grievance was also redressed during this session. We have already witnessed the failure of attempts that had been made to satisfy the claim of dissenters to be allowed to have their marriages celebrated with such religious rites as they preferred. This question was now taken up as part of a greater whole, and dealt with in a more comprehensive manner than had hitherto been attempted. Up to this period the only register of births, deaths, and marriages was that kept in the churches. Of births there was no official registration at all, but only of baptisms; and this of course was very imperfect, as it did not contain the names of the children of persons of the Baptist persuasion, or of members of the Society of Friends, or of persons who for some reason or other had not been baptised in their infancy. All marriages were performed and registered in the churches. This was also the case to a great extent with regard to burials, but not entirely, as even then some cemeteries existed as well as a few nonconformist burial-grounds, and though in such places registers were usually kept, yet they were often kept very carelessly. It was therefore desirable that some general and uniform system of registration should be established, and that copies of all registers should be collected in a central place, where they could be referred to in case they should be required to establish claims to property, or for other purposes. Thus the question of dissenters' marriages was merged in the larger question of a general registration. This question was dealt with in two bills; the first of which was for the registration of births and deaths, and the other for the registration of marriages. These measures, with the working of which we are all familiar, effected a very great and desirable change with very little interference with existing practices. Baptisms, marriages, and funerals continued to be celebrated in the churches after the passing of the bill exactly as they had been before. And the dissenters obtained the boon of celebrating their marriages in the manner most in accordance with their religious convictions, without being subjected to the vexations which the measures previously introduced imposed on them. But these are by no means the only benefits which have resulted from this measure. It has imposed on the registrar-general and his subordinates throughout the kingdom the duty—a duty which has been admirably discharged—of collecting an immense body of statistical facts of the greatest possible value to the government, the legislator, the medical man, the philosopher, the man of science, and the nation at large; facts which never could have been obtained if some such plan as that we are now recording had not been adopted, and which will exercise a most beneficial influence on the march of scientific discovery, on the sanitary legislation of Parliament, and on the sanitary proceedings of our various corporations, enabling them to discover and remove the causes of disease, to watch its course, and to study the efficiency of the various means that may be employed to contend with it. It was a fortunate circumstance for the country, in reference not only to this, but to many other measures that were brought forward about this time, that the Opposition in the two Houses was led by two men so candid and straightforward as the Duke of Wellington and Sir R. Peel. It was due in a great degree to their influence, that these two important bills were read a second time in both Houses without opposition, and that government had no reason to complain in any respect of the treatment they received in committee in either House of Parliament. A few alterations of no great moment were made in the details of the measures. The old practice of proclaiming the banns in the churches, which the bill, as at first drawn, had abolished, was retained. It was ordered, for the sake of securing greater publicity, that notices of intended marriages should be read at the meetings of the guardians of the poor. This provision was strongly opposed by the representatives of the dissenting interest in the House of Commons; but a large majority, listening to the advice of Lord J. Russell, decided to accept it rather than run the risk of losing the bill. Thus passed a law which, though it did not attract the attention bestowed on some other measures of less intrinsic value, which, involving as they did the fate of parties and administrations, were the objects of vehement struggles and stormy debates, was nevertheless little, if at all, inferior in utility and importance to any of the great measures which had been introduced and carried by the representatives of the reforming party. If little else had been effected during this season, the government might yet have pointed to this measure as a sufficient atonement for many other failures.

The ecclesiastical commission, which had been called into existence by Sir R. Peel, continued its labours, the places which had originally been occupied by members of the late administration being now filled by their successors. This alteration, however, did not at first produce any great change in the character of its recommendations. It was in fact doing quite as much in the way of church reform as could be expected from a body containing so large a proportion of bishops. The commissioners set themselves to work with exemplary diligence to remedy many of the more glaring abuses of the church. They proposed to diminish the inequality that existed between the incomes of the different bishoprics, and so to remove the chief inducement to translations from one see to another. Some of these inequalities were enormous. Thus, while the bishop of Durham had a revenue of 19,480*l.* per annum, the archbishop of Canterbury 18,090*l.*, the bishop of London 13,890*l.*, the bishop of Rochester had only 1,400*l.*, the bishop of Oxford 1,600*l.*, and the bishop of Llandaff 1,170*l.* It is true that many of the more poorly endowed bishops hold deaneries, canonries, or other rich preferment, *in commendam*, as it was termed; but this was another abuse, and another source of unpopularity to the church. It was proposed therefore to fix the income of Canterbury at 15,000*l.*, of York and London at 10,000*l.* each, of Durham at 8,000*l.*, Winchester at 7,000*l.* and to equalise more nearly the incomes of the other sees, fixing them at 5,000*l.* or 4,500*l.*, per annum. It was proposed also to suppress the bishoprics of Bristol and Sodor and Man; to establish new sees at Ripon and Manchester; and to adopt such new circumscriptions of dioceses as the change in the population and the alterations of circumstances seemed to render desirable.

Coming down to cathedral dignitaries, it was proposed to deal with the incomes of deans on the same principles as the incomes of bishops—not bringing them to an exact equality, but establishing a much nearer approach to equality among them than had hitherto existed. There was to be a great reduction in the number of canons and minor canons. Many ecclesiastical sinecures connected with the cathedrals were to be suppressed altogether; and the dignities that were allowed to remain in the different cathedrals were to be more nearly equalised. Still, great differences in this respect were allowed to continue. Thus, while the dean of Durham retained a revenue of 4,594*l.*, and the deans of Westminster and Oxford each 3,000*l.* per annum, the dean of Chester was only to have 441*l.*; and while each canon of Durham was to receive 2,000*l.* a year, each canon of Chester was to have only 187*l.* These inequalities arose from the different value of the estates belonging to the different cathedrals: a difference which it was thought desirable to respect, because, if all should be brought nearly down to the level of the lowest, their incomes would be too much reduced; and if all should be raised nearly to the level of the highest, the fund which was wanted for other important purposes would be seriously diminished.

In consequence of these arrangements, a large revenue would be placed at the disposal of the commissioners; and it was proposed that it should be applied to the augmentation of poor livings in populous places and public patronage, thus diminishing the glaring disproportion which existed in many instances between the duties which the ministers of the church were expected to perform and the emoluments they received. There were many parishes of the metropolis and of Lancashire and Yorkshire, with populations of twenty or thirty thousand persons, under the nominal charge of one minister, receiving an income often less than 150*l.* per annum, and that arising from fees and pew rents; there were many country livings, with very small populations, in which the salary of the minister amounted to 3,000*l.*, 4,000*l.*, and even 7,000*l.* per annum. Anything like a complete redress of these inequalities was rendered impossible by the existence of lay patronage, recognised by the law as a private and saleable property; for any transfer of the revenues of these livings to others would diminish the value of the patron's property, and any augmentation of them would enable him to sell the advowson or next presentation for a larger sum than he could otherwise have obtained. For these reasons, the commissioners limited their operations to benefices in public patronage; and this was fortunately the case with regard to the great majority of parishes situated in those parts of the kingdom in which the population had been and still was growing most rapidly.

Such were the chief recommendations of the ecclesiastical commissioners. The government determined to embody them in bills, and introduce them into Parliament. They encountered, however, a very vigorous opposition from the radical and dissenting sections of the ministerial party, who objected strongly to the amount of the salaries still proposed to be left to the bishops and other dignitaries, and desired to see the principle of appropriation, which had already been sanctioned by the House of Commons in dealing with the Irish church, applied to her English sister, or, at all events, to see the church-rate question settled before a measure calculated to strengthen the church was adopted. But in spite of this opposition, the government persisted in urging forward their measures, and, by the aid of the conservatives on the one hand, and the neutrality of Mr. O'Connell and his followers on the other, they succeeded in carrying the Bishops Bill; but the chapter reform bill and that for the regulation of pluralities were dropped for this session. Bills were also passed to prevent the creation of new vested interests in certain cathedral offices which it was intended to abolish; for the suppression of the secular jurisdiction of the bishop of Durham and the archbishop of York; and for restricting the renewal of leases by ecclesiastical persons. This delay afforded those persons whose interests or whose prejudices were touched by the proposed measures—and they were numerous—as well as all who for any reasons objected to them, an opportunity of agitating the country against them. Many of the bishops declared strongly against the proposed chapter reforms. The deans and chapters themselves petitioned against them, and so did a great number of the clergy; the dissenters likewise agitated against them. But more formidable than all their other antagonists was Sydney Smith, now canon of St. Paul's, London, who, in his three celebrated letters to Archd. Singleton, put forth all his unrivalled powers of wit, argument, and raillery against the proposed measures. But all was in vain. The ministry was too deeply committed on the question to draw back, and the recommendations of the ecclesiastical commissioners were too manifestly right and reasonable to be withstood, even by the wit, eloquence, and wisdom of the great canon; but as long as the English language endures, the memory of the ecclesiastical commissioners will be handed down in the humorous and argumentative letters of their formidable antagonist.

It was found absolutely necessary to introduce some changes into the Corporation Reform Act in the course of this session. There were defects in it which had caused the validity of the election of several mayors and other municipal officers to be disputed. The act had also made a temporary provision for the management of charities, which would come to an end on the 1st of August, 1837, and which must therefore be dealt with by the legislature either in this or the following session. On these questions the two Houses differed. The Lords made certain amendments in the bill sent to them from the Commons, which were agreed to by the ministers, but which the majority of the lower House were nevertheless unwilling to accept. The Duke of Wellington complained that after an amendment had been assented to by the lord chancellor its rejection should be moved by the attorney-general. Conferences and free conferences took place, but to no purpose. Bills were, however, introduced embodying those provisions on which the majorities in both Houses were agreed, and these were passed.

This session witnessed the abolition of a most barbarous and absurd practice of the English courts. Up to this time prisoners accused of felony were not allowed to have counsel to defend them. The prosecution might be carried on by the ablest advocates at the bar, while the defendant, often a poor unlettered man, was compelled to plead his own cause against them. This practice, like every other established abuse, did not want its apologists. More than twelve years had elapsed since the subject was brought under the notice of the House of Commons by Mr. George Lamb; and still there were many persons, high in office and of great legal authority, who defended this time-honoured absurdity. It was urged that the judge was counsel for the prisoner, though it was well known that the accused person had no opportunity of consulting with him, or of putting before him the facts and the arguments on which his defence ought to rest, except in open court. Bills which, if carried, would have had the effect of removing this anomaly in our judicature, had in two successive sessions passed through the Commons, but had been rejected in the upper House. This time, however, the advocates of justice and common sense were more successful. The measure went through the House of Commons without much difficulty. In the House of Lords it had the good fortune to fall into the hands of Lord Lyndhurst, who had formerly opposed the change, but now supported it zealously, and with his usual great ability.

'Distinctions,' he said, 'are drawn even between different classes of crimes, which do not seem to rest on any rational foundation. Treason, the highest of all crimes, and misdemeanour, the lowest kind of offences, are placed on the same footing. In both of them the prisoner is allowed the benefit of counsel to address the jury on the facts of the case; and yet in the intermediate class—that of felonies—the same privilege does not exist. Thus certain offences regarding the coin constitute only a misdemeanour when committed for the first time, but become felony in case of a previous conviction. The consequence is, that a man may be tried for a first offence as a simple misdemeanour, and his counsel may address the jury: if he is found guilty, and immediately tried upon a second indictment for a similar offence, it is now felony; his counsel can no longer address the jury; they can only examine witnesses and speak to points of the law.' After considering the reasons which had been urged in favour of the practice by Lord Nottingham and Serjeant Hawkins, and stating that he himself had formerly defended it, though he had subsequently seen reason to change his opinion, he thus proceeded: 'England and Ireland are the only countries in Europe in which a prisoner is not allowed to defend himself by counsel. In Scotland that power is given to the counsel in every case. The same thing is done in our British possessions. If the system is bad, why should it be continued in any part of the country? if it is good, why should it not be extended to all? And what are the evils that are dreaded from the change? It may lead, it is said, to a great consumption of time—the duration of assizes and sessions would be greatly prolonged. But this could never be stated as an objection to the principle of the measure; for where life and liberty are at stake, no time could be grudged that may be necessary for going into the case in the fullest manner. Again, it is objected, that if counsel are allowed to address the jury, instead of trials being conducted as they now are with temper and firmness, there would be warmth and zeal on both sides of the court, which would detract from the gravity and decorum of its proceedings. But is it found in Scotland that trials are conducted with more zeal and warmth or with less decorum than in England? No one ever pretends that it is so, and the evidence proves the contrary. It may be true, that in nine cases out of ten it is almost immaterial to the result whether there are counsel in the case or not; the facts are so clear and conclusive. Yet there are many cases where the aid of counsel is of the utmost importance to the elucidation of the truth, and of great service to the judges who try the case. Another objection is, that if counsel addressed the jury for the prisoner, the judge would reply to him, and thus be placed in the unseemly position of appearing to be an advocate against the accused. The best answer to this objection is a reference to the cases of misdemeanour, where the judge interferes no farther than to point out the errors and sophisms into which the counsel may have fallen, which it would be his duty to do in any case.'

The bill, as originally sent up from the Commons, not only provided that the prisoner accused of felony might be defended by counsel, but also gave him the last word in every case. To this part of the bill Lord Lyndhurst and several other law lords strongly objected, contending that it would substitute one anomaly for another; and notwithstanding the strenuous opposition of the lord chancellor, this provision was expunged. The Commons at first were disposed to adhere to their original opinion; but, finding that the Lords were resolved to maintain their amendment, they gave way, consoling themselves with the reflection, that much was gained by the bill as it stood; and, with the promise of Mr. Ewart, who had the care of it, that he would in a future session introduce a new measure embodying those provisions, which for the present he found it expedient to abandon.

The cause of humanity gained another victory during this session. Hitherto the law had required that persons convicted of murder should be executed the next day but one after their conviction, unless that day should happen to be a Sunday, in which case they would be executed on the Monday. In the interval between the sentence and its execution they were to be fed on bread and water, and no person was to have access to them except the gaoler, the chaplain, and the surgeon. The statutes containing these provisions were repealed, and a longer interval allowed to elapse between the sentence and its execution. Other bills of less importance affecting our judicature were introduced. It was enacted that medical witnesses before coroners' juries should receive a guinea for their evidence, and two guineas for a post-mortem examination. On the other hand, bills for the abolition of imprisonment for debt under certain circumstances, and for separating the judicial functions of the lord chancellor from his parliamentary duties, miscarried.

Since the destruction of the old Houses of Parliament, a select committee had been busily engaged in making arrangements for the erection of new buildings, and after careful examination of the plans submitted to them, had given the preference to that of Mr. Barry, by whom the building of the new Houses was accordingly superintended. They had, however, determined to make several alterations in his plans, and to carry the buildings farther along the river from Westminster-bridge than had been originally contemplated, as well as to extend them considerably in the direction of Abingdon-street. Mr. Hume proposed a change of site, and made a motion for that purpose. The committee hoped by the removal of some superfluous ornaments, to be able to keep the cost of the building down to 500,000*l.*, or at most 700,000*l*. Mr. Hume, on the contrary, insisted that, in spite of the proposed alterations of the plan, the expense of the building would be at least 1,300,000*l*. He also presented a petition from the unsuccessful competitors, complaining on various grounds of the preference given by the committee to Mr. Barry's plans, and asking either that they might be allowed to be heard by counsel at the bar of the House, or that the report of the committee might be submitted to the judgment of some competent persons. This claim of Mr. Barry's disappointed competitors was not seriously entertained by the Commons. The question had been decided after long and laborious investigation, and they were unwilling to reopen it.

The proposal to admit ladies to hear the debates was carried this year by 132 against 90, and the chancellor of the exchequer, while avowing his own strong objection to their admission, proposed, in deference to the decision of the House, that the sum of 400*l*. should be applied to defray the cost of fitting up a portion of the gallery for their accommodation. In the debate on this vote, different members of the government took different sides, Lord Palmerston expressing himself strongly in favour of the innovation, while the president of the board of control as strongly opposed it; adding that he would have been in his place to vote against the resolution which had been passed, if he had not regarded the proposal of such a thing as a jest. He declared that he thought there was something indecent in introducing high-bred and virtuous-minded females within the walls of Parliament to listen to the multifarious debates that were carried on there. At last the speaker was requested to deliver his opinion on the subject, and accordingly he made the following observations: 'As the House has twice decided in favour of the admission of ladies to the strangers' gallery, I have felt it a matter of great doubt whether I ought to give any opinion at all on the question; but as I have been called on by the House to do so, I must say that, having well considered the subject, and looking at it as a question of considerable importance with reference to the order and decorum of the House, and with reference to the influence that might be exerted on the House, I have come to a distinct and positive conviction that the measure is most undesirable. I have formed and expressed this opinion without reference to those whom it may please or displease, and in the discharge of what I conceive to be my duty to the House.' This declaration was fatal to the proposed innovation; for though the motion for the admission of ladies to the gallery of the House had been carried by a majority of 42, the proposal to furnish the sum necessary to the carrying out of this resolution was refused by 42 against 28.

We have seen the representatives of the agricultural interest coming year after year before the House with statements, only too well founded, of agricultural distress, and with various ineffectual applications to the House for the relief of that distress. This year the government determined to anticipate them, and at the very commencement of the session, on the 8th of February, Lord J. Russell proposed the appointment of a select committee to deliberate on this question. The committee sat till the 21st of July, when its chairman announced that his colleagues had come to the conclusion that they would not make any report, but content themselves with publishing the evidence they had taken. Without waiting for this result of the committee's labours, but no doubt with a full foreknowledge that they would be altogether fruitless, 'farmers' friend' Lord Chandos brought forward a motion of his own on agricultural distress, urging that any reduction of taxation that might be made, the interests of agriculture should be considered.

This motion was resisted, not only by Lord J. Russell, but also by Sir Jas. Graham and Sir R. Peel; but notwithstanding the opposition of the leaders of the two great parties in the House and very conclusive reasons urged against it, there were 178 votes in favour of the motion to 208 against it.

The great feature of the budget of this year, and that which excited the warmest enthusiasm on the one hand, and called forth the greatest alarm and the most vehement opposition on the other, was the proposed reduction of the stamp duty on newspapers from 4*d*., minus the discount to 1*d*., without any discount. An attempt was made to get rid of this part of the government plan by Sir C. Knightley, who proposed that the duty on soap should be reduced instead of the stamp duty on newspapers. He said: 'The duty on soap is one that not only presses severely on the working classes, but also presses on them unequally in comparison with the more wealthy, the soap of the poor man being taxed at 75 per cent., and that of the rich man at only 30 per cent. The reduction of this tax, by aiding cleanliness, would promote the health and comfort of the people; the lowering of newspaper stamps will tend to introduce a cheap and profligate press, one of the greatest curses which could be inflicted on humanity. Are the necessaries of life to be taxed in preference to luxuries and superfluities? Or is such knowledge as is likely to be communicated through a cheap newspaper so vitally important as to be worth acquiring at the expense of inflicting filth and disease on the very persons whose minds are to be thus illuminated? Neither the farmers nor the growers complain of the want of cheap newspapers, but all complain of the want of cheap soap. It is absurd to say that even the poor are debarred from reading the newspapers; for in a coffee-shop they can have a cup of coffee and a sight of every newspaper published in London for three-halfpence, being only half the price at which it will be possible to publish the newspapers even after the duties have been reduced. Nor has any application for this reduction proceeded from the proprietors of newspapers; even those journals which are most favourable to the government have protested against it.'

Mr. C. Barclay, the seconder of this motion, argued that

the loss to the revenue by the reduction of the duty on soap would certainly not be greater than the loss sustained by the proposed reduction of the duty on the newspaper stamp. As one principal reason assigned for the reduction of the duty was the impossibility of punishing offenders, he urged that this difficulty might easily be overcome, as each sheet of every printed paper bore the printer's name.

The chancellor of the exchequer thus replied: 'One reason for preferring a reduction of the stamp duties to a reduction of the soap duties, is that the former is a diminishing, and the latter an increasing duty. The quantity of soap bought in charge in 1831 was 109,000,000 lbs., and in 1833 was 133,000,000 lbs. The consumption of soft soap in the first of these years was 9,600,000 lbs., and in 1833 it was 12,103,000 lbs. But the stamp duties on newspapers, which in 1831 had yielded 483,000*l.*, yielded in 1835 only 455,000*l.* Now it is a principle of finance, that in reducing public imposts the comparative productiveness of different taxes should be kept in view. Besides, the soap duty has already been reduced one half, while the stamp duty has been kept at its maximum. The loss to the revenue by the reduction of the soap duty would be twice the amount of loss that is anticipated from the reduction of the newspaper duty. Besides, when the improvements in the manufacture of soap and the reduced price of the alkalies are taken into account along with the present low rate of duty, I do not think that this is an article which calls most pressingly for relief.

'On the other hand, the condition and consequences of the newspaper stamp duty call loudly for alteration, unless the disregard of the law is to be encouraged, and those who obey it are to be left without protection. The diminution which has taken place in the produce of these duties does not arise from any falling off in the education of the people, or in their anxiety for political information. Accordingly, every man would have expected that the revenue yielded by the newspapers would have increased. It is the tax that prevents the increase. Here, as in every other case, a duty raised above the legitimate amount leads to successful smuggling, and supplies the public demands without contributing to the public revenue. I am far from thinking that all the knowledge that it is desirable to circulate among the people is to be found in newspapers; but they are the means of diffusing political knowledge of a very important character. I entertain no apprehension of the consequences of facilitating the spread of this knowledge; but even if it were desirable to confine it to the present high-priced papers, it would be impossible. In London and throughout England an active agency has been employed for the purpose of violating the law by circulating newspapers without a stamp. The total number of stamps taken in the United Kingdom is 36,000,000. On one occasion the officers of the stamp department seized an incomplete publication amounting to 40,000 sheets. This gave for a weekly paper 2,000,000 sheets per annum, being equal to one-eighteenth of the whole stamped press: and this was only a single instance. It is true that every sheet bears the printer's name, but it is often a false one. The law officers of the crown have given their opinion, that the existing law is wholly ineffectual to put down the evil. I believe that any attempt to cure the evil by increasing the severity of the law would be wholly ineffectual. I will not, however, as some desire, repeal the duty altogether, but bring it back from its present amount of 4*d*. to its original amount of 1*d*. This will equalise the whole of the press, raise its character, and enable parties who are anxious to give religious instruction to the people to combine it with knowledge of a political nature.'

Mr. Goulburn: 'In reducing public burdens the first question ought to be, what reduction would confer the greatest benefit on the greatest portion of the community; from which it follows as a corollary, that in all reductions of taxation we should retain those that are burdens on luxuries, rather than those which affect the necessaries of life. To propose a diminution of the stamp duties instead of the soap duties is to sin against both these plain principles. The chancellor of the exchequer accordingly has maintained, that the reduction of the latter would occasion a positive loss, which the revenue could not sustain, because he anticipates that no great increase of consumption would follow on the reduction, and that because a very limited increase had ensued on the former reduction of the duty by half its amount. This is a fallacy. The former reduction led to no great increase because the duty still remained too high to exclude the contraband trader from the market. The metropolitan manufacture of soap the year previous to the reduction of the duty amounted to 32,900,000 lbs. In 1835, after the reduction, the amount brought to 'change in the city of London was only 32,400,000 lbs., showing a reduction of 500,000 lbs. In Scotland previous to the reduction in 1833 there had been brought to 'change 11,800,000 lbs.; and in the year after the reduction 10,400,000 lbs., being a reduction little short of 1,000,000 lbs. In some rural parts of the country, where the same facilities for smuggling do not exist, there has been some increase; but it is not proportionate with the amount of reduction. Thus the reduction, so far from impeding the smuggler, has given him additional vigour and incitement to carry on his trade; and a further reduction is necessary in order to put the fair dealer on a par with the smuggler.

'The chancellor of the exchequer cannot justly apply to this question the principle, generally a correct one, that a diminishing tax ought to be selected for reduction instead of an increasing one; for the newspaper stamp duty is not in fact a diminishing one. It is said that it yielded in 1831 488,000l., and in 1835 only 435,000l. But this is not a fair comparison, because the political excitement of 1831 raised it to an enormous amount in that year. The same thing happened in 1813, when every one was anxious to gain the earliest intelligence of what was passing on the Continent. In that year the newspaper duty yielded the then unprecedented amount of 394,000l. But in the following year it fell to 363,000l., a reduction greater than that which had taken place between 1831 and 1835. If periods are taken which give a fair average, this is an increasing duty.

'As, then, there is no reason for preferring newspapers on any of these grounds, look at the comparative value of reduction in these two articles to the country. It appears from the stamp returns that there are but 300,000 persons who take in newspapers; while the soap duty applies to the entire population of 15,000,000. Besides, the relief given to the public in the case of newspapers would be but one-twentieth part of a penny, while that in the article of soap would be 4½d., or 3d. at the least. Even this is not all. I have no objection that the poorest classes of the community should be supplied with all the passing events of the day, provided that information is correctly and fairly given. But will the proposed reduction have this effect? Will the labouring classes be able to take in a daily or even a weekly paper which would cost 4d. at least? Why should they do so? Are they not in the habit of associating together for the purpose of reading the newspapers taken in for their accommodation in coffee-houses and other places? The poor man who thus pays for the paper will not be a gainer by the reduction: the publican will be a gainer, and not his customers; the master of the family, and not the servants and dependents to whom he lends the paper after he has read it himself. But it is said that it is necessary to reduce the duty in order to prevent the smuggling—that is, the sale—of unstamped newspapers. But does any man maintain that smuggling is not as mischievous and extensive in the soap manufacture, and that it does not call still more loudly for a similar remedy? The stamp duty protects the editor of a London journal—who is compelled to incur enormous expenses in procuring parliamentary reports, in obtaining foreign intelligence, in anticipating the arrival of the post by expresses, and in having correspondents in every quarter of the world where matters of interest are going on—against the conductors of the predatory publications, who go to no expense, but simply copy the contents of the other journals. And with all this you will still have an unstamped press to restrain; for the retained duty will be treated as the existing duty has been.'

After a long and earnest debate cheap newspapers triumphed over cheap soap by a majority of 33; there being 241 in favour of the former, and 208 for the latter.

Other changes were made in connection with this of the stamp duty. Newspapers exceeding 1530 square inches of the printed part of the sheet were to pay an additional half-penny. If the sheet exceeded 2295 square inches or had a supplement, an additional penny was to be paid. Every newspaper was to have a distinctive stamped die. Two proprietors of each newspaper were to be registered with its editor and its publisher; and, by a clause subsequently carried, every proprietor was to be registered. This last provision was struck out by the Lords, who made no other change in the bill; but this amendment was rejected by the Commons as being a breach of their privileges. They, however, passed another bill exactly similar in all respects to that which had been thus dealt with, except that it did not contain the clause of which the Peers disapproved, and it went through both Houses without opposition. Thus this important change became the law of the land, with results very different from those which its opponents had foretold. Since it passed, newspapers have become much cheaper, and their tone and character instead of being lowered has been greatly elevated, and in every respect improved.

While moderate and steady progress was thus being made at home, Canadian discontent pushed to the very verge of insurrection, needless and improper intermeddling in the internal affairs of Spain by a legion composed of British subjects under the command of Colonel Evans, and other attempts to force on 'liberal principles' by interference in the affairs of continental nations, were creating alarm and uncertainty at home, and rendering necessary an addition of 5000 men to our naval force, and a corresponding increase of our naval estimates. Parliament was prorogued on the 20th of August by the king in person.

The year 1837 commenced with some symptoms of political life and activity. The different parties, each in its own way, made their appeal to the nation. At Bath and Middlesex, represented by Messrs. Roebuck and Hume, the two foremost leaders of the radical party, political banquets were held, at which the views of that party were strongly advocated. At Leeds Lord Morpeth, at a similar celebration, upheld the ministerial policy ; while at Glasgow Sir R. Peel, who had been elected lord rector of the university, after a contest with Sir J. Campbell, the attorney-general, proclaimed and justified the policy he intended to pursue, in a very telling speech vociferously applauded, the audience rising at parts of it in order to give full vent to their enthusiasm. In Dublin a great Protestant meeting was held, which was attended by a large number of peers and members of the House of Commons, and, as was asserted, by 3000 or 4000 persons, at which the cause of Irish Protestantism was strenuously maintained. As for O'Connell, he was carrying on his usual course of agitation. Thus all the different parties made their appeal, not to the comparatively few who composed the meetings we have enumerated, but through the press to the country generally, and prepared the way for the parliamentary campaign which was about to commence.

The session of 1837 was opened by commission on the 31st of January. The king's speech was more than usually vague and deficient in interest, provoking little criticism and no direct opposition. As usual, Irish questions occupied the most prominent place in this address. To an objection raised by Mr. Plumtre, member for East Kent, that the speech did not contain the usual recognition of divine providence, Lord J. Russell replied, that if every speech contained such a recognition, it would become a mere matter of form, and lose its intended effect.

The expectation raised by the speech, that Irish questions would again monopolise a large portion of the session, was not disappointed. In the first place, the Irish Corporation Reform Bill, which was rejected last year by the Peers, was reintroduced with some modifications. The bill, having passed its third reading in the House of Commons, by a majority of 55, was read a first and second time in the Lords without opposition; but when, on the 5th of May, the order of the day for its committal was read, the Duke of Wellington moved that it should be deferred to the 9th of June, in order that their lordships might see what course ministers would take with regard to the tithe bill, intimating at the same time that if the church question should be dealt with in a manner calculated to meet the views of the majority of that House, they would be prepared to make great concessions on the question of corporation reform. Lord Melbourne, Lord Brougham, and other supporters of the ministry, objected strongly to the adoption of the duke's motion, and urged the House to proceed at once with the consideration of the bill, without regard to any measure which might follow it; but the duke's motion was carried, in spite of their remonstrances, by a majority of 77. The tithe bill had, however, only reached its second reading in the House of Commons on the very night fixed for the committal of the municipal bill in the House of Lords; but the peers were now, of course, well aware of the nature of that measure, which was not calculated to meet their views, or to abate the objections they entertained to a measure the necessary effect of which would be to transfer the management of the greater part of the municipalities of Ireland from the Protestants to the Catholics, now avowedly aiming at the disestablishment and disendowment of the Irish church. Lord Lyndhurst therefore proposed a further postponement of the committal of the Irish corporation bill; and his motion, notwithstanding an earnest deprecation of further delay on the part of Lord Melbourne, was carried by a majority of 86.

The measure for which the Lords thus resolved to wait was the fifth legislative attempt to settle the question which had been made in the course of the last three years. It was introduced into the House of Commons on the 1st of May, and, as we have just mentioned, read a second time on the 6th. The old appropriation clauses no longer figured in this bill, but the plan of appropriation was revived in another shape. It provided that all future bishops, dignitaries, or beneficed clergymen, should be required to pay a tax of ten per cent. on their incomes, to be devoted to the purpose of general education in Ireland. In justification of this provision, a statute of the 15th of the 28th of Henry VIII. was cited to the following effect: 'That every incumbent in each parish in Ireland shall keep, or cause to be kept, within his parish a school to learn English; and that every archbishop, bishop, &c., at the time of the induction of any clergyman to his benefice, shall give to the person so inducted a corporal oath that, being so admitted or inducted, he shall to his best endeavour himself to teach the English tongue to all that are under his rule and governance.' The same act imposed penalties on all bishops and clergymen who should be guilty of a breach of this statute: for the first offence the clergyman was to be fined, for the second he was to be fined more severely, and for the third to be deprived. It was further stated, that the act was still in force, and that every rector or vicar on being inducted into his benefice was compelled to take the following oath: 'I will teach or cause to be taught an English school within the said rectory or vicarage, as the law in that case requires.' This bill was read a second time on the 9th of June, in spite of the opposition of Mr. Sherman Crawford and a few others, who declared that they would be satisfied with nothing short of a complete release from all taxation in support of the Irish church. Irish poor-laws and Irish education also occupied a large share of the attention of the legislature; but the discussion of these important measures led to no result during the session.

The electors of Westminster had for some time past been not unnaturally dissatisfied with the state of their representation. In fact they were unrepresented. Colonel Evans, one of their members, had during the last two years been in Spain, commanding the British legion there. Some of his constituents strongly disapproved of this intervention of a British force in the internal affairs of another country; others complained of his absence from his parliamentary duties; both called upon him to relinquish either his command or his seat. The conduct of the other member for Westminster was also of a nature to give umbrage to many of his constituents. On all the great divisions on party questions which for some time past had taken place in the House of Commons, Sir F. Burdett had been absent. His neglect was for some time excused on the plea of advanced years and failing health; but it began to be rumoured that this was not the true explanation of his conduct, but that it was owing to a great change in his political sentiments; that his heart was with the conservatives, and that if he felt himself free to follow the bent of his own inclinations, his vote would be with them too. Sir Francis had now represented the city of Westminster about thirty years. He had been a reformer—nay, a radical—at a time when to avow such opinions was sure to exclude the man who held them from all aristocratic society. He had suffered fine and imprisonment for expression of his opinions. Up to this time, he had consistently supported every measure of reform which had been brought forward, and was still regarded as an advanced liberal by those who knew him only as a public man. But the proposals of government with regard to the Irish church had alarmed his sensitive Protestantism, and completely alienated him from the party with which he had hitherto acted. The change which had taken place in his sentiments had not escaped the notice, or at least the suspicions, of many of his constituents. A meeting of the electors of Westminster was held on the 24th of April, at which resolutions were passed expressive of dissatisfaction with the conduct of their representatives, and calling on them to resign their seats. In anticipation of their compliance with this requisition, Sir G. Murray was brought forward by the conservatives, and Mr. Leader by the radicals. Sir Francis at once accepted the Chiltern Hundreds, announcing at the same time that he would again present himself as a candidate for the suffrages of the electors. He declared that he should come forward as the supporter of the laws and institutions of the country, and as a 'resolute opponent of all the new-fangled notions, shallow doctrines, and crude projects now afloat.' He denied that he had changed his opinions, but charged those who accused him of inconsistency with having abandoned theirs. He called on the electors of Westminster to join him in struggling against 'an unnatural alliance, and odious and ludicrous combination of Irish agitators, popish priests, and paid patriots, operating on a well-intentioned but weak and vacillating administration.' There could be no mistake with regard to the import of this language.

It was a curious spectacle to see the old ultra-radical, now become an ultra-Tory, present himself once more to the electors of Westminster, in the hope that, partly by the votes of those who had so often supported him before, and did not like now to cast him off, partly by the suffrages of old opponents and reactionary liberals, he might once more carry his election. Sir G. Murray withdrew from the contest, leaving Sir Francis and Mr. Leader to fight out the battle, for the sake of which Mr. Leader resigned his seat at Bridgewater. But though Sir Francis had certainly abandoned his old friends, and seemed also to have abandoned his old principles, the Westminster electors were faithful to the man whom in his younger days they had so enthusiastically supported, and by whom they had so long been represented. The baronet was returned by a majority of 515 votes.

This result was hailed with great exultation by the conservatives, and severely mortified the ministerial party. That Westminster, which had so often upheld the liberal party in the days of its adversity, which had been faithful to Fox at a time when Fox's political creed was most unpopular, should now return as one of its members a man who had distinctly avowed his attachment to the Tory party, was a heavy and unexpected blow. As for Sir Francis himself, he regarded his reëlection as stamping the approval of his constituents on his conduct, and releasing him from the necessity of farther concealment. He openly took his seat on the opposition side of the House, and spoke against the government measures amidst the uproarious cheers of his new friends.

But a yet heavier blow was in store for the liberal party. The chief English measure of the session was a bill which the government had introduced for the settlement of the question of church rates. The scheme was explained to the House of Commons on the 9th of March by Mr. Spring Rice. It was computed that a sum of 225,000*l.* might be gained annually by putting an end to the system of leasing church lands which then prevailed, and by the better management of them, with which intent the bill proposed to invest them in eleven commissioners. From the saving thus effected, eked out by pew-rents, the repairs of all churches were to be made. This was, in fact, a plan similar to that which had already been adopted in Ireland for the purpose of getting rid of the grievance of church cess, and which had been found to work well there.

On the 12th of March fifteen bishops, being the whole of those who were at that time in town, met at Lambeth Palace, and unanimously resolved to oppose a measure which proposed to take from them the management of their episcopal estates; and on the evening of the same day the archbishop of Canterbury took the opportunity of the presentation of petitions against the abolition of church rates, to express in strong and decided terms his objections to the government plan. To this declaration Lord Melbourne, evidently much mortified, replied with unusual asperity and vehemence, and was answered by the bishop of London, who denounced the scheme as a 'sacrilegious spoliation,' loudly complaining that a plan considered and rejected by the ecclesiastical commission, on which many members of the government sat, should be brought forward by the government.

These appeals were addressed to the country, and a strong agitation commenced against the bill. While numerous petitions in favour of it were got up by the dissenters, petitions still more numerous, though less numerously signed, were got up against it by the clergy and their flocks. The old cry of 'the church is in danger,' was raised again with something of the old effect. Every possible influence was brought to bear on members of the House of Commons in order to defeat the bill.

When the resolutions on which the bill was to be founded were brought before the House on the 22nd of May, a division took place, and the second reading was carried by a majority of five. The smallness of this majority made it evident that a bill founded on the resolutions would have no chance of getting through the House of Commons, and the measure was abandoned by the government; but Lord J. Russell, in order to pave the way for future legislation on the question, moved that a committee should be appointed 'to inquire into the present mode of holding and leasing the property belonging to bishops and chapters, with a view to ascertaining the probable amount of any increased value that might be obtained by an improved management, with a due consideration of the interests of the established church and of the present lessees of such property.'

This motion gave rise to several divisions which threw light on the state of parties in regard to the church-rate question. A motion by Mr. Harvey for the entire and uncompensated abolition of church rates was rejected by a majority of 431. The motion for inquiry was carried by a majority of 86. An attempt made by Mr. Goulburn to pledge the House to appropriate any surplus revenues that might be obtained through the means indicated by Lord J. Russell's motion to the extension of religious instruction by ministers of the establishment, was defeated by a majority of 26. These numbers show that the conservative reaction evidently going on was due in a great measure to the exertions of the clergy, who were now recovering the influence and popularity of which they had for the moment been deprived partly by their opposition to the national will during the reform struggle, and partly through those gross abuses which were now being gradually corrected. The clergy disliked the measures of the ministers, and distrusted their professions of attachment to the church, and, with very few exceptions, exerted all the influence they possessed against the government. On the other hand, the conduct of ministers themselves tended to promote a conservative reaction. Instead of keeping alive the enthusiasm of their supporters by bringing forward the ballot and other measures which the popular voice called for, they regarded themselves as having already achieved all the great changes which could safely be made, as having now entered the promised land flowing with milk and honey, and as being entitled to sit down and govern a grateful people in a kind of political millennium. But there was yet another cause of the conservative reaction, which was probably more potent than either the influence of the church or the improgressive character of the administration; and that was, the circumstance that three successive good harvests had spread plenty and conservatism through the land, rendering the mass of the people indifferent to those party politics which had so deeply stirred them when distress and poverty overshadowed their country.

This session was remarkable for an unusually large number of abortive motions. Some of these we have already had occasion to mention. Others, proposed by the radical party, in favour of great and organic changes in the constitution, failed through the opposition offered to them by the government. Among these were Mr. Grote's motion for the ballot, Sir Wm. Molesworth's for the abolition of the property qualification, Mr. Lushington's for the exclusion of the bishops from the House of Lords, Mr. Duncombe's levelled against the system of proxies in the upper House; an attempt made by ministers to graft on a motion made by Mr. Williams for the repeal of the duty of one pound payable on the admission of freemen into corporations; an amendment deferring the time of the payment of rates under the Reform Bill from April to October; Mr. Tennyson d'Eyncourt's motion for shortening the duration of Parliaments; and a motion for the abolition of the law of primogeniture. Of these motions, some were rejected; others lost for want of sufficient time to carry them through.

So great a change as that which had been made by the new poor-law could not be effected without producing much incidental hardship, and causing a good deal of discontent. Although from the very beginning the good results of the new law were patent, and manifestly preponderated over the hardships it produced in individual cases, yet the evil effects of the change were felt at once, while the greatest part of the good was produced by the slow and gradual operation of the measure in improving the habits and feelings of the working classes, and in substituting reliance on their own industry and economy for reliance on the public purse. Yet, even now, the framers and advocates of the new poor-law could point with triumph to the results it had already achieved. The amount of the rates and the number of able-bodied paupers had been enormously diminished. The vicious practice of supplementing wages by payments out of the rates had almost entirely ceased, and the remuneration which the labourer received had increased. But some of those who found themselves compelled to exchange luxurious idleness for hard labour were greatly dissatisfied. Others, more deserving of compassion, whom a temporary depression of their trade had compelled to take refuge in the workhouse, and to sell off their little property, complained that the diet provided for them in the workhouse was insufficient, and inferior to that which was supplied to prisoners confined in the gaols. The vicious and turbulent elements which the old system had produced were in a state of exasperation, that might easily be fanned into insurrection. Their distress and irritation had been increased by the sufferings which an unusually long and severe winter had caused. Under these circumstances the poor-law commissioners were strongly urged to relax, in some degree, the stringency of their regulations, and to allow some return to the old system of out-door relief. They were placed in a very difficult position: for they saw that by yielding to this cry, they would run a risk of opening the door to all the abuses which the new poor-law had removed, and of the lavish expenditure it had corrected.

The flame of discontent was at this time fanned by the powerful influence of the *Times* newspaper, which fiercely attacked the new poor-law board. A meeting on the subject was held in the west riding of Yorkshire, which was said to have been attended by from 250,000 to 300,000 persons. On this subject the ultra-tories were found in coalition with the extremest radicals. Every effort was exerted to hinder and deter the commissioners from extending the operation of the law to the manufacturing districts, into which as yet it had only very partially penetrated. It was stated by the Earl of Harewood, the lord-lieutenant of

Yorkshire, that in some places the commissioners had gone into towns for the purpose of assisting in introducing the law, and had been obliged to leave them in consequence of the resistance which was offered. But this feeling of hostility to the new law was confined to places where it had not yet been introduced; in those places where it had been fully tried, as Lord Brougham justly remarked, the measure was not an odious but a favourite law with the well-disposed labouring men. However, in deference to the strong feeling that prevailed, a committee of the House of Commons was appointed to inquire into the operation of this law. Among other members placed on that committee was Mr. Walter, member for Berkshire, and the proprietor of the *Times*, who had all along manifested the same hostility to the poor-law that was displayed in the columns of that powerful journal. This gentleman brought the question before the House of Commons, by moving for a select committee to inquire into the operation of the act; to which Lord J. Russell moved an amendment, asking for the appointment of a select committee to 'inquire into the administration of the relief of the poor, under the orders and regulations issued by the commissioners appointed under the provisions of the new poor-law amendment act.' In proposing this amendment, Lord J. Russell said: 'My only difficulty is to compress within any moderate compass the voluminous mass of evidence with which I have been furnished from persons of all classes—from noblemen, landowners, clergymen, farmers, and labourers—all tending in the strongest manner to show the great advantages that have resulted from the measure. This has been especially the case with regard to the employment of the workhouse system as a test of destitution. In East Kent, formerly one of the most pauperised districts, out of 160,000 inhabitants 55 has been the maximum of able-bodied labourers in the workhouses at the same time. But it is said to be cruel to force the disabled and infirm into the workhouse. The degree and manner in which this has been done is, no doubt, a very proper subject of inquiry with the committee. In the meanwhile, however, I can refer to returns which have been received from eighty-eight unions, showing that the number of in-door paupers was 8850, while the number of out-door paupers is 54,417. In these eighty-eight unions, nine-tenths of the disabled and infirm receive out-door relief. This, then, is the working of that cruel system which is represented as driving every disabled and poor person into prison! But while I make this statement, I do not dissemble my belief, that when the new system has been brought into full operation, out-door relief will be entirely abolished, except in cases of sickness; and I think that it ought not to constitute a permanent part of the system.

'With regard to the kind of relief afforded in the workhouses. From the return of the Easting union it appears that, whereas the amount of annual payments for bastardy was formerly 300*l*., there is now no instance of a charge on that account. The amount of poor-rates collected for the year ending March, 1835, was 16,900*l*.; the amount collected for the year ending December, 1836, was 8965. The diet of the inmates of the workhouses is ample, wholesome, and substantial, the medical attendance prompt and considerate, the clothing suitable, and the moral and religious improvement duly attended to. The children of both sexes are reared and trained in a manner far surpassing that enjoyed by the children of independent labourers.'

Mr. Harvey, the ultra-radical representative of Southwark, denounced the new law and its administration. He stigmatised the act itself as 'one of the most cruel, heartless, and selfish bills that ever was passed into a law.' He declared that the funds 'were administered with the most barbarous and heartless severity.' Mr. Hume, on the other hand, though generally agreeing with Mr. Harvey on political questions, on this occasion spoke strongly in defence both of the act itself and of the manner in which it was being administered. After a long debate, the amendment proposed by Lord J. Russell was adopted, and the committee at once entered on the investigation it had been appointed to make.

Mr. Walter and Mr. Harvey, who had been placed on this committee, soon found that the course its inquiries were taking was not calculated to promote their views. The former of these gentlemen moved, unsuccessfully, the addition to the committee of six members whose opinions on the subject were in accordance with his own. The latter took the far more extraordinary course of publishing in the *Sun* newspaper the evidence as it was daily taken. Ultimately both retired from the committee, complaining that it was partial and one-sided; that the poor-law commissioners were allowed to produce any evidence they pleased, while the poor were practically debarred from putting before it any evidence at all. These statements were strongly rebutted and fully replied to; and the committee continued its labours, the results of which were embodied in a report presented to the House of Commons a short time before the end of the session. This document stated that the introduction of the new law had been attended with a considerable improvement in the character and condition of the poor; that labourers and widows with large families under age for work suffered severely from the loss of the allowances they had before been accustomed to receive, but that their sufferings had been much mitigated by a considerate administration of the laws; that the operation of the law was satisfactory and ought to be maintained, and that its administration both by boards of guardians and poor-law commissioners had been, in the main, judicious; lastly, they recommended that the inquiry should be resumed next session, and suggested certain points to which they thought it advisable that the attention of a future committee should be directed. The favourable opinion of the law expressed by the committee was corroborated and confirmed by a great number of important facts contained in the report made this year by the commissioners. The conduct of Mr. Harvey in publishing the minutes of the evidence taken before the committee, in disregard of the remonstrances of the speaker, who had warned him that in doing so he was committing a breach of privilege, was brought under the notice of the House by Lord J. Russell.

Another, and a very much more important question of privilege, also came before the House during the session. Messrs. Hansard presented a petition, in which they stated that they were authorised, by certain resolutions of the House, to sell all parliamentary reports and papers to the public at a rate below the actual primo cost. In accordance with the permission thus given them, they had printed a report of the commissioners for inquiry into the state of the prisoners, in which it was alleged that many of the prisoners were found reading certain obscene works which had been published by J. J. Stockdale. This firm commenced an action against Messrs. Hansard for libel, in the Court of King's Bench, laying their damages at 20,000*l.* It was pleaded in justification, that the report had been printed under the order of the House of Commons. On this plea lord chief justice Denman gave it as his opinion, that the authority of the House of Commons would not justify the publication of a libel; and the jury, acting under his direction, rejected the plea. The question was taken up by Lord J. Russell on the 13th of February, and on the 16th of the same month he moved for a committee, on the report of which a resolution was founded, declaring the power of the House to order the publication of such papers as it shall think conducive to the public interests, and affirming that any action for the purpose of bringing the privilege of Parliament into discussion before a tribunal elsewhere than in Parliament, is a high breach of privilege; and farther, that for any court or tribunal to assume to decide on matters of privilege inconsistently with the determination of either House of Parliament thereon, is contrary to the law of Parliament and a breach and contempt of the privileges of Parliament. These resolutions being in accordance with the general opinion of the House, and supported by the votes of Sir R. Peel, and many of the most distinguished members of his party, were carried in spite of the strenuous opposition of Sir R. Inglis. It was remarked at the time, that the statesmen were in favour of the resolutions, and the lawyers against them.

Canada was now affording nearly as much trouble and anxiety to the English government as Ireland, and the discontent of the two countries arose from causes not dissimilar. When Lower Canada came into possession of the English crown by the peace of 1763, it contained a population which, in habits, language, and sympathies, was thoroughly French. An attempt to give to the new colony law and institutions modelled on those of England failed, partly on account of their intrinsic unsuitableness to the genius and character of the people on whom they were to be imposed, and partly in consequence of the war which was being carried on between England and the United States of America. However, in 1791 Mr. Pitt, feeling that under the circumstances in which we were then placed, Canada must at any price be more closely attached to the mother country, formed a new constitution for the colony. He gave it what he termed an executive council, corresponding with our cabinet, to be named by the governor; a legislative council, also named by the governor, composed of hereditary and life members, and answering to the English House of Lords; and lastly, an elective assembly, a sort of Canadian House of Commons, but possessing only a limited control over the supplies. This constitution, however, had not worked much better than its predecessor, and had at last come nearly to a dead-lock. The colony did not contain the materials out of which an aristocracy could be created; and the legislative council, with far less weight and authority than the English House of Peers, was far more obstructive. The Canadians were exasperated to the highest pitch when they saw measures demanded by the almost universal desire of the colonists defeated by a set of men whose opinions had little weight, and whose motives were very questionable. But the chief cause of the discontent which prevailed in Lower Canada was that, like Ireland, it suffered under the ascendancy of a small minority of its inhabitants, which was enabled to dominate over the majority by the support it obtained from the mother country, and the consequent preponderance it enjoyed in the executive and legislative councils. Thus a state of things prevailed very similar to that which existed in Ireland, but aggravated by the existence of a separate legislature, by the distance between the colony and the mother country, and by the proximity of the United States. The Whig government in 1831 conceded to the assembly that full control over the supplies which had hitherto been denied to it; and the consequence was, that the supplies had been refused and the judges and the other government officers were unpaid. The government wisely resolved to meet the difficulty, not by strong measures, but by a redress of those grievances of which the Lower Canadians had reason to complain; they therefore considered in a conciliatory spirit the complaints that were made by the Canadian assembly, and endeavoured to establish a good understanding between the mother country and her colony. With this view Lord J. Russell brought forward ten resolutions, in which the plan of the colonial assembly to make the legislative council elective was refused; the government proposed to improve its composition, declared their determination to maintain inviolate the privileges of the American company, and held out the prospect of certain advantages to the inhabitants of Lower Canada. These resolutions, strenuously opposed by Mr. Roebuck, the paid advocate of the Canadian legislature, and by the other leaders of the radical party, were supported by Sir R. Peel, and adopted by both Houses; Lord Brougham alone objecting and protesting in the House of Lords. We shall see hereafter how this attempt at conciliation was received in the colony.

This was a year of great disorder and derangement in the money market, apparently brought about by a sudden and rapid extension which had taken place in the number of joint-stock banks since the renewal of the Bank charter. These banks had been originally established in virtue of an act of Parliament passed in the year 1826. At first, the number which this act brought into existence was very small: in 1826 there were only three, in 1827 four, in 1828 none; the highest number that had ever been created in any one year was eleven in 1834, in 1835 there were only nine new banks; but in 1836 no fewer than forty-two were established, many of them carrying on their operations on a very extensive scale. This great increase in the number had been followed by a considerable drain of bullion from the Bank of England, and by a consequent rise in the bank discount. In a short time, several of the new joint-stock banks were found to be in a very critical condition, and the embarrassments thus produced were severely aggravated by still greater embarrassments in the United States of America, where, owing to the measures adopted by the government of General Jackson, the president of the States, every bank had suspended payment, and fraudulent transactions had been practised on a large scale, by which many joint-stock banks in England, and even of the Bank of England itself, were very seriously compromised. A bank called the Agricultural, which had been established in Ireland, and which had thirty branches, was compelled to stop payment. The Northern and Central bank in Manchester, with a capital of 700,000*l.*, was in an almost equally critical position. Blind confidence was succeeded by blind panic. In this emergency the directors of the Bank of England came forward to sustain the credit of the Manchester bank. In doing so, they avowedly acted in violation of many of the principles by which their administration had been hitherto regulated; but they arrested a panic, the consequence of which might have been most disastrous. In 1836 a committee had been appointed to inquire into the causes of these monetary derangements, which even then began to create alarm, though they had not by any means manifested the serious character which they afterwards assumed. The committee had not been able to come to any agreement, either as to the causes of the mischief, or the remedies which should be provided for it. It was therefore renewed this year, with the understanding that it should extend its inquiries to the sister country, and with the feeling that the state of our banking and monetary operations was such as demanded a searching inquiry and a prompt decision.

Another subject brought under the notice of Parliament was the British intervention in the affairs of Spain. It was justified by the ministry on the ground, that it was in accordance with the conditions of the quadruple treaty, and calculated to maintain the cause of liberal and constitutional government in Spain against despotism. But it was justly argued not only by the conservatives, but also by Mr. Roebuck, that unless liberal institutions were maintained by the feelings and wishes of the Spanish people, they were little likely to hold their ground, and still less so if forced on the majority of the nation by the aid of foreign bayonets. However, the policy of the government was sanctioned by the majority of the House of Commons; but in June, Colonel Evans, disgusted at the manner in which he was treated by the Spanish ministry, resigned his command, and the British legion ceased to exist as a separate body.

We have already seen how bill after bill of the government had been brought forward, carried on to a certain stage, and then either dropped or defeated. Under these circumstances, and with continually dwindling majorities in the Commons, there was little chance of their being able to force forward their measures against the hostile phalanx arrayed against them in the House of Lords. To restore the balance by a large creation of new peers was out of the question. The only resource left to the government was to dissolve. But it was very doubtful whether much would be gained by another appeal to the country; while it was quite certain that the king was very unwilling to resort to it, and would probably accept the resignation of the ministry rather than sanction it. Sir R. Peel had publicly declared in the House of Commons that he was prepared to resume office. The government therefore found themselves unable to carry the measures to which they were pledged, and which they could not allow to be thrown aside without incurring much discredit and seriously damaging the party they represented. It is not easy to see how they could have extricated themselves out of these difficulties, and it seemed only too probable that, when the session was over, the king might do, and with some show of reason, as he had done last year—take from them the seals of office, and put them again into the hands of Sir R. Peel. But an event occurred which probably saved the ministry for a time, and exercised a very considerable influence on the political destinies of the country.

William IV. was now in his seventy-second year. His health, which before his accession was feeble, had greatly improved after that event. The duties which devolved on him had evidently produced a beneficial effect on his constitution. But in the spring of this year his old bad symptoms had recurred; and it was perhaps the foresight of his death, or the desire to spare him the trouble and anxiety of another change of ministry, that had led the government—notwithstanding the declarations they had made at the commencement of the session—to acquiesce in the frustration of the measures they had deemed it their duty to introduce in the course of this session. About the beginning of June, William underwent an attack of hay fever, a complaint to which he had been annually subject before his accession, but which had not returned since he became king; and the progress of this disease caused much anxiety. It was feared that his constitution was too feeble to contend with the disease. He nevertheless continued to transact business. On the 15th of June the *Times* announced that his death was certain and imminent; but the disease unexpectedly took a more favourable turn, and a bulletin issued on the

16th announced that his condition was so far improved, that three of his physicians had returned to London, their attendance being no longer deemed necessary. However, on Sunday, the 18th, the symptoms again became urgent, and the Archbishop of Canterbury—who had been sent for to administer the last rites of the church of England to the dying monarch—was greatly edified by the patience and resignation he displayed.

On Tuesday morning, the mournful tolling of muffled bells announced to the Londoners that their king had departed during the night. The reign of William IV. was not indeed of long duration; but it was marked by greater and more beneficial changes than had been effected during much longer reigns. The political improvements carried out in the course of it have already been dwelt on; but there were other kinds of progress effected which were the indications and the causes of still greater progress in material prosperity. At the commencement of this reign there were in the British dominions 315 steam-vessels, with a tonnage of 33,441; before its close, there were 600 steam-vessels, with a tonnage of 67,969; and at the time of the king's decease there were steam-ships in construction of far greater size and power than had ever been built before, intended to try the experiment, of which many high authorities confidently predicted the entire failure, of crossing the Atlantic. At the commencement of this reign there was not a single railway of any importance open for goods and passenger traffic in the whole of England; but before its close, railways were either completed or in the course of being laid down connecting the metropolis with Birmingham, Liverpool, Manchester, the chief towns of the iron and pottery districts, Winchester, Southampton, Bath, and Bristol, besides a considerable number of provincial railways serving important towns and traversing wealthy districts.

When Parliament assembled after the decease of the king, three eminent men, all of whom had filled the office of his prime minister, said a few words in eulogy of the departed monarch. Lord Melbourne praised his 'assidnity and industry,' and declared that he was 'as fair and just and conscientious a man as ever existed—always willing to listen to any argument, even though opposed to his own previous feeling—a sterling quality' (Lord M. observed) 'in any man, but peculiarly good, sterling, and valuable in a monarch. The Duke of Wellington spoke of 'the firmness, candour, justice, and true spirit of conciliation' of the deceased monarch. Earl Grey said, that 'a man more sincerely devoted to the interests of his country—that a man who had a better understanding of what was necessary to the furtherance of those interests—that a man who was more patient in considering all the circumstances connected with those interests—that a man who was more attentive to his duty on every occasion—never did exist.'

These were no insignificant encomiums. They came from men who had enjoyed the amplest opportunities of forming the opinions they expressed, and whose characters are too high to allow us to suppose that their eulogies were insincere. But on the other hand they only presented one side of the picture; they had far too much good taste and good sense to utter at such a moment anything that could detract from the commendations they bestowed on their deceased master. There were other features of his character which on such an occasion it would have been improper to touch. It is therefore necessary that we should try to fill up the outline which they thus generally sketched. The character of William IV., in its excellences as well as its defects, is best described by the epithet which was so often and so generally applied to him during his lifetime—'the sailor king.' At an early age he was sent by his father, George III., to rough it on board ship as an ordinary midshipman. He saw a good deal of service, and acquired that plain downright bluntness of manner and that frank honesty of purpose by which the naval officers of his time were generally distinguished. He was affable, kind, good-natured, but very undignified both in his gait and conversation; he had moreover a propensity for gossiping, which sometimes led him thoughtlessly to reveal matters which should have been kept strictly secret. He had a strong yet not excessive love of popularity; yet he did not know how to keep it; and he made a complete sacrifice of it when, allowing himself to be carried away by the alarms of the court, he dismissed Earl Grey, and called in the Duke of Wellington. But this mistake proved more injurious to the king who made it than to the country, which it roused to a high pitch of political excitement. For this error he deserves pity rather than blame. It should always be remembered to his honour, that by his good sense and popular conduct at the commencement of his reign he probably saved England from the revolution which would almost infallibly have occurred if his elder brother George IV., or his younger brother the Duke of Cumberland, had occupied the throne at that critical period. Take him for all in all, we must conclude that he was one of the best, and if not one of the wisest monarchs who have sat on the English throne, yet one of the most useful.

www.ingramcontent.com/pod-product-compliance
Lightning Source LLC
Chambersburg PA
CBHW051740300426
44115CB00007B/645